THE OTHER SIDE OF RUSSIA

The Other Side of Russia

A Slice of Life
in Siberia
and the
Russian Far East

Sharon Hudgins

TEXAS A&M UNIVERSITY PRESS | *College Station*

Library of Congress Cataloging-in-Publication Data

Hudgins, Sharon.
    The other side of Russia : a slice of life in Siberia
and the Russian Far East / Sharon Hudgins.
        p. cm.–(Eastern European studies ; no. 21)
    Includes bibliographical references and index.
    ISBN 1-58544-237-2 (cloth : alk. paper)
    1. Siberia (Russia)–Description and travel.
2. Hudgins, Sharon–Journeys–Russia (Federation)–
Siberia. I. Title. II. Series: Eastern European
studies (College Station, Tex.) ; no. 21.
DK756.2H83   2003
915.704'86–dc21   2002013749

TO TOM,

with all my love—

and for taking the adventure one step farther,

to Russia

CONTENTS

~

ILLUSTRATIONS

～

MAPS

~

ACKNOWLEDGMENTS

Several people deserve recognition for their contributions to this book during various stages of its development. All of them were familiar with Russia firsthand, having lived, worked, or traveled there themselves—yet each had a different perspective on this complex country. Special thanks are due to Birgitta Ingemanson and Julian Jones, who read the lengthy first draft of this book and offered many insightful observations and constructive comments that ultimately influenced the final text. Julian Jones also read the revised text, as did Victor L. Mote, Kira Van Deusen, Carol Chappell, and Glenn Mack, all of whom provided useful suggestions for fine-tuning the manuscript. I am indebted to Maria Lebedko in Vladivostok and to Birgitta Ingemanson in the United States for sharing with me their unpublished and published works about Vladivostok and the surrounding area. I am also grateful to George P. Morgan, Jr., for letting me read his unpublished manuscript about his own experiences in Siberia, and to William Craft Brumfield, Rosemary Hoffmann, and Robert Sweo for providing recent information about Vladivostok and Irkutsk for the Postscript.

Among the Russians who were such an important part of my life in Siberia and the Russian Far East, certain colleagues merit special mention. Vladimir N. Saunin, director of the Baikal Education Complex at Irkutsk State University, was an outstanding administrator whose personal integrity and straightforward manner won him the respect of all the Americans who taught in the program there. Alexander V. Diogenov, dean of the Siberian-American Faculty of Management at Irkutsk State University, and his wife Nelli V. Ilina, head of the English-language program in that department, were both highly committed and very effective educators who have had a positive influence on the lives of hundreds of students there. At Far Eastern State University in Vladivostok, Anna A. Khamatova, dean of the Russian-American Joint Faculty for International Economic Relations and Management, was an energetic organizer and an evenhanded administrator who contributed significantly to the program's success. And of course University of Maryland University College in the United States gets credit for sending me to Russia in the first place.

I also owe many words of thanks to our colleagues Gennadiy N. Konstantinov and Nataliya V. Mikhalkovskaya in Irkutsk, to our friends Alla S. Brovko and Pëtr F. Brovko in Vladivostok, and to all of our other colleagues, students, and friends in Siberia and the Russian Far East who invited my husband and me to their homes and dachas, welcomed us at their places of work, took us on picnics, hikes, and train trips, prepared sumptuous feasts for us, and gave us so many opportunities to see how Russians lived, worked, and played in such diverse places as Angarsk, Ust'-Orda, Bol'shaya Rechka, and Ulan-Ude, from the shores of Lake Baikal to the outback of Primorskiy Kray.

I also greatly appreciate all the people in the United States who graciously agreed to read my account of these Russian experiences and to offer their endorsements of this book: Alfred Friendly, Jr., Helen S. Hundley, Larry McMurtry, Victor L. Mote, and Bill Richardson.

The publishing staff at Texas A&M University Press was a pleasure to work with. Noel Parsons, editor-in-chief at the time I submitted the proposal for this project, convinced me that his press would be the best publisher for my book. Thanks, too, to Tony L. McRae for drawing all the maps and to everyone at Texas A&M University Press who participated in the production of this book.

Finally, I owe much more than a few words of gratitude to Tom Hudgins, my constant companion during three decades of travel around the world. Knowing my longtime interest in Russia, he agreed to give up the comforts of life in Germany, our home at the time, for the uncertainties of a new adventure on the other side of the globe. A good sport and intrepid traveler, he always managed to maintain his sense of humor despite the difficulties that were often a part of daily life in Russia. And after we returned to the United States, he supported the writing of this book in many ways, not the least of which were all the fine Russian meals he cooked as inspiration for me when my mind was miles away, completely focused on finding the best way to word a sentence or to organize a chapter. *Spasibo*, Tom.

PREFACE

⌣

In 1993 my husband and I went to Russia to teach in a new education program established by University of Maryland University College in Siberia and the Russian Far East. During the early period of political, economic, and social change after the breakup of the Soviet Union, we were among the first Americans to live and work in the Asian part of Russia, the "other side of Russia" that extends across eight time zones from the Ural Mountains to the Pacific Ocean.

Prior to going to Russia, I had worked abroad for many years as a university professor and as a food and travel writer. Realizing that I was one of the few American women working in Asian Russia in the mid-1990s, I decided to take advantage of that opportunity to record my impressions of everyday life in the "new" Russia—from the difficulties of living in high-rise apartment buildings that often had no electricity or running water, to the cultural differences I encountered almost every day at work, to the friendships I made with Russians from many walks of life.

The result is this personal narrative of a specific place and time: southern Siberia and the Russian Far East, in the early post-Soviet period between 1993 and 1995, when a market economy was emerging, when some of the country's long-established institutions were no longer powerful or relevant (and, in some cases, no longer in existence), and when many of the old, familiar ways of thinking and acting were being challenged by the new social, political, and economic environment. It was an exciting time to live in Russia, to observe those changes as they occurred, and to participate, even if only in small measure, in helping educate some of the next generation who will inevitably make Russia of the twenty-first century very different from the country in which they were born.

My job was to teach Russian undergraduate students in the new degree programs offered by University of Maryland University College at two Russian state universities, in Irkutsk and in Vladivostok. As the American program

*Traditional Siberian "wooden lace" on an old house
in Ulan-Ude, Buryat Republic.*

coordinator at each location, I also served as a liaison between the American faculty in Russia and several different groups: the Russian students, faculty, and administration; the local Russian community; the small local American community (U.S. government and Peace Corps personnel, employees of nongovernmental organizations, visiting scholars, and business people); and our own university administration, which at that time was located in College Park, Maryland.

That job provided many opportunities for me to meet a wide range of Russians, from high-ranking officials to harried housewives, from university students to *mafiya* gangsters, from optimistic entrepreneurs to disillusioned pensioners. In addition to recording my personal observations about daily life, I interviewed Russians at home and at work; gave psychological tests and opinion surveys to my Russian students; visited schools, colleges, and universities in major cities and small towns; spoke at World Bank symposiums in Siberia; participated in international conferences in Vladivostok and Irkutsk; traveled extensively by public transportation to a variety of places in the Asian part of Russia; and listened to many, often differing, opinions about the causes and effects of the historic changes that were occurring there.

While living in Russia I wrote the notes for this book on whatever paper was handy in a country still suffering from shortages: envelopes, dinner napkins, theater programs, printed flyers, food labels, bus tickets, school notebooks, graph paper, even toilet paper (not the typical Russian crude gray "sandpaper," but squares of precious, good-quality white writing paper, the best paper I ever saw in Russia, which had somehow been packaged as toilet paper). But despite the trend toward more "openness" in post-Soviet Russia, attitudes toward the control of information had not changed as rapidly as some other aspects of the society. My efforts to learn more about everyday life were occasionally viewed with suspicion by those Russians who still feared the free flow of information and ideas. My notes for this book were tampered with, my E-mail intercepted, and some of my computer disks destroyed. When I discovered what was happening, I made copies of all those materials and sent them back to the United States with friends willing to carry them by hand. Thus I was able to preserve a complete collection of the impressions that I recorded while living in Irkutsk and Vladivostok.

After returning to the United States, I continued my research on the history, customs, foods, education systems, and economic development of Siberia and the Russian Far East. Although this book is based on my own personal experiences of everyday life in Asian Russia, it also contains background information about many social, cultural, historical, and economic factors that have shaped contemporary life in that part of the world.

Throughout the book, I have used the term "Soviet" to mean a citizen of the Soviet Union and "Russian" to mean a citizen of the Russian Federation, regardless of that person's ethnic identity. I have used the term "ethnic Russians" when referring specifically to that particular ethnic group. In the Russian Federation, however, the term "Russian" usually refers only to ethnic Russians, not more broadly to any citizen of that country.

Transliterating Russian words into English for a book of this type always requires a compromise between consistency and readability, a choice between adhering to a single system or using the most common spelling of Russian words already familiar to English-language readers. In general most Russian words in the text have been transliterated according to the system of the United States Board on Geographic Names. Exceptions include direct quotations from other sources that have used a different system and the names of Russian authors that have been transliterated differently when their works were published in English. Russian words that have come into English are rendered in their most familiar form and printed without italics (glasnost, perestroika, taiga, tsar). I have also chosen to use the more common "Baikal," instead of "Baykal," when referring to the lake and to proper names, including place names, based on that word, but I have adhered to the spelling "baykal" (with italics) whenever transliterating from an actual Russian text. For ease of readability, I have omitted the Russian soft sign (') in people's names (Sofya, Igor, Yeltsin, Lebedko). And for the convenience of English-language readers unaccustomed to Russian names, I have used only the first, and sometimes also the last, names of Russians identified in this book, rather than the proper Russian form of a person's first name and patronymic (a Russian's middle name, derived from the name of his or her father).

The dollar value of each ruble amount noted in the text has been calculated at the official exchange rate at the particular time for which the figure was quoted. And all temperatures are given in degrees Fahrenheit, although the Russians use Celsius. I have avoided the use of many statistics, however, because anyone who has lived in Russia with open eyes and an open mind soon learns that official statistics compiled by the Russians are often highly unreliable—not surprisingly in a country with a tradition of public prevarication from the Potëmkin villages of the eighteenth century to the more recent publication of falsified figures about the fulfillment of five-year plans.

A book of this sort can ultimately be only one person's impressions of a highly complex society. But I hope that it will at least give the reader a picture of the people and places that I came to know so well "on the other side of Russia." I wrote it to answer many of the questions that I have been asked about life in Asian Russia; to give the reader a better understanding of the Russian people and the problems that they faced during that historic period of transformation in their country; and to dispel some of the many misconceptions that Westerners have about Siberia and the Russian Far East. If the reader comes away from this book with a richer knowledge of Asian Russia, then I will have succeeded in this endeavor.

INTRODUCTION

～

Russia—and Siberia in particular—has always appeared rather forbidding in the Western mind, an impression largely shaped by best-selling books from Boris Pasternak's *Doctor Zhivago* to Aleksandr Solzhenitsyn's *The Gulag Archipelago*. In popular fiction, nonfiction, still photography, and motion pictures, the Asian part of Russia has usually been depicted as a place of frozen tundra, snowy steppes, dense forests, icy wastelands, and grim prison camps. But Asian Russia is also a region of great natural beauty, abundant raw materials, thriving cities, and proud people. Today Siberia and the Russian Far East are home not only to reindeer herders and ice fishermen but also to millions of Russian citizens who live and work in modern metropolises, attend technical schools and universities, own cars and dachas, and have a rich cultural life. Asian Russia is traversed by the Trans-Siberian Railroad, the longest continuous railroad on the globe. Far inside Siberia's interior it curves around one of the natural wonders of the world, Lake Baikal, the largest, deepest, and oldest body of fresh water on earth. Asian Russia encompasses three-quarters of the Russian Federation's land mass and the majority of its natural resources. By many measures Asian Russia is certainly a land of superlatives.

During the second half of the twentieth century, prior to the collapse of the Soviet Union, few Americans had an opportunity to live, work, or travel widely in the Asian part of Russia because much of this vast area was off-limits to foreigners. Most of the Westerners who visited Russia went to the more accessible European side of the Ural Mountains, particularly to Moscow and Leningrad (now St. Petersburg). Almost all the foreign journalists and government employees assigned to work in the Soviet Union lived in Moscow, in special "foreigners' compounds." Whenever they wanted to journey beyond twenty-five kilometers (about sixteen miles) from the city center, they had to obtain permission from the Soviet authorities. The Soviets discouraged, controlled, and often prevented foreigners from traveling outside a few carefully designated areas of the country—and those who did get permission to travel to places such as Siberia were limited in what they were allowed to see. Even during the Gorbachev era of budding glasnost, much of Russia remained closed to foreign visitors. Similarly, many cities were also closed to Soviet citizens living in other parts of the country, unless they obtained special permits to visit friends or relatives residing in those restricted areas.

Foreign tourists crossing Russia on the Trans-Siberian Railroad were usually assigned to special cars that effectively segregated them from Soviet passengers on the train. Itineraries were controlled by the Ministry of Foreign Affairs and by Intourist, the official government travel agency that also kept track of visitors to the Soviet Union. Many cities along the Trans-Siberian route—including Vladivostok, Russia's major eastern port and home to the Soviet Pacific Fleet—were completely off-limits to foreigners. If, on an impulse, a foreign traveler wanted to get off the train at some station not included on his preplanned trip, the Soviet authorities erected bureaucratic obstacles in an attempt to thwart any deviation from the approved route. Contact between foreigners and ordinary Soviets was discouraged, and, until the late 1980s, Soviet citizens could even be prosecuted by the government for having unofficial contacts with foreign visitors.

After Mikhail Gorbachev came to power in 1985, some of these impediments to travel in the Soviet Union began to change—slowly at first, then more rapidly between 1989 and 1991, as the pace of political change in the Soviet Union also accelerated. After the collapse of the Soviet Union in late 1991, the Russian Federation became even more accessible to outsiders, with trips organized by Russian and foreign travel agencies taking tourists to parts of the country that previously had been difficult or even impossible for them to visit. But much of Asian Russia remained unknown to outsiders, as it still does.

In the early 1990s Moscow, St. Petersburg, and a few other cities of European Russia attracted the first waves of Western business people, educators, and employees of governmental and nongovernmental organizations. Fewer people set their sights on Asian Russia. A small number of investors and developers from foreign countries were attracted by Siberia's rich natural resources, including gold, diamonds, timber, oil, coal, and natural gas. Multinational companies, especially from Pacific Rim nations, saw Asian Russia not only as a source of raw materials, but also as a potentially vast new market for manufactured products from abroad. In 1992 the United States opened a consulate in Vladivostok, the first U.S. consulate in that city

*A typical Siberian wooden house in the village of
Listvyanka near Lake Baikal.*

since 1948. And in 1992 the first group of fifty-one Peace Corps volunteers
was sent to the Russian Far East to help train Russians in establishing and
operating small businesses of their own. But the number of Westerners actually living in, or even visiting, this part of Russia has always remained
considerably smaller than in European Russia.

During the period of increasing openness under Gorbachev, University of Maryland University College became the first U.S. university in history to offer an American-accredited bachelor's degree program for students in the Soviet Union (soon to be the Russian Federation), taught entirely in Russia. This joint Russian-American program was established both at Irkutsk State University, the oldest institution of higher education in Eastern Siberia, located in the city of Irkutsk near Lake Baikal, and at Far Eastern State University in Vladivostok, which was still a closed military city at that time. The goal of the program was to prepare Russian university students for positions as business managers in the market economy that was just beginning to develop in a country whose official economic system was still a socialist one.

The first classes commenced in August 1991, shortly after the unsuccessful coup in Moscow that led to the breakup of the Soviet Union four months later. Some historians have concluded that the collapse of the Soviet Union that year was at least partially a result of Gorbachev's misunderstanding of the forces unleashed through his policies of glasnost and perestroika during the late 1980s. The effects of those forces were becoming even more evident by the the the summer of 1993, when I arrived in Russia. And during the following sixteen months I lived through a time of rapid social, political, and economic change in Russia's early period of transition from an authoritarian to a democratic government, from a state-owned to a market economy, from a closed society to a more open one.

In the first half of the 1990s those processes of change were still in their initial stages. From the summer of 1993 through December, 1994, Russia—which had already seen the dissolution of its empire, the Soviet Union, and its collective security alliance, the Warsaw Pact—experienced a number of changes whose effects are still being felt today: the privatization of part, but not all, of the state-owned economy; a sharp decline in industrial production and a sudden increase in the importation of foods and other consumer goods; hyperinflation, the collapse of the ruble's value, and an enormous flight of capital from Russia; a rapid rise in unemployment and a significant reduction in social services, including health care; a substantial increase in crime, overt corruption, and *mafiya* activities; a bloody confrontation between Boris Yeltsin, the first democratically elected president of Russia, and members of the Russian parliament in Moscow, culminating in the storming of the parliament building by troops loyal to Yeltsin and the loss of more than 140 lives during that two-week political crisis; parliamentary elections, which brought contingents of Communists and ultranationalists into the Duma, the lower house of parliament; the adoption of a new constitution, which increased the power of the presidency; and the Russian invasion of the breakaway republic of Chechnya, the beginning of a bitter and bloody war there. During that same period, the number of foreigners traveling to Russia—which had begun to increase in the early 1990s—declined significantly, as a result of negative news stories coming out of Russia about crime, living conditions, and the economy, as well as several Aeroflot plane crashes in 1993 and 1994.

In June, 1993, two months before we moved to Vladivostok, my husband, Tom, and I made our first trip to Russia, to visit Moscow and St. Petersburg. In retrospect I realize how important it was to see those two cities—the traditional European centers of Russian political power—before I went to Asian Russia, because that experience gave me a better perspective on some of the differences between Russians living east and west of the Ural Mountains. When I began writing this book about life in Siberia and the Russian Far East, I chose to title it *The Other Side of Russia* because, from my first days in both European and Asian Russia, it was clear to me that Russians had not only a geographical but also a psychological "them and us" attitude toward their fellow citizens living on opposite sides of that immense country.

Part of this attitude stems from the size of the country itself, a nation that extends across eleven time zones—more than six thousand miles from west to east, from the Baltic Sea to the Bering Strait, and three thousand miles from north to south, from well above the Arctic Circle to the shores of the Black and Caspian Seas. Part of it can also be attributed to the historical isolation of large segments of Russia's population—a result of poorly developed transportation and communication systems in so vast a land, as well as political and societal obstacles to the kind of personal and professional mobility that we take for granted in the West. But part of this attitude also comes from the Russians' sense of living in, or being from, a particular town or city or region itself. Seventy years of government propaganda about the all-encompassing Soviet state did not entirely erase the individual's feeling of belonging first to a specific geographic place within the country and only secondarily to the nation as a whole.

I was soon to discover that Siberia is not only a geographic location but also a state of mind. Native-born Siberians of European Slavic ancestry have such a strong sense of themselves as a people separate from European Russians that they proudly call themselves *Sibiryaki*. This term also distinguishes them from the many indigenous Siberian peoples who belong to other ethnic groups, such as Buryats, Evenks, Chukchi, and Sakhans (Yakuts), as well as from more recent "immigrants" to Siberia from European Russia—although it should be noted that, throughout the centuries, marriages and liaisons between people of European ancestry and indigenous Siberians have produced a large number of Siberians of mixed ethnic and racial heritage. Asian-born Russians descended from European forebears also distinguish themselves from Asians such as Chinese, Japanese, Mongolians, Koreans, Vietnamese, and others. Regardless of their own ethnic identification, however, many residents of the Asian side of Russia often refer to their own part of the country as "Siberia" or "the Russian Far East," reserving the term "Russia" only for the European side, west of the Urals. Some even refer to European Russia as "the mainland" or "the continent," as if Asian Russia were an island separated from Europe not only by an arbitrary geographical boundary, but also by an ocean of differences.

More than a century ago, the Russian writer Anton Chekhov noted the same phenomenon during an eight-month, roundtrip journey from Moscow to Sakhalin Island in the Sea of Okhotsk off Russia's far eastern coast. In 1890 he wrote, "my God, how far removed life here is from Russia! . . . While I was sailing down the Amur [River, east of Lake Baikal] I really felt I wasn't in Russia at all, but somewhere in Patagonia or Texas. Quite apart from the strange, un-Russian scenery, I constantly got the impression that our Russian way of life is completely alien to the old settlers on the Amur . . . and that we who come from Russia appear as foreigners."

Traveling eastward from the low line of mountains that divides Europe from Asia, one soon discovers that Siberia itself contains a large number of geographical, political, ethnic, cultural, and psychological divisions seldom recognized in the West. Westerners tend to think of Siberia as a single geographic entity, encompassing all of Russia's land and people between the Ural Mountains and the Pacific Ocean. But when I lived there in the mid-1990s, that vast area of 5.3 million square miles was broadly divided into three macroregions (which actually had no formal political authority within the Russian Federation): Western Siberia, Eastern Siberia, and the Russian Far East—geographic configurations whose boundaries were based on a combination of historical, political, and economic factors, some of which have changed over time. Each of these macroregions was composed of several smaller administrative subdivisions known as *respubliki* (republics), *oblasti* (regions), *kraya* (territories or provinces), and *okruga* (districts). In the 1990s the new Russian Federation comprised a total of eighty-nine of these administrative subdivisions, twenty-nine of which were in Asian Russia. Many of the people inhabiting those areas east of the Urals also made a distinction between "Siberians," who lived in Western and Eastern Siberia, and residents of the Russian Far East, who lived in the easternmost part of the Russian Federation.

Despite its immense size, Asian Russia has, for a number of reasons, remained beyond the mainstream of contemporary mass media reportage in the West. Although numerous books and articles about the Russian Federation have been published in Europe and North America and several documentary films shown on television there, the Western media have focused their attention primarily on the most easily accessible parts of European Russia—particularly Moscow and St. Petersburg—not the huge and distant Asian side of Russia. Even the scattering of travel narratives published about post-Soviet Siberia and the Russian Far East have been written mainly by people who spent a few weeks traveling in those parts of the country, not actually living and working there for any length of time. As a result most people in the West still know little about the details of daily life in Asian Russia today.

My own sojourn in Asian Russia was one of the most intense learning periods I have ever experienced. Everyday life ranged from fascinating to frustrating, but it was seldom dull. Sometimes the absurdities I encountered left me feeling like I was living on "The Far Side" of Russia, not just "the other side." I quickly learned that the best way to cope with the many challenges I confronted each day was to be a good sport, to be flexible, and to appreciate (if not always accept) the ironies of life in such a complex and often contradictory country. I also discerned that for foreigners to live successfully in Russia, they must be able to take daily life with a grain of salt—perhaps a grain from the small saltcellar atop the loaf of bread that Russians customarily offer as a sign of hospitality when a guest arrives in their country or at their front door.

After more than four years as a foreign correspondent in Moscow, Michael Binyon summed up the situation well in his 1983 book, *Life in Russia:* "Russia is a country that demands constant effort. It demands patience, tolerance, and a sense of humor. It is a country of hardship, frustration, and oppression, insecure at home, encircled by enemies abroad, facing an uncertain future and grappling with political and economic difficulties that look awesomely intractable. But it is also a country where life has an intensity and sharpness that few know in the West. Shorn of the affluent ease that cocoons us in the West, personal relationships seem stronger, values, emotions and choices harsher and more real." Similarly Birgitta Ingemanson, director of Russian Area Studies at Washington State University, observed in 1990, "Yes, Russia is bleak, dreary, and badly organized; but it is also true that as nowhere else, life can come sparkling to the surface in the swiftest of seconds. We, too, are richer when we become attuned to the magic of this contrast."

I tried to stay attuned to the magic of that contrast throughout my time in Russia. But when I returned to the United States and recounted my stories of everyday life, many people asked me why I ever wanted to go to Russia in the first place—and, given my experiences there, why I stayed so long. This book is my reply.

For both Tom and me, living in Russia was an unprecedented personal adventure, an experience both of us would certainly repeat despite the difficulties we encountered, the hardships we endured, and the glaring differences between life in the modern Western world and in Asian Russia of the late twentieth century. Although much of the material I have included in this memoir might seem negative (to Russians and Americans alike, sometimes for different reasons), I have tried to report life as I saw it, without any attempt to achieve some kind of contrived balance between the good and bad aspects of what I experienced there.

The first half of this book describes the locations where I lived, worked, and traveled in Siberia and the Russian Far East, including Vladivostok, Irkutsk, the Buryat lands, and Lake Baikal. The second half focuses on specific aspects of everyday life, from housing conditions to the workplace, from the consumer society to the celebration of holidays old and new. Since so little has yet been written about daily life in Asian Russia during the post-Soviet period, I felt that it was especially important to document the details of what I observed—not only the continuation of old ways in a new and sometimes rapidly changing context, but also the material aspects of everyday life, from the sudden influx of imported products to the kinds of foods that people prepared at home, from the discontinuities of the new market economy to the public utility crises that still plague parts of the Russian Far East today.

Although no foreigner who goes to Russia can ever claim to know what it is like to be born and raised there, the interested and observant outsider can still seek to delve beyond facile stereotypes and superficial impressions. I tried to do this while living in Russia—and later, while writing this book. I also tried to heed the advice of those who have warned against making broad generalizations based on one's own particular experiences in that country. As Michael Binyon noted in *Life in Russia:* "even those [Westerners] who have lived a generation in the Soviet Union—and there are one or two—never fully understand the country. It is aptly symbolized by those painted wooden dolls you find in any souvenir shop; you open one and there is another inside. When you are confident that you really know how Russians think and react, that is the time to beware, for you can be mightily deceived."

THE OTHER SIDE OF RUSSIA

CHAPTER 1

✌

The Road to Russia

When I told my family and friends in the United States that I was moving to Siberia, the following conversation invariably occurred:

"What are you going to do there?"
"Teach at two Russian universities," I replied.
"There are *universities* in Siberia?" they asked incredulously.
"Yes, several major universities," I said.
"Where are they?" was always the next question.
"In the big cities," I replied. "Vladivostok, Irkutsk, and Novosibirsk
    all have populations over half a million."
"There are *cities* in Siberia?" they gasped, as if I had just told them
    there were health spas on the moon.

A pause. And then the last, inevitable question:

"Do they have *meat* in Siberia?"

Regardless of their own images of Russia, few of the people who knew me well were surprised to hear that I had accepted a job there. As a child growing up in a small Texas town during the 1950s, I had become interested in the Soviet Union at an early age. Like most other Americans at that time, I viewed the Soviet Union as a superpower, a nuclear threat, an enemy to be reckoned with. The decade of the fifties was an era of bomb shelters in the backyards and "duck-and-cover" civil defense drills in school. Newsreels at local movie theaters, and news programs on my family's first television set, reported the horrors of the Korean War; the hearings of the House Committee on Un-American Activities, with its "Red-scare" rhetoric and dire warnings of a "worldwide Communist conspiracy"; the death of Josef Stalin in Russia in 1953, and that same year the execution of Julius and Ethel Rosenberg as Soviet spies in the United States; the Hungarian uprising in 1956 and its brutal suppression by Soviet troops; the launch of *Sputniks I* and *II* in 1957 and subsequent Soviet successes in space; the building of the Berlin Wall in 1961; and the Cuban missile crisis of 1962. Each of those newsworthy events was depicted not only as a black-and-white image on the screen, but also as a black-and-white choice in the mind: Communist or anti-Communist, either-or, them-or-us, wrong-or-right. But as a child I also learned something about other, less-stereotyped aspects of the Soviet Union, about the human side of life in that country, through the books of popular writers such as John Gunther and Irving R. Levine, as well as the personal tales of one of my cousins who traveled there during the Khrushchev era.

That cousin was an unlikely source of positive information about the Soviet Union. After serving in England as a cryptographer with the U.S. military during World War II, he had established John Deere farm equipment dealerships in Illinois and Idaho during the late 1940s. Twice he testified before committees of the U.S. Senate and House of Representatives, against the power of American labor unions. Later he pursued a second career as a stockbroker while also becoming a speaker on the Knife and Fork Club circuit throughout the United States. A popular raconteur with a serious interest in international politics, he traveled to the Soviet Union three times during the late 1950s and early 1960s, ostensibly to gather material for his professional speaking engagements. I was never quite sure about the real reasons behind his trips to Russia during those dark days of the Cold War, but I do know that he returned with a repertoire of entertaining stories about travel in that still-secretive place.

I listened with fascination to his anecdotes about hotel "key ladies," collective-farm workers, kindly grandmothers, surly shop girls, and obfuscating bureaucrats. He recounted visits to Russians' homes and meals around their kitchen tables, religious services at Baptist and Russian Orthodox churches, harrowing flights on Aeroflot planes, and trips by car through the Russian countryside. He told about finding Russian farm machinery that had been replicated down to the last detail from John Deere machinery sent to the Soviet Union under the Lend-Lease program during World War II. Once at a trade show where such a Russian-made tractor was on display, he asked the

Russian representative to explain the function of a metal ring welded onto it. "We don't know," replied the Russian. "It was on the one we copied."

Some of my cousin's experiences in Russia gave him an opportunity, unusual for an American at that time, to see beyond the hard outer shell of the "official" Soviet Union. And although he was an anti-Communist, staunchly conservative businessman who voted Republican at home, in his descriptions of daily life in Russia he was careful to separate people from politics—his own and theirs. He characterized the Russians he had met as people who were often friendly, humorous, generous, and kind, sometimes also stubborn, duplicitous, and deceitful, but always proud of their own country and curious about America—in other words, just like people everywhere on the globe. Even today, now that I have lived in Russia myself, I find that the observations he made about Russia and its people remain accurate and insightful almost half a century later.

My initial interest in Russia stemmed from those early influences of the American mass media, bolstered by my cousin's personal stories about his own experiences in the Soviet Union when I was still a child. Several years later, that interest led me to specialize in Soviet and East European Studies as an undergraduate at the University of Texas in Austin and to study international politics, with a focus on U.S.-Soviet strategic relations, as a graduate student in political science at the University of Michigan in Ann Arbor.

During the summer of 1968, just before I entered graduate school, I worked as an intern for the United States Information Agency (USIA) in Washington, D.C., in the section that dealt with the Soviet Union and East Europe. My office was adjacent to that of Alexander Barmine, a tall, distinguished-looking, very likeable, elderly gentleman who held a high position in that branch of USIA. Barmine's life story seemed to come straight out of my Russian history books. Born in Byelorussia in 1899, he had joined the Red Army as a nineteen-year-old private, fought in Russia's civil war following the Bolshevik Revolution, graduated from a school for Red Army officers, and held several commands on the western front in 1920 during Russia's war against Poland. He subsequently graduated from the General Staff College in Moscow, then retired from the army in 1922, with the rank of brigadier general, at the ripe age of twenty-three.

A member of the Bolshevik Party since 1919, Barmine had also served as a political commissar in the Red Army during his military career. Between 1923 and 1937, he held a variety of Soviet government positions in Russia, Persia, France, Italy, Belgium, Poland, and Greece. In 1937 he defected to the West from his post in Athens during the height of Stalin's purges, fleeing

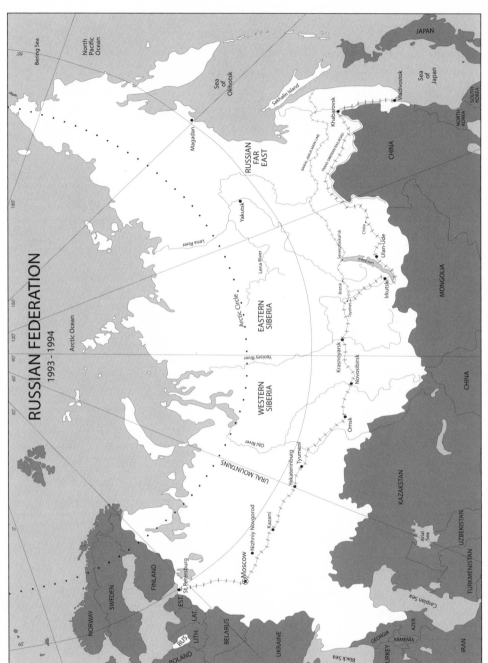

MAP 1. *Russian Federation, 1993–94 (boundary lines are approximations).*

first to Paris where, condemned to death, in absentia, by the Soviet government, he managed to evade the Soviet secret police for two years. In 1940 he immigrated to the United States, and in 1942 he enlisted as a private in the U.S. Army—surely the first and only former brigadier general from Russia ever to have held that rank in the American military.

Barmine wrote a book about his extraordinary experiences, which was published in 1945. Titled *One Who Survived: The Life Story of a Russian under the Soviets*, it was later translated into twenty-three languages. When Barmine died in 1987, at the age of eighty-eight, his obituary in the *New York Times* quoted Edmund Wilson's review of that book in the July 14, 1945, issue of the *New Yorker* magazine: "For a foreigner who really wants to learn what has been happening of recent years in Russia—as distinguished from demanding support either for faith or for hostile prejudice—this is probably the one book that ought to be read."

Alexander Barmine was always very kind and helpful to me at work, where he encouraged me to think critically, to question sources of information, and to look beyond superficial impressions. But interns tend to be viewed as fifth wheels in federal government offices. To give me something to do while I was drawing a full-time salary, Barmine assigned me to a highly classified, but low-priority, task: translating from Russian into English a rather grainy, photocopied manuscript written by someone I had never heard of, a Russian physicist named Andrei Sakharov. Shortly before I finished the translation, however, I was scooped by the *New York Times*, which published Sakharov's historic essay, "Reflections on Progress, Peaceful Coexistence, and Intellectual Freedom," on July 22 of that year. My only consolation was that my own translation was almost identical to that of the *Times*.

A month later, on the morning of August 21, 1968, I checked the Teletype machine as usual when I arrived at work at USIA. As the block letters clacked unevenly onto the flimsy yellow paper, forming words that slowly flowed into sentences, I couldn't believe what I was reading. Other people in the office soon gathered around the Teletype machine, where we all watched in shock as a succession of reports from abroad described the Warsaw Pact invasion of Czechoslovakia. Many of my coworkers broke into tears as they imagined the fate of friends and relatives there—and feared for the lives of others in adjacent countries if the international crisis were to expand beyond the borders of Czechoslovakia.

Twenty-one years later, in November, 1989, I vividly remembered that fateful August day as I stood among the thousands of demonstrators crowded into Prague's Wenceslas Square during what came to be called the "Velvet Revolution." As I listened to speeches by Alexander Dubček, the former Communist leader who had been deposed in the late 1960s for seeking to give socialism "a human face," and Václav Havel, the dissident playwright who was soon to become the president of a democratic Czechoslovakia, I— like so many others in that hopeful crowd—felt that history had come full circle, from the Soviets' crushing of the Prague Spring movement in the summer of 1968 to the recent events in Central and Eastern Europe during that momentous autumn of 1989, including the opening of the Berlin Wall only two weeks before. And, as the Communist bloc continued to crumble that year, I was gratified that Alexander Barmine had survived to see the first stirrings of glasnost and perestroika in the Soviet Union, and that Andrei Sakharov, who died in December, 1989, had lived long enough to witness the beginning of the end of the Cold War.

Despite my longtime interest in the Soviet Union, however, my own life had taken a turn away from Russia during the previous two decades. In 1970 I had moved to Western Europe, where I lived successively in France, England, Germany, and Scotland. While in Europe, I had also married Tom Hudgins, a former classmate from the University of Texas. A graduate student in economics when he was drafted into the U.S. Army in the late 1960s, Tom had had the good fortune to be sent to fight the Cold War in Germany instead of the much more deadly one in Vietnam. Together we eventually returned to the United States, earned additional graduate degrees in film production, and worked for a time as photographers, filmmakers, and multimedia producers.

But we missed the adventure of living abroad. In 1975 we both accepted teaching positions with the European Division of University of Maryland University College, on a one-year contract that turned into sixteen years as itinerant instructors with the university's overseas education programs at U.S. military bases in Germany, Spain, Greece, Japan, and Korea. By the time Maryland offered us the opportunity to work in Russia in 1993, I had already lived in twenty-six cities in nine countries on three continents, and I had traveled in more than forty countries around the world. The transfer to Russia would be my fiftieth household move in less than three decades.

Prior to 1993, however, I had never been to Russia itself. But during the previous fifteen years I had traveled extensively in Central and Eastern Europe between the Balkans and the Baltic—from the mountains of Macedonia, Bosnia, and Kosovo, to the forests of Croatia and Slovakia, to the plains of Hungary and Poland. I was in Hungary, Germany, and Czechoslovakia dur-

ing the autumn of 1989, when Communist governments were collapsing in
Central Europe, and where I had the opportunity to witness firsthand some
of the major political events that changed the course of recent history. Those
same events soon created unexpected opportunities for Americans such as
Tom and myself to work in parts of Russia where it would have been un-
thinkable for us to live only a short time before.

Along with boxes and bags full of winter clothing, herbs and spices, office
supplies, and dozens of books, I carried to Russia my own knowledge of
that country's history, culture, politics, and language. But I didn't tote along
any conscious ideological baggage. As someone who had the good fortune
to be educated by scholars who seldom let their personal political prefer-
ences influence their teaching of history and politics, I had no preconcep-
tions about Russia as either a worker's paradise or a Stalinist gulag. My
teachers, colleagues, mentors, and friends were people of many different
backgrounds who had lived, worked, studied, and traveled in tsarist Russia,
the Soviet Union, and the Soviet bloc at various times during the first nine
decades of the twentieth century. Some had dealt directly with Josef Stalin
and other major officials in the Soviet Union; with Tomáš Masaryk, Jan
Masaryk, and Edvard Beneš in Czechoslovakia; with anti-Communist revolutionary leaders in Hungary; with Josip Broz Tito in Yugoslavia; with political dissidents in several East Bloc countries; and with key advisers on
foreign policy and national security in the United States. So when I finally
went to Russia myself, I approached the country as a realist, with an open
mind, with interest and curiosity, but without Red-tinted glasses or conservative blinders.

Shortly before Tom and I left for Russia, we had an opportunity to meet
two young Russian officials who were visiting the United States—Even E.
Harlanov, one of Boris Yeltsin's economic advisers, and Vladimir I.
Milovankin, deputy chief of the Department of Foreign Investment in the
new Russian Federation. Both were quite frank about the economic and
social problems that Russia was facing in the early 1990s. And both expressed their hope that new education programs such as ours would focus
on teaching Russians the practical aspects of business and economics, not
abstract theories that had little relevance to the realities of present-day
Russia. "Russia has already had enough theories," Harlanov noted sardonically. Later, as we shook hands to say good-bye, I told Harlanov and
Milovankin how much I was looking forward to living in their country.
"Yes, it's a good time to be going there," Harlanov replied with a straight
face. "Such times occur only once every seventy years or so."

CHAPTER 2

~

Vladivostok

CAPITAL OF RUSSIA'S WILD EAST

All the passengers applauded as our Aeroflot plane bumped to a landing on the washboard runway at the airport in Khabarovsk, just north of the Chinese border, in the Russian Far East. Tom and I were scheduled to transfer to another Aeroflot flight the next day to reach our final destination, Vladivostok. But when we checked in for that flight, the airport officials said the plane going to Vladivostok was too small to carry us and all of our luggage, too. They suggested we take our scheduled flight on to Vladivostok—and let them send our luggage on another plane later in the evening.

We were jet-lagged after two days of air travel from Texas to California to Alaska to Russia. But we weren't stupid. There was no way we would leave a year's supply of winter clothing, lecture notes, books, medicines, and other essentials with the reputedly corrupt airport officials at Khabarovsk. Politely, but firmly, we refused their offer. Which meant that new tickets would have to be obtained for a later flight on a larger airplane—and that we would have to spend who-knew-how-many-more hours in one of the dirtiest, most depressing air terminals I had ever seen.

Granted, we had a lot of baggage—fifteen pieces total, including six large, heavy boxes of textbooks and supplies for our university program. We had already paid several hundred dollars in overweight baggage charges to Aeroflot in San Francisco when we boarded the international flight to Khabarovsk. Now Aeroflot wanted to charge us again for the "domestic" leg of the journey, the last four hundred miles to Vladivostok.

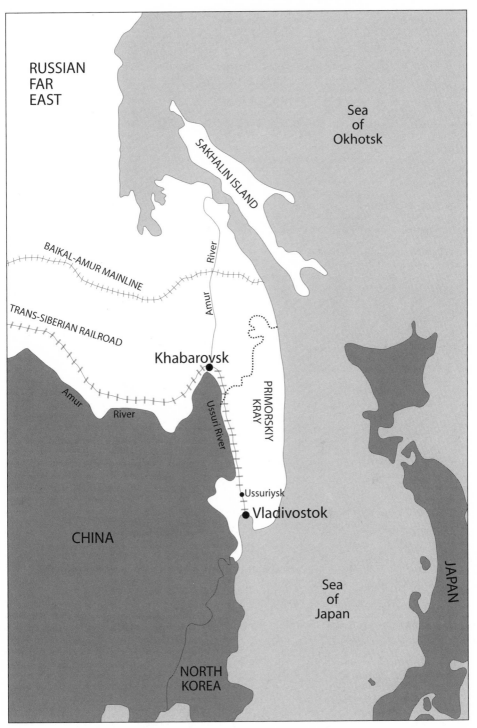

MAP 2. *Southeastern part of the Russian Far East*
(boundary lines are approximations).

It took more than an hour to get our tickets changed to the later flight. Then we had to negotiate with the airport officials for another hour in regard to the baggage. They weighed the luggage again and assessed an exorbitant price, 450 dollars, for the excess.

"But the Russians ahead of us paid much less money for a similar amount of baggage," I protested.

"That's because we have two rates," the official replied. "One for foreigners and one for Russians. You pay a higher rate and you pay in dollars. They pay a lower rate and they pay in rubles. It's simple."

We sat down on the luggage piled in front of the check-in counter and calculated the financial damage. Those final four hundred miles from Khabarovsk to Vladivostok were going to cost us as much as the five thousand miles from the United States to Russia. There was nothing we could do except pay and get on the plane.

Round One—and the Russians were the winners.

The Russian official had already told us he could not accept our travelers' checks. We would have to pay cash. Fortunately we had come prepared for such a situation, with 3,000 dollars in small bills divided between us and stashed in well-hidden money belts. It was getting late, the flight would be boarding soon, and we were the last passengers who hadn't checked in their luggage.

"Okay," Tom finally said to me. "I'll go find the men's restroom and get enough dollars out of my money belt to pay for this and get us on to Vladivostok."

By the time Tom came back, the airport official had disappeared. We waited and waited, becoming more anxious as each minute ticked away. Our plane was already on the runway, and the waiting room was empty. Tom went to find someone else who could check in the luggage. Not long after Tom left, the Russian official returned to the check-in counter and asked me if we were going to board the flight or not.

"Yes," I replied, "but my husband has the money for the baggage, and I don't know where he's gone." I had enough money to pay for it, too, but I couldn't leave the luggage unattended while I went to the women's restroom and stripped down to my own money belt.

Just then Tom returned. "Where have you been?" I asked. "Pay this guy quickly so we can get on that plane."

Tom started to count out the 450 dollars and hand them to the Russian behind the counter. The man shook his head no.

"What's the matter?" Tom asked.

"It's too late," the man replied. "It's after five o'clock. The person who is authorized to take dollars has already gone home."

"So will you accept rubles?" asked Tom.

"Of course," said the airport official.

Tom took out his pocket calculator and began to figure the ruble equivalent of 450 dollars.

"Where can I get these dollars changed into rubles?" Tom inquired.

"Over there," said the man, nodding his head toward an unmarked door. Tom started off in that direction. "But it's too late," the Russian called out to him. "The exchange office has already closed today."

Tom turned back with a hard look in his eyes. "Then where *can* I get these dollars exchanged?" he asked, trying to keep his voice as even as possible, when he felt like shouting in anger and frustration.

"I can do it for you," the Russian calmly replied.

"Okay, okay," said Tom, pulling out his calculator again and knowing that we were going to get taken in this illegal financial transaction. "What's your rate?"

"One thousand and twenty rubles for a dollar," the Russian replied, which was quite close to the official exchange rate.

Pleased at this surprising turn of events, Tom began counting out the dollars again, to exchange them into rubles. When he got to 50 dollars and started to put another ten-dollar bill on the counter, the Russian stopped him, saying, "No, no. That's enough."

"I don't understand," said Tom. "The overweight baggage charge is 400 dollars more than that."

"Yes," the Russian replied. "That was the foreigners' price if you paid in dollars at the exchange office before five o'clock. Now it's after five o'clock and you are paying in rubles, so you pay the same rate as Russian travelers. That will be 45,900 rubles, which is 45 dollars." He took out a calculator, checked his own figures again, reached into his pocket, and gave Tom the ruble equivalent of 5 dollars in change. Then he smiled, tagged the luggage, and sent it out to be loaded onto the plane.

Round Two—and we were the winners.

Welcome to Absurdistan.

We had arrived in Khabarovsk at eleven o'clock the night before, on a fully loaded Aeroflot flight from San Francisco via Anchorage and Magadan. Two of our University of Maryland colleagues were on the same flight; together we comprised four of the seven faculty members sent by the university in August, 1993, to teach in Russia during that academic year. On board we also happened to meet four Russian students enrolled in our program, returning home after a two-month summer vacation in the United States. I soon discovered that these students and their families were among the class of Russians who, because of their political and business connections, rated as VIPs on such flights—the group of people who sit in special airport waiting rooms; who board and leave the plane first, on vehicles separate from the rest of the passengers; and who go through a different, much faster, passport and customs inspection.

Aeroflot's domestic flight from Khabarovsk to Vladivostok the next day was noticeably worse than its international flight from the United States. There were no reserved seats, and passengers scrambled to find ones that weren't occupied or broken, as well as places to put all their boxes, bundles, and bags. The windows were dirty, the upholstery was grungy, and large pieces of scrap metal littered the floor. The cabin was full of flies, and a worm crawled around on the seat in front of me. The stewardess, who looked like she would rather be anywhere else than inside that plane, served us nothing but carbonated mineral water that tasted like rusty Alka-Seltzer and smelled like rotten eggs. "Where Aeroflot begins, order ends," quipped one of our students, quoting a modern Russian saying.

After landing at the airport in Vladivostok, we had to remain inside the plane until the VIPs, including our four new students and their families, had debarked to two large black cars and one unmarked van that drove straight across the tarmac and up to the aircraft. We sat in the hot, stuffy cabin and watched as their drivers unloaded boxes of new television sets, videocassette recorders, and computers from the plane's baggage compartment and stashed them in the waiting vehicles. Only after the VIP cars had pulled away were the rest of us finally allowed to get off the plane.

Soon we were in a blue Toyota van bouncing down the potholed highway toward Vladivostok, the city that Nikita Khrushchev once dubbed "the San Francisco of Russia" because of its hilly terrain and scenic location by the sea. In 1913 the Norwegian explorer Fridtjof Nansen had compared Vladivostok to Naples, albeit without Mount Vesuvius smoking in the background. Local Russian boosters called it "the Pearl of the Golden Horn," in reference to the Golden Horn Bay, one of several bays and gulfs of the Sea of Japan that wash the shores of the city. But even before we arrived in Vladivostok, we also knew that this capital of Primorskiy Kray (Russia's Maritime Territory) had the dubious reputation of being "the Capital of

Russia's Wild East," a city beset by organized crime, corrupt government, and a breakdown of social and municipal services.

The largest and most important city in the Russian Far East, Vladivostok in the mid-1990s had a population of 650,000, with a total of nearly a million people living in the greater metropolitan area. Located on approximately the same latitude as Monaco, Madrid, and Milwaukee, Vladivostok is the southernmost capital city in Asian Russia and one of the most southerly cities in the entire Russian Federation. It has a unique microclimate, influenced by the mountains and the sea, where subtropical vegetation and arctic plants grow side by side. Summer temperatures sometimes soar above ninety degrees Fahrenheit, but in winter the thermometer can drop to twenty degrees below zero. Icy winds blow off the ocean, and rare Siberian tigers stalk their prey in the snowy forests nearby. Tigers and anchors, two suitable symbols of the geographical location, appear on the city's coat of arms, as well as on the emblems of Primorskiy Kray and the coast guard of the Russian Pacific Fleet.

Vladivostok was originally established in 1860 as a naval base and military outpost for tsarist forces in the eastern part of the country. Its name in Russian means "Ruler of the East"—and indeed, during most of its history, Vladivostok's primary functions have been to provide a port for Russian naval forces in the Pacific Ocean, an administrative center for the Russian military in the Far East, and a balance of power vis-à-vis other nations in the area, especially China and Japan. Not long after it was founded, Vladivostok also became an important commercial port, and in 1880 the Russian government granted the settlement the official status of a city. Nine years later, when Vladivostok was declared to be a fortress of the Russian military, construction began on the first of several sets of fortifications designed to protect the city and the men stationed there. In the 1990s, in keeping with an old tradition of fortress cities in Russia, a large artillery piece was still fired every day at noon, from the peak of Tiger Hill, its percussive boom a reminder of the city's historical role as a bastion for Russia's military forces in the Far East.

Strategically situated near the point where the borders of Russia, China, and North Korea converge, Vladivostok is also only an hour away from Japan by air. Vladivostok is actually closer to its U.S. sister city of San Diego than it is to Moscow, which is seven time zones and 5,771 railroad miles away. European Russians' attitude toward the city's distant location on the other side of Russia is apparent in the often-quoted announcements made by conductors on the Trans-Siberian Railroad when passengers begin to disembark at Vladivostok: "Take your time, ladies and gentlemen, you have reached the end of the world," and "Ladies and gentlemen, you don't have to hurry, because Russia ends here and there is nowhere else to go."

Historically—except for the period when it was a closed city—Vladivostok has served as Russia's primary Asian gateway, its easternmost window onto the world and the major Pacific port of entry to Russia itself. Prior to the Bolshevik Revolution of 1917, Vladivostok was a cosmopolitan, multicultural, polyglot city, host to consulates from a dozen nations. In 1917 its population numbered just over 130,000, and its residents included sizable groups of Chinese, Japanese, Koreans, and various Europeans, as well as a large military contingent of Russian sailors, soldiers, and officers, and the civilian members of its commercial shipping fleet. Factories, theaters, hotels, social clubs, newspapers, and even a racecourse had been established. In addition to several Russian Orthodox churches, Vladivostok also had a number of buildings where its Lutheran, Catholic, Jewish, Buddhist, and Shintoist communities gathered for worship. Few of these religious edifices remain in the city today; most were destroyed or converted to other uses after the Bolshevik Revolution. Destruction was also the fate of the monumental triumphal arch that had been built in 1891 to commemorate the visit to Vladivostok that year by Tsarevich Nikolay Aleksandrovich Romanov, the future Tsar Nikolay II, the last monarch to rule Russia before the revolutions of 1917.

During the chaos of the civil war in Russia following the Bolshevik Revolution, eleven foreign nations—including the United States, Britain, France, and Japan—sent expeditionary forces to the Russian Far East in pursuit of a variety of different, sometimes conflicting, and often ill-defined goals, some of them political, others economic or military. In the summer of 1918, only three months before the end of World War I, President Woodrow Wilson dispatched nine thousand American troops to Asian Russia—officially, to help other Allied forces in keeping the eastern section of the Trans-Siberian Railroad open to traffic during the continued fighting of the Russian civil war. The majority of the Americans remained in or around Vladivostok until they were withdrawn in April 1920. The Japanese, who were seeking to extend their influence in that part of Asia, kept their much larger military force of more than seventy thousand men in Russia until 1922. After the Soviets finally consolidated their power in Siberia and the Russian Far East, and after all foreign troops had departed, the Soviets continued for the next seven decades to denounce this foreign intervention during their civil war, citing it as indicative that other countries still had designs on Soviet territory.

For more than forty years after World War II, from 1948 to 1992, Vladivostok was closed to most foreigners, particularly those from non-Communist countries—and, at various times, closed to nonresident Soviet citizens, too. The Soviet government declared the city to be off-limits because of its strategic location, its military installations, and its function as the nerve center of both the military and civilian intelligence organizations of eastern Russia. But sometimes the door opened a crack. In 1974 President Gerald Ford and an entourage of U.S. government officials and journalists were invited to travel to Vladivostok briefly for Ford's summit meeting with Soviet leader Leonid Brezhnev. In 1988 during the Gorbachev era, the city was opened to Soviet citizens from elsewhere in the country, who no longer had to obtain special permission to go there. By the late 1980s, Soviet companies in Vladivostok had undertaken joint ventures with businesses in several non-Communist countries, and Far Eastern State University had established ties with institutions of higher education in the United States, Japan, and the Republic of Korea. On January 1, 1992, soon after the breakup of the Soviet Union, Vladivostok was officially opened to foreigners—although groups of academics, business people, and even military and government representatives from the United States and other non-Communist countries had been allowed to visit the city earlier, primarily as a result of Gorbachev's policy of glasnost.

Shortly after the Soviet Union collapsed, Western business people, Chinese traders, Japanese and South Korean entrepreneurs, Taiwanese and Australian investors, and a ragbag of con men, carpetbaggers, speculators, hustlers, prostitutes, drug dealers, and gangsters—both locals and outsiders—all began to take advantage of the new openness to seek their fortunes in Vladivostok, legally or illegally. Missionaries arrived to make converts. Educators came to teach Western business methods and foreign languages, particularly English, which was in great demand. U.S. Peace Corps and consular personnel, employees of the U.S. Information Agency and the U.S. Agency for International Development, and representatives of a number of nonprofit and nongovernmental organizations came to Vladivostok to assist Russians in making the transition to a democratic state and a market economy. Democracy was the new ideal, capitalism the new savior, and *biznes* the new buzzword.

Post-Soviet Vladivostok quickly became a city of opportunity and instability, excitement and energy, corruption and crime. In some ways it was not unlike Vladivostok during the unsettled period of the Russian civil war, which one observer in 1919, Konstantin Kharsky, described as a city of

"Morphine, cocaine, prostitution, blackmail, sudden riches and ruin, dashing autos, a cinematic flow of faces . . . uniforms from every kingdom, empire, republic, monarchist clubs, leftist rallies, complete isolation from Moscow." Vladivostok in the mid-1990s was similarly a city of contrasts: sailors, soldiers, and students; merchants, mobsters, and military cadets; ragged beggars and chic women; homeless drunks and wealthy businessmen; *mafiya* molls and burly bodyguards.

Even under the Soviets, before the city was opened to outsiders, Vladivostok's crime rate was reported to be the highest of any urban area in the country. In the newly opened city of the 1990s, criminal behavior became more open, too, as previously established institutions of social and political control began to break down. By the time I arrived in Vladivostok in 1993, Primorskiy Kray had almost double the annual crime rate of Russia as a whole. As one of my Russian friends observed, "In times when there is a lack of power, the dark powers are the ones who rush in to fill the void."

Ordinary citizens became victims of burglary, armed robbery, assault, extortion, and murder. One of Tom's Russian students was stabbed in the chest outside a nightclub on Vladivostok's main street when he refused to give the attackers his new leather jacket. Twice on his way home from class, one of my students was held up at knife point and robbed of everything but his underwear. An American woman was severely beaten on the street near a bus stop. An American friend of ours was slipped a mickey by a Russian visiting his apartment and woke up later to discover the place stripped clean. The Russian had also stolen the keys to his office downtown and heisted thousands of dollars' worth of electronic equipment. Statistics showed that the Chinese in Vladivostok were far more likely than other outsiders to be targets of crime—but the city's reputation of being similar to Chicago in the 1920s exacerbated the fears of many of its foreign residents, both Westerners and East Asians, some of whom even hired bodyguards of their own. As Vladivostok's murder rate reached an average of two per day in 1994, many people—Russians and foreigners alike—became afraid to go out after dark, and some even carried knives, gas pistols, or cans of Mace for protection.

Much of the criminal activity was perpetrated by organized groups ranging from small-time gangsters to major *mafiya* members with business interests in commercial shipping, drug trafficking, arms dealing, prostitution, and protection rackets. These groups were also implicated in contract killings and car bombings, with victims ranging from powerful businessmen to hapless bystanders. Local newspapers published reports of people being maimed or killed by hand grenades, plastic explosives, and gunfire. On the roads southwest of Vladivostok, a gang led by a former traffic control officer posed as policemen in uniform, stopped cars coming in from China, murdered the occupants, and stole the vehicles. Some of the most notorious—and financially successful—of the organized gangs were the "port thieves" operating at the city's commercial and military docks, who stole whatever they could get their hands on, from automobiles to automatic weapons. In a *Vladivostok News* article about the city's rising crime rate, Andrey Ostrovskiy, a local Russian journalist wrote, "My great-grandparents have lived in this city all their lives. 'Times were different,' they say, 'but they've never been so bad.'"

Sartorially, it was sometimes difficult to distinguish the local *mafiya* "businessmen" from their bodyguards, many of whom hung around the newly restored Hotel Versailles in downtown Vladivostok. In their shiny silk suits, black nylon shirts, narrow white ties, white socks, and mirrored sunglasses, they all looked like gangsters in old black-and-white Hollywood B movies. Some of the lower-level hoods rode around town in flashy black limousines; others favored less conspicuous, but well-armored, Japanese cars. The truly powerful people operated behind the scenes, reputedly in collusion with the political authorities and the police. Corruption in Vladivostok was as well established and pervasive as elsewhere in Russia and worked according to long-standing traditions. As a Russian proverb says, "It's easy to steal when seven others are stealing, too."

The Western press perpetuated Vladivostok's unsavory reputation with newspaper and magazine articles such as "Once Secret Vladivostok Now Heart of 'Wild East'" (*International Herald Tribune*), "Russia's Wild East: A Yeasty Boom" (*World Press Review*), and "Lawless Thugs Rule Russian City" (*Chicago Tribune*). But locals sometimes had a different reaction to this characterization of their city. Over a sumptuous meal at one of the city's best restaurants, a senior Russian official who had just returned from a trip to the United States told me that he objected to the American media's reporting only "the dark side" of Russia, picturing it as a violent and chaotic country. He thought this was hypocritical because America had such a bad crime rate of its own. I agreed with him about America's high rate of crime, but I pointed out that Russia too had serious problems with crime, including organized crime, and surely he understood why the American media would find that a newsworthy subject. He replied that he had recently discussed *mafiya* activities in Vladivostok "with certain local 'officials,' if you know what I mean," who assured him that there were just "twenty-nine groups of organized crime [operating in the city], totaling only five hundred people." I stared at him while trying to think of some response to this star-tling, matter-of-fact statement that implied so much by saying so little. After a short pause, he added, "Of course, *all* the customs people are corrupt, thoroughly corrupt."

Such attitudes on the part of powerful local Russians contributed to the double-edged cynicism that some Americans developed during their stay in Vladivostok. Many of those who had earned their stripes by living and work-ing in the city for a fair amount of time were well aware of the level of corruption and the depths to which some people sank in search of money, power, or merely a higher place in the pecking order. But they also justifi-ably disdained the "instant experts," those Western journalists who spoke no Russian, came to Vladivostok for a week, stayed in the best hotel, and went back home to write long articles about their harrowing experiences in the crime capital of the country. "They never get it right," complained an American who had lived in Vladivostok for more than a year. He was refer-ring, only half in jest, to a recent *Chicago Tribune* article reporting that unknown attackers had tortured an outspoken Vladivostok journalist with a blowtorch. "They didn't use a blowtorch," said my informant, "just lighted cigarettes."

Russian residents of Vladivostok understandably preferred to focus on the more positive aspects of their city. They pointed with pride to the city's eclectic architecture, with building styles ranging from neo-Muscovite to Oriental, from classical revival to German neogothic and neobaroque, from art nouveau to art deco, from early Soviet modernist to later socialist realist. Almost all the interesting edifices were located in the central core of the city, most of them constructed prior to the Stalinist era. Many were in disre-pair, but behind the crumbling facades, tucked away in the bowels of the buildings, were labyrinths of dark, dank hallways with doors that opened onto hidden, unsuspected sights: a contemporary photographer's studio equipped with only one camera, a wood-and-brass 8-by-10-inch, wet-plate apparatus on a wooden tripod, both dating from the nineteenth century; a brightly lit office with modern Scandinavian furniture, the latest electronic equipment, a garishly lacquered samovar, and a jungle of potted plants; a library of leather-bound books preserved in dusty, glass-fronted bookcases, surrounded by mounted specimens of butterflies; a private, well-appointed, wood-paneled dining room, with stained-glass windows, white linens, stemmed wine goblets, and vases of fresh flowers, nicer than any public restaurant in the city. Peek through other doors, however, and you would find Kafkaesque rooms piled to the ceilings with old papers spilling out of disintegrating cardboard boxes; a grungy sauna, with chipped grayish-yellow ceramic tiles and the odor of mildew mingling with the smell of human sweat; a jumble of junk in what looked like a long-forgotten storage closet, until you realized that someone actually ate and slept every day in that cramped, inhospitable space. The interiors of many of those buildings seemed to have been designed as an afterthought, a misleading maze contradicting the standardized symmetry of the exteriors. They struck me as a metaphor for the Soviet ideal versus the Russian reality—the desire for an external appearance of achievement and order versus the natural disorder of internal feelings and emotions that cannot be contained in any social or architectural blueprint.

Perched on the hills in the central city were also blocks of ill-kept five-story brick apartment houses, with older three-story stuccoed structures behind them, shadowed by narrow rows of rickety wooden storage sheds stacked on top of each other. There were still even a few traditional one- and two-story wooden houses like those pictured in historical photographs of Vladivostok. Most were at least fifty years old, having somehow survived not only the fires that had swept through the city, but also several waves of urban renewal. Some were painted green or blue, others were merely raw, weathered wood, and almost all of them were in dilapidated condition. Many were located on unpaved streets and had no running water or indoor plumbing. Inside, they ranged from musty, filth-ridden shacks to neat, sparsely furnished homes of people who, for a variety of reasons, lived in these simpler, more Spartan accommodations instead of the modern, prefabricated concrete high-rise apartment blocks that surrounded the city. One of those old wooden houses in central Vladivostok was located on a street named "Victims of the Revolution." Painted on an exterior wall was an example of ironic post-Soviet graffiti, crudely printed in large white letters: "WE are the victims of the Revolution." That bitter statement stayed on the building during the entire time I lived in Vladivostok, the white paint remaining fresh while the rest of the house continued to decay.

Less evident to the casual visitor were the buildings that housed thousands of political prisoners and common criminals in or near the city—not only during the Stalinist period, but also from earlier tsarist times to the recent past. In the tsarist era, Vladivostok had been both a transit point and a final destination for prisoners and exiles from European Russia, many of whom were confined in the *katorzhnaya* (convict) area that later became known as the First River district. In Stalin's time, Vladivostok continued to be a major transit point for prisoners from elsewhere in Russia, who arrived there by train on their way to the notorious labor camps of the gulag, including some of the worst penal colonies located in the regions of Sakhalin, Magadan, and Kamchatka, far to the north of Vladivostok itself. In 1938 the Russian poet Osip Mandelstam perished in a Vladivostok transit camp near the site of today's Second River food market, many of whose buyers and sellers are probably unaware of that district's dark past. Other Russian writers who survived that infamous era, such as Eugenia Ginzburg and Aleksandr Solzhenitsyn, wrote vivid descriptions of the horrors of those camps in the Russian Far East, from the transit prisons of Vladivostok to the deadly mines of Kolyma.

But a city is much more than its history and its buildings. The longer I stayed in Vladivostok, the more I came to appreciate those aspects of daily life that only time and experience can reveal: the changing light during different seasons, the salty smell of the sea, the salmon-colored sunsets over low-lying islands, the people I met, the friends I made, the swirl of urban life.

Autumn was my favorite season in Vladivostok, after summer's stifling heat and humidity had finally faded away and before winter's winds gathered force to howl off the frozen bays. On warm, sunny afternoons, Tom and I often went downtown to the central square, strolled along the harbor, and watched the occasional three-masted sailing ship glide through the sun-sparkled water of the Golden Horn Bay. Behind us towered a modern twenty-two–story government office building faced with white marble and nicknamed "the White House," home of the regional administration of Primorskiy Kray. In front of us on the square stood a massive monument to "The Fighters for Soviet Power in the Far East," dominated by the bronze form of a heroic trumpeter facing the sea, his trumpet in one hand and a swirling banner in the other. Below that reminder of Russia's past, local bands played American show tunes, Dixieland jazz, and sixties rock music. Sea smells mingled with the stench of diesel fuel and the smoke from burning coal, while albatrosses circled slowly overhead in the hazy blue sky.

Sitting on wooden benches in the golden autumn light, we watched a juxtaposition of images worthy of a film by Sergey Eisenstein: Two teenage girls in maroon jogging suits riding on horseback across the square. A fully furnished, American-made, double-wide mobile home, one side completely cut away and open to view, like a giant doll's house, being towed by truck down the street in front of several ships anchored in the harbor. Hare Krishnas chanting rhythmically in their saffron-colored robes. A middle-aged woman charging 200 rubles (16 cents) for people to weigh themselves on her old bathroom scale. Welders working without goggles or gloves, showering sparks

БОРЦАМ
ЗА ВЛАСТЬ
СОВЕТОВ
НА
ДАЛЬНЕМ
ВОСТОКЕ
1917 - 1922

Monument to "The Fighters for Soviet Power
in the Far East," a landmark overlooking
Vladivostok's Golden Horn Bay.

on the pedestrians nearby. A Gypsy palm reader—a brown-skinned, mustachioed, roughly handsome rogue—telling fortunes to a long line of women on the crowded sidewalk of Svetlanskaya Street, Vladivostok's main thoroughfare that parallels the harbor and passes by the central square. Amid the hustle and bustle of shoppers and gawkers, the fortune-teller played his part well, looking deeply into his customers' eyes as he spoke about life and love, then graciously accepted payment of 1000 rubles (80 cents) for each forecast of a better future. Business must have been good: his wife, a stocky, well-dressed Gypsy weighted down by gold jewelry, picked him up after work in a late-model Mercedes-Benz sedan.

Among the crowds of people in downtown Vladivostok were many attractive, well-dressed women who surely spent much of their hard-earned income on clothing and cosmetics. On my first day in the city, a university administrator—a pretty, flirtatious, rather coquettish middle-aged Russian woman—had warned me to keep an eye on Tom, because the women in Vladivostok were reputed to be the most beautiful in all of Asian Russia. They were certainly better attired than most of the women I saw elsewhere in that part of the country. Colorful mohair sweaters, well-tailored wool skirts, long leather coats, and high-heeled leather boots were common on women under the age of fifty. Dingy beauty salons, full of outdated equipment and plenty of customers, provided permanents, facials, manicures, and pedicures. At the first hint of cool weather, it seemed like half the women in the city donned fur coats and fur hats, the latter often hiding blonde- or henna-dyed hair carefully styled like that of housewives in America forty years ago. This focus on fashion and femininity—which would appear almost quaint in much of urban America today—was characteristic of Russian women even during Soviet times, when dressing well was much harder to do. And in the 1990s it was an understandable reaction of middle-aged Russian women against the deprivations of the former Soviet era. For the younger generation, however, it seemed to be more an expression of optimism about the future and of changing attitudes toward sexual freedom, as well as an assumption of increasing material prosperity, all heavily influenced by the recent influx of television programs, advertising, and consumer magazines from the West.

Compared to smaller cities and towns that I visited in Asian Russia, Vladivostok had a vitality that was lacking in more provincial places. But, despite its large population, Vladivostok still sometimes seemed more like a village itself than a major metropolis. Often while waiting for Tom at the central square, I encountered people whom I had met at this or that official conference, neighbors from our distant suburb, students from the university, shop girls I knew from a food store in another part of the city, vendors I recognized from an open-air market several miles away. Yet urban life inevitably revealed its underside, too, with scenes that still linger in my memory: Poor people scavenging for empty liquor bottles to exchange for a few rubles to buy their next shot of vodka. A glassy-eyed man at a beer stand, holding out a plastic bag to be filled with the bubbly brew, then wobbling away as he tried to focus on pouring the bulging bag of beer down his throat. A local bus driver using a tire iron to beat up a man outside the bus, while the passengers on board watched impassively through the mud-splattered windows. A heavy-set old woman wearing a cheap, black wool coat and carrying an orange string bag with three green cabbages in it, standing forlornly in the fog next to a gray metal utility box with "FUCK YOU" chalked onto it in English in big bright orange letters, each letter artistically outlined with a white chalk border. A filthy young tramp sitting cross-legged in the middle of a large pile of garbage, holding up a woman's compact mirror and staring dully at his own face.

During our first autumn in Vladivostok, the weather was mild throughout September and much of October, with daytime temperatures sometimes reaching well above fifty degrees even as late as mid-November. A Russian superstition similar to ours about Groundhog Day says that if the weather is sunny and clear on September 14, then autumn will be warm—but if it rains on that day, fall will be cursed with heavy downpours. That prediction held true: September 14, 1993, was a beautiful day, the start of a month of Indian summer, called *bab'ye leto* (older woman's summer) in Russian, because the season corresponds to that time in a woman's life just before she turns fifty, when she still retains some of her former youthfulness—and perhaps even blossoms once again—before the inevitable fading of beauty, sex, and life itself. But in the following year, 1994, mid-September brought the first of several devastating typhoons that flooded Vladivostok and Primorskiy Kray that autumn, with part of the region receiving 25 percent of its annual rainfall in one day alone. People, houses, animals, roads, bridges, power cables, and telephone lines were washed away, causing the entire region to be declared a national disaster area. A week later, when we were finally able to reconnect with a telephone line and send E-mail messages to friends abroad, Tom's first line to them was "Have you ever considered what it really means to be living in a place that has been designated a national disaster area in *Russia?*"

"What is it about *October?*" asked one of my students in the autumn of 1993, referring to both the Bolshevik Revolution of 1917 and the current insurrection in Moscow during which more than 140 people were killed. Seven times zones away from the capital, we tried as best we could to keep abreast of the events unfolding in Moscow, given the limitations on Russian news reporting, which included government censorship and intermittent news blackouts, as well as occasionally odd translations on the English-language radio broadcasts. Soon after the confrontation began between President Boris Yeltsin and hardline members of the Russian parliament, Radio Moscow World Service reported that the entire Russian officer corps had "pledged its unanimous disobedience to the decrees issued by the unlawful government of Aleksandr Rutskoy." And a later announcement informed listeners that inside the Russian parliament building "five hundred to six hundred weapons are in the hands of people whose intellect is not very well developed."

On Monday, October 4, when I turned on the television to see the latest news report from Moscow, I immediately realized that something significant must have happened. Instead of the regularly scheduled national news program, Russian television was showing a classical music concert that had been videotaped in St. Petersburg in early June, 1993. I knew the exact date of that concert because Tom and I had been in the audience that evening—and there we were on the screen, standing on the second floor of the Great Philharmonic Hall in St. Petersburg, while Valeriy Gergiyev conducted the Mariinsky Theater Orchestra in a performance of selections from Wagner and Shostakovich. Feeling as if I were suddenly thrust back into the earlier Soviet era, when the mass media played innocuous classical musical programs as a form of "media black-out" while important political events were taking place, I turned on the radio—only to hear Radio Moscow World Service broadcasting a continuous repeat of a folk-music show that I had already heard the Saturday before.

As the crisis unfolded that day, with Yeltsin's troops attacking the parliament building in Moscow, the television stations in Vladivostok broadcast a Brothers Grimm fairy tale, followed by rock-music videos interspersed with short reports from Moscow showing Russian tanks firing on the insurgents still inside the parliament building. Occasionally those reports were accompanied by snippets of voice-over commentary in English, not intended to be heard, by CNN broadcasters who thought their microphones were turned off: "Do you want some chocolate?" asked one reporter. "Should I update my packet?" asked another. "Yeah, because mine was done in a real rush," replied his listener. "We're on our stomachs on the ground," giggled another reporter, followed by laughter as the screen showed pictures of the Russian parliament building on fire. And at the end of one short CNN report, an anonymous voice candidly commented, "That didn't make any sense at all."

By the evening of October 4, Moscow time, the insurrection was over. The next day Radio Moscow World Service reported that security forces in the capital were "liquidating snipers and separate groups of militants remaining in the city," and on television Channel 1 broadcast a historical film about the 1917 Bolshevik Revolution and the ensuing civil war. On October 6, Radio Moscow declared that "the feelings of political dissent have been uprooted in Russia" and on the following day reported that "in a major operation in this city last night, five criminal gangs were wiped out and a large number of weapons captured." Meanwhile the victorious Yeltsin had addressed the nation that night, denouncing "that dirty conspiracy [that] brought together Communists and fascists—the hammer-and-sickle and the swastika together." And later that week Radio Moscow reported that "the government, free from the constraints of the legislature during the next two months, has the opportunity to advance reforms on all key fronts." Democracy was still on a very fragile footing in the young Russian Federation.

But none of the Russians I knew in Vladivostok seemed particularly worried about those unsettling events in Moscow. No one I spoke with thought that the insurrection would spread very far beyond Moscow or that civil war would break out elsewhere in the country. And only a few of my students—those most interested in politics—cared about the insurgents' challenge to the democratically elected government of Russia or questioned their government's violent response to that situation. Most of the people I knew were more concerned about their own personal hardships than any political crisis in the distant capital. Power outages, pollution problems, price inflation, and an overburdened public transportation system all contributed to lowering the quality of life for many residents of Vladivostok that autumn, as Russians on fixed incomes struggled to make ends meet— while looking enviously at the city's successful new entrepreneurs, who appeared to be profiting at everyone else's expense.

A Russian woman who worked at the U.S. consulate in Vladivostok told me that the city had been a much nicer place to live when it was a closed city—safer, cleaner, and in better repair. But Americans who came to Vladivostok after it was officially opened in the early 1990s had a different point of reference. Many felt as if they were living in a time warp, in a badly colorized version of an old black-and-white film about the Great Depression of the 1930s. Except for the more modern clothes and cars of Vladivostok's nouveaux riches, almost everything else seemed to belong to a neglected past. Even the most recently constructed public buildings looked as if they had been deteriorating for decades. Cracks marred the masonry, paint peeled off the walls, and large chunks of plaster fell from the facades after every rain. Public utilities—water, heating, electricity—were notoriously unreliable. Streets were pitted with potholes. Open manholes in the middle of sidewalks and roads posed a constant safety hazard, especially at night in a major metropolis with almost no streetlights. One American jokingly surmised that in such a land of shortages there were only half as many manhole covers as needed and that city workers were kept employed by moving the scarce covers from one hole to the next in an apparently random manner. But scarcity had its consequences, and the dangers were real. During the flash floods of 1994, a Russian woman in Vladivostok escaped from her car on an inundated street, only to step unknowingly through the water into one of those uncovered manholes and be washed away through the sewers, never to be seen again.

Vladivostok was also a city plagued by pollution. For decades the centrally planned economy had emphasized industrial and agricultural production, with little regard for the deleterious effects on people and the environment. With its massive military, commercial, and fishing ports, and with its many arsenals, fuel storage tanks, and chemical waste dumps, Vladivostok was particularly prone to ground and water pollution from toxic materials. Raw sewage, industrial effluents, and untreated medical wastes were discharged directly into Vladivostok's beautiful bays, where oil slicks on the surface of the water occasionally caught fire. In 1992 a series of explosions at a local naval ammunition depot showered debris over the city for two days. And in 1993 that same arsenal caught fire again. Radioactive materials seeped from decommissioned submarines, and mercury leaked from a ship anchored in the Golden Horn Bay. Citizens complained about piles of uncollected garbage rotting in the streets and beaches littered with rubbish and broken glass. A local newspaper reported a study by the Primorskiy Geological Association, which found high concentrations of heavy-metal pollutants—including lead, cobalt, arsenic, and mercury—throughout Vladivostok, with the inner city being the worst affected area. Some sites registered levels of harmful heavy metals more than one thousand times the maximum allowable limits.

Public transportation was also a problem in a city suffering from both insufficient revenues and the inability of local politicians to improve the transportation system. Since we lived so far from work and did not have cars, our university provided a chauffeured Toyota van to take all the American professors to and from school every day. This spared us the minimum hour-and-a-half commute, each way, by foot, bus, and tram between our apartments on the edge of the city and the classroom building located near the center of Vladivostok. But after work, on weekends, and at night, we had to rely on public transportation—which meant that we might spend two hours traveling one-way to a dinner party in another section of town.

Public transportation in Vladivostok was not for anyone with a faint heart or a sensitive nose. At almost any time of the day, crowds of people waited at each stop for buses, trolleys, and trams that were already packed with pas-

sengers by the time they arrived. Only by pushing and shoving was it possible to get on board, and often we just gave up entirely, in the vain hope
that the next vehicle to come along might not be so jammed. Seldom did
public transportation operate on any discernible schedule, however. Sometimes after waiting an hour or longer for buses that were supposed to arrive
every fifteen minutes, we finally flagged down a passing car and offered to
pay the driver to take us to our destination—a practice that our Russian
friends considered extremely risky in crime-ridden Vladivostok. Other times,
out of necessity or simply because it was faster, we walked to wherever we
wanted to go, even if it was several miles away and we were lugging shopping bags full of groceries through fog, rain, or snow.

In summer the buses, trolleys, and trams, none of which were air-
conditioned, reeked of body odors, fish, and fresh produce. In winter the
unheated vehicles smelled of wet wool and musty furs. Crowding was so
bad that only twice in ten months did I ride sitting down. The rest of the
time I stood pressed so tightly against the other passengers that I could
hardly breathe. In such a situation it was almost impossible for the drivers
to collect fares, which were priced so low they provided less than 10 percent
of the required operating revenue for the city's public transportation system. So in August, 1993, the mayor of Vladivostok decided to let everyone
ride for free, with the city financing the municipal transportation system by
a tax on local businesses. We all enjoyed this benefit until December, 1994,
when a fare of 300 rubles (9 cents) was officially reinstated. But the transportation system was just as overcrowded as before, with fares still artificially
low and just as difficult to collect.

Heavy rains, hail, snowstorms, and power outages always brought public
transportation to a halt, stranding thousands of people all over the city. In
August, Vladivostok was as hot and muggy as Houston was, followed by an
autumn of wildly fluctuating temperatures and torrential downpours. Winter brought lows of twenty degrees below zero, fierce gales, and sudden
blizzards, with wind-chill factors of seventy degrees below—the kind of climate where, when a man has to urinate outdoors, the puddle begins to
freeze before he finishes his business (an experience that Tom has never
forgotten). The hilly streets were especially treacherous in such weather.
Vladivostok is the only place in the world where I have ever been blown
uphill by the wind, on an ice-covered street that sloped forty-five degrees
down to the university where I worked. Only by locking arms with two
other colleagues were the three of us able to form enough mass to slide
down the street together and get to class on time.

Private vehicles were at the mercy of the weather, too. City streets were built unbanked and without drainage ditches, so when it rained in hilly Vladivostok, even the paved roads turned into rivers of water, mud, and gravel. In many places the cheap asphalt broke up and washed away with each downpour. In winter the snow would partially melt during the day, freeze again at night, then melt and refreeze, again and again, until the streets were covered with thick layers of ice. But little effort was made by the city government to clear the slick streets or even to spread grit on them. "I've lived here for twenty-three years," a Russian colleague told me. "We've had good times and bad times, good leaders and bad leaders, but no matter what, the roads in winter always stay the same."

Traffic was a major problem in a city where Russians were buying cars faster than the government could build roads to accommodate them. The streets downtown were often clogged with private vehicles, many of them secondhand Japanese sedans that had a right-hand drive in a country where traffic drove on the right. Jeep Cherokees, Toyota Land Cruisers, and other macho models were favored by the local *mafiya*. Less affluent residents who were able to buy a car usually had to settle for Russian-made Ladas, Zhigulis, and Moskviches or flimsy, underpowered Ukrainian Zaporozhetses, sometimes referred to as "soap dishes" because they were the smallest automobiles sold in Russia.

Service stations were few and far between, and most looked dilapidated if not deserted, leading me to wonder where all those cars found the power to run. When fuel shortages occurred, rusty tanker trucks reminiscent of those in the film *Road Warrior* would park along the crowded highways to sell gasoline directly to motorists, thus slowing the pace of traffic even more. Automobile mechanics were as scarce as gas pumps, and spare parts were difficult to find. At the poorly equipped repair shops, cars were simply flipped onto their sides when mechanics needed to fix the exhaust systems. But most automobile owners had to make their own repairs, working at nights and on weekends inside old metal shipping containers that served as makeshift garages. And scattered around the city were the skeletons of cars that had died on the spot, then been stripped bare, their empty, rusting shells littering the landscape like huge crab carapaces on an urban asphalt beach.

The famous Russian sense of fatalism seemed to surface whenever people got into an automobile—not surprising in a city where a driver's license could be bought on the black market for 200,000 rubles (164 dollars) in the autumn of 1993. I seldom saw Russians use seat belts in the few cars that

were equipped with them. And many drivers went for months without replacing their "headstrike windshields," patterned with spider webs of broken glass bulging outward from the places where passengers' heads had
hit. Wrecks were common, as kamikaze drivers fought their way through
the traffic with utter disregard for the rules of the road. Traffic lights and
ONE-WAY signs were often ignored. Without warning, drivers shifted into
reverse and drove backward down the streets to get where they wanted to
go. And when traffic was especially dense, some drivers didn't hesitate to
barrel down the sidewalks or take shortcuts through footpaths in the city
parks. The situation became so bad that in the summer of 1994 the city
government finally passed several new traffic ordinances making it illegal
to drive on sidewalks and curbs, to drive in reverse in intersections and
crosswalks, and to drive through intersections when pedestrians were still
in the street. And as of July 1, 1994, drivers were also required to use their
headlights at night.

Political infighting often resulted in a paralysis of government as archrivals
Yevgeniy Nazdratenko, the governor of Primorskiy Kray, and Viktor
Cherepkov, the mayor of Vladivostok, vied for power on issues ranging
from energy crises to economic development. As city and regional services
continued to deteriorate, local officials failed to devise any workable plans
of their own. Instead they looked to the federal government in Moscow to
bail them out financially, while simultaneously shunning any outside control by the authorities in the capital. They also courted foreign investors
from rich countries such as Japan and the United States, who they hoped
would inject large sums of hard currency into the unstable local economy.
The political crisis came to a head in the spring of 1994, when rivals of the
mayor accused him of corruption, and armed militiamen removed the mayor
bodily from his office. Although the mayor had his own fair share of obvious shortcomings, many people in Vladivostok thought that particular sting
operation was surely a set-up. Governor Nazdratenko then appointed one
of his close friends to be acting mayor and canceled the upcoming elections for the city and regional legislatures. As a commentator on Radio
Moscow noted that spring, "History has its own laws, and political ambi-
tions have theirs."

While the politicians bickered, essential services such as state-provided
health care continued to decline. Every morning on the way to work I passed
a branch of the local medical institute in Vladivostok, a somber-looking
building with a morgue in back. Stacks of simple wooden coffins, painted
shiny red, stood near the rear door, like the entrance to an amusement-park

house of horrors. Through the windows I could see classrooms, laboratories, and medical equipment, all of which looked as if they dated from the 1930s. And, indeed, Western doctors who worked in Russia in the 1990s told me that the overall level of medical care was at least six decades behind that of Western Europe and the United States. Worse yet, Russian state funding for the already inadequate system of national health care was cut almost in half between 1989 and 1993.

In Russia the average life expectancy for men dropped from sixty-five years in 1989 to just over fifty-seven years by 1995, while that of women decreased by three years, from seventy-four to seventy-one, during the same period. (By comparison, the average life expectancy for American men in 1995 was seventy-two years; for women, seventy-nine years.) Meanwhile, during the early to mid-1990s, children in Vladivostok suffered from an increase in birth defects, chronic illnesses, skin diseases, and infant mortality. A Russian friend who had a diabetic son attended a local medical conference about the disease and reported to me that the incidence of diabetes in Primorskiy Kray was three times higher than in the rest of Russia. Adults succumbed to cancer, heart disease, strokes, tuberculosis, alcohol poisoning, suicide, and accidents, with high stress levels, excessive drinking, and heavy smoking contributing to many deaths. Infectious diseases such as cholera and diphtheria spread rapidly, the latter reaching epidemic proportions in the Russian Far East when I was there during the autumn of 1994. In January of that same year, the *Vladivostok News* reported that the city had one of Russia's highest mortality rates from infectious diseases, trauma accidents, and poisonings. And in the early 1990s, Vladivostok also had the dubious distinction of being not only the murder capital of Russia but the suicide capital as well.

A different set of problems stemmed from racism and other forms of discrimination, which were not only pervasive but also openly expressed by many people there. The former Soviet Union's 287 million people had included more than one hundred different "nationalities," with only 51 percent of the population classified as ethnic Russians. In the mid-1990s, the much smaller Russian Federation had a population of 148 million, 80 percent of whom were ethnic Russians. And many of those Russians didn't hesitate to classify other people according to those categories that the Russian government still calls "nationalities," based on national, ethnic, or religious affiliation: Ukrainians, Belorussians, Latvians, Poles, Germans, Chechens, Armenians, Tatars, Buryats, Jews, and others. Even if two centuries had passed since someone's parents had emigrated from Germany to

Russia or been exiled from Poland to Russia, that person was still catego-
rized according to his or her ancestors' ethnic group or place of origin. And
implicit in such classification was the position of each group in a hierarchy
of "nationalities," with Russians at the top and other Slavs just below them,
followed by Jews, indigenous Siberians, and people from other Asian countries toward the bottom.

Because of our Northern European features and European attire, Tom
and I usually blended in with the Russian majority on the streets. Russians
who spoke to me in public places—food stores, tram stops, buses, trains—
often mistook me for one of their own. But when I replied, they were always surprised at my limitations in their language. When they realized that
I was not Russian myself, they invariably retorted, sometimes unkindly,
sometimes just matter-of-factly, "Why don't you Estonians ever learn to
speak Russian correctly?"

Had Tom or I belonged to a non-Caucasian race—or were merely darker-
skinned Caucasians like Indians, Pakistanis, or Gypsies—we would have been
far less accepted in Russia. Even many well-educated, relatively sophisticated Russians who had traveled in their own country and abroad didn't
hesitate to make disparaging comments about Asians, blacks, Jews, and other
groups of people whom they considered "different." I heard schoolteachers
and university professors refer to Jewish students and their families as "'those'
people." A Russian colleague confided to me that "'Those' people always
know how to make the most money, and they always get it *first*." A Russian
friend of mine was convinced that cholera had been brought to Vladivostok
by Moldovan Gypsies. Another described a concert by a Russian symphony
orchestra composed entirely of dwarfs. "What an oddity it was!" she exclaimed.
"The music was excellent," she went on to say, with a note of genuine surprise in her voice. "But can you imagine why anyone would want to teach
music to such people?"

When I arrived in Vladivostok in 1993, there were only three black people,
all of them African Americans, living in the city. One was a retired business
executive from the Midwest, a man in his sixties who was a Peace Corps
volunteer. The other two were a younger Peace Corps administrator and his
wife, a lawyer, both from Washington, D.C. Laura, the lawyer, was a large,
nice-looking, well-dressed woman whose dark skin and often flamboyant
attire attracted much attention on the streets of Vladivostok. As the only
black woman in the city, she was often the object of stares by Russians who
had never seen someone black in person and to whom she must have seemed
like some exotic being from another world.

Several of our Russian friends were shocked, initially, when I invited Laura to join us on a group shopping excursion to an open-air market in the city of Ussuriysk, seventy miles north of Vladivostok. But they were soon won over by Laura's warm personality, her openness, and her attempts to speak their language. At the market in Ussuriysk, however, Laura stood out like an ebony apparition among the crowd of Russians, Chinese, Koreans, Gypsies, Georgians, and Armenians hawking their wares that day. As she and I walked around the market together, people kept coming up to me, tugging on my sleeve, and asking in Russian, "*Negrityanka? Negrityanka?*" ("Negress? Negress?") as if they couldn't believe their eyes. "Yes," I replied with a smile, at which point Laura turned to them and charmed them with a few Russian phrases. During the entire time in Ussuriysk, we were followed around by a small group of locals who seemed to think that Laura's presence there was the most exciting event of that market day.

A few days later one of the Russians on the trip, an elementary school-teacher in Vladivostok, told me how much she had enjoyed meeting Laura— and added how impressed she had been with Laura's natural ability to seem at ease in situations where she was obviously so "different." But my friend the schoolteacher had a natural tendency to be more open-minded than many Russians I knew. She told me about taking her class of third-grade students down to the central square to see a public concert performed by U.S. Navy musicians when an American naval vessel had visited Vladivostok that fall. All the children were dressed in their best clothes—the little boys in white shirts and dark pants, the girls in their finest dresses, with big organza bows in their hair. Each child carried a single red carnation. At the end of the concert, their teacher said they could present the flowers, individually, to any of the American sailors they chose. The entire class surged forward to give their carnations to an African American trumpet player on the back row of the band, completing ignoring the conductor and other members of the group. "Why did you give all the flowers only to *him?*" asked my friend, who had expected her students to present them either to the conductor alone or to various members of the band. "Because he's treated so badly in America," replied the students, who obviously wanted, in their own small way, to redress the wrong. "I was so embarrassed," she added. "You see, these youngsters are still a product of our socialist education. They were taught that white people in America oppress all the Negroes, so they gave all their flowers to this 'poor black man' out of pity for him. These young people—these third graders!—have already learned that kind of propaganda. And they're our *future* generation, too!"

Probably because they live in such close proximity, Asian Russians' attitudes toward their other Asian neighbors also seemed particularly pronounced. Historically, Vladivostok and the Russian Far East have had relatively large populations of ethnic Chinese, Koreans, and Japanese, whose influence on the history, culture, and economic development of the region is still evident today. From the 1860s until the early 1920s, different waves of immigration brought settlers and seasonal workers from China, Korea, and Japan to the Russian Far East. Most of them came for economic reasons—to open businesses, to establish small farms, or to earn money as laborers in the agricultural sector, in the shipyards of Vladivostok, or on construction crews of the Trans-Siberian Railroad. According to the 1897 census, Vladivostok had just over twenty-eight thousand residents, half of them Chinese, Japanese, and Koreans. And, by the census of 1912, Russians still constituted only 58 percent of the people living in the city.

Before the 1917 Bolshevik Revolution, Vladivostok had its own Japanese, Korean, and Chinese districts—the last a geographically small, densely populated ghetto called "Millionka" where a number of Chinese businesses catered to the various tastes and needs of the city's residents, from textiles, jewelry, and housewares, to foods, medicines, opium, and sex. In enterprises both legal and illegal, Chinese merchants and businessmen played an important part in the commercial life of Vladivostok during the late nineteenth and early twentieth centuries.

But Russians also developed an ambivalent attitude toward many of these Asian neighbors. On the one hand, they established an Oriental Institute in Vladivostok in 1899—the first institution of higher education in the Russian Far East—to teach Asian languages, history, and culture, and to train students for work in administrative and commercial positions in that easternmost part of Russia. On the other hand, Russians resented Asian economic successes, particularly Chinese, in the same way they resented Jewish ones. During the mid-1930s more than three hundred thousand ethnic Chinese and Koreans living in the Russian Far East were sent back to their countries of origin or were deported, with great loss of life, to Central Asia. Many others disappeared into the Soviet gulags. After the reopening of the Russian Far East in the early post-Soviet era, thousands of Chinese, Koreans, and Japanese began to return, to take advantage of the economic opportunities suddenly available there. A few came as big-scale entrepreneurs, others as small-time farmers, merchants, and traders, some as construction workers, others, particularly North Koreans, as forestry and agricultural laborers bound to their Russian or foreign employers by a system similar to indentured servitude.

Russian prejudices against the Chinese were especially strong—a result of historical phobias dating from the Mongol invasions in the thirteenth century to more recent fears fueled by border disputes, including armed clashes, between the Russians and the Communist Chinese. In the 1990s the large immigration of Chinese into the Russian Far East only added to the Russians' apprehensions. When I lived in Vladivostok, the Chinese were blamed for everything from bringing deadly diseases into the city, to perpetrating most of the crimes, to trying to colonize the region and take over the economy. But most of the Russians I knew were unable to provide concrete evidence of these allegations. Many were even unable to differentiate among their neighbors. They called all such people "Chinese"—or, more derogatorily, "Yellows"—whether they were Chinese, Koreans, Japanese, Mongolians, or Vietnamese. And they certainly were not displeased when, in the summer of 1994, large numbers of Chinese in Vladivostok and the surrounding area were rounded up by the police and sent back to China—recalling similar actions not only in the Soviet period but also during the tsarist era, when local officials periodically tried to expel the Chinese from Vladivostok and to restrict their activities in the region.

In the autumn of 1994, while the Russian Duma (the lower house of parliament) in Moscow was debating a law that would require all foreigners staying in Russia for more than three months to be tested for AIDS, Primorskiy Kray was the only region in the country to make AIDS testing for foreigners immediately mandatory. Some people surmised that since AIDS testing was not required for Russian residents of Primorskiy Kray—nor for Russian sailors returning there from abroad—the real reason for this regional rule was to provide a legal pretext for forcing thousands of Chinese in the Russian Far East back across the border to their homeland.

As Americans working in Vladivostok, Tom and I came under this rule. In order to renew our residence visas after living in Vladivostok for ninety days, we had to go to the only clinic in the city that was equipped to test blood for the HIV virus. It turned out to be an old brick-and-stone building, with badly blue-washed walls and flaking white paint around the windows. "This place looks like a spruced-up slaughterhouse," muttered Tom, as we warily opened the front door. Inside, the clinic was a bare and cheerless place, poorly constructed but surface-clean, with a mixture of materials covering the floor and patches of mismatched paint on the mildewed walls. AIDS-prevention posters similar to those in the West were taped to the walls, and a few scraggly potted plants almost succeeded in adding a bit of color to the anemic atmosphere.

Sanitary conditions in Russian medical facilities were so bad that foreigners going to Russia were advised to carry their own supplies of sterile,
disposable, single-use syringes and needles, and to avoid blood transfusions
and dental work except in emergencies, to reduce the possibility of con-
tracting AIDS. So I was worried when the Russian nurse looked at my packet
of sterile needles and said she couldn't use any of the small hypodermics for
drawing blood. I was ready to get up and walk out of the clinic when she
rummaged through the packet, found a larger needle with a butterfly attachment (and no syringe), and pronounced it suitable. She took hold of my
wrist and tied a well used, ragged strip of cloth around my upper arm, then
pulled a wooden test tube holder over beside me. With its twenty-five glass
test tubes, all open at the top, it looked like a nineteenth-century exhibit in
a medical museum. While I watched with an air of detached fascination, the
nurse smoothly slipped the needle into my vein. The blood immediately
spurted out, arcing through the air and landing directly inside the only
cracked test tube in the holder. I have to admit that she had a very good
aim—although I did feel rather like Joan of Arc being bled by her tormen-
tors in that unforgettable scene in Carl Theodor Dreyer's classic silent film.
And I wondered how accurate the HIV test could be, given the large crack
in the glass tube collecting my stream of warm blood.

For many Americans who came to Vladivostok in the early post-Soviet
period, experiences like that—along with the high crime rate, the low standard of living, and the considerable cultural differences—made it difficult
for them to adjust to life in Asian Russia. For some, the negative experiences outweighed the positive ones, causing them to cut short their stay and
return home. One new Peace Corps volunteer went back to the United States
after only two days in the Russian Far East. Other Americans remained,
even if reluctantly, until their work contracts were completed. And a few
married Russians and decided to settle there for the indefinite future.

From our own perspectives, Tom and I viewed life in Vladivostok as an
adventure, a unique episode in our lives, and an opportunity to learn more
about a people and culture quite different from our own. While coping with
the challenges of daily life and the demands of our jobs at the university, we
also made a special effort to take advantage of the cultural and leisure activities available in the city, to participate in private and public social events,
and to make friends with many local Russians as well as members of the
foreign community.

Vladivostok offered a variety of cultural amenities—concerts, plays, operas,
ballets, films, puppet shows, circuses, museums, and art galleries—although

far fewer than one would find in a Western city of the same size. Some of the performances and exhibitions were of a quality equal to those in major European and American metropolises; others were frankly a disappointment. But the concert halls, theaters, and auditoriums were almost always full and the exhibitions well attended, despite decreased state funding for the arts and the resulting increase in ticket prices. A small number of nightclubs, casinos, video arcades, and amusement parks also provided other forms of entertainment. Children and adults took lessons in drawing, painting, music, knitting, kickboxing, karate, and judo at the local Dom Kul'tury (Palace of Culture). And behind the unmarked doors of nondescript buildings were meeting places for chess players' and stamp-collectors' clubs, literary and historical societies, chamber music ensembles, and folk-dancing groups.

Russians also participated in a wide range of sports, indoors and outdoors, singly or in groups. Team sports such as soccer, basketball, and ice hockey were especially popular. On weekends in the summer, crowds of people left the city on buses or local electric commuter trains for short trips to outlying areas where they could swim in the ocean, picnic on the beach, hike in the forest, or stroll through the botanical garden. Many people also owned small boats that they sailed on the surrounding bays when the weather was good. And in winter they drilled holes in the ice and patiently fished for an often meager catch.

Twice Tom and I sailed to Reyneke Island south of Vladivostok with a group of Russian and American colleagues on a research boat that belonged to Far Eastern State University. Along the way we fished off the side of the boat, catching the ingredients for *ukha*, a fish-and-potato soup that the Russians cooked on board while we all snacked on salmon caviar and imbibed too much vodka in the stifling summer heat. Later in the evening we sailed back toward the Golden Horn Bay, past harbors full of gray military vessels and rusty commercial ships, most of which had seen better days. As we neared Vladivostok on one of those trips, a Russian friend turned to me and said, "See that boat over there, the white one?" I looked in the direction she was pointing and spotted what seemed to be a sleek, new, brightly painted coastal patrol boat, standing out among the other ships like a trumpeter swan in a flock of bedraggled gray geese. "Before perestroika," she sighed, "all of our boats were white like that."

Such nostalgia for the past was often expressed by Russians, especially those over the age of forty, who thought that Vladivostok was deteriorating under the new political and economic system. One of my students said it was probably a good thing that her grandfather had died in 1988, because he was a KGB colonel who would never have been able to adapt to what was happening in Russia now. A middle-aged schoolteacher told me that "It was better when it was worse"—a sentiment shared by many residents who longed for the stability and predictability of the Soviet era, when they could count on a steady monthly paycheck, subsidized housing, and fixed prices for consumer goods. Few of them were willing to admit that selective memory filtered out recollections of the political repressions, the limited opportunities, and the drabness of daily life under the old Communist regime.

Tom and I first lived in Vladivostok from August, 1993, until the middle of January, 1994. When we returned to Vladivostok in August, 1994, we noticed many improvements made during the seven months we had been away. Several buildings in the central part of the city had been cleaned up and repainted. The historic train station—no longer "that nasty green color," as one of my Russian friends had described it—was being restored to a pretty pale yellow hue and topped with copper spires. Communist Party slogans on fading billboards were being replaced by colorful commercial signs that read SNICKERS, DOVE BARS, and AVON: YOUR PATH TO BEAUTY. Some of the dingy old stores were now shiny new shops, selling everything from canned tamales to body-building equipment. A few of the streets had even been repaired, and construction was progressing on Vladivostok's first highway overpass.

When that overpass was completed in December, 1994, after almost two years of work, a big crowd turned out for the opening ceremonies. City officials made the expected speeches before cutting the wide red ribbon strung across the multilane bridge. The first vehicle to drive over it was a black-and-white American police car (part of a fleet recently purchased by the Vladivostok municipal government), followed by a colorful, motley parade of local folksingers and musicians dressed in traditional Russian costumes, Orthodox priests draped in golden robes, uniformed Cossacks on horseback, and even a bride and groom in an automobile festooned with ribbons, bows, and flowers for their wedding. Plenty of vodka and champagne kept the whole crowd in high spirits. That event seemed to me a perfect example of the spirit of Vladivostok: a much-needed public work, its completion long overdue because of mismanagement and corruption, was finally being celebrated with a boisterous, boozy expression of public pride.

In mid-January, 1994, after finishing our first semester of teaching in Russia, Tom and I began packing for the move to our next assignment in Irkutsk, more than two thousand miles away, deep inside Siberia. On our last evening in Vladivostok, we had dinner with Alla and Pëtr Brovko, Russian neighbors who had become our close friends during the past five months. Pëtr was chairman of the Department of Geography of Asian Pacific Countries at Far Eastern State University. Alla taught English at an elementary school near our apartment building and spent much of her precious spare time trying to help the new American faculty at the university adjust to daily life in Russia.

Alla was also an excellent and inventive cook, with a natural ability to locate a wide variety of foodstuffs in a land of scarcity and combine them so that every dish seemed grander than the sum of its separate ingredients. That evening she made one of my favorite recipes from the Russian Far East—fiddlehead ferns sauteed with paprika, onions, and garlic. Her main course was roasted chicken that Alla had basted—in a moment of inspiration—with some mayonnaise that I had brought along in a box of kitchen supplies I was leaving behind. Dessert consisted of large, lacy *blinchiki* (Russian-style crepes) as dainty as crocheted doilies, served with homemade cherry jam and local citrus-scented honey, accompanied by delicate china cups of chicory-flavored coffee. But the festive food was a stark contrast to the mood around the table, which was somber and subdued because we were all so sad about parting.

After dinner Tom and I returned to our apartment just as the electricity, heating, and hot water all went off—a common occurrence in Vladivostok that winter. The temperature outside was five degrees below zero, and a blizzard was blowing in. Strong winds pushed the snow into drifts against the building and made ghostly swirls of trash on the rocky embankment below our windows. While I grumbled about having to finish packing by candlelight, Tom stirred up soothing cocktails concocted from the remnants of our last bottle of vodka and the juice from a jar of preserved pears. And in the dark we offered a toast to a brighter future—literally—in Irkutsk.

Shortly before midnight Alla and Pëtr arrived at the front door with Igor, the driver of our university van. After the men had carried all of our baggage down the five flights of dark stairs, Alla joined Tom and me in the living room. For several minutes we sat together, silent and still, until Alla stood up and said it was time to go. We had just observed an old Russian custom of "sitting the house" before its occupants leave on a long journey or move to another place—a superstition meant to protect against danger en route. Thinking we were seeing our Vladivostok apartment for the last time, Tom and I said good-bye to it in our own way, too, then locked the door behind us and headed off through the snowy night to board a train to Siberia.

CHAPTER 3

~

Riding the Rails

THE TRANS-SIBERIAN RAILROAD

Vladivostok's historic train station gave off an eerie green glow in the dim street lights obscured by the snow. More than a century before, in 1891, Russia's crown prince, Nikolay, had laid the cornerstone of this building, using a silver shovel and silver wheelbarrow crafted especially for the occasion. During the following decades, revolution, civil war, and renovations had altered the building's original design, while lack of money for maintenance had also taken its toll. But the arched windows, curved portals, and architectural embellishments on the exterior still hinted at the former beauty of this Russian-Byzantine–style building, the eastern terminus of the Trans-Siberian Railroad.

With the help of our Russian friends Alla and Pëtr, an American colleague, and Igor, the van driver, we struggled to lug our seventeen pieces of baggage through the heavy snow to the station platform. We were scheduled to leave at 1:00 A.M. on train Number 7, appropriately named *Sibir'* (Siberia), which plied the route between Vladivostok and Novosibirsk, the largest city in Siberia, thirty-seven hundred miles to the west. Although we had already paid in advance for a sleeping compartment on the train, the conductress would not let us board until we gave her an extra 40,000 rubles (32 dollars)—apparently a "tax" that she personally levied on foreigners to supplement her own salary. Appalled at her request for money, Alla and Pëtr argued loudly with the stocky, stubborn conductress for several minutes before Tom suggested that we just hand over the rubles and get on the train before it left without us.

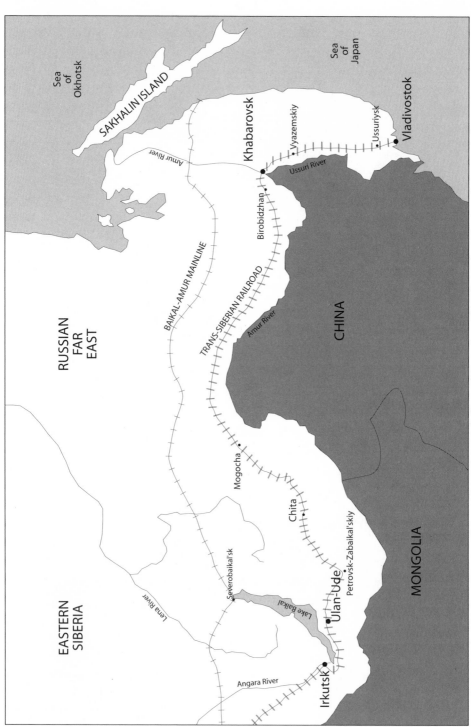

MAP 3.   Trans–Siberian Railroad route between Vladivostok and Irkutsk (boundary lines are approximations).

The men hoisted our heavy bags and boxes onto the passenger car, while Alla and I dragged each piece down the narrow hallway to the sleeping compartment. I was surprised at how much the small compartment could hold, with plenty of storage space underneath each berth and inside a large alcove extending over the ceiling of the corridor outside. By the time we squeezed the thirteenth piece of baggage into the tiny room, however, the conductress adamantly refused to let us bring any more luggage aboard. Tom and I looked in dismay at the four boxes still standing on the station platform. We couldn't leave them behind: they contained all of our university textbooks and lecture notes, plus several cans of crabmeat and salmon caviar, and precious supplies of spices, dried peppers, and bottled hot sauces not replaceable in Siberia. I suggested slipping the conductress twenty dollars for the remaining boxes, but Alla and Pëtr were opposed to any more bribery. The conductress wouldn't budge. Pointing toward the other end of the train, she told us to take the boxes to the baggage car. We had planned to keep all the luggage in our own compartment, because theft was reputedly so common on the baggage cars of Trans-Siberian trains. But suddenly we were forced to part with our four most valuable boxes, leaving them in the care of a stranger whom we had no reason to trust.

There was nothing else we could do. Tom and Pëtr shouldered the heavy boxes and hurried off toward the baggage car. The engine's horn hooted. Alla quickly hugged me good-bye and got off the train. Metal doors slammed shut, and the horn sounded again, but Tom was nowhere to be seen. In the last few seconds before the train started moving, he came running along the snowy platform, reaching our car and jumping on just as the conductress was closing the door. As the train slowly pulled out of the station, we peered through the frosted window and waved to our friends. The image receding from view could have come from the pages of a nineteenth-century Russian novel: lonely groups of two or three people, bundled in fur coats and fur hats, standing by the lampposts on the murky platform, surrounded by pools of aqueous green light, silhouetted against the peeling stucco of the station, with snowflakes sifting softly over the scene.

We were traveling in the train's best accommodations, a first-class sleeping compartment for two people, in a car containing nine double compartments plus the conductors' quarters. Inside our room, on each side of a narrow aisle, was a single, bed-length berth, its worn-out red-plush upholstery covered by a thin cotton-batting mattress, with a length of beige linen sacking stretched across the backrest. The walls were paneled with dun-colored plastic and the floor covered in dingy brown linoleum partially hidden by a threadbare rug. White cotton curtains printed with dark green leaves scrimmed the lower half of a wood-frame window between the berths. A small table jutted out just below the sill. Clothes hooks, storage racks, and towel bars provided places for personal items, and three large mirrors gave the illusion of more space than there actually was. Like all but a very few "deluxe-class" sleeping compartments on Russian trains, this one had no private toilet, no sink, no shower.

Each passenger car on the Trans-Siberian Railroad normally had two attendants—two male conductors (*provodniki*) or two female conductresses (*provodnitsy*), or sometimes a husband-and-wife team—with their own tiny cabin at one end of the car. Our car had only one attendant, however, a young conductress who soon knocked at the door to request 3,000 rubles ($2.40) for the sheets, pillowcases, and towels for our sleeping compart-ment. Initially we thought this was merely another money-making scam, but later we learned that all passengers had to pay extra for such items on Russian trains. The towels were small and scrimpy, sufficient only for blot-ting hands and faces, but I was surprised to find the sheets made of linen fine enough to be used as tablecloths for a formal meal.

Tom and I made up the beds ourselves, kneeling on the four boxes of books we had squeezed into the narrow floor space between our berths. We finally crawled into bed around 2:00 A.M., but I couldn't sleep because of the draft seeping through the double-glazed windows, so cold it formed a layer of ice on the inside of the interior pane of glass. Still awake an hour later, I was nearly blasted out of bed by bad rock music blaring through an even worse sound system. Assuming it to be a radio or cassette deck playing in the next passenger compartment, I lay awake wondering why the conduc-tress allowed such a racket to continue. But the next day I discovered that the awful noise actually came from the train's own sound system, piped into the corridor and compartments at the whim of the conductress, who turned it on and off whenever the spirit moved her. A white plastic knob above my bed controlled the volume but would not turn the sound completely off. Either we were living in a land that still had not banished Big Brother, or, more likely, we were merely at the mercy of another small piece of Russian technology that had failed yet again.

During the night the train traveled north from Vladivostok, skirting the border between China and Primorskiy Kray, the most populous part of the Russian Far East. Its 2.3 million people lived in a land known for an unusual variety of flora and fauna, unlike that of any other region in Russia. A local legend said that when God was creating the earth, he was so busy that he forgot about this remote area near the Great Ocean. When he realized the oversight, he shook out the remnants in his bag, showering that small corner of the planet with the unique combination of plants and animals found there today.

Almost 2,000 different plants grow within the borders of Primorskiy Kray, including 250 species of trees and shrubs. Deciduous trees turn the forests into flames of color every autumn. Spring and summer blossom with irises, lilies, jasmine, and rhododendrons. Subtropical vines curl around conifers, rowan trees live next to lotuses and lianas, cork trees tower over hot-pink orchids. Summer and early fall are the seasons for wild grapes and wild garlic, horseradish and mushrooms, cranberries and cloudberries, Manchurian walnuts and Siberian filberts, apples and apricots, plums and pears. And hidden in the forests is the precious "root of life," wild ginseng, a prized ingredient in traditional Asian medicines and an important cash crop for the people of Primorskiy Kray today.

Those same forests shelter a wealth of wildlife, including rare Amur leopards. Spotted deer live both in the wild and on special deer farms; their young, unossified antlers are harvested annually to produce an extract used in Chinese medicine, for which the Chinese are willing to pay dearly. But Primorskiy Kray's most famous mammal is the Siberian tiger—also called the Ussuri tiger, or Amur tiger—the world's largest feline, which now lives mainly in the region north of Vladivostok. Thousands of these beautiful animals used to inhabit a much larger area of Northeast Asia, but by the mid-1990s there were only between 300 and 400 members of this endangered species still remaining in the wild. Their numbers had been decimated by poachers, who made fortunes selling tiger pelts, bones, and organs to China and other Asian countries where tiger parts are highly valued for their use in traditional medicines, including aphrodisiacs. In Primorskiy Kray it was widely believed that many of those poachers were in league with local politicians and police. And the few poachers who were actually apprehended usually got off with nothing more than a fine, costing much less than the profits from the sale of a single slaughtered tiger.

Logging operations in Primorskiy Kray were also destroying the reclusive tigers' habitat, forcing them to seek prey nearer to human settlements, including Vladivostok. Residents recounted stories of household pets being devoured by tigers prowling near the edges of the city. In the mid-1980s a tiger was killed at an outlying trolley stop in Vladivostok, and in the 1990s

there were still reports of people being attacked by tigers in the area. While
we were in Russia, one of my American friends, a Peace Corps volunteer
living in the region just north of Primorskiy Kray, reported seeing a Siberian tiger twice during his two years there. But the future of these magnificent
beasts was sadly uncertain in Russia's economically troubled times. In 1994
a high-ranking American diplomat in Vladivostok told me that Primorskiy
Kray officials had made it very clear to her that "if it's a matter of saving
tigers or saving jobs, there's no question."

Our *Sibir'* train from Vladivostok took all of the first night and much of
the next day to traverse the 477 railroad miles between Vladivostok and
Khabarovsk, the second largest city in the Russian Far East, located at the
confluence of the Ussuri and Amur rivers, which mark much of the border
between Russia and China. On the way to Khabarovsk we passed through
villages large and small, with unpaved streets and row after row of *izby*—
small, single-story wooden houses made of logs or clapboard, all with snow
oozing slowly down their roofs like globs of marshmallow creme. Many of
the frame houses were covered with black tar paper or warped, weathered
planks of unpainted wood; others were painted blue, green, or soft yellow-
beige, with windows and doors highlighted in white, maroon, dark blue, or
dark green. Picket fences enclosed small yards, some with a single evergreen tree customarily planted when the family's first child was born. A
modern air-conditioning unit perched incongruously on the window ledge
of an old log house. Bunches of golden corn hung under the eaves of a
dilapidated barn. People wearing padded cotton coats and hats with earflaps
pulled sleds loaded with large metal milk cans. In the fields stood short
round hayricks capped with snow, like giant bran muffins spread with a
thick layer of vanilla icing.

As we pulled into Vyazemskiy, south of Khabarovsk, I noticed a crowd
of people clad in fur coats, fur hats, and felt boots who were lined up on
the station platform beside big bundles on wooden sleds. I thought they
were passengers waiting to come aboard, but as soon as the train stopped,
they opened up their packs and took out bottles of vodka, honey, kefir, jam,
and tomato sauce to sell to the travelers passing through. Meanwhile, in
the hazy winter light of midday, an old tractor drove up, pulling a rusty
cart filled with buckets of coal, which the crewmen began shoveling into
every passenger car of the train. This was the fuel for the train's heating
system, including the big cast-iron boiler at the end of every corridor that
provided a continuous supply of hot water for the passengers. Although
steam locomotives were officially phased out on the Trans-Siberian Rail-

road in the 1980s, the smell of coal smoke from these boilers in each car still recalled an earlier era, before the big black steam-belching engines were replaced by their sleeker, but less romantic, diesel and electric descendants.

Leaving Khabarovsk later that day, our train rumbled over a bridge across the broad expanse of the frozen Amur River and headed west toward Siberia. When the 22-span, 1.5-mile bridge over the Amur River was completed in 1916, it was the longest bridge on the entire line and formed the last link of the Trans-Siberian Railroad, the longest railway in the world.

Begun in 1891—with the initial construction on the Ussuri Line between Vladivostok and Khabarovsk—the Trans-Siberian Railroad took twenty-five years to complete. Constructed at great cost in both rubles and human lives, the Trans-Siberian Railroad was built by hand, without heavy machinery, mainly by unskilled laborers equipped with nothing more than picks and wooden shovels. Construction crews were made up of convicts, Russian army units, and migrant workers from the Orient and Central Asia, as well as skilled stonemasons from Italy who built many of the bridges across Siberia's largest rivers. They had to cut through dense forests, tunnel through mountains, slog through swamps, and lay tracks over permafrost. Living and working under often inhuman conditions, they suffered from poor housing, shortages of food, debilitating diseases, plagues of mosquitoes and black flies, raids by bandits, attacks by wild animals, and extremes of heat and cold. A combination of difficult terrain, cheap materials, corrupt management, poor planning, and shoddy workmanship resulted in rails that buckled, ties that broke, and tunnels that collapsed. Floods and landslides also destroyed bridges and huge sections of track. By the turn of the century, much of the line built during the past decade was already in need of repair or replacement. Despite these difficulties, the Trans-Siberian Railroad was one of the greatest engineering achievements of its time. When the bridge over the Amur River at Khabarovsk was opened in 1916, passengers could travel entirely by train for more than six thousand miles from St. Petersburg on the Gulf of Finland to Vladivostok on the Pacific Ocean without leaving Russian soil.

Many foreigners think of the Trans-Siberian Railroad as a single ribbon of steel stretching from one end of Russia to the other, traversed by a special train called "the Trans-Siberian Express" (similar to the original Orient Express that ran between London and Istanbul). But there is no single train named "the Trans-Siberian Express." Instead a number of passenger and freight trains ply the route, in both directions, some of them covering the

*Passenger car on the Trans-Siberian train Rossiya, which
runs between Moscow and Vladivostok.*

entire distance of the Trans-Siberian line between Moscow and Vladivostok,
others traveling shorter distances of only a few hundred or a few thousand
miles (like the *Sibir'* train on which we rode). Likewise the railroad is not a
single line but a whole system that includes branch lines, feeder lines, and
spurs intersecting the main line like tributaries of a great river, all of which
provide freight and passenger service to several parts of Siberia, as well as
to Central Asia, Mongolia, and China.

Late in the afternoon of the first day of our own trip on the Trans-Siberian
tracks, the train stopped briefly at Birobidzhan, the capital of Russia's Jewish Autonomous Region. In 1927 Stalin had established this region as a so-
called national homeland for Soviet Jews. But only a small number of them
were ever willing to leave their settled lives in European Russia, Ukraine,
and Belorussia and move thousands of miles away to this remote, sparsely
populated territory of the Soviet Far East. By the 1990s Jews made up only
4 percent of the population of that region, their presence only hinted at by
the faded Hebrew letters spelling out "BIROBIDZHAN" on the train station
in the hazy dusk.

After we left Khabarovsk, the landscape had become flat and uninterest-
ing, but just before the train reached Birobidzhan we spotted the outline of
low mountains on the horizon, their shapes bluish-purple in the late after-

noon light. Beyond Birobidzhan the winter night came on quickly, and in
the dark I could see only my own distorted reflection in the frosted window,
superimposed over the backsides of a few snow-covered buildings along the
tracks, strobe-lighted by the passing train. I went to bed early but slept
fitfully. Our private compartment, which had been freezing the night before, was now so hot and stuffy that I felt like I was trapped in a mobile
sauna. The windows were locked shut, and even the draft leaking through
the warped wooden frames was not enough to overcome the continuous
blast of heat from the coal-stoked boiler. Periodically I was also jolted awake
by the thud of someone's fists beating on the door to the next compartment,
the pong of hammers as workmen checked the cars' undercarriages whenever we stopped, and the heavy-metal sounds of the train as it lumbered
and lurched over rough stretches of track.

I woke the next morning to a scene straight out of nineteenth-century
paintings of the American West: a wide, flat valley bordered by a range of
mountains covered with mixed conifer and deciduous trees, and, in the
foreground, a large village of closely spaced log houses with snow capping
the roofs and smoke drifting lazily out of the chimneys. According to the
map, I had awakened just in time to see the town of Never, a Russian name
that easily lent itself to jokes in English. The night before we had passed a
place called Progress. As Tom sipped his morning tea and gazed out at the
log-cabin town, he remarked, "Only in Russia can you go to sleep in Progress
and wake up in Never."

Although we had been on the train for thirty-five hours—almost half the
total time of the trip—we were still in the part of the country known as the
Russian Far East. In the late 1500s, Russians from Europe began moving
eastward past the Ural Mountains into the vast Asian land that came to be
called Siberia. Russia gained the easternmost parts of this territory during
three centuries of exploration, conquest, and colonization, beginning with
the first Cossack forays into the Far East in the mid-1600s. In the latter half
of the eighteenth century, Empress Catherine the Great divided the large
land mass of Siberia into two administrative units, with the area designated
as Eastern Siberia extending more than two thousand miles from the Yenisey
River to the Pacific Coast. In the late 1800s, part of the Far Eastern territories of Siberia were separated from the governor-generalship of Eastern
Siberia and made into an administrative subdivision of their own. And in
the 1920s, after the Bolshevik Revolution and the ensuing civil war, these
Far Eastern territories—the last regions of Russia to come under Bolshevik
control—were incorporated into the Soviet Union.

Both the concept and the definition of the Russian/Soviet Far East have varied over time, with the inclusion or exclusion of certain territories. In 1994 the geographic-economic macroregion known as the Russian Far East comprised nine political subdivisions of the Russian Federation, ranging from the relatively small Jewish Autonomous Region to the huge Sakha Republic (formerly Yakutiya), which is twice the size of Alaska and which is now constitutionally an independent republic within the Russian Federation. These easternmost lands of the Russian Federation covered an area two-thirds the size of the United States and extended across four time zones, constituting the largest subdivision of Russia in geographic terms but one of the least developed regions in terms of economic output. Nearly eight million people inhabited the 2.4 million square miles of the Russian Far East, 75 percent of which is mountainous and 70 percent of which is classified as permafrost. From the lush forests of Primorskiy Kray to the frozen tundra of Sakha, from the smoking volcanoes of Kamchatka to the mountain ranges of Magadan, the Russian Far East is a sparsely populated land rich in both scenery and natural resources. But decades of Communist rule had left the region a legacy of bad leadership and poor economic development, as evidenced by the low standard of living, the pervasiveness of corruption, the plundering of natural resources, and the degradation of the environment.

By the second day of our Trans-Siberian journey, Tom and I already felt at home on the train called *Sibir'.* The day before, we had taken turns leaving the compartment to wander through the rest of the train, locating the dining car and squeezing through the crowded corridors of the several second-class passenger cars. Even though we could have left the compartment together and asked the conductress to lock it for us, we had been warned by Russian friends not to leave our room unattended. Enterprising thieves on the Trans-Siberian Railroad had skeleton keys for the sleeping compartments and—sometimes in collusion with the conductors—stole whatever they could find while the passengers were away. We also kept the door locked when we were inside the compartment, because robbers were bold enough to enter even when the passengers were present—a frightening experience we'd had a few months before on the Moscow-St. Petersburg overnight express. Just before we left Vladivostok, my friend Alla—fearing the worst—had offered to give me her treasured can of Mace. She seemed truly disappointed when I refused to accept the gift, and I think she doubted my confident assertion that simple prudence, along with the Swiss Army knives we always carried, would be sufficient to see Tom and me safely through the trip.

The second day of the trip started with the single restroom in our car in very bad condition. There were no private toilets on standard Trans-Siberian trains, but every first- and second-class sleeping car had a single restroom at each end, for use by male and female passengers alike. However, the conductors often locked the restroom adjacent to their own compartment, reserving it exclusively for themselves, leaving only one toilet at the other end of the car for the eighteen passengers in first-class or the thirty-six people in second-class accommodations. In our particular car, the lone conductress not only kept one restroom for her own use, she also seldom bothered to clean the other one. A tiny room with barely enough space to turn around in, it contained only a minuscule sink and a filthy toilet, with no seat and no toilet paper. It was also bitterly cold: a hole was worn completely through the floor, perilously close to the toilet, exposing the ground below and sucking in icy air from outside. By the end of the first day, the sink had stopped up and overflowed onto the already foul floor. The room also reeked of urine, because few of the passengers bothered to flush the toilet. When they did flush, the contents were supposed to drop through the drain hole directly onto the tracks. But in the Russian winter, all the liquid froze before it reached the ground, forming a funky stalactite just below the drain hole, which grew larger and longer with each flush, until the whole system completely stopped up.

The conductress on our car was a lazy, sullen young woman, so sour of disposition that we nicknamed her "Rassolova," from the Russian word for pickle or brine *(rassol)*. When the toilet and sink both backed up so badly they were completely unusable, she was finally stirred to action. She filled an old green hot water bottle with water from the boiler at the end of the car, connected a rubber hose with an enema attachment, and stuck this device down the drains to thaw them out. Then she took an already dirty rag and swabbed the slimy restroom floor, after which she used the same rag for "cleaning" the corridor outside the compartments, thus spreading the muck over a much wider area.

When she finished "cleaning," she added insult to injury by hanging the hot water bottle and its snaky attachment on the boiler next to the spigot from which everyone in the car drew hot water for making tea. I had heard that conductors on the Trans-Siberian trains traditionally provided hot tea for the passengers, but our conductress apparently disdained such hard labor. So Tom and I brewed our own tea throughout the day. We and the other passengers also used hot water from the boiler to cook packages of Oriental instant noodles in our compartments. Having been warned about the poor quality and limited selection of food served in the dining car, we had brought enough provisions for all of our meals on the trip: several plastic containers of Korean noodles, a package of Chinese ham, Danish and American sausages, three kinds of Russian cheese, a loaf of Russian bread, Dutch chocolates, Russian gingerbread cookies, plenty of tea bags, and a few peppermint candy canes left over from decorating our Christmas tree in Vladivostok. We had also brought along food supplies for the next semester, including bags of dried fiddlehead ferns and dried mushrooms whose earthy aromas permeated the stuffy air in the closed compartment. Just before we left Vladivostok, Tom had also purchased two whole smoked salmon to carry with us to Irkutsk. When the salmon began to warm up and exude too fishy a fragrance in our tiny room, Tom took them out to the vestibule at the end of the car and hung them on the inside door handle to cool off. We also chilled our beer in the vestibule, because that part of the train was like a refrigerator locker—so cold that ice crystals formed on the gray metal ceiling and walls, then floated down to the floor like snowflakes. After only a few minutes in that frigid space, the salmon lost their fishy smell, and the tepid beer became cool enough to drink.

The frozen vestibule was also the only area where smoking was officially permitted, the place where passengers gathered for a quick cigarette before the bitter cold drove them back into the overheated corridor. In the narrow hallway outside the compartments, people walked around, stretched their legs, and viewed the scenery outside the train. We were the only Americans. Except for two rough-looking Chinese men who kept to themselves in the compartment next to ours, all the other passengers were Russians. Most of the men had on cheap Chinese-made track suits, and a couple of the women went around in long housecoats all day. Almost everyone wore flimsy, floppy slippers on their feet, seldom with socks; one woman proudly sported a pair of fuzzy hot-pink house shoes that nicely matched her bright pink bathrobe. At first these fellow passengers seemed wary of making eye contact with each other, but they became more relaxed by the second day of traveling in close quarters. And except for someone who pounded on doors in the middle of the night, everyone else in our car was quiet and reserved. They passed the time by reading, knitting, playing chess, or just staring out the windows—unlike some of the passengers in the second-class cars, who drank heavily, sang loudly, and seemed to party around the clock.

Between Vladivostok and Irkutsk the train made eighteen scheduled stops, plus a few unscheduled halts for reasons I could never figure out. A timetable posted in the corridor told the official length of each stop—from two to twenty minutes, depending on the station—but the list turned out to be only an approximation, with some stops lasting much longer while engines were changed or repairs were made. During the day the train creaked along at a pleasantly slow pace, but at night it often sped over the tracks, apparently making up for time lost to repairs and other delays. The entire twenty-five hundred–mile trip would take seventy-two hours, at an average speed, with stops figured in, of thirty-five miles per hour.

Whenever the train halted for five minutes or more, many of the passengers got off to purchase food from the vendors lining the station platforms. At some of the major stations colorfully painted wooden kiosks marked "ICE CREAM," "MEAT PIES," or simply "MARKET" apparently offered foodstuffs in the summer but were vacant in the depth of the Russian winter. The only sellers were hardy *babushki* (grandmothers, elderly women), bundled up against the cold, who rolled their wares to the station in old-fashioned baby carriages. The first time I saw a group of these *babushki* waiting on the platform, I wondered why so many old ladies had brought their grandchildren out in the frigid weather to meet the train. But as the train slowed to a stop, I watched the *babushki* quickly unpack their "babies" and set up an instant outdoor buffet on the snow-packed ground.

While I stayed on guard in our train compartment, Tom got off at every station to see what foods he could forage for us. At various stops along the way, he returned with roasted Siberian pine nuts, salted sunflower seeds, baked whole potatoes, chunks of boiled potatoes napped with butter or mayonnaise (sometimes garnished with mushrooms or fried onions), and *pirozhki*, small, individual Russian "pies," baked or fried, made of dough completely enclosing a filling of meat, potatoes, or sauerkraut. All of these homemade foods were wrapped in whatever scrap paper was available: sunflower seeds in a cone made from a page torn out of a Russian novel, fried *pirozhki* surrounded by a scholarly article from an education journal, steamy hot potatoes enclosed in old newspapers. As we peeled off these recycled wrappings, we laughingly remembered an American colleague who had once purchased a portion of roasted peanuts at an open-air market in South Korea, where the nuts were handed to him in a paper cone made from a U.S. military document stamped "TOP SECRET."

All day our train rolled along just north of the Chinese border, through a winter landscape of snow-dusted steppes, undulating hills, and low rounded mountains, under a cloudless blue sky brightened by the pale winter sun that both rose and set to the south. Through forests of larch and birch standing thin and naked in the hazy light, their spindly branches laced with hoarfrost and punctuated by crows' nests. Past villages of stolid log houses, a film of wood smoke hovering over the sloping roofs. By small, turn-of-the-century train stations painted in pastel colors and decorated with fretted woodwork. Over frozen rivers, their glassy surfaces brocaded by wind and snow. Through tunnels glistening like caves of ice. By steam locomotive graveyards, black and forlorn, next to modern snow-clearing equipment, shiny and proud. Past female road crews in orange safety vests and heavy eye makeup. Near former gulags and present prisons. By lonely cemeteries, the graves marked with faded red Soviet stars or the eight-pointed crosses of the Russian Orthodox Church.

Not far past the town of Yerofey Pavlovich we crossed from the Russian Far East into Eastern Siberia. Our train was traveling toward the setting sun, in the opposite direction of those Europeans who first ventured into Siberia several centuries before. Although a few Europeans had penetrated a short distance beyond the Urals as early as the ninth century, Siberia remained until the sixteenth century terra incognita to people living west of the continental divide between Europe and Asia. But in the 1500s the Russians succeeded in subduing the two Tatar khanates that had formed a boundary between Europe and the uncharted lands "east of the sun." As a result of those victories, an immense expanse of northern Asia was suddenly opened to European exploration, conquest, and colonization.

Less than six decades after Russians and other Europeans began their eastward expansion into the vast territory that the Russians called *Sibir*, "the Sleeping Land," Russian explorers reached the Asian shore of the Pacific Ocean. The following three centuries witnessed a succession of expeditions, conquests, fortifications, and settlements, along with varying degrees of agricultural and industrial development in the newly charted lands of the east. Many of those Europeans who set out for Siberia made their fortunes, built their reputations, and left their mark on the land. But many more died in obscurity, victims of fate in that contradictory place of hope and despair, freedom and imprisonment, opportunity and exile.

Siberia's wealth of natural resources initially attracted trappers and traders in search of "soft gold"—the furs of sable, marten, fox, ermine, and squirrel—followed by prospectors seeking the "hard gold" of Siberia's massive mineral wealth, and later by petroleum engineers hoping to tap the "black gold" of Siberia's huge oil reserves. When the first Europeans set their sights on Siberia, however, the entire territory of more than five million square miles had a population of only 175,000 native people belonging to some 140 tribes and groups. During the ensuing centuries, these small numbers of Kirghiz, Tungus, Buryats, Yakuts, Evenks, Chukchi, and other indigenous people were eventually subjugated and overtaken, numerically and technologically, by successive generations of Russians, Ukrainians, Poles, Belorussians, Moldovans, Balts, and other Europeans who made their way to Siberia, voluntarily or involuntarily: peasants forcibly resettled by the tsar from European Russia; pioneers who came of their own free will; runaway and, after 1861, emancipated serfs; religious dissenters; exiles from Russia and deportees from conquered lands; Cossacks and convicts, adventurers and fortune seekers, misfits and malcontents—so many, in fact, that people of Slavic origin make up 95 percent of Siberia's population today.

Prior to the construction of the "Great Siberian Railroad," as the Russians called it, the only way to cross the vast land mass of Siberia had been on foot, or by horse-drawn wagons or sleighs, along the Great Siberian Post Road—the *Trakt*—the single dirt trail that, in conjunction with Siberia's rivers, served as the primary route for transportation and communication in that part of the world. Sometimes called the "Convict Highway," the *Trakt* was also the route followed by those unfortunates condemned to prison or exile in Siberia. With the building of the Trans-Siberian Railroad, the Russian government was able to move people—soldiers, settlers, convicts, and exiles—into Siberia and to take raw materials out of Siberia, much more rapidly than before, thus speeding up both the colonization and the economic development of Asian Russia, while at the same time exerting more control, politically and militarily, over the great expanse of land between the Ural Mountains and the Pacific Ocean. Today, as a result of the railroad's influence on this part of Russia, the majority of Siberia's population still lives either in the major cities situated on the railroad line—such as Novosibirsk, Irkutsk, and Ulan-Ude—or in the small towns and villages scattered along its thousands of miles of tracks.

Late in the afternoon on the second day of our own Trans-Siberian journey, we arrived in Amazar, the first railroad stop in Eastern Siberia. On the snowy platform in front of the blue-and-green-painted station, *babushki* were selling *pirozhki* stuffed with meat, turnips, and sticky rice; *vareniki*, Ukrainian-style boiled dumplings shaped like half moons and filled with sauerkraut; loaves of brown bread; two kinds of *bliny* (Russian pancakes), beige ones made with white flour, darker ones made of buckwheat; and chocolate ice cream in unwrapped cones, frozen solid and stacked in open boxes with no fear of melting in the frosty air. While I watched from the window of our compartment, Tom got off the train to photograph the old steam locomotives rusting on the sidings and to buy freshly cooked food for supper that night. But I decided to see what the dining car had to offer that evening. Before we reached the next stop at Mogocha, I left Tom behind to guard our compartment while I went in search of a Trans-Siberian restaurant meal.

The *Sibir*'s dining car looked like an American roadside diner from the 1950s. A row of red leatherette booths with white Formica-topped tables lined the car on either side of a center aisle. Fake wood paneling, chrome fixtures, and fluorescent lighting completed the 1950s retro scene. At the far end of the car was a cramped, dimly lighted kitchen. The two booths nearest the kitchen were reserved for the staff, all of whom were remarkably friendly and good-natured for Russian restaurant personnel: a large, middle-aged female cook, with a dirty apron and dyed bright-yellow hair; a wiry young busboy-dishwasher in a grimy white cotton coat; and an attractive waitress in her mid-30s, wearing a black straight skirt, crisp white blouse, and a flashy black leather blouson jacket. One of the tables displayed the choice of drinks for sale: cans of Miller Draft beer and bottles of Russian champagne, Italian fizzy white wine, Rasputin vodka, and Fiesta orange soda. On the same table, a Michael Jackson tape wound its way through a big Korean boom box.

I sat alone in a booth near the kitchen. On her way to deliver food to the other customers, the waitress stopped by to say that goulash was the meal for that evening. Given no other choices, I agreed to take the goulash, then waited a long time before the waitress finally came back with a small white cotton cloth to spread on my table. As she unfolded it, we both noticed that it was smeared with big black blotches that looked like axle grease. She grinned, shrugged, and flipped it over so the grease was on the bottom. For some reason I felt strangely honored—perhaps because the waitress had singled me out as the only person in the dining car who rated a tablecloth, even a soiled one.

A few minutes later she returned with several slices of stale Russian bread and a plate of "goulash," which was nothing more than chunks of tough meat smothered with a tasteless, pasty brown gravy. On the same plate were a few brownish noodles, half a large pickled red tomato, and a surprisingly tasty cabbage-and-carrot salad garnished with canned green peas. All the customers shared around the dining car's single, faceted-glass saltshaker (missing its lid), and the substitute for a pepper shaker, an old canning jar half full of very hot paprika, which I sprinkled liberally over the bland meat.

When I finished eating, the waitress brought me a large glass of hot, sweet, chicory-flavored coffee, just as the train pulled into the town of

Mogocha in the blue winter light. As soon as the train stopped, two well-dressed women, in fur coats and fur hats, entered the dining car and asked the cook, "What do you have?" "Butter," replied the cook. "How much?" asked the women. "Four," answered the cook, meaning 4,000 rubles ($3.25) for a kilogram. "What else?" inquired the women, apparently in a hurry to make a transaction. "Oranges, chocolates, cookies," said the cook, although I couldn't hear the prices because obnoxious rap music was now blaring out of the boom box on the drinks table.

The cook led the women to the opposite end of the dining car where several cardboard boxes were stacked, full of butter slabs, oranges, small individually wrapped chocolates, and two kinds of sugar cookies. The ladies' order was quickly placed into plastic bags, and money changed hands just as swiftly. Already the narrow aisle of the dining car was beginning to fill up, as other locals boarded the train to purchase whatever the restaurant staff had to offer. One was a nice-looking man in ski pants and an anorak who, with his wire-framed glasses, charming grin, and pleasant demeanor, had the appearance of a young college professor. He must have handed the waitress a large denomination hard-currency note that required much change in return, because suddenly she started pulling big wads of rubles from inside her leather jacket and tossing them onto the table behind me. She kept throwing money on the table until it was entirely covered with a pile of 100- , 200- , 1,000- , and 5,000-ruble notes. Then she nonchalantly told him to pick his change out of that mess of money, while she went on to help the other customers. The man asked her to repeat the price of his purchase, to confirm it. When he heard the amount, he laughed and said, "But I'm not a Chinese!" They both laughed together, and she immediately quoted him a lower figure. As I left the dining car, local customers were still crowding in to buy food, the boom box was playing rock music, and the waitress was still bantering with the handsome fellow while she set up a display of German Advent calendars for sale, their Christmas scene of an old, snow-covered European village merely a romanticized reflection of the real Siberian village just outside the train.

On the third morning of our journey, the sun rose dark red over southern Siberia, but it was soon hidden by low gray clouds that brought the first snow flurries of the trip. "Sneg! Sneg!" ("Snow! Snow!"), I exclaimed to the Russian woman standing next to me at the window in the corridor, as both of us watched the falling flakes. "Only a little now," she replied gaily, "but more—much more!—as we go into Siberia!" She was right: the first two days of the trip, the sky had been blue and cloudless, the land covered with only a few inches of snow. But as we went farther into Eastern Siberia, the blowing snow obscured the landscape, blotted out distances, and grew deeper and deeper on the ground. Peering through the ice patterns on the window, as snow accumulated in the corners between the double panes of glass, I wondered what the temperature was outside the train. But I knew the Trans-Siberian Railroad had a long way to go before it would ever reach the high-tech level of the InterCity Express trains that I had ridden in Germany, with their computer terminals at the end of each car, which displayed instant information about the cities along the route, including the latest weather conditions.

By the third day and the third time zone of the trip, Tom and I had begun to feel the full effect of "Trans-Siberian time warp," a kind of train lag similar to jet lag where you aren't sure whether the train is ahead of, or behind, your own internal clock. To keep the official railroad schedule consistent over the line's eight time zones, Trans-Siberian trains ran on Moscow time— and along the way, the station clocks showed Moscow time instead of local time, which just added to one's own constant chronological confusion. For example, at the beginning of the trip we had left Vladivostok at 1:00 A.M. on Tuesday, January 18 (Vladivostok time), but the train had officially departed at 6:00 P.M. on Monday, January 17 (Moscow time). Even though we gained only one hour of real time each day as we entered a new time zone, by the second day of the journey, we began waking up at dawn and getting hungry for lunch by mid-morning. All day long, we napped and snacked whenever we felt like it, and by evening we were no longer certain what time it was anymore. By the third day we didn't care.

The morning of that third day the train stopped at two Siberian towns, Chita and Petrovsk-Zabaikal'skiy (also known as Petrovskiy-Zavod), both famous in Russian history as places of imprisonment and exile for the Decembrists. In the early nineteenth century, this group of young, idealistic, progressive-minded members of the Russian aristocracy, many of them military officers, had hoped to overthrow Russia's autocratic form of government, establish a constitutional monarchy or a republic, and abolish serfdom. But in December, 1825, they failed in their poorly organized attempt to unseat the tsar. The following year five of their leaders were hanged, and another hundred men involved in the plot were condemned to long terms of imprisonment, hard labor, and exile in Siberia. Many of them died in that distant land, far removed from family and friends in European Russia. Some lived long enough to benefit from a decree of amnesty by Tsar Aleksandr II in 1856, but many of the survivors, elderly men by then, chose to remain in Siberia, where they had spent most of their lives.

Outside the pale yellow train station at Petrovskiy-Zavod stood a rather strange-looking monument to those Decembrists, its stucco badly painted in yellow and turquoise, with busts of eight of the ill-fated aristocrats inside oval niches and a domineering statue of Lenin on top. On a building nearby was a large, modern, more attractive ceramic-tile mural commemorating the Decembrists and the eleven courageous women who gave up their aristocratic titles, their fortunes, and, in some cases, even their children, to follow their husbands and fiancés into exile in Siberia. These well-educated Decembrists and their wives were credited with raising the level of education, science, and culture in nineteenth-century Siberia, making a lasting impression on the history of the regions where they lived and the people whose lives they touched. Their influence continued even into the twentieth century, when the Soviets found it convenient to appropriate the history of these unfortunate Russian nobles, using them as symbols of early Russian revolutionary spirit and turning their story into a kind of Communist morality tale.

Our train continued to clank and clatter, rumble and rattle across the Siberian countryside to the north of Mongolia. The much-romanticized rhythm of the rails was more of a syncopated beat as the train lurched along the uneven roadbed, the cars bouncing and bumping as if pulled by a horse of flesh and blood, not one of iron. For miles and miles the tracks paralleled the routes of frozen rivers, their solid surfaces serving as ice roads for the occasional truck or horse-drawn sled. As the train climbed over the Yablonovy Mountains, reaching the highest point on the line at more than three thousand feet, great vistas of valleys and peaks opened up before us, revealing grassy steppes surrounded by forests of fir and pine. When the sun broke through the clouds, every element in the landscape stood out in sharp contrast to its neighbor: white snow, black rocks, dark brown tree trunks, dark green conifers, black-and-white magpies. On a broad white plain, a dozen brown and black Mongolian horses raced alongside the train, while others pushed their muzzles through the snow to graze on the grasses below. The mountain scenery was reminiscent of Montana or Wyoming. When the prairie predominated, the landscape reminded me of the seemingly endless Great Plains in Hungary and the United States. In such a setting, I wouldn't have been surprised to see a band of Sioux Indians suddenly appear on the horizon or a horde of Mongol horsemen come riding across the grasslands, sweeping over the steppes like the wind-driven snow.

As we neared Ulan-Ude, the largest city on the line after leaving Khabarovsk, we passed villages more closely spaced than before, with livestock huddled in the fenced farmyards behind small wooden houses. Stacks of firewood reached

Vendor selling home-cooked food at a railroad station in Siberia.

up to the eaves, and pots of cactus, jade plants, and geraniums soaked up the sparse sunlight behind double-glazed windows. Almost all the villages along the eastern Trans-Siberian route were low and flat, composed of single-story houses made of logs or planks, with roofs of wood shingles or corrugated tin, television antennae on top and privies out back. Occasionally I saw long, two-story wooden buildings, like barracks, or a few brick buildings, two- or three-stories tall, that looked like factories, hospitals, or schools. But only rarely was the view broken by the dreary gray high-rises and rusting industrial sites that blight Russia's bigger cities and towns.

The train was scheduled to stop for fifteen minutes in Ulan-Ude, but for some reason it stayed much longer, giving us an unexpected opportunity to linger over the wares of vendors at the salmon-pink station: breads and buns in a surprising variety of shapes and sizes, bottled drinks, boiled eggs, homemade *pirozhki* and *vareniki*, candy bars from Germany, sticky sweets from China and Korea. Some of the sellers were heavy-set *babushki* in woolen shawls and thick felt boots; others were slim, well-dressed younger women with children in tow. Many of the vendors were local Buryat-Mongolians, for Ulan-Ude is the capital of Siberia's Buryat Republic. It is also a major industrial city: that day a pall of factory smoke hung in the air, further dimming the late-afternoon light, as steam from the trains' boilers mingled with the cigarette smoke and condensed breath rising from the crowds of people milling around on the snowy station platform.

Past Ulan-Ude, in the gray-white twilight of the Siberian winter, I caught my first glimpse of Lake Baikal. I had been standing with the other passengers in the train corridor for almost an hour, looking out the windows in hope of seeing the legendary lake before night enshrouded it. Suddenly, beyond a bend in the track, there it was: a great flat expanse of snow-covered ice stretching unbroken to the gray horizon. Lake met sky at exactly the midpoint of the window, drawing a sharp, straight line across the field of view like a color chart that states unequivocally: This is White. This is Gray. Five minutes later the sky was completely black, and I could see nothing more beyond the windows except a small strip of sooty snow along the tracks, illuminated by the passing train.

At eleven o'clock that night, seventy-two hours after leaving Vladivostok, the *Sibir'* pulled into Irkutsk, the city that was to be our home for the next five months. The Russian dean of our university program met us at the station with two students to help unload all our luggage from the train. "I don't like guys with guns," remarked one of the students as he warily watched four sinister-looking men get off the train and begin circling around us, casing the growing pile of baggage on the dark, almost deserted platform. While the students and I guarded the luggage, Tom went to the baggage car to retrieve the four boxes he had consigned to the baggage handler back in Vladivostok. Much to Tom's surprise, all the boxes were still there and still intact. Apparently the eighteen dollars he had given the baggage car attendant had been sufficient "protection money" for the entire trip. Later, when we unpacked the boxes at our apartment in Irkutsk, we discovered the only casualty of the journey: our single, treasured bottle of Tabasco sauce had frozen solid in the baggage car and shattered into several pieces.

Tom and I thought that trip on the Trans-Siberian Railroad would be our first and our last, a once-in-a-lifetime journey that in later years we would fondly recall as the high point of our travel experiences in Russia. But ten days after arriving in Irkutsk, we were on the train again, heading back to Ulan-Ude to speak at a World Bank conference there. And during the next nine months we rode the rails many times, using the trains as the Russians do, to cover long and short distances in Siberia and the Russian Far East, where travel by rail, despite some of its discomforts, was usually safer and more dependable than long hauls by automobile on Russia's sparse and badly surfaced roads, or by airplane with the increasing number of crashes in Russia that year.

Several times during the spring in Irkutsk we also rode the *elektrichki*, electrically powered commuter trains that ran between the main train station, outlying urban districts, and nearby small towns. Form followed function in the passenger cars of those short-haul trains, with the seating nothing more than closely spaced rows of hard wooden benches bolted to the floor. But it was not until early June that we experienced true "hard class" on a long-distance Russian train. On a weekend trip to Ulan-Ude we traveled in the lowest category of sleeping car on the Trans-Siberian Railroad, third class or dormitory class. In those cars there were no separate compartments, just open rows of hard, plastic-covered bunks, like broad shelves, on which the passengers sat during the day and slept at night, with no privacy whatsoever. Along one side of the car eighteen rows of double-decked bunks were situated perpendicular to the windows, each with a third shelf near the ceiling that could be folded down for a luggage rack. On the other side of the off-center aisle two hard, narrow, single fold-down seats faced each other under every window, with a tiny table in between; at night each set of these facing seats could be converted into a single bunk for sleeping. Along that same wall were brackets for attaching a second bunk above the fold-down seats, parallel to the wall and extending across each window, with a third shelf for luggage above that. Officially these open-style dormitory cars were supposed to accommodate a maximum of fifty-four passengers, but the Russian trains were often so crowded that extra passengers bribed the conductors to let them sleep on the upper, luggage-rack shelves, thus increasing the total capacity of each car to eighty-one people.

During my stay in Russia, I made three long trips in these dormitory cars, and each time I felt like I was riding backward in time, inside settings that recalled Russian films produced half a century before. The interiors of these passenger cars had walls of gray-and-white plastic paneling, with cheap chrome fixtures, blue plastic-covered berths, dirty reddish-brown linoleum floors, and windows that needed washing thousands of miles ago. The single restroom at one end of the car looked and smelled worse than a derelict outhouse. The whole effect of chrome, plastic, filth, crowding, and lack of privacy was that of a prison train, or perhaps a train of retreating troops in wartime.

The passengers in these dormitory cars were Russians who could not afford better accommodations, or who, like us, had been unable to obtain seats in a first- or second-class car. Most of them were shabbily dressed in cheap clothes bought at local street markets. More than a few reeked of vodka and body odors. Typical was the middle-aged man on the berth next to mine, wearing grubby blue jogging pants with a red stripe down the side, floppy slippers with no socks, a beige nylon shirt buttoned to the neck, and a shiny brown polyester suit coat with three rows of military medals pinned on his breast pocket. When he spoke, he flashed a mouth full of stainless steel teeth. And, as on all classes of Russian trains, some of the passengers traveled with their pets: a puppy on a crude string leash, a kitten tucked inside a jacket. Never did I see an animal in a modern plastic or wicker pet carrier like those in the West.

The mood of each dormitory car depended on the character and group dynamics of its passengers—sometimes quiet, courteous, and friendly, with meager food supplies shared among strangers; other times tense, suspicious, and withdrawn, or rowdy and unruly, with too much vodka fueling fights over minor matters made large. On one of our trips to Ulan-Ude, a large group of Gypsies boarded the train at Slyudyanka near Lake Baikal. Attired in a jumble of clothing, the Gypsy women paraded down the aisle in a panoply of patterns and prints—bright magenta, turquoise, and red—accented by gold teeth, gold jewelry, and gossamer scarves glistening with gold lamé threads. Loud and laughing, they disrupted the relative quiet of the car like a flock of noisy parrots suddenly landing in the midst of a group of gray pigeons pecking at the ground. As the train rolled on, Gypsy children raced up and down the car, while the women chattered, sang, and clapped. Their men cast surly glances at the other passengers and occasionally slapped a Gypsy woman for some imagined offense. Soon the smell of fish enveloped the car, as the Gypsies began eating salted *omul'* from Lake

Baikal. Meanwhile the Russian passengers visibly recoiled from this color-ful chaos, either pointedly ignoring the Gypsies or making snide comments about them behind their backs.

That weekend excursion to Ulan-Ude in early June was our first journey by train beyond Lake Baikal after the last snow had melted. Gray clouds still caressed the mountain tops, but the hillsides, meadows, and stream banks were a palette of spring colors: the lime green of new birch leaves, the soft green of larch needles, the dark green of Siberian pines, the lacy white blossoms of bird-cherry trees, the purple clusters of lilacs, the yellow dots of dandelions, the pink and orange petals of flowers too tiny to identify from the train window. In the villages *babushki*, still bundled up as if it were winter, sat on wooden benches outside their log houses, their weath-ered faces turned toward the welcome warmth of the sun. Small children ran around naked while their parents tilled the family's garden plot. Teen-agers swam in the rivers, dogs chased each other in the streets, and cats snoozed on the depleted woodpiles. In the Siberian summer light, the sur-face of the Selenga River shimmered silver like the scales of the *omul'* that swim upstream to spawn. And in the forest a nude couple engaged in their own private rite of spring, oblivious to stares from the passing train.

At the end of June, Tom and I left Siberia, retracing our route on the Trans-Siberian Railroad from Irkutsk to Khabarovsk. This time the train was Number 2, the *Rossiya* (Russia), which took six-and-one-half days to traverse the entire intercontinental line between Moscow and Vladivostok. The green locomotive, still displaying its Soviet red star, pulled a baggage car, seventeen passenger cars, and a dining car located in the middle of the train. Occasionally a vendor came through the passenger cars selling beer, oranges, and packages of snack foods. More often, however, trade went the other way. Whenever the train stopped, the dining car staff stacked their boxes of foodstuffs in the vestibule and sold beer, soft drinks, fruit juices, and chocolates to Russian customers crowding the platforms at each sta-tion, while the passengers got off to purchase fresh red radishes, cabbage salads, and green onion tops from the local *babushki* with their well-stocked baby carriages.

The train was packed with summer travelers, mostly Russians and Chi-nese. The only way Tom and I could reserve a sleeping compartment for just the two of us was to buy all four places in a second-class, four-person compartment. In Russia, however, such an obvious solution to a simple problem seldom took into account the obstacles that could be devised by petty bureaucrats. Western expediency came head-to-head with Russian obduracy in the form of the ticket seller who initially refused our request. Her attitude, like that of many older Russians, was "Why should two passengers, just because they have the money, buy two seats they don't use and thus deprive two other people of those seats on the train?" I understood her objection—and could agree with it in principle—but I wasn't about to spend two-and-a-half days in a hot, crowded four-person room with two strangers, when Tom and I could afford to pay the 695,504 rubles (358 dollars) to reserve the entire sleeping compartment for ourselves.

We were assigned a compartment on the first passenger car at the head of the train, adjacent to the quarters of the two conductresses, a team who worked alternating twelve-hour shifts. One was a short, small, rather shy but pleasant, middle-aged woman; the other, named Nadezhda (Hope), was as jolly and extroverted as she was tall and fat. But both were just the opposite of the slovenly, ill-tempered "Rassolova" of our first trip on the Trans-Siberian Railroad. They took us under their wings, brought us hot tea more often than we wanted it, and let us (and only us) share the clean restroom they had reserved for themselves at our end of the car. Early in the trip Nadezhda decided that I spoke Russian much better than I actually did, and she took every opportunity to talk with me about the United States, about her own country, about whatever came to mind. Whenever she was on duty, Nadezhda also regaled us with American music piped through the passenger car's sound system—"When the Saints Go Marching In," "Rock around the Clock," "See Ya Later, Alligator," and Credence Clearwater Revival's cover of "Good Golly, Miss Molly"—while I tried to imagine how Americans would react to Russian rock being played for twelve hours each day on Amtrak with no way to turn off the sound.

The weather was foggy and cool when we left Irkutsk early that morning at the end of June. Five hours later our last sight of Lake Baikal was of gray water melding with the leaden sky, but soon after the train headed up the Selenga River toward Ulan-Ude, the day became sunny, hot, and dry. In January we had ridden into Siberia with the winter snow; now, as we rode away from Siberia, the sky was filled with the "summer snow" of fluffy poplar seed puffs floating lazily through the air. And during the rest of the two-thousand-mile trip we watched a panorama of summer scenes pass by the window. A dozen horses waded in the shallows of the Selenga. A pair of large waterbirds, like peach-colored flamingoes, glided to a landing in a lime-green marsh. Hawks circled over the grassy steppes. A profusion of wildflowers carpeted the meadows, like an Impressionist painting exuberantly expanding beyond the limits of canvas and frame: undulating shades of yellow, gold, and blue, maroon and magenta, soft pink and pristine white, the pale purple globes of wild onions gone to seed, thousands of red-orange tiger lilies, whole fields of dark purple Siberian irises, and occasionally a single red poppy or two, like a stubborn symbol of politics past. Outside Chita a small lake glistened under the midnight moon. Near Birobidzhan the mountains to the north of the train rose charcoal gray through the morning mist. A pair of Siberian cranes—a symbol of long life and an omen of good luck—preened themselves in a bog pool against a background of deep purple mountains looming up from China to the south.

As the train rolled along near the Chinese border, Russian armored personnel carriers churned up clouds of dust on the dirt roads parallel to the tracks. Huge metal radar scanners circled slowly on the hilltops. To the north were grim-looking prisons surrounded by guard towers, barbed wire, and search lights. Beside a river stood a large wooden stockade, like a cavalry fort in a John Ford movie. In a forest clearing, workers cooked a meal over a smoky campfire next to a hut built of railroad ties. Miles from any settlement pitiful little cemeteries lay desolate and abandoned, set in the woods as if the dead could find comfort in the company of trees.

On the third morning of the trip I awoke to a landscape so lush and green that if I were a grazing animal I would have wanted to devour it. Old women in loose cotton smocks tended their gardens and tilled their potato patches next to weathered wooden houses reminiscent of rural homes in the American South of my childhood. Younger women, clad in 1940s-style printed cotton sundresses and white kerchiefs on their heads, cut hay by hand with long scythes and raked it into rows in the fields. On the back porch of a frame house a woman sat treadling her spinning wheel. Heat and humidity hung in the air like a heavy sigh of relief after the long Siberian winter. As we neared the end of our journey, I reflected on the variety of scenery between Lake Baikal and the Pacific Ocean—and wondered why so many writers from the West have persisted in promulgating the myth that Siberia is a vast, monotonous expanse of nothing but taiga and tundra, where the landscape barely changes from one end to the other of the entire Trans-Siberian route.

The last time I traveled by train in Russia was in the autumn of 1994, to the village of Krylovka, 225 miles north of Vladivostok. The trip had been arranged by Larisa, a Russian friend who taught English at an elementary school in Vladivostok. She and her husband had bought a small wooden house in the village, which they used as a summer home and weekend retreat. Larisa invited Tom and me to accompany her to Krylovka one weekend in mid-October, when she planned to harvest the last vegetables from her garden and close up the house for the winter. The journey would take more than six hours each way by train, followed by two bus rides that, with waiting time for connections, added another four hours to the trip.

The Vladivostok train station was closed for restoration, so we met Larisa on Friday evening at the adjacent Morskoy Vokzal (Sea Terminal) on the Golden Horn Bay. In a stuffy waiting room that reeked of stale cigarette smoke, unwashed bodies, and dirty clothes, we sat for more than two hours on molded-plastic chairs, watching a surrealistic scene of several shabby drunks carrying bunches of red flowers and beating up on each other. Throughout the melee bored-looking *babushki* sat stoically on big bulging bundles piled on the floor, while a gold-toothed hag played with a tiny tabby kitten tucked into her threadbare coat.

Larisa had bought tickets for the overnight train that left at 11:00 P.M., booking the three of us into one of those eighty-one–person, open-dormitory, hard-class sleeping cars. It turned out to be the dirtiest one I had ever seen, with chewing gum stuck on the walls, no backrests for the seats, and a single toilet so filthy we could smell it throughout the crowded car. Soon after the train left Vladivostok, the conductress came by with sheets, pillowcases, blankets, and small towels for the passengers to rent for 3,000 rubles (now worth only 1 dollar) per person. Although the linens were of far worse quality than those I had used on other Russian trains, I was grateful for anything to cover the grimy pillow and grungy mattress on my bunk. Before we finished making up our beds, however, the conductress turned out all the lights, suddenly casting us into an unwanted darkness in an unfamiliar place. Still fully clothed, we crawled into our berths, but sleep was difficult in a room packed with eighty other people, the sour stench of body odors mingling with the sounds of snoring and the clack-clack-clack of the train. As the cold lights of empty train stations flashed through the bare windows, I tried to retreat from the reality of Russia by pulling the skimpy blanket over my head. But the cloth was so full of dust that I began coughing and sneezing, adding my own disturbance to the fitfully slumbering car. The only hint of civilization in that squalid setting was a jam jar full of bright red roses that one of our fellow passengers had placed on the little fold-down table between our berths.

The return trip was no better. After spending the weekend at Larisa's house, the three of us returned together to Vladivostok, retracing our route

Meeting the train at a Trans-Siberian railroad station.

by bus and train on Sunday night. At the train station nearest Krylovka, we waited for more than an hour in the crackling cold, watching as militiamen with submachine guns milled around inside, occasionally stopping some-one to check identification papers. To my surprise the station was full of well-dressed people, many of them in their late teens and early twenties. The young men had on coats and ties, and several of the women were decked out in party frocks, fur coats, and high-heeled shoes—not the sort of attire you normally saw in the waiting room of a provincial Russian train station. Larisa—an elementary schoolteacher who worked hard just to make ends meet—regarded them with a mixture of envy and contempt. "They're university students in Vladivostok," she said, forgetting for the moment that Tom and I taught at that same university. "But look at them, they have so much money they can do anything they want. See how they dress? They can buy whatever they want. And on weekends they have plenty of time to go to parties in the country instead of studying like other students have to do." But richness is only relative, I thought, reflecting on the fact that all these so-called privileged people were returning to Vladivostok on the same squalid train as the rest of us.

Shortly after midnight, Larisa suddenly told us to gather up our bags and get ready to board the train. We couldn't understand her tenseness and sense of urgency as she hustled us out of the station and motioned us to follow her across the tracks. As at most Russian train stations—even the major ones—there were no pedestrian walkways, so all the passengers had to scramble over the rails in the dark, lugging their baggage with them. "Hurry, hurry!" urged Larisa as we heard the sound of the train in the near distance. Taking us by hand, she led us well beyond the station platform, as we stumbled over the uneven, unlighted ground beside the tracks, unable to see more than a few feet in front of us. I couldn't imagine where she was going, but Larisa knew what she was doing, as did the large group of Russians following right behind us, including those fashionable young women teetering along in their high heels. Just then the train pulled into the station, the engine stopping next to the small platform, with the passenger cars trailing off into the darkness beyond.

The conductor opened the door to our third-class car, but didn't lower any stairs down to the passengers on the ground. The lowest step on the train was higher than my head, and I couldn't see how anyone could climb aboard without a ladder. Suddenly the crowd surged forward, pushing a young man up onto the train. He turned around, reached down, and helped hoist the next passenger aboard. A piece of luggage followed, then another passenger, and so on, until it was my turn to be pushed and pulled onto the train, too. Working together, in a spontaneous collective action, the crowd of passengers overcame the uncaring idiocy of the Russian railroad system and managed to get all of themselves and their luggage onto the train during the two-minute stop at that little station, despite the darkness and disorder.

Our dormitory car that night was even worse than the one that had brought us from Vladivostok two days before. Although the weather had turned cold that weekend, there was no heat inside the train. The single toilet in our car was locked, forcing people to search in the dark for another one somewhere else on the train. I went to bed fully clothed under the dirty blanket on my bunk, dreading the thought of having to wear those same clothes to work at the university a few hours later. Sleep eluded me, however, as cockroaches crawled over my face during the night. The next morning, some of the passengers were so appalled at conditions on the train, they circulated a petition protesting the situation. When the impromptu document was handed to Larisa, she signed it readily. Then, with a note of weary triumph in her voice, she turned to me with tired eyes and sighed, "At last our people are beginning to fight back."

CHAPTER 4

Irkutsk

THE PARIS OF SIBERIA

It was not a typical Tuesday in Siberia. Two days before, Nobel Laureate Aleksandr Solzhenitsyn had arrived by train in Irkutsk, traveling with his personal entourage in two private railroad cars, like a modern-day tsar, accompanied by a phalanx of news reporters from around the world. Twenty years after being expelled from the Soviet Union for criticizing the Communist regime, Solzhenitsyn had returned to the Russian Federation in May, 1994, landing first in Vladivostok, then embarking on an eight-week journey by rail across Russia to Moscow, to reacquaint himself with his homeland. Along the way he stopped off for several days in Irkutsk, where he stayed in the best hotel in the city, the Intourist, on the so-called American floor customarily reserved for visitors from the West who paid for their rooms in hard currency.

On Tuesday evening Solzhenitsyn was scheduled to hold a press conference for local and foreign reporters. Earlier that day, Kathy Lally—an American journalist covering Solzhenitsyn's trip for the Baltimore *Sun*—spent several hours with us at Irkutsk State University, interviewing the students, faculty, and staff in our Russian-American program. After she left for a late-afternoon appointment to interview Solzhenitsyn at the Intourist, Tom and I also headed for the hotel to meet a group of Oregonians who were visiting Irkutsk on a Rotary Club trip. In the lobby we ran into several other Americans recently arrived in Irkutsk, including businessmen, U.S. government employees, and an eccentric ecologist from Arkansas who had

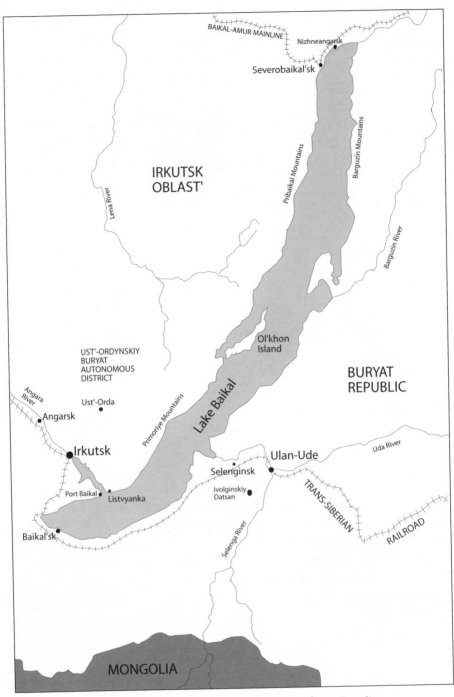

MAP 4. *Lake Baikal and surrounding area (boundary lines are approximations).*

come to do research at Lake Baikal. Summer seemed to be the season for foreigners in the city. We had not seen that many Americans during the previous four months in Irkutsk, and certainly never that many in a single day.

After dinner at the hotel, Tom and I left the Intourist by taxi at half past ten. Even at that late hour the twilight still lingered in southern Siberia, as the calendar approached the summer solstice. Just as the taxi started to cross a bridge over the Angara River, we noticed a large militia van parked on the bridge, with a militia car stopped directly ahead of it. We assumed there had been an accident on the bridge, but when our taxi slowed down to pass the police vehicles, the cause of the commotion became clear: a totally nude woman, about fifty or sixty years old, was standing in front of the militia car, making a speech. As she continued to declaim and wave her arms around—like a naked Mother Russia addressing the Duma—several young policemen stood nearby, looking up in the air or down at the water with embarrassed expressions on their faces, obviously unwilling to interrupt her deranged diatribe. Our first reaction was to laugh at the strange spectacle, but the poker-faced taxi driver never cracked a smile. Maybe he saw scenes like that every night. Or maybe he just considered it impolite to laugh at Mother Russia.

That nude *babushka* was only one of many sights I never expected to see in Siberia. None of the books I had read on the history, geography, and politics of Russia had prepared me for some of the surprising images of everyday life that sometimes seemed surreal in the context of southern Siberia: biplanes and hot-air balloons, bikinis and baseball caps, hydrofoils and horse-racing tracks, Buddhist temples and Baptist missionaries, swimming pools and tennis courts, motorcycles and Mercedes-Benzes, Hula Hoops and Slinky toys, Dove Bars and Dr Peppers, sailboats and skateboards, miniskirts and mirrored sunglasses, bumper cars and Ferris wheels, French poodles and Siamese cats, air conditioners and neon signs, cowboys on horseback herding cattle, Cossacks in colorful uniforms carrying cavalry whips, a Cyrillic-lettered movie poster for Oliver Stone's film *JFK*. Such are the realities from which modern myths are made.

When Tom and I arrived in Irkutsk by train in mid-January of 1994, the temperature that night was eighteen degrees above zero—a Siberian heat wave in a city where the mean temperature in January is six degrees below zero and where winter temperatures can easily drop to forty degrees below. As we rode from the train station to our new apartment in a high-rise hous-

ing development on the edge of the city, my first impressions of Irkutsk
were of cold, dry, crackling crisp air; hoarfrosted trees standing ghostly
white against the black, star-studded sky; and old wooden houses, shut-
tered against the cold, deeply asleep under a thick blanket of snow.

During the following week, we explored the city that has been the capital of Eastern Siberia for more than two hundred years. Founded by Cossacks as a military outpost in the mid-1600s, Irkutsk officially became a
town in 1686. Situated near the confluences of the Angara, Irkut, and
Ushakovka rivers, about forty miles from Lake Baikal, the wooden fort of
Irkutsk was originally a center for the collection of *yasak*—a tax, payable in
furs, levied by the tsars upon the native Buryats who lived in the lands
around the lake.

Located in the southern part of Siberia, not far from China and Mongolia,
Irkutsk soon developed into a major transportation hub and commercial
center on the trade routes between Europe and Asia. The fur trade initially
formed the basis of Irkutsk's economy, its importance symbolized by the
city's coat of arms, which features a mythical, tigerlike animal called a *babr*,
an emblem of power, holding in its mouth a sable, representing wealth.
Trade with China also enriched the coffers of businessmen in Irkutsk, as
caravans of Chinese tea, silks, spices, and porcelains came northward to
Irkutsk on their way to Europe, and Russian furs and ancient mammoth
tusks were sent to Chinese customers in the south. And the sale of salt and
minerals from Siberian mines, as well as timber from its virgin forests, brought
additional revenues to the residents of Irkutsk.

During the eighteenth and nineteenth centuries Irkutsk developed into
Eastern Siberia's major city, a metropolis with schools, libraries, learned
societies, museums, theaters, orchestra, and choral groups, which was reputed to have a higher level of culture than other cities in Siberia. Many
Russians at the time also viewed Irkutsk as the eastern edge of the civilized
world. Expeditions organized and funded in Irkutsk set out from there to
explore the rest of unknown Siberia, to the east and to the north. Others
ventured even farther, to North America, from the Bering Strait to the coast
of present-day California, where several small Russian settlements were
established in the late eighteenth and early nineteenth centuries. During
that time, people in Irkutsk called the North American lands claimed by
Russia "the American district of Irkutsk," and some even envisioned a political union between Siberia and the United States.

In the 1880s the economy of Irkutsk boomed when gold was discovered
in the Lena River basin, several hundred miles to the north. The influx of

new and sudden wealth produced a "gold rush" atmosphere similar to that of California in the mid-1800s, and Irkutsk soon came to be known as the capital of Siberia's Wild East, long before Vladivostok acquired that moniker. Travelers to Irkutsk during the late nineteenth century described it as a city of traders and trappers, soldiers and smugglers, prostitutes and professors, exiles and ex-convicts, freebooters and fine ladies, gold miners and government officials—where the nouveaux riches delighted in displaying the fruits of their conspicuous consumption: French champagne, Parisian fashions, Bohemian chandeliers, gilded furniture, fine china, silver samovars, and sparkling crystal. The city's social and cultural life, along with its abundance of luxury goods, earned Irkutsk another sobriquet, "the Paris of Siberia"—a phrase sometimes spoken with irony in the salons of European Russia, but one that residents of Irkutsk (as well as many visitors) thought was an appropriate description of the city's prosperity and level of cultural attainment in comparison with other urban areas of Siberia at that time.

By the end of the 1800s, Irkutsk was the second largest city in Siberia, with a population of more than fifty thousand. Within its confines were twelve thousand buildings, including two Russian Orthodox cathedrals and twenty-nine Orthodox churches, a Roman Catholic church, a Lutheran church, two synagogues, and a mosque. Many of its wealthy citizens had constructed stately stone mansions in a variety of architectural styles, and the city had erected several grand public buildings, some even with electric lighting and telephone service. But throughout its history Irkutsk was plagued by earthquakes, floods, and fires. In the summer of 1879 a huge fire burned for three days and three nights, destroying 75 percent of the city. Many of the old wooden buildings went up in flames, and thousands of people were left homeless. Over the next ten years, as money flowed in from the gold fields north of Irkutsk, much of the city was rebuilt, this time in more durable brick and stone.

When I moved to Irkutsk in the last decade of the twentieth century, it was a modern metropolis with more than half a million inhabitants. Located two thousand railroad miles from Russia's Pacific coast and more than three thousand miles from Moscow, Irkutsk was still considered the capital of the entire macroregion of Eastern Siberia—although in the Russian Federation, the city was officially the capital only of Irkutsk Oblast', a region larger than France, England, and Scotland combined. Although the economy was now based on industry instead of trade, Irkutsk in the mid-1990s seemed, on the surface at least, to be less polluted than many other Russian industrial cities of its size—yet it ranked high on the list of cities with the worst air pollution in the country. As in Vladivostok, however, locals were quick to claim that the city had been cleaner in Soviet times, when residents were expected to participate in monthly *subbotniki*—Saturday clean-up details for public spaces, such as streets and parks—organized by their school or place of work. But despite increasing urban problems with pollution and crime in the early post-Soviet era, residents of Irkutsk still retained a particularly strong attachment to their city, which they considered to be "the heart and soul of Siberia."

Almost all the interesting buildings in Irkutsk were located in the city's compact center, which, with its wide streets and lack of tall buildings, had a feeling of spaciousness not often found in Russia's major urban areas. Facing the Angara River, on a pleasant, tree-lined esplanade, was the Bely Dom, Irkutsk's own "White House," a three-story colonnaded stone edifice built in the early nineteenth century in Russian Empire style. Formerly a wealthy merchant's home, it served as the residence of the governors-general of Eastern Siberia from 1838 to 1917, when it was badly damaged in a ten-day battle between Red and White forces during the early days of the Russian civil war. In the mid-1990s the restored Bely Dom housed the main library of Irkutsk State University, and its reconstructed tsarist-era rooms provided an elegant setting for university conferences and important ceremonies. Across the street stood the whimsically Moorish-style Irkutsk Museum of Regional Studies, home of the region's best historical and ethnographical collections. But surrounding the older city center were the inevitable Soviet-style apartment blocks—five-story buildings from the Khrushchev era and prefabricated concrete high-rises built since the 1970s—row after row of cookie-cutter dwellings that seemed symbolic of the triumph of collectivism over individuality.

Only a few of Irkutsk's many Russian Orthodox churches survived the battles of the civil war and subsequent Stalinist demolitions, but those that remained—with their soaring bell towers, copper-covered spires, and golden domes—attested to the glory of Russian ecclesiastical architecture of previous centuries. The Roman Catholic Church of the Assumption of Our Lady, a handsome neogothic structure erected by Polish exiles in the late nineteenth century, was spared from destruction and later converted to a concert hall with a large East German pipe organ replacing the original altar. In 1994 Irkutsk also had a functioning synagogue, an unprepossessing blue wooden building that had recently been defaced by "Yeltsin = Yid" and a Star of David, both crudely drawn on the front in red paint.

Despite the scourge of recurring floods and fires, more than three hundred old one- and two- story wooden buildings still remained in Irkutsk, some of them simple log houses chinked with moss, others covered with shingles of Siberian stone pine or with clapboard nailed onto the original logs to give the buildings a more "modern" appearance. Many also had wooden shutters, window frames, door jambs, eaves, pilasters, pediments, cornices, and corbels all decorated with carved fretwork—known in Russia as "wooden lace"—featuring floral, geometric, or baroque motifs often painted blue, green, or white. Even in winter begonias and geraniums bloomed behind double-glazed windows etched with ferns of frost. And on the window sills, in the space between the outer and inner panes of glass, residents often placed large wads of thick cotton batting, or wide strips of colored construction paper folded into arcs, decorated with tinsel, glitter, colored glass balls, evergreen boughs, pine cones, or sprigs of bright red and orange berries, to brighten up their homes during the winter holiday season.

Most of these old wooden houses fronted onto unpaved streets where wooden planks served as sidewalks. Some of the buildings tilted at odd angles, their foundations sunk deep into the mud. As elsewhere in Russia, even in the major cities, few of these picturesque old wooden houses had running water or indoor plumbing. Outdoor communal pumps or taps, spaced two or three city blocks apart, provided the nearest source of water. A common sight in such neighborhoods was a heavy-set old woman trudging down the rutted, muddy street, her shoulders burdened by a wide wooden yoke with a big bucket of water suspended from each end.

When I asked a Siberian colleague what these houses were like inside, she seemed surprised that I would even think to pose such a question. "I wouldn't know," she replied curtly, with an air of condescension, "I don't know anyone who lives in such houses." Despite my curiosity about older domestic dwellings, I could understand her reaction to my inquiry. Putting aside any romantic images of Russian architecture, it was easy to see why most urban Siberians preferred to live in more modern apartment buildings made of brick or prefabricated concrete, which were connected to city utilities, including electricity and central heating. Yet I also knew other city dwellers who longed for the rustic aesthetics of rural villages and tried to reproduce them in the exterior decoration and interior decor of their own small dachas on little plots of land outside of town.

During the past three centuries the architecture, economy, public institutions, and cultural life of Irkutsk were shaped by the people who came to live there, from the earliest Cossacks to more recent arrivals from Europe and Asia. By the 1990s modern Irkutsk was a city peopled by the descendants of political exiles—including Russians, Ukrainians, Belorussians, Germans, Balts, and Poles—gulag survivors, prisoners of war, native Siberian Buryats and Evenks, immigrants from other parts of Asia, and the many European Russians who voluntarily "went east" in search of adventure and better opportunities for themselves in the lands beyond the Ural Mountains.

Some historians have compared the "opening" of Siberia by Europeans to that of the American West, drawing parallels between the Russian and American experiences of migration and settlement, of taming the wilderness and subduing native peoples. And many Siberians did seem to possess a spirit of independence and initiative, self-reliance and persistence, similar to the pioneers who settled the American West. But other historians have pointed out that the so-called awakening of the Sleeping Land of *Sibir'* was unlike the unfettered freedom of westward expansion in North America. In pursuit of its own political and economic goals, the Russian government sought to control and direct emigration from the European to the Asian part of the country, turning Siberia into not only a land of opportunity for some, but also a place of imprisonment, exile, and forced settlement for others.

Still standing in Irkutsk were the wooden houses of two noble Decembrist families, the Trubetskoys and Volkonskys, who settled in the city in the 1840s. After their failed attempt to overthrow Tsar Nikolay I in 1825, Prince Sergey Trubetskoy and Count Sergey Volkonsky served prison sentences of several years at hard labor in the Transbaikal region, before being released to live in exile in Siberia. Socially the highest-ranking people in a city where, as elsewhere in Siberia, there was officially no titled aristocracy, these Decembrists had a pronounced influence on the social, intellectual, and cultural life of Irkutsk. Local residents lauded the efforts of Count Volkonsky's wife, Mariya, to establish hospitals, charities, schools, a drama theater, and a concert hall. A princess in European Russia before she gave up her title to follow her husband into exile, Mariya Volkonskaya came to be known in Irkutsk as "the Princess of Siberia," in recognition of her social status and her many good works for the inhabitants of the city.

Irkutsk's Decembrists were but a few in the long line of people who were forcibly sent to Siberia between the late 1500s and the last decades of the Soviet era. At the beginning of the nineteenth century, the tsarist government sent an average of two thousand people to Siberia every year, but, by the end of that century, the number had risen to twenty thousand annually. Lenin, Stalin, Trotsky, and many other Russian revolutionaries served time in Siberia before the Bolsheviks gained power in 1917. During the purges of the 1930s, those people not shot or otherwise done to death in the prisons of Moscow and Leningrad were sent to die a slower death in the labor camps that dotted the map of Russia like the pockmarks on Stalin's face. Even in the mid-1990s, I knew Russians who spoke about exiles still living in Siberian villages and towns less than a decade earlier, as if the existence of exiles in the late twentieth century was merely a normal fact of life.

Despite official restrictions on their professional activities, many of the well-educated people sent to Siberia over the past three centuries contributed significantly to the scientific, cultural, and educational development of Asian Russia. They taught in schools and colleges; practiced medicine and conducted scientific research; engaged in ethnographic studies; wrote poetry, short stories, novels, and plays; translated works from foreign languages; published periodicals; composed and performed music; produced paintings, prints, and sculpture; and developed their own styles of folk art. But I found it interesting that the Russians I met in Irkutsk seemed to have a different attitude toward their own past than the ones I knew in Vladivostok. My friends in Vladivostok readily admitted that they or their ancestors had come to Russia's Pacific coast from other parts of the former Russian or Soviet Empires, whether in the nineteenth century or in the 1930s or only a few years ago. Out on the eastern edge of Asian Russia, those contemporary residents of Vladivostok often spoke about their family members still living in European Russia or in the now-independent states of the former Soviet Union; many of them even traveled several thousand miles back to visit their relatives every year. They also possessed a restlessness often found among immigrants, along with a wider view of the world, their own horizons extending far beyond Vladivostok to other shores washed by the seas. In contrast, many of the people I knew in Irkutsk were vague about how they or their European ancestors came to live in Siberia. They seemed to think of themselves solely as modern *Sibiryaki*, settled in Siberia and uninterested in where they came from or in going anywhere else. Siberia was their world, their present and their future, and the past was a place to be forgotten.

At first I was surprised by this attitude on the part of my Siberian students, colleagues, and friends, particularly given their pride in Siberia as a land inhabited and energized by a people with a special, pioneering spirit, different from that of European Russia. As a child in Texas, I had grown up listening to my own family's stories about my maternal great-grandmother who had emigrated to New York from a village in Prussia in 1867, when she was only four years old. In 1883 she and her new husband had traveled west in two covered wagons to the Dakota Territory, where they built a

*One of several historic Russian Orthodox
churches in Irkutsk.*

ranch near the Standing Rock Indian Reservation and befriended Sitting
Bull and his band of Lakota Sioux during the last years of Sitting Bull's life.
But the Siberians I spoke with had no similar stories of how or why their
European ancestors came to Irkutsk Oblast', how they interacted with the
indigenous Buryats and Evenks, or how they survived to bear the children
whose descendants live in that part of Siberia today. Not only had much of

Russia's national history been revised, distorted, or suppressed under the Communist regime—even many individual family histories, in this very family-centered society, were also a blank.

Given Siberia's long history as a land of imprisonment and exile, it was understandable that many Siberians might have wanted to conceal or forget the circumstances that brought their own European ancestors to Asian Russia. But after I became better acquainted with some Siberians, they occasionally disclosed a small piece of their past, telling me personal stories that are hard for foreigners to fully appreciate without having experienced the Soviet Union's seven decades of Communist rule, including twenty years of Stalinist terror and four years of world war that left twenty-seven million Russian soldiers and civilians dead.

One of my Russian friends told about living for a year in an exile village, a four-hour drive by truck from Irkutsk, in the early 1950s when she was a child. While her parents were sorting out their marital difficulties in Irkutsk, she had been sent to stay with her uncle, the military commandant of the village, which was composed entirely of people who had been deported to Siberia from the Baltic countries after World War II. Since there was no village when the exiles arrived at that remote spot in the Siberian taiga, they had to cut down trees and build their own log houses by hand. All the exiles were confined to the village and a specific area around it, defined by fences and guard towers. Once a week each person had to report to the commandant's office to prove that he or she was present in the village, and no one was allowed beyond the perimeter without a pass signed by the commandant. My friend went on to say that there were many exile villages like this, as well as several prison camps, in rural areas near the city of Irkutsk.

Another story described the plight of a friend's uncle who served two years in prison for taking half a sausage from the meat-packing plant where he worked as a teenager, during a time when food was especially scarce in Siberia. And another woman told me about her father, a Soviet soldier during the Great Patriotic War (as Russians call World War II), who was reported missing after a battle against the Germans. Since his body was never found, the Soviet authorities declared that he must have surrendered to the Germans—and, because of his "treachery" against the Soviet Union, the state refused to provide a survivors' pension to his widow and children, a benefit they would have received if he had "officially" died defending the motherland. With tears in her eyes, my friend remembered the hardships of her life in Siberia during the years following World War II and how her family had suffered the shame of being labeled "traitors" by those veterans who had been fortunate enough to return home after the war.

For many of the people who were born in Siberia or went there voluntarily, or even those who stayed after release from prison or exile, Siberia was a place where they could establish a homestead, advance in their professions, earn higher salaries, or find a relatively comfortable niche away from the more stratified society of European Russia and the central political authority of Moscow or St. Petersburg (Leningrad)—an attitude expressed in the often-quoted Siberian adage: "God is high in his heaven, and the tsar is far away." Even when contemporary Siberians mouthed this maxim, with the hint of a smile, they were still expressing a shared feeling derived from their sense of freedom and opportunity in the physical and social environment of Siberia—a feeling that sometimes transcended the other inevitable constrictions of daily life in a country with a tradition of collective endeavor and a long history of authoritarian rule.

I was particularly interested in the attitudes of Siberians who were living through—and in some cases effecting—the initial political and economic transformations in Russia after the collapse of the Soviet Union. During that time of uncertainty, many Siberians whom I met—especially those over the age of forty—still preferred to keep their opinions to themselves. Others might express their views in private, but were wary of saying the same things outside their own circle of trusted friends. At a Russian wedding party in our apartment building that spring, fifteen guests crowded around a small dining table laden with platters of home-cooked food and bottles of booze. Suddenly a well-dressed young man whom I had never met before asked me why NATO was bombing the Serbs in Bosnia. "The Serbs are our allies," he went on. "They've done nothing wrong, yet NATO continues to bomb them. Why are they being attacked by your country?" I tried to put the situation into perspective, explaining that from the viewpoint of most American and Western European policy-makers, the Bosnian Serbs were the aggressors in that particular conflict, in much the same way that the Germans were the aggressors in World War II. That silenced him for a while, but he soon began arguing the Serbs-as-victims side again. Finally the bride's mother declared that a wedding party was not the place to discuss the war in Bosnia— but only after she and several of the other guests had made it very clear that they disagreed with the breakup of the Soviet Union and could not understand why the Balts, Caucasians, and Central Asians did not want to remain a part of Greater Russia. So it was no surprise that most of the people at the party did not approve of the breakup of Yugoslavia, either.

As some of the tipsy guests began dancing to a Patsy Cline tape in the tiny room, the man across the table brought up the subject of Bosnia again, repeating the official Russian position that the Serbs were innocent victims of NATO aggression. When I discovered that he had never been to Yugoslavia himself—and had never even traveled beyond Irkutsk Oblast'—I explained that I had a longtime interest in the history and politics of the Balkans, had traveled in all the regions of former Yugoslavia, and knew people who lived in Bosnia, Croatia, Serbia, Macedonia, and Kosovo. I was genuinely curious about his views on the Bosnian conflict and why he held them. So I suggested that if he wanted to continue the discussion, I would be quite willing to speak with him any time during my office hours at the university, where he could reach me by phone to make an appointment. Up to that point, he had been assertive and insistent, but polite and articulate, in arguing his side of the issue. But when I mentioned meeting at the university to discuss it further, he suddenly held up his hands, palms toward me, and backed away, saying, "No, no, I can't do that, I can't do that," his whole body language indicating that he was fearful of pursuing the conversation in another location. Not understanding the reason for his extreme reaction, I gently reiterated that there would be no problem in our getting together to talk about this topic sometime at my office. "It's impossible, it's impossible," he repeated, as his voice rose higher and higher. "I have a wife and child," he stammered. "I have a wife and child! I don't have time to talk with you about such things!"

Far more outspoken were Viktor and Galina, a well-educated, seemingly sophisticated, middle-aged Siberian couple with whom Tom and I had a series of personal discussions that spring, during which they didn't hesitate to express their own strong opinions about history, domestic politics, and current events. Over dinner one evening at their large, well-furnished apartment in Irkutsk, we discussed the breakup of the Soviet Union and the subsequent political and economic changes occurring in Russia. Both Viktor and Galina had been vehemently opposed to the disintegration of the Soviet Union and felt that Russia had been betrayed by its leaders. Referring to a referendum held in the USSR in the spring of 1991, Galina complained that "Seventy per cent voted to preserve the Soviet Union, but the leaders let the country break up against the wishes of the people." I pointed out that I thought the majority who had voted in favor of preserving the Soviet Union were ethnic Russians living in the Russian Republic, which was only one of the fifteen state republics that made up the Soviet Union, albeit the largest and most powerful one. Both Viktor and Galina disagreed with me and refused to believe that the percentages were any different in the republics that ultimately broke away from the Soviet Union. They did concede, however, that the three Baltic states—Latvia, Lithuania, and Estonia, which they considered "inferior countries"—would probably have broken away from the Soviet Union anyway. But they felt strongly that "Russia should have kept all the others." When I mentioned that some analysts had predicted that Russia itself might someday break up into three countries—European Russia, Siberia, and the Russian Far East—Viktor reacted angrily. Just then, his grandson toddled into the room. Viktor pointed to the little boy and said, in a tightly controlled voice, "I would tell my grandson that if he ever heard someone say that, he should take a machine gun and blow them away!"

Both Viktor and Galina felt that Russia needed a strong leader to bring order to Russia and to restore the Russian Empire. "Those are *our* Ukrainians," asserted Viktor. And they were pleased to hear that a survey I gave to our university students in Irkutsk showed that many of them favored the restoration of a tsar and the establishment of a constitutional monarchy in Russia. Viktor contended that currently in Russia there was only "permissiveness, not democracy," and he went on to complain that "the mass media are destroying our cultural values. I would put a bomb in Ostankino [the state-run television station] if I could."

This highly opinionated couple had an attitude toward Stalin similar to that of many other Russians that I knew. Among intellectuals it was now politically correct to say how much they abhorred Stalin—but some, like Galina, would immediately temper that statement by reciting a well-worn litany of the "many good things" that Stalin had done: industrialized the Soviet Union, collectivized agriculture, eliminated illiteracy, won the Great Patriotic War. And they would inevitably say how surprised they had been to learn, long after Stalin's death, about the bad things that had also occurred during his regime, acts they only hinted at, but never specified. Galina still referred to Stalin as "the Great Helmsman," and both she and her husband believed that recent revisionist history had given Stalin an undeservedly bad reputation. Remembering or imagining a more stable era, they claimed that people were "more polite to each other during Stalin's time," and that "culture was on a higher level then." Galina—who had trained for the stage—once passionately confided to me how she had cried uncontrollably when Stalin died. But I also had the sense that Galina, the actress, was watching to see how I, as an American, reacted to her overly dramatic disclosure. Would I be shocked? Would I be surprised? I already knew that millions of Russians had grieved the same way at the news of Stalin's death, and I think my neutral silence in response to her banal revelation was a disappointment to her. As an actress, her performance had failed.

Like many Russian nationalists, Viktor and Galina believed that the solution to Russia's many problems lay not only in the restoration of a tsarist government, but also in the reinstatement of other traditional Russian institutions and the return to "traditional Russian values." Viktor considered it "a sin to own land, to buy and to sell it," and he believed that all land in Russia should belong only to the aristocracy and the Russian Orthodox Church. Contrary to any logic, he contended that "the aristocracy are not interested in material wealth," and he argued that an aristocracy was necessary in Russia because "they are the preservers of the cultural values of our society." I thought that Viktor and Galina's attitudes about property and material wealth were not only confused but also disingenuous, given the amount of time, effort, and money they had obviously spent acquiring fine furnishings and decorations for their unusually spacious and well-appointed apartment. Apparently from their point of view, their household possessions were not true material wealth—and therefore not "sinful," in the way that owning land or a house would be. They seemed to be the sort of people who, in a society of scarcity, could rationalize the possession of valuable belongings as merely the personal expression of their own "cultural values."

Given Viktor and Galina's views about Russian society, I wasn't surprised to learn that they considered Valentin Rasputin to be Russia's greatest living author and philosopher. Rasputin—who was born in a village on the Angara River in 1937 and moved to the city of Irkutsk in 1954—is indeed one of Russia's finest contemporary writers of novels and short stories, as well as an outspoken activist against the industrial pollution of Lake Baikal. But he is also a Russian nationalist and a conservative reactionary, whose graceful prose is sometimes marred by the expression of graceless beliefs, and whose public anti-Semitic and antidemocratic statements have offended many people both within Russia and abroad. Aleksandr Solzhenitsyn is another Russian literary icon whose social and political views are similar to Rasputin's, but the Siberians I knew in Irkutsk liked him far less than they did Rasputin. Some considered his writings inferior to Rasputin's. Others, conveniently forgetting that Solzhenitsyn had been expelled from Russia by the Soviet authorities, resented him for spending two decades in wealthy comfort in the West. When Solzhenitsyn returned in 1994, they dismissed his pronouncements about Russia, saying that he was out of touch with his homeland and had no basis for his opinions. "He's been gone for twenty years," they sneered. "What does he know about Russia now?"

The Siberia of the mid-1990s was like a deep body of water or dense mass of air, with some layers that were almost stagnant and other currents that were shifting at different rates of speed. Some Russians, particularly the younger ones, were able to surf the waves of their changing society as easily as they surfed the Internet. Others preferred to stay in the calm waters or still air of the perceived past, where they felt comfortable with the old, familiar ways of doing things. Caught in between, however, were those very people described as the "middle" in more economically developed societ-ies: middle-aged members of the former Soviet middle class, who had ris-ing expectations of the opportunities that the new Russia could provide, but many of whom had little idea of how to actually take advantage of those opportunities for their own benefit.

No special insight was required for the few Westerners in Siberia to feel that they were living in the early-twentieth-century past overlaid with an ever-changing veneer of late twentieth-century present. Consumer goods were beginning to trickle in from the Orient and the West, a few elite schools had been equipped with computers, and new private shops had begun to open their doors. But the texture of everyday life in Siberian cities was still far removed from that of the urban, industrialized West. And it was often the little things that were most striking to me—not just the lower standard of living, which was apparent to the most casual observer, but more so the ways in which people carried out daily tasks, their acceptance of the status quo, their attitudes toward change, their approach to solving everyday problems.

One day I went to the main post office in Irkutsk with Tom and three American colleagues, all of us wanting to purchase a large number of enve-lopes and air-mail stamps. But the Russian clerk sitting behind the cast-iron grille repeatedly refused to sell them to us, even though we could see that she had all the envelopes and stamps that we needed. Instead of ac-cepting the situation and walking away, as many Russians would have done, we reacted in a typically American manner by asking "Why?" until we got an answer. Finally a Russian student who was with us gravely explained, "There is no opportunity"—because we would deplete her supply and thus deprive other people of the opportunity to buy envelopes and stamps. We asked if the clerk could get more stamps and envelopes somewhere else, but the reply was the same: "There is no opportunity." We asked if we could buy part of them from her and the remainder from the clerk next to her, who also seemed to have an ample supply, but again we heard: "There is no

Old wooden house in the center of Irkutsk.

opportunity." We finally gave up and purchased the very limited amount that she was willing to sell. But that sentence soon became a running joke among our small group of American professors. Whenever we became frustrated because something could not be obtained, arranged, or achieved in Siberia—which was often—we would all look at each other and say, in unison, "There is no opportunity!" before breaking into hysterical laughter.

A Russian who worked at our university inadvertently supplied another slogan that provided an overarching explanation for all the absurdities we encountered in Siberia. The American faculty used our department's photocopy machine every day, but we were constantly frustrated by the paper's jamming in the machine. We knew *why* the paper jammed: Instead of purchasing reams of standard-size photocopy paper, the university had obtained huge rolls of blank paper, like newsprint—one meter wide and hundreds of meters long—which the Russian departmental staff had to cut by hand, with the office's single pair of scissors, into thousands of individual sheets supposedly the correct size for the photocopy machine. At least one-third of those hand-cut sheets would not even feed into the photocopier, and many of the pieces of paper that did go into it caused the machine to malfunction immediately. I finally asked one of the Russian staff why our department insisted on using this labor-intensive, misshapen, hand-cut paper that obviously caused everyone so much trouble. Was it because standard photocopy paper was not available in Irkutsk? Or was it because they had no money to buy anything else? Or was it simply because someone had donated those huge rolls of paper to our department? With a look of intense concentration on his face, the man considered my questions for a long time before he answered. Then—as if a light bulb had suddenly switched on above his head—he smiled broadly and replied, "It is because we live in Russia!"

"Because we live in Russia!" became our shibboleth, our stock answer to the many unanswerable questions about Russia that always began with the word "why." But we never found an equally succinct phrase to sum up the sense of isolation that all of us felt during our stay in Siberia. The American faculty lived and worked in a new urban development still under construction on the edge of the city, none of us had a telephone or a car, and we often had difficulty getting accurate information (or even any information at all) about activities available in and around Irkutsk. Despite the difficulties of transportation and communication, however, we organized dinner parties at our apartments, played Trivial Pursuit together, went hiking and skiing in the forest, attended ice hockey and basketball games, and arranged excursions to Lake Baikal. But compared to the more cosmopolitan Vladivostok, Irkutsk was a city that moved at a slower pace. There were fewer restaurants, a much smaller international community, and not nearly as many opportunities for us to socialize with a wide range of people outside the university environment.

On the other hand, residents of the Paris of Siberia justifiably took pride in the cultural life of their city, which they saw not only as a form of entertainment, but also as evidence of a civil society deep in the Siberian heartland. In 1994 Irkutsk boasted four theaters for live productions, six movie theaters, two concert halls, and several museums, including a fine arts museum and an ethnographic museum with major Siberian collections—not a large number of theaters and museums compared to Western European cities of that size, but a significant quantity of cultural institutions in such a relatively remote location.

During that spring Tom and I attended two art exhibitions, a concert of Russian symphonic music at the Philharmonic Hall, and performances of Verdi's *La Traviata* and Offenbach's *La Vie Parisienne* at the ultramodern Irkutsk Musical Theater—which, despite being the city's newest and costliest theater, had very bad acoustics. Ticket prices for these events were ludicrously low, ranging from 1,400 rubles (80 cents) to 3,000 rubles ($1.70).

But the financial problems of municipally owned theaters in the post-Soviet era were evident in such anomalies as the staging of *La Traviata*, where the costumes included period clothing from mid nineteenth-century Europe, 1950s-style chiffon ball gowns, and Scottish tartan outfits that looked like they had been recycled from a production of *Brigadoon*.

Cultural differences between Russia and the West were also apparent at these performances. The printed programs at the Irkutsk Musical Theater listed two or three possible players for each part, with a checkmark next to the names of the people actually performing that evening, laboriously penciled by hand on each of the hundreds of programs. At the Philharmonic Hall, an announcer came onto the stage before each musical piece and loudly declaimed the official ranks, titles, honors, and awards of the conductor, the soloists, the first violinist, and other worthy members of the orchestra, a ritual whose repetition seemed redundant after the initial recitation. In the production of *La Vie Parisienne*, the cancan dancers were clad in skimpy, sexy, Las Vegas–style costumes, and the choreography was a cross between ballet and go-go dancing, with almost no reference to the real French cancan itself. During intermissions the audience—most of them dressed in modest street clothes—milled around the lobby, buying cans of beer, soft drinks, and packaged snack foods that cost much more than the ticket price itself, all sold by vendors sitting behind folding metal tables. And despite musical performances that ranged from above average to excellent at all these events, many members of the audience persisted in carrying on conversations with each other during the performances—a common occurrence in Russian theaters, which was apparently acceptable behavior to the Russians, but which, from our own perspective, always seemed blatantly rude and disruptive.

One Saturday we attended a ballroom-dancing competition with participants from several cities in Russia, including prizewinning professional pairs from Moscow and St. Petersburg. The daylong contest was held at a modern concrete-and-glass municipal cultural center, in a wood-paneled hall that looked like a typical high-school auditorium in the United States. Many of the competitors were local amateurs, all highly skilled, ranging in age from six to their early twenties, including one of our students who placed third in the jive-dancing category. Most of the men wore tuxedos or tails, and the women were decked out in beautiful ball gowns and colorful costumes made of shimmering satin, sequins, and chiffon, which surely much have been sewn by hand from materials hard to find in Russia. But the aura of elegance was tarnished a bit by the recorded music used for the dances—

mostly American middle-of-the-road electronic disco tapes, which, except for the rhythms, were not at all appropriate for the waltz, samba, tango, or paso doble being performed on stage.

We went to all these cultural events on public transportation, our primary means of getting around the city. As in Vladivostok, the buses, trolleys, and trams were usually jam-packed, with passengers squeezed into every available space. In winter the floors were continually wet from tracked-in snow. In spring they were slick with mud. Vehicles sometimes broke down en route, forcing the passengers to get off and wait for the next, equally crowded one to come along. Often it took an hour and a half to travel one way between our apartment and the central part of the city where most of the shops, restaurants, and theaters were located.

Russians seemed to passively accept the crowded, dirty conditions on their poorly maintained transportation systems. But occasionally their frustrations surfaced as rudeness or rage. Once Tom was riding on a trolley during the evening rush hour when an old woman lugging a large wooden sled came aboard. As the trolley filled up with people going home from work, the *babushka* and her sled kept being shoved down the aisle toward the center of the car. Just before the stop where she wanted to get off, the old woman tried to push through the packed throng of passengers toward the exit. Some of the people pushed back, making nasty comments that everyone could hear. When she finally neared the exit door, a big fellow picked her up, sled and all, and threw her off the trolley into a snowbank. The doors closed, and the trolley moved on, as if nothing out of the ordinary had happened.

On another closely packed trolley, a scruffy young man with crazed eyes and a sweet smile insisted that I take a chocolate ice cream cone that he handed to me. Then, with the same senselessly benign look on his face, he pulled out a long knife and held it between us, as he peered through me to some other place that only he could see. While the trolley lurched on up-hill, Tom edged me away from the knife, moving slowly and carefully toward the exit door. We got off at the next stop and walked the rest of the way home in the snow, shivering from more than the cold.

Early one evening during a heavy snowstorm, Tom and I got on a trolley in downtown Irkutsk that was even more crowded than usual, with people returning home carrying shopping bags stuffed with groceries. Tightly squeezed between the other passengers standing in the aisle, I watched as more people tried to push on board, to get out of the blowing snow. Finally the driver shouted at the crowd still attempting to climb aboard, then he closed the doors, and the trolley slowly started off. Filled far beyond its designated capacity, it was barely able to climb the icy incline to the next stop. At that halt, no one got off, but even more people tried to get inside. One who succeeded was a huge, exceedingly ugly man, with a broken nose, cauliflower ears, and a pock-marked face, his bulky body wrapped in a big bearskin coat. For no discernible reason, he began pushing his way down the packed aisle, much to the dismay of the other passengers. But no one was willing to oppose him. When he tried to press past me, he forced me so hard against the metal edge of a seat that I cried out in pain. Looking away from me as if he hadn't heard, he smashed his fist into my thigh. Then he slowly turned his head and peered straight into my eyes, with an expression of cruel satisfaction on his face. I was so shocked that I spat out the first Russian word that came to mind. "*Smertnik!*" I exclaimed loudly. The effect was instantaneous. The brute immediately pulled back, a look of fear on his face. The crowd of passengers suddenly became silent, quickly glancing in our direction, then turning away as if trying to distance themselves from the situation. Only then did I realize the full import of calling someone a *smertnik*—a prisoner condemned to die—in a place like Siberia.

The weather that winter in Irkutsk was milder than usual, according to Russians who had lived in the city all their lives. Russians joked that "in Siberia winter lasts for twelve months and the rest is summer." Another adage said that "in Siberia one hundred kilometers is no distance at all, one hundred years no age at all, one hundred rubles no money at all [when one hundred rubles was worth much more than it is today], and one hundred grams of vodka no drink at all"—often with the weather tag lines, "and a day without sunshine is unusual" or "forty degrees [below zero] is no frost at all." Siberians don't ask, "How cold is it?" They ask, "How many degrees is it?" And the reply is a number never preceded by "minus" or followed by "below zero," which is simply taken for granted. But the climate in Irkutsk was not nearly as harsh as outsiders usually imagine. The winter I was there, the temperature outside our apartment never dropped lower than sixteen degrees below zero. In summer the mean temperature in Irkutsk is sixty-six degrees in July, the warmest month, but even in June the mercury sometimes reached well into the nineties on sunny days.

Irkutsk is the "sunhole of Siberia," with an average of three hundred days of sunshine annually, more than any other city in Russia. And, despite the heavy snowfall in winter, the climate is dry, with little wind. The first snow usually falls in mid-October, and the ground remains covered with several inches of snow until mid-March, because the temperature never rises above freezing during those five months. But I seldom actually saw it snow in Irkutsk. The clouds usually crept in at night, silently scattered their burden over the city, then departed before morning. I would wake to a clear, deep blue sky, with bright sunshine sparkling off the pristine snow. The sky would remain clear for several days, while a thin layer of gray grime settled over the covering of white, followed by another snowfall, and so on, forming alternating rows of soot and snow that became compacted into a solid mass. City road-clearing crews then came along and chopped up the icy accumulation, shoveling it onto the sides of walkways and streets where it formed jagged, gelid piles that looked like hundreds of frozen gray-and-white napoleon pastries heaped haphazardly on the ground.

I became so acclimated to the cold that whenever the temperature rose above ten degrees Fahrenheit, I declared it to be a warm day and went outdoors without hat or gloves. The Russians—who seemed to spend the entire winter bundled up in several layers of clothing—were convinced that I would succumb to all sorts of dreaded diseases. "Where is your hat? Put on a hat!" the busybody *babushki* would say to me at the market. "Why aren't you dressed warmly?" strangers would ask me on the street. Even when the temperature finally began to creep above freezing in mid-March, Russians warned me that spring was a very dangerous time of year in Siberia, and I should dress more warmly or risk becoming gravely ill.

Although people dressed less fashionably in Irkutsk than in Vladivostok, prestige furs warmed and adorned the heads of men and women alike. Mink, sable, fox, and wolf were especially popular, as was less expensive muskrat, which looked like Little Richard pompadour wigs perched atop of the Russians' heads. For women, the fur of white arctic fox was particularly prized: some of the hats had the full fox tail attached in back, rather like an haute couture version of a Davy Crockett coonskin cap. And it was always a surprise to see Siberian women wearing their fur hats indoors in winter, even in the stuffy, overheated buildings that were so characteristic of Russia—a country that, contradictorily, both embraces and fears the cold.

One warm, sunny day in April I climbed aboard our university van to ride into town with several of my Russian colleagues. Vladimir, the only man in the group, grinned at me, then swept his gaze around the five other women sitting in the van. "Who is the *real* Siberian woman here?" he declaimed dramatically, looking at my unbuttoned cotton coat, lightweight synthetic sweater, cotton skirt, bare legs, and flimsy flats. "Not me!" I riposted in an equally grandiose manner. "It couldn't be. I'm not dressed for the part." Vladimir and I laughed heartily, but the Russian women only smiled tightly, almost defensively, as if my attire constituted a challenge to their stamina. Despite temperatures in the sixties that day, all five of them were wrapped in heavy coats, fur hats, and wool mufflers, with woolen gloves and high leather boots. I would have suffocated in such swaddling, but those Siberian women seemed completely comfortable in their cocoons, convinced that all their clothing would protect them from a host of illnesses just waiting to attack anyone foolish enough to be underdressed for the season. Later I asked another professor why people in Russia dressed that way when the temperature did not warrant it. "We Russians dress for the *season*," she replied, "not for the *temperature!* If it's autumn, we have to put on autumn clothes, even if the temperature outside is still summer. That's just the way we are."

Despite the warming weather, no one in Irkutsk was ready to define March or April sartorially as spring. At that time of year, mothers tell their children, "Don't put up your boots yet, or it will snow again." And indeed, there were occasional snow flurries well into mid-May—the kind of weather where the sun shines in one part of the sky, while snow pelts down from another. In previous years, Irkutsk had even seen snowfalls as late as June and as early as August. And prudent local gardeners, fearing a late frost, always waited until mid-June to plant their hothouse seedlings outdoors.

During March and April the beautiful Siberian winter melted into the truly mucky "mud season," as the city slowly emerged from its mantle of snow like a sepia-toned photographic print in a tray of chemical developer. Unlike the soft shades of spring in more temperate climates, brown was the dominant color of March and April in Irkutsk, when even the budding white birches seemed dingy and drab. The roads turned into rivers of mud, which froze overnight into deep and treacherous ruts, then thawed during the day into clogged arteries of squelching mire. The only signs of spring were the first few silvery catkins on the branches of pussy willows, and the street cleaners, usually old women, hunched over their brushwood brooms like worn-out witches sweeping away the wiles of winter.

In mid-May spring suddenly burst forth from the liberated landscape as wildflowers, wild garlic, and fiddlehead ferns emerged from the earth, and cuckoos called from the blossoming bird-cherry trees. (Siberians say that if you hear a cuckoo singing, count the number of "cuckoo" sounds it makes, and that's how many more years you will live.) As if winter had also released them from its hold, our Russian students, colleagues, and friends invited us to all kinds of social events—official functions at the university, dinners at their apartments, a weekend at a dacha, a daylong hike through the taiga, and trips by car, train, and boat to several sites in southern Siberia. Our last six weeks in Irkutsk were filled with a flurry of activities, more than in the previous four months combined. At the same time, Tom and I were also finishing up the school term, grading final exams, making arrangements for a summer trip to England and the United States, and packing for our move back to Vladivostok the next autumn. Yet the Russians seldom seemed to comprehend that we might have professional and personal commitments that took precedence over spur-of-the-moment social invitations. As an American friend wrote to me from Vladivostok that spring: "Nothing of consequence in Russia is ever done slowly and deliberately. It is always done in a crisis mode, at the very last second, as quickly as possible and preferably with as many last-minute complications as conceivable." To which Tom added his own twist, noting that "Russians never put off until the last minute anything that can be left until even later."

On May 9 the university was closed in honor of Russia's Victory Day, marking the end of World War II in Europe. In Irkutsk that day of national remembrance was observed with a rally at Victory Square, the site of the city's stone-slab memorial to the Soviet People's Victory in the Great Patriotic War of 1941–45—a monument guarded year-round by goose-stepping groups of high-school students in paramilitary uniforms. Forty-nine years after the Allied victory, the square was filled with veterans, both men and women, some dressed in their old military uniforms, many proudly wearing rows of ribbons and medals on their chests. A few hoisted red satin banners with gold embroidery identifying their military units or proclaiming victory over the Germans. Others carried colorful flags, most of which I could not identify. But the hammer-and-sickle ensign of the old Soviet Union outnumbered them all.

Some of the veterans were pleased when I asked to take their pictures, posing for the camera with big smiles. But when they learned that I was an American, their attitude changed abruptly. "Why did America wait so long to open a second front?" they demanded, repeating a commonly held Russian belief that the United States and its other allies deliberately delayed attacking Germany from the west until the Soviet Union and Germany had both been severely weakened by fighting each other. I had no satisfactory reply. And indeed the Russians had every right to complain, having suffered such terrible losses in that war—half of all the casualties in World War II—

from the siege of Leningrad to the battle of Stalingrad to the conquest of Berlin. But if I spoke Russian better, I would have countered with several questions that should have been asked of the Russians themselves: "What about Stalin's purges of thousands of Soviet military officers and countless civilians before the war? What about the Molotov-Ribbentrop Non-Aggression Pact—and the subsequent partition of Poland and the Soviet annexation of the Baltic States? What about Lend-Lease and all the food, materiel, and medical supplies the Western allies sent to the Soviet Union? What about the Normandy landing?" But that was neither the time nor the place to argue with those old Russian veterans who had assembled that day to honor their heroes and mourn their dead. On that sun-drenched square in southern Siberia, the present was merely a place where myth and memory came together to shape the past.

"Every day in summer is an event," remarked one of my Siberian students, and it certainly seemed that way to me, as our social calendar filled up during May and June. In mid-May, Vladimir, one of Tom's older married students, invited us to join him and his family on an outing to gather *cheremsha*, the wild garlic that grows in abundance in southern Siberia that time of year. At first I was surprised by the spot he chose for a picnic—the site of a former prison camp several miles from Irkutsk. In the forest clearing where we searched for the green shoots of garlic, we soon turned up traces of the painful past: rotted fence posts, rusty barbed wire, and the remnants of a railroad track running to nowhere. But these grim reminders of Soviet Russia were tempered by the warm Siberian sunshine, the wildflowers in full bloom, and the trilling of songbirds in the trees. Surrounded by these sights and sounds of eternal Russia, we grilled shashlik over an open fire, munched on spring onions and pickled green tomatoes, drank homemade berry juice, and finished the meal with a Siberian specialty brought by Vladimir's mother: a rich cake made from the finely ground pits of bird-cherries, baked with sugar, eggs, and sour cream. Yet I could not escape the feeling that our presence in that place was somehow an affront to whatever spirits of the past still lingered there.

On a sunny weekend in May, we traveled by hydrofoil down the Angara River from Irkutsk to the city of Angarsk, skimming over the muddy water through a landscape that looked like a setting from *Huckleberry Finn*. Our Russian colleagues could not fathom why we wanted to visit Angarsk, and anyone arriving there by river might well have agreed with them. The boat dock for this city of 280,000 people was only a small, rusty pier, surrounded by forests and seemingly deserted, with nothing else around it except a few sad old grave markers and a dirt road through the trees. Pavel, the student who had invited us to visit his hometown, met us at the dock and soon we were driving down the dusty, rutted road toward the city itself. To my surprise Angarsk was unlike other cities I had seen in Siberia. Built in 1956, it was a new, seemingly well-planned metropolis with broad boulevards, clean-looking neighborhoods, pleasant parks, and many pale-yellow stucco buildings, all of which gave it an almost Italianate aspect. The only graffiti I spotted the whole day was a spray-painted homage, in English, to the rock band Red Hot Chili Peppers. But—as so often in Russia—appearances were deceiving. Only later did I learn that Angarsk had been a closed military-industrial city until the early 1990s and that it still suffered from some of the worst industrial air- and soil-pollution in that part of Siberia.

As the time neared for us to leave Irkutsk that summer, all the American faculty became increasingly worried about returning to the United States on Aeroflot, the former Soviet state airline that had broken up into more than three hundred smaller regional airlines (most of them still called Aeroflot) after the collapse of the Soviet Union. We joked about flying on "Aeroflop, the world's worst airline," where it was all too easy for passengers to earn "frequent crasher points." But Aeroflot's miserable safety record over the past sixteen months was a real cause for concern: fourteen crashes in 1993 and six crashes during the first four months of 1994, including a Tupolev-154 that had departed from Irkutsk in January and gone down with 120 people on board, and an Airbus-310, carrying seventy-five passengers, that had crashed in Siberia in March after the pilot let his teenage son take over the controls. In late April the International Airline Passengers Association advised its members "not to fly to, in, or over Russia. It's simply too dangerous," because of "overloaded airplanes, lack of cockpit discipline, pilot error, aging aircraft." Shortly thereafter the U.S. Department of State issued a warning to travelers not to use Russian airlines, at least for flights within the country. In May we began hearing radio reports on the Voice of America, the BBC, and even Radio Moscow warning people not to fly on Aeroflot for either domestic or international flights. Aeroflot pilots even went on strike to protest the lack of safety standards at the airline. Returning by train to Irkutsk from a trip to Ulan-Ude, Tom and I shared a second-class sleeping compartment with an Aeroflot pilot who had chosen to spend eight hours traveling overland by rail instead of flying back to Irkutsk, which would have taken him only one hour by plane. When pilots start taking the train, you know there's a problem.

The American professors in Irkutsk finally protested to the University of Maryland about our being booked on Aeroflot for return flights to the United States. So the university agreed to pay for us to leave Russia on a foreign airline instead. But when I told our Russian dean about the change of plans, he was obviously displeased. The son of a former Aeroflot official in Irkutsk, he seemed offended by our apparent disparagement of his country's airline, a source of pride, power, and prestige for many of the people associated with it. I tried to reason with him, citing international radio reports, the IAPA and State Department warnings, and recent articles from *Time* magazine and major American newspapers, all describing Aeroflot's poor safety record. But Russian pride won out over fact and reason. He scorned those sources of information, claiming that the entire situation was "an international conspiracy to hurt Aeroflot and reduce the number of tourists to Russia." When I pointed out that even Radio Moscow had reported these stories, he countered that the radio station was merely a mouthpiece for Western interests that were trying to ruin Aeroflot. And when I reminded him about the most recent Aeroflot crash in March, he tried to defend the airline by saying that the plane "wasn't a Russian airplane, it was an Airbus"—implying that because it wasn't made in Russia, then Aeroflot couldn't be blamed.

In the end the Russians reluctantly made alternative, more expensive travel arrangements for the American professors to leave Irkutsk that summer. Tom and I chose to travel the first two thousand miles by rail to Khabarovsk, the nearest city in Russia where we could get an Alaska Airlines flight to the United States. Given Alaska Airlines' good safety record at the time, we had every reason to expect a smooth, uneventful journey back to America. But we began to have doubts when the plane took off after a refueling stop in Magadan and the pilot's voice came over the public address system, asking the passengers to "fasten your seat belt lights." And as we neared the airport at Anchorage, Alaska, after a ten-hour flight of more than four thousand miles, the pilot turned on the public address system again to let us know that "We're now beginning our descent into Seattle."

CHAPTER 5

~

Lake Baikal

THE SACRED SEA OF SIBERIA

Feeling excitement tinged with fear, I carefully climbed out of the Russian van parked on the frozen expanse of Lake Baikal. Beneath my feet the lake looked dark and foreboding, like a smoky mirror that concealed more than it reflected. But apprehension soon turned to delight as I slithered around on the ice and marveled at the changing patterns made by the wind swirling snow over its obsidianlike surface, as if I were looking through a kaleidoscope filled with bits of black-and-white glass.

Suddenly I heard a low rumbling that sounded like distant thunder in the clear blue sky. Then came a loud *crack!*—like a rifle shot—followed by an eerie silence, then another *crack!* I looked around to see who was firing a gun, when I heard the rumbling again and another *crack!* even closer this time. Next to my boot a long fissure fractured the seemingly solid surface of the ice, which had been unbroken only seconds before. At that moment I realized what natural force had created all the long white lines, intersecting at odd angles, that streaked the ice on Lake Baikal, making it look like a huge slab of dark gray marble shot through with intrusions of white igneous rock.

On the distant shore jagged blocks of ice glistened in the afternoon light, like abstract sculptures made of broken blue glass. Nearby a group of men cheered an ice hockey game, while an iceboat sailed past in the background. Two cars raced each other across the frozen surface from shore to shore. An off-road vehicle spun around in crazy circles on the ice. Fishermen sat on folding stools beside big metal bores, like giant corkscrews, used for drilling holes in Baikal's wintry crust. An old motorcycle roared past, with a sidecar carrying three drunken, disheveled men looking like characters out of a Dostoyevsky novel. Brilliant sunlight, refracted through millions of ice crystals, shimmered over the surreal scene.

My first sight of Lake Baikal had been on that snowy afternoon in January when our Trans-Siberian train bound for Irkutsk inched its way along the southern shore of Siberia's "inland sea." Peering through the dim gray dusk, straining for a glimpse of the famous lake, I could hardly wait for a chance to return and view it in full daylight. My first close encounter with Baikal came a month later, when its entire 12,000-square-mile surface was still frozen up to a depth of six feet. And during the next four months I visited Lake Baikal several times, traveling by car and by boat, as the seasons changed and the frozen lake thawed from its southern tip to its northern-most shore.

By most measures Baikal stands as a colossus among the world's lakes. The oldest and deepest lake on earth, Baikal was formed between 25 and 30 million years ago when a massive tectonic shift created the deepest rift in the earth's surface. Today the lake reaches a depth of more than one mile and contains one-fifth of all the fresh water on the planet—more than any other single lake and more than all of North America's Great Lakes combined. Long and narrow, its crescent shape extends from 395 miles in length to 50 miles at its widest point. Three hundred and thirty-six tributaries flow into Lake Baikal, but only one river, the Angara, runs out of it, ultimately joining the Yenisey River to carry Baikal's waters thousands of miles to the north, past the Arctic Circle and into the Kara Sea.

Such a body of water was bound to inspire legends and myths. One story recounts how Old Man Baikal had 337 daughters until one of them, the restless and rebellious Angara, fell in love with the mighty warrior Yenisey and ran off to join him more than a thousand miles away. In a fit of rage, Old Man Baikal hurled a huge rock at Angara to block her flight, but she had already cut a deep cleft in the earth and escaped from her father's hold. Known today as the Shaman Rock, this massive granite boulder can still be seen at the southwestern end of the lake, in the wide outlet where the Angara River begins flowing away toward Irkutsk. Another story says that Old Man Baikal was brought gifts of water by his 336 sons, but his only daughter, Angara—jealous of her many brothers—carried the precious water away from

Baikal, out into the world beyond. Not all Siberians think of the Angara as feminine, however; some of my Russian friends in Irkutsk referred to the forcefully flowing river as "Father Baikal's only son."

Revered in ancient and modern times by the people living on or near its shores, Lake Baikal has acquired a number of honorary names indicative of its hold on the human imagination: "the Blue Eye of Siberia," "the Sacred Sea of Siberia," "the Blue Pearl of Siberia," and several similarly evocative appellations. Legends tell of Baikal's creation, of the spirits and gods who inhabit its waters, of lovelorn maidens and wicked winds, of its connection with the Mongol warrior Genghis Khan. The Buryats still venerate sacred sites on its islands and shores. And Russian writers celebrate the great lake in poetry, fiction, and song.

Lake Baikal is the prime tourist destination in Siberia, for Russians and foreigners alike, even though there are few tourist facilities near the lake itself. (This lack of development is actually one of Baikal's major attractions.) For many Russians a journey to Lake Baikal is the dream of their lifetime. Newlyweds come to have their wedding pictures made on Baikal's beaches, against a backdrop of blue water and purple mountains in summer, or on the white expanse of its frozen, snow-dusted surface in winter. Visitors take home talismans of Baikal stones, glistening with mica, feldspar, and quartz, rounded and polished by the motion of the water. Some follow an old Buryat custom of tying strips of cloth to bushes and trees near the shore, as a prayer to the powerful god of the lake. And some who swim in Lake Baikal believe that its invigorating water will add twenty years to their lives.

But when the dam across the Angara River at Irkutsk was built in 1956, the water level behind the dam rose between Irkutsk and Lake Baikal, submerging part of the river banks between the city and the lake and encroaching on the famous Shaman Rock at the river's outlet, leaving only its tip showing above the surface of the rushing water. First-time visitors to the lake often find this legendary landmark to be a disappointment, having heard the many stories about the origin of the Shaman Rock and the rituals and superstitions associated with it. One says that a person must speak nothing but the truth in the presence of this rock. Others tell of the sacrifices made on the rock to the Invincible White God who dwells within it. And others tell how the local Buryats would take an alleged wrongdoer out to the rock by boat and leave the accused person there overnight. The next morning, if the transgressor had not died of fright or cold or been washed away by the river, then he or she would be pardoned and welcomed back into the community. Today the Shaman Rock serves only as a tourist attraction and a challenge to vandals armed with paint, rather than a site of divine judgment by the spirits said to inhabit Lake Baikal.

On a hillside overlooking the Shaman Rock is the leading scientific center for the study of Lake Baikal, the Limnological Institute of the Siberian Branch of the Russian Academy of Sciences. Inside its Baikal Ecological Museum several rooms of exhibits detail the geologic history of the lake, as well as the flora and fauna that live in and around it. Also proudly displayed are bottles of clear water from Lake Baikal, which is considered to be some of the purest water on earth. Despite problems with industrial pollution of the southern part of Baikal, most of its water is so pure that it can be drunk, untreated, directly from the lake. High in oxygen and low in mineral content, Baikal's water is the product of a self-cleaning ecosystem in which a tiny crustacean, the *epishura*, filters out algae and bacteria that form in the lake, while other crustaceans scavenge for larger forms of organic matter. The label on a commercial brand of bottled water from Lake Baikal features a color photograph of its icy blue water, with a drawing of a fat, bewhiskered *nerpa*—the unique freshwater seal that lives in Baikal—and states (in English) that the bottle contains "Water of the Last Century Purity," with "no preservatives." The influence of Western advertising is blatantly apparent in further claims that "The World's Most Pure Water Will Keep Your Health" and "Each sip of this water, taken from 400-metre depth, will give you longevity, cheerfulness and love!"

Lake Baikal's crystal-clear water supports more than twenty-five hundred species and subspecies of plants and animals, approximately 70 percent of which are found nowhere else on earth. Beneath the lake's surface live four kinds of *omul*, a trout-sized, white-fleshed fish belonging to the salmon family, which the Russians eat raw, salted, smoked, dried, boiled, baked, or fried; the Baikal *osëtr*, a type of sturgeon that can grow to six feet in length and produce up to twenty pounds of caviar per fish; endemic varieties of shrimp, crayfish, mollusks, and sponges; and the strange-looking, inedible *golomyanka*, a translucent, iridescent, pink-colored fish with large eyes and no scales, that gives birth to live offspring. Thirty-five percent of the *golomyanka*'s body weight is oil, rich in Vitamin A, which the Baikal Buryats have traditionally used for making medicines and as fuel for lamps.

Lake Baikal is ringed by mountains, some of whose snow-capped peaks reach more than nine thousand feet. Locked within them are deposits of rare metals, valuable minerals, and precious stones: lapis-lazuli, jasper, amazonite, serpentine, purple charoite, pink quartz, lavender marble, green jade, garnets, and gold. National parks and nature preserves line the east and west shores of the lake, encompassing a landscape of dense forests and grassy steppes, lush wetlands and harsh deserts, rocky islands and rugged cliffs. Mixed forests of tall evergreen and deciduous trees shelter a multitude of mammals, from brown bears and mountain sheep to sables, ermines, and minks. Cormorants and capercaillie, woodpeckers and wagtails, swans and seagulls, falcons, cranes, geese, and ducks can be spotted in the trees, on the rocks, or on the water.

Multicolored lichens dapple the massive boulders scattered among the trees and along the shore. Rare ferns, Icelandic mosses, and dark red bergenia cover the forest floor. Spring is heralded by carpets of snowdrops—yellow, blue, or lilac—and a profusion of purple Daurian rhododendrons. Summer brings golden-orange Siberian globeflowers and bright yellow Alpine poppies, followed by bluebells, violets, and jonquils, white camomile, yellow daisies, purple thistles, and wild roses. People and animals alike feast on an abundance of late-summer berries before autumn weaves a flaming tapestry of yellow, orange, red, and gold against a background of dark evergreens. Then winter comes to create its own beauty of crystalline white.

Baikal's highly changeable weather follows its own rules. In one direction the lake might be wrapped in fog and mist, while in another the sky remains clear and sunny, with the mountains reflected perfectly in Baikal's mirror-smooth surface. Suddenly a storm will blow in from another direction, churning up the water, blotting both lake and land from view. Then, just as quickly, the clouds will part, sending shafts of sunlight streaming from on high, like the golden fingers of a god reaching down to touch the water, bringing a rainbow to grace the space between earth and sky. Siberians familiar with Baikal's chameleon nature say that you can stand on its shore all day long, every day of your life, and never see the lake the same way twice.

Fewer than three dozen towns and small settlements dot Lake Baikal's 1,250-mile shoreline and its thirty islands (most of which are uninhabited). Some of these towns are situated on the Trans-Siberian Railroad line that runs along the southern curve of the lake. Others are connected by a single road, often nothing more than a dirt track passable only in summer and early autumn. No road runs around the entire perimeter of the lake, and hundreds of miles of Baikal's sparsely populated region have no roads at all. People living in the remote settlements on Baikal's shores rely on the lake as their primary route for transportation and communication. In winter it serves as an "ice road" for cars, trucks, motorcycles, and sleds; in summer, as a waterway for boats. But many of Baikal's small communities are virtually isolated in autumn and spring, when ice forming or melting on the lake makes driving on its surface dangerous and boat routes unnavigable.

During the second half of the twentieth century, when three major dams were built on the Angara River that flows out of Lake Baikal, the rising water submerged several old villages along the river's banks. Before those villages were destroyed, a few of their most important traditional wooden buildings were dismantled and transported to the Museum of Wooden Architecture and Ethnography, an open-air museum at the settlement of Tal'tsy on the right bank of the Angara River about ten miles from Lake Baikal. There they were reassembled as part of the museum's exhibits of Siberian village life. When I visited the museum in 1994, it comprised a collection of seventeenth- to nineteenth-century traditional wooden buildings (originals and replicas) from the Irkutsk region, including farmhouses and outbuildings, two churches, a one-room schoolhouse, several Buryat eight-sided log cabins (shaped like felt yurts), and a reconstructed watchtower for a wooden fort. The houses contained simple country furnishings and household implements: handwoven and embroidered linens, rag rugs, handmade pottery, carved wooden saltcellars, nickel-plated samovars, painted distaffs, a wooden loom. Some also had a large traditional Russian stove made of bricks or clay, constructed as part of the house itself. Used both for cooking and for heating the rooms, many of these stoves were built with flat ledges where children and old people often slept during the winter to keep warm.

As a collector of antique textile implements, I was especially interested in the wooden distaffs on display. I mentioned my interest to Marianna, a Russian colleague who was visiting the museum with us that day, and I casually asked if she knew any place where I might buy an old Russian distaff or spinning wheel to add to my collection. Marianna inquired at the museum's administrative office, and a few minutes later a middle-aged man in work clothes, felt boots, and a fur hat came up to us and said he had a distaff that he would sell to me. At first I thought he might be selling something from the museum's warehouse, and I didn't want to engage in such a transaction. But then he said, "Come with me. It's at my house in the next village."

Marianna, Tom, and I trudged behind him across fields deep with snow to a small village of wooden houses overlooking the Angara River. Inside his tiny two-room house, the heat was stifling from the big Russian stove occupying a large part of the low-ceilinged space that served as a combination

kitchen, living room, and bedroom. White light reflecting off the snow outside filtered through lace curtains over the single window, and pot plants
bloomed on the sill. Surprised by our unannounced arrival, the man's wife
rushed around to shoo several chickens back into their wooden cage near
the stove. Then she motioned for the three of us to sit down on the two
narrow beds placed against the wall, since there were no divans or chairs in
the room. Once the chickens were secured, she pulled up a short wooden
stool for herself.

We waited and waited in that stuffy room while the man rummaged around
in a small shed beside the house. A black cat named Chernoshka jumped
up beside me and was soon purring in my lap, while a tabby cat called
Murka settled contentedly on Marianna's fur coat. Marianna tried to make
small talk with the man's wife, but she was a quiet woman who seemed to
prefer sitting on her stool and staring at the two Americans who had suddenly shown up at her house. I was beginning to think we had all been
taken on a Russian wild-goose chase, when her husband finally appeared
with an old, two-part, wooden distaff, unpainted and uncarved, so plain-
looking that I wouldn't have given it a second glance at a flea market. For a
moment I wondered if it had been rescued from the woodpile just before
being burned in the stove. But after all the time we had spent on this impromptu quest, I could hardly refuse to buy it from him. So I paid the ten-
dollar asking price, without even bargaining, knowing that those few American dollars would mean much more to the man and his wife than they did
to me.

Carrying the distaff under his arm, the man walked back with us across
the snowy fields to the open-air museum. Then, looking somewhat sad, he
handed the distaff to me. "It was my mother's," he said. "But she's no longer
alive. She has no need of it."

"What was her name?" I asked. "Alexandra Ivanovna," he replied. "She
was an Evenk from the northeastern end of Lake Baikal." With a sense of
modest pride, he added that his father was a descendant of a famous Polish
revolutionary who had been exiled to Siberia in the nineteenth century,
when part of Poland belonged to the Russian Empire. I recognized his family's
name from my history books. Just before the man turned to leave, he looked
at the distaff once more, paused, then said to me, "Remember my mother's
name when you use it."

The Museum of Wooden Architecture and Ethnography was one of the
few tourist attractions along the two-lane, forty-mile highway that runs parallel to the river between Irkutsk and Lake Baikal. The road itself was of

*Reconstructed seventeenth-century watchtower at the
open-air Museum of Wooden Architecture and
Ethnography near Lake Baikal.*

surprisingly good quality in a country where the surfaces of paved roads often had more potholes than asphalt. Residents of Irkutsk called this highway "the Eisenhower Road," because Nikita Khrushchev had ordered it paved in preparation for a state visit to Russia by President Dwight D. Eisenhower in 1960. Eisenhower had asked to visit Lake Baikal, so the Russians spruced up the city of Irkutsk, paved the road, constructed special guest houses at the lake for the president and his entourage, and even built a golf course for his use. Eisenhower's trip was canceled, however, after the Russians shot down an American U-2 spy plane in their airspace and captured its pilot, Francis Gary Powers. But more than three decades after that international incident—which soured Russian-American relations at the time—people in Irkutsk were still fond of saying, "Every time we drive on this road, we thank your President Eisenhower for getting it paved for us."

Despite the good highway from Irkutsk, we continually felt frustrated by the difficulty of finding transportation to Lake Baikal during the winter months. Russians in Irkutsk warned us that bus schedules were erratic and that we might get stranded at the lake if we relied on public transportation. But every time we arranged an outing by private vehicle to Lake Baikal, the Russians we were dealing with canceled the trips at the last minute. Paraphrasing Tsar Peter the Great's observation that "Russia is the land where things that don't happen, happen," Tom summed up the situation as "Russia is the place where things that *could* happen, *don't*." On one occasion in early April, when we had planned to spend the weekend of my birthday at a guest house on the lake, we received a handwritten note from the Russian woman making the reservations. "Dear friends," it read, "The date is settled on 2/IV–3/IV. But you should find a car. You will go on ice (about 20 minutes by car), that's why think twice before going." When we asked her to explain the note, she replied matter-of-factly, "If you try to cross lake by car, car can drown." Since we couldn't find anyone willing to risk having his car fall through the ice, our plans for the excursion fell through instead.

The difficulty of finding transportation to Lake Baikal became a running joke among the American faculty. "Did you enjoy your canceled weekend at the lake?" we would ask each other on Monday mornings. But our Russian university colleagues never seemed to understand why all the Americans had such a desire to "get out and *do* something," particularly during the Siberian winter. So we were pleasantly surprised when the head of our department told us late one afternoon that we were going on a trip to Baikal the next day. None of us could figure out the sudden change of attitude on the Russians' part, but we didn't question our good fortune.

Dressed for a winter excursion to the frozen lake, all five Americans arrived promptly at work early the next day. Squeezed into a small van with four Russian university officials, we headed toward the elusive Lake Baikal, all the while wondering what special activities the Russians had planned for us. Only when we arrived at the lake and kept on driving around its southern shore did we discover that we were actually on our way to the town of Baikal'sk, to meet officials of the Baikal'sk Pulp and Paper Complex, who were being courted as financial supporters for our Russian-American education program in Irkutsk.

Inappropriately attired for such an important business meeting, we arrived just in time for lunch in the plant's executive dining room. Our host was Anatoliy Steinberg, the company's deputy director for Reorientation and Foreign Economic Relations. Knowledgeable, articulate, and Western-oriented, Steinberg was candid about the problems facing his company in Russia's new market economy. He was well aware of the difficulties the company would have in obtaining new capital investment, meeting environmental standards, and converting to the production of goods that could compete in the global economy. But he also emphasized its responsibility to continue providing jobs for the six thousand people of Baikal'sk, a company town whose residents were dependent on the pulp-and-paper-mill complex not only for their livelihood, but also for their housing, schools, stores, hospital, cultural center, and sports stadium.

After lunch we were taken on a tour of the plant, a modern facility by Russian standards. The small section that we were allowed to see was clean and well lighted, but the safety standards for workers appeared well below those of the West. No one wore hearing protectors against the din of the massive machines, and the only hard hats we saw were stacked in a corner, like props waiting to be used for another performance. No alarms sounded to warn workers to stand clear when tons of material were transported by big pulleys across the factory floor. As we stood watching enormous sheets of white cellulose pulp rolling through huge machines, Tom suddenly jerked me away from an overhead mechanized trolley whose moving block and tackle would have knocked me out if Tom hadn't been so quick on his feet. After our tour of this showcase section of the factory, we asked about visiting other parts of the plant, but were told that only authorized people could go there. Resigned to accepting the inevitable, our group of Americans looked at each other and said once again, "There is no opportunity," knowing that we had all just been given the official Potëmkin Tour.

Constructed between 1960 and 1966, the Baikal'sk Pulp and Paper

Complex was originally built to produce a special type of durable viscose rayon cord used for making airplane tires. By the time the plant began operating, however, rayon cord was already an obsolete material for heavy-duty tires, having been supplanted by superior synthetic products strengthened with metal. The plant eventually shifted production to other cellulose-based materials, including pulp cord and pulp rayon for the paper and textile industries, as well as wrapping paper, twine, and by-products such as turpentine and pine oil. Meanwhile a second cellulose plant, the Selenginsk Pulp and Cardboard Complex, began operating in 1974 on the Selenga River that flows into Lake Baikal.

These industrial behemoths in southern Siberia became the focus of the first public environmental protection movement in the Soviet Union. Scientists documented their detrimental effects on Lake Baikal, citing the air and water pollution resulting from the chemicals used in the cellulose-making process and the discharge of industrial effluents into the lake. Well-known writers such as Valentin Rasputin publicized the problems and called for the plants to be closed, and concerned citizens protested against the existence of smoke-belching industrial eyesores near the shores of the country's most revered and renowned natural wonder.

Environmentalists became especially concerned when they discovered that the by-products of cellulose manufacture were killing the *epischurae* at the southern end of the lake, thus upsetting the ecological balance provided by the tiny crustaceans most responsible for the purity of Baikal's water. They were also worried about the depletion of *omul'* in Lake Baikal—the backbone of the Baikal fishing industry—from the pollution of their spawning grounds in the Selenga River, caused by the logs floated downstream to the Selenginsk Pulp and Cardboard Complex. Finally in response to a variety of pressures, both domestic and international, the Soviet government decreed in 1987 that the Baikal'sk Pulp and Paper Complex had to "reprofile" itself into "an ecologically clean works" by 1993. In 1989 the company installed a new sewage treatment system for industrial wastes and drainage water at the plant, and by the early 1990s company officials claimed that the quality of the "treated sewage waters of the Baikal'sk mills exceed[s] the state standard specifications for drinking water"—an assertion disputed by environmentalists who said that the company had a history of fudging its figures and that Russian standards for drinking water were a joke.

To counter such bad publicity, the Baikal'sk Pulp and Paper Complex published a large full-color booklet, in several languages, presenting an array of positive environmental statistics about the plant. Visitors to the

Baikal'sk plant were customarily offered glasses of clear-looking, treated industrial waste water to drink. And the company's booklet featured a full-page color photo of a *nerpa* in a pool of clear water, with the caption (in English): "Quality of the treated sewage waters is testified by the excellent mood of the seal Nataly living in the basin at the institute of ecological toxicology." At the end of our tour of the plant, we asked to see the famous *nerpa*, but were told that he had recently been purchased by the Japanese. Later, one of my students in Irkutsk said the Japanese had paid the Baikal'sk plant the equivalent of five thousand dollars in hard currency for its single showcase seal.

Our first excursion on our own to Lake Baikal wasn't until early May, when we finally found someone in Irkutsk willing to rent us a van with a driver to take us out to the lake for a day. Several Russian friends had tried to discourage us from going, warning that the lake would still be frozen at that time of year. But—as so often happened in Russia—their information was completely wrong. When we arrived at the village of Listvyanka, near the place where the Angara River flows out of Baikal, the weather was sunny and warm, and Old Man Baikal no longer groaned under his armor of ice. Together with our three American colleagues, we spent the day hiking in the hills surrounding Listvyanka and picnicking on a beach beyond the village. Pooling the foods we had carried to Baikal in our backpacks, the five of us feasted on smoked chicken, slices of dark bread slathered with butter and topped with caviar, the season's first red radishes, juicy fresh tomatoes and crisp cucumbers, my own homemade brownies, a store-bought German pound cake, and plenty of vodka, beer, cider, and white wine, which we iced down in a hummock of melting snow on Baikal's rocky shore.

At the end of that fine day we headed back to Listvyanka to rendezvous with our rented van. Walking over a hill above the lake, we passed a large group of Russians eating a picnic spread out on the hoods of a new white Toyota sedan and an older Lada. At first glance the gathering looked like a family reunion, with several men, two young women, and an old *babushka* eating and drinking together, while a bunch of small children played nearby. Music blared from a tape deck, the kids were laughing, and everyone seemed to be having a good time. Just to be friendly, I waved and said hello. The Russians waved back and motioned for us to join them. Soon we were all drinking vodka together out of plastic cups and eating an excellent home-made pâté spread on whole-wheat bread.

When we introduced ourselves as Americans teaching at Irkutsk State University, the Russians replied that they were students at the Polytechnic

Institute in Irkutsk. But with their expensive clothing and new Toyota car they appeared more affluent than most students I had met in that part of Siberia. One of them wasn't a student, they went on to say, laughing and pointing at a big, stocky, square-headed fellow with close-cropped hair, who looked just like a caricature in a George Grosz drawing. "He's a butcher," the Russians said, all breaking into laughter again. Later, when we complimented the Russians on their homemade pâté, they pointed to "the Butcher" and said he had made it himself, before they all burst out laughing once more.

Someone turned the volume up even louder on the tape deck, and a hatchet-faced fellow, who seemed to be the headman of the group, came up to me, held out his hand, and commanded in English, "Shar-*own*, we must dance!" I had a feeling it was an offer I shouldn't refuse. But I couldn't keep up with the rapid rhythm of the music, a folk tune from the Caucasus, and after a few turns I took leave of my partner, thanking him for the dance. Just at that moment a weaselly looking little fellow in a leather jacket began dancing by himself in the midst of the revelers. He was so good that everyone else stopped dancing, formed a circle around him, and began clapping faster and faster. Suddenly he pulled a large revolver out of his jacket, waved it around his head in time to the music, then deftly slipped it back inside the jacket, ducked his head, and grinned sheepishly, displaying a mouthful of gold teeth. My American companions began backing away from the crowd, but I suggested that we shouldn't make too hasty an exit. One of our group, George Morgan, disagreed, as he discreetly steered me over to the Toyota and pointed out a snub-nosed revolver lying on the back seat. So as soon as it was politely possible, we thanked the group for their hospitality and started to leave. But the Russians wouldn't let us go without a parting gift. When the headman opened the trunk of the Toyota, we started moving away, not knowing what might happen next. But he merely pulled out several bottles of German Henninger beer and insisted that each of us take one as a symbol of Russian-American friendship.

Two weeks later Tom and I were dining at a Chinese restaurant in Irkutsk with our friend George and three visitors from the American Embassy in Moscow when in walked Hatchet-Face-the-Headman from Lake Baikal, sporting a shiny sharkskin suit. Right behind him was the bulky Butcher, dressed in a gray silk suit exquisitely tailored to fit his beefy body. No cheap Russian polyester for those guys. And anyone doubting their real profession needed only to look at the width of their lapels to gauge the extent of their influence in the local business community.

"Uh-oh, here come your friends," muttered George, winking at me and adding, "'Shar-*own*, we must dance!'" The visiting Americans looked around innocently for someone who might be joining us for dinner. Just then the Butcher caught my eye and headed toward our table, followed by Hatchet Face. "What's going on?" asked the savviest American from Moscow, as the Butcher deftly maneuvered his bulk between the chairs in the crowded restaurant. I was a bit apprehensive as they approached, but the Butcher's smiling eyes and genial grin disclosed his genuine delight at finding a foreign "friend" on his home turf. Maybe he remembered my compliments about his pâté. I returned the smile and stood up to greet them. "Shar-*own*, we must dance!" commanded the Butcher's boss, as Hatchet Face took me in his arms and whirled me around several times in the tiny space beside the table. Then he suddenly stopped, smiled broadly at me and everyone else in our group, and just as quickly faded away to another table along with the Butcher.

"Who was *that?*" asked the Americans from Moscow. "Just some friends of mine from the *mafiya*," I replied nonchalantly, as I began to sip my Chinese hot-sour soup. Tom and George tried to stifle their laughter, as they concentrated on chewing their wontons. The other Americans looked around the restaurant with a mixture of confusion and uncertainty, while the Butcher and Hatchet Face, now seated at the best table in the place, nodded back at me and raised their vodka glasses in a silent toast. George later joked that with friends like that, I would never have trouble getting a reservation at that restaurant again.

On another trip to Lake Baikal that May, we stopped at the home of a well-known craftsman who lived in Bol'shaya Rechka (Big Stream), a small town on the Angara River, near the lake. Slava Ogarkov was a former journalist, once blacklisted by the KGB, who now earned his living by crafting beautiful boxes out of birch bark. Each of Ogarkov's boxes was an original, with different colors and layers of birch bark intricately laced together to form round, oval, and square containers ranging in size from tiny ring boxes to ones large enough to hold a full-size Russian fur hat. Some of the boxes were made of birch bark that had been cut, pierced, and stamped like tooled leather. Others had semiprecious stones from the Baikal region incorporated into their designs. When one of these small masterpieces of Siberian folk art was about to depart with a foreign buyer, Ogarkov would say, "My spirit is inside each box, and it will go with you all over the world."

Ogarkov lived surrounded by rustic beauty in a new log house overlooking the river. The carved wooden decorations on the exterior of his home echoed the motifs of the master craftsman's own birch box designs. Inside, his house was the most attractive of any private dwelling I visited in Russia, with pine-paneled walls, a flagstone fireplace, and a balconied loft extending around two sides of a spacious living room. Potted plants and an eclectic collection of folk art, small paintings, and original prints decorated the rooms, along with several of Ogarkov's favorite, most beautiful, birch-bark boxes that he had kept for himself.

Just down the street was another distinctive wooden house, its exterior adorned with layers of lacy wooden fretwork and big panels of white birch bark framing dark, expressionist wood carvings reminiscent of writhing snakes. The house was surrounded by a picket fence with larger-than-life-size carved wooden heads atop the end posts. Several phantasmic totem poles made of natural, unpainted wood stood like silent sentinels in front of that singular structure. Each pole was covered with the carved likenesses of Lenin, Stalin, and other well-known Communist figures, along with nameless faces and skulls representing the millions of people who perished under Communist rule. The effigies of those anonymous victims peered out from the totem poles like wooden ghosts who had returned to accuse their killers. The artist who created those haunting images was not at home when we stopped in Bol'shaya Rechka that day, but later I saw a television documentary film that featured a segment about him and his work. Exiled to Siberia during Stalin's time, he was now an old man in the last decade of the twentieth century. "When the repression ended and democracy came to Siberia," he said, "at last I was free to express myself. . . . We must remember what we had—and appreciate what we have now."

Not long after our visit to Bol'shaya Rechka, Tom and I finally got a chance to go boating on Lake Baikal. When our American friends Carol Chappell and Pete Kamarainen came from Vladivostok to visit us in May, we couldn't let them leave Irkutsk without an excursion to Siberia's "sacred sea." But when I asked several Russians in Irkutsk how to make arrangements for a boat trip on Baikal, they all replied that such an outing wasn't possible in May. "The lake is still frozen," they persisted in telling me, even though I had already seen it thawed near the southern shore. "No boats are operating at this time of year," they insisted. "You and Tom probably won't even get to boat on Lake Baikal before you leave Siberia next month." We couldn't fathom why our Russian friends kept feeding us false information and discouraging us from going to Baikal on our own. Maybe they feared for our safety. Or perhaps it was merely a mindset left over from the Soviet period, when most foreigners were prohibited from traveling around Russia without an official escort.

Lake Baikal in summer.

Although Siberia's changeable weather sometimes sifted snow over the
wildflowers of May, the day we took Carol and Pete to Lake Baikal was
warm, sunny, and bright, with the snow-capped mountains standing in stark
relief against the calm blue water. When we arrived at the village of
Listvyanka, several fishing boats were busy at work far from shore. With no
particular plans for that day, the four of us boarded the local ferry for the
twenty-minute trip to Port Baikal on the opposite shore—just so all of us
could say that we had indeed once "sailed" on Lake Baikal.

The five Russians on board the ferry got off at Port Baikal, a tiny, unim-
pressive village that didn't even seem worth a visit. We stayed on the ferry
for the return trip to Listvyanka, and since no one else came aboard at Port
Baikal, we were the only passengers on the boat. After the ferry pulled away
from the dock, the captain came downstairs to the salon and asked if we
would like to charter the boat for an hour's excursion on the lake. We readily
agreed and negotiated a price that didn't seem too extravagant, split four
ways, for such a private tour. I think we all felt a twinge of guilt at disrupting the ferry's schedule and inconveniencing any passengers who might be
waiting on the shore, but we couldn't pass up the chance to spend even a
little more time on Lake Baikal.

As the ferry slowly headed southward, away from both Listvyanka and

Port Baikal, Tom and I gazed at the now-familiar scenery from our new perspective on the water, while all of us reveled in the unexpected luxury of having the boat completely to ourselves. A few minutes later, the captain came downstairs again and invited us up to the bridge. There he introduced us to his girlfriend, a plain-looking, round-faced, cheerful woman in her early thirties, dressed like any Russian housewife you would see at the local market. Soon she and Carol and the captain were chatting together in Russian. Small world: it turned out that the captain also had a wife, who happened to live in Vladivostok on the same street as Carol—a matter that the captain didn't seem to mind discussing in front of his local Siberian girlfriend, who took it all in good stride. But their conversation was cut short by the static crackling of the ship's radio. "You idiot! What are you doing? Come back!" shouted his boss on the shore. The captain just laughed and ignored the first two or three messages, but as the voice on the radio became more frantic, he eventually decided that it might be prudent to head back to Listvyanka. We had sailed on Lake Baikal for only forty minutes of the hour we had bargained for, but we didn't mind the excursion's being cut short. And when the ferry docked at Listvyanka, we were relieved that no irate passengers were waiting on the pier for the wayward boat.

After the northernmost part of Lake Baikal had thawed in mid-June, boat service became available from one end of the lake to the other. As soon as the schedule was posted, Tom and I booked passage for June 19–20 on the hydrofoil that sailed between Port Baikal on the southwestern shore, at the head of the Angara River, and Severobaikal'sk, the only sizable town at the northern end of the lake. (The city's name means North Baikal'sk, to distinguish it from the other Baikal'sk, where the paper plant is located, at the southern end of the lake.) The roundtrip journey was almost eight hundred miles, but tickets for the two-day trip cost only 105,150 rubles (54 dollars) per person, including roundtrip fare by boat from Irkutsk to Lake Baikal itself.

We left early on a bright sunny morning from the *Raketa* (Rocket) boat landing in Irkutsk, where we boarded a small hydrofoil for the 1¾-hour trip up the Angara River to Port Baikal. There we changed to a larger boat, a hydrofoil named *Kometa* (Comet) that would take us on to Severobaikal'sk— a trip of at least ten hours, depending on the weather. Modern and sleek, the European-made hydrofoil had an interior like a wide-bodied jet, with rows of airplane seats for 105 passengers. Only 40 people were making the trip that day; since none of the seats were reserved, the passengers settled themselves and their luggage wherever they wanted. Soon we were pulling away from Port Baikal, heading past the old wooden houses in Listvyanka on the opposite shore, out onto the open lake surrounded by high mountains still streaked with snow.

As the hydrofoil skimmed over the surface of Lake Baikal, I watched the scenery on shore change from blue-tinged mountains to dense green forests to barren drylands. A herd of horses waded in the shallow water of a sheltered cove. Granite cliffs towered over sandy beaches. Gnarled trees, twisted into strange shapes by the wind, stood on lonely ledges like lookouts guarding the lake. The faces of men and animals suddenly seemed to appear as silhouettes on rocky outcrops, then just as quickly disappeared as the direction of the moving boat changed my line of view.

Traveling northward along the western side of the lake, we passed only a few small settlements of wooden houses nestled on narrow strips of land between the mountains and the water. On the opposite side of the lake was the Selenga River delta, next to Fallen Bay, where a series of massive earthquakes during two days in 1861 sank 120 square miles of land and three Buryat villages into Baikal. The whole area around the lake is an especially unstable part of the planet, rocked by two thousand earth tremors each year. Midway along the route, near the western shore, was Ol'khon Island, the largest island in the lake, which had separated from the mainland several million years ago during one of these cataclysms. North of Ol'khon Island the mountains on both sides of the lake became higher and more dramatic, their snowy peaks tinted iridescent purple by the late afternoon light. And near the northern extremity of Baikal's crescent, chunks of ice floated in the frigid water, with ridges of ice still clinging to the shore.

Tom and I were the only foreigners on board the *Kometa* that summer day. All the other passengers were Russians using the boat as the fastest, most direct way to reach Baikal's northern shore, a journey that would take much longer on Siberia's sparse and mostly unpaved roads. Some of the passengers on the boat were as interesting to watch as the sights on shore. One was a man traveling alone, carrying a woman's large straw hat festooned with colorful ribbons and silk flowers, like a Dickensian Dolly Varden or a froufrou chapeau in a French Impressionist painting. I had never seen a hat like that for sale in Russia (much less on any Russian's head), and I wondered how far, and for whom, he was toting that fanciful treasure. Was it a gift for his wife, for his girlfriend, for his daughter—and if so, where would any of them wear such a hat in Siberia?

Several of the Russians were traveling with their pets, which they carried by hand, restrained with only a homemade leash around the animals' necks.

Two giggly girls had brought along their gray tabby cat, Dima. Another passenger played with Elipa, his spunky, part–German shepherd puppy. A young man in a punkish outfit of black jeans and heavy-metal jewelry doted on his white rat, Sena, which crawled around in the fellow's black leather jacket, sat contentedly in his shirt pocket, and slept with him when he stretched out on the seats across the aisle from us. He seemed particularly pleased that I took an interest in his rat, and he proudly showed me the cardboard box he had fashioned into a comfortable, portable home for his friend.

The boat had three sections for passengers: a front salon that seated twenty-seven people, which was locked during most of the trip, except for an hour when the crew set up a small television and videocassette recorder to show cartoons to the kids; a main salon with seventy-eight seats, in the middle of the boat, where most of the passengers sat or slept; and a small, back salon with one end open onto a deck. The single toilet was cramped and none too clean, with toilet paper made from pages torn out of a lurid Russian novel titled *Sword over Moscow*, each sheet cut neatly in half.

The back salon also had a tiny galley where a woman prepared food for the crew and a small buffet counter where she sold chocolate bars, fruit juices, beer, vodka, champagne, and coffee to the passengers. But when I tried to purchase a few of the fresh *bliny* from a steaming stack of them that she cooked during the voyage, she just laughed and said they were all reserved for the captain. Experience had already taught us to carry extra food whenever we traveled in Russia, so Tom and I ate our own standard Russian picnic fare for lunch that day: hard-boiled eggs, pickled green tomatoes, chunks of cheese and sausage, and half a loaf of bread. Too late did I learn that we should have brought along enough food for the entire two-day trip.

No stops were scheduled on the route to Severobaikal'sk, so I was surprised when the hydrofoil's engine slowed to a halt about three-fourths of the way to our destination. The boat was a considerable distance from the shore, with no port in sight. Before I could find a crew member to ask what was happening, I heard the sound of outboard motors as three small aluminum boats sped toward us from a hamlet on the nearest shore. When they pulled up alongside the hydrofoil, I noticed that the plastic windshield of one had previously been broken into several irregular pieces, each neatly and laboriously laced back together, with lengths of heavy twine, like pieces of animal hide—a necessary repair in a region where replacement parts were as scarce as paved roads. The hydrofoil crew began handing boxes of supplies and packets of mail down to the men in the smaller boats. Since this was only the second trip of the *Kometa* that year, the villagers seemed delighted with the goods delivered to them—particularly a large calendar, which, in June, was only six months late. Given the expressions on the men's faces, it was obvious that the calendar's timeliness was of far less importance than the girlie pictures illustrating each month.

When we docked at the port of Severobaikal'sk at eight o'clock that evening, all the other passengers disembarked to an old bus and a couple of private cars waiting on the pier. Standing on the almost-empty quay outside that remote Siberian city, Tom and I began to wonder where we were going to spend the night. We had tried to phone ahead from Irkutsk to make a hotel reservation in Severobaikal'sk—an exercise as futile as trying to reserve a room on the moon. I asked the last crew member remaining on the *Kometa* where we could find a hotel, and he pointed to a modern, but dilapidated-looking, multistory building just beyond the broken concrete pier.

From outside, the hotel looked dark, dreary, and deserted. Cautiously we pushed open the dingy front door and peered into the dim light of a clean, well furnished lobby, devoid of people and deadly silent. I called out, asking if anyone was there. No answer. I tried again, already imagining having to bribe the caretaker to let us sleep in the lobby because the hotel had not yet officially opened for the summer season. Finally the desk attendant emerged from the gloomy recesses of the cavernous hall. She turned out to be a pleasant young woman who seemed amazed that we actually wanted to stay there. I suspected that we were the first Americans she had ever met.

I soon learned that we were the only guests in the large hotel, where we were given a spacious, comfortable room on the third floor with an excellent view over Lake Baikal. But when I inquired about a place to eat, the desk attendant said the nearest food to be found was in the city of Severobaikal'sk itself, about three miles away. I asked if there was any transportation available, but she shook her head no. The entire area around the port and the hotel seemed completely deserted at that time of night, so Tom and I walked uphill to the nearest road and eventually flagged down two Russian men in a beat-up old Lada who gave us a ride into town.

We had foolishly thought that food would be available in Severobaikal'sk, a city of thirty thousand people. But despite its being the main transportation hub for that part of Siberia, Severobaikal'sk seemed on that Sunday evening in June to be nothing more than a sleepy, Soviet-style backwater. Built in the mid-1970s as a major stop on the Baikal-Amur Mainline Railroad (BAM), Severobaikal'sk was a company town of uniform five- and six-story prefabricated concrete buildings, surrounded by a shanty town of makeshift dwellings without electricity, running water, and indoor plumbing. Promising higher pay, larger apartments, a cleaner environment, and better opportunities, the Soviet government had enticed blue-collar workers and white-collar professionals from other parts of Russia to settle in Severobaikal'sk during the 1970s and 1980s. But for many the dream was never achieved. The government never managed to construct enough housing for the population, and the BAM never lived up to its promise of spurring the economic development of the eastern half of Russia. In the mid-1990s thousands of former railroad workers and their families still lived in poverty in Severobaikal'sk, in rusty railroad cars, metal shipping containers, and wooden shacks made from materials scavenged from construction sites.

The Russians who had given us a lift tried to help us find some place to eat, but we soon discovered that the city's few restaurants were already closed, as were most of the kiosks, the little street stalls that sell a jumble of items from candy to vodka to cigarettes. The Russians dropped us off in the center of Severobaikal'sk, where we walked a few blocks down an eerily empty esplanade to the city's large, modern train station. There we finally found a scrawny roasted chicken and some stale bread at the station's sparsely stocked buffet. A nearby kiosk supplied two other essentials, toilet paper and beer.

After taking a taxi back to the hotel, Tom and I hungrily devoured a late picnic supper in our room, as we gazed out the picture window at the lingering summer light on Lake Baikal. Rosa, the hotel's calico cat, must have smelled the chicken, because she soon presented herself at the door of our room. We let her in, gave her the meager chicken scraps, and watched her strip the bones clean. Afterward I put her out into the hall, but later that evening I opened the door again, and there was Rosa, holding a kitten in her mouth. Following a strong survival instinct, she'd apparently decided to move her kittens from their cozy box behind the check-in desk in the lobby, up to our third-floor room where good food was suddenly plentiful.

The next morning we nearly missed the return boat. Scheduled to depart at seven o'clock, it took off ten minutes early, leaving behind anyone who might not have shown up until the posted departure time. The weather was bright and sunny again, but it was already much warmer than the day before. I later learned that the mercury reached ninety degrees in Irkutsk that day, the warmest temperature so far that year.

Among the passengers on the southbound boat was Sasha, an attractive teenage girl who was traveling with Dima, her fluffy black-and-white cat.

Sasha was a mobile fashion show: during the twelve-hour trip, she ducked into the tiny toilet and changed clothes six times! Four of her outfits were completely different, and two were mix-and-match costumes—all very stylish except for her choice of color combinations. When she wasn't changing clothes, Sasha played with the children and animals on board or just walked aimlessly around the middle salon in a completely unselfconscious manner, as if it were perfectly normal to wear six different outfits during one day on a boat in the outback of Siberia. She seemed the sort of girl who would grow up to be a kind-hearted kindergarten teacher, if she didn't succumb to the lure of fashion modeling instead. The last time I saw her, she was decked out in a dark purple miniskirt and light purple leggings, with a huge hot-pink nylon bow in her hair and Dima the cat poking his head out the front of her chic, stone-washed, blue denim jacket.

Ninety minutes after leaving Severobaikal'sk, the hydrofoil suddenly stopped running. By then we were far out into Lake Baikal, with no settlements in sight on shore and no motorboats speeding out to meet us. The crew got out their tools and began tinkering with the engine, while we sat dead in the water for almost half an hour. Finally the diesel motor started up, and the boat slowly began moving again. But we had been underway only five minutes when I smelled something burning and saw black smoke pouring from the engine. I ran to tell the crew, who quickly stopped the boat and set to work on the motor once more. The other passengers seemed unconcerned about the problem, stoically accepting the situation as if it were an everyday occurrence. No one complained about the delay or seemed worried about missing connections at the other end. For many of the men, the extra time was just an opportunity to drink more beer and vodka or to sleep off the effects of earlier indulgences.

While the crew was trying to repair the engine, Tom and I sat on the deck enjoying the spectacular scenery on both sides of the lake, as the still air around us heated up under the relentless summer sun. I fantasized about being stranded in the middle of Lake Baikal, with rescue boats eventually taking us to the nearest little settlement and our overnight trip stretching into several days of unplanned adventure. But the downside of such daydreams was the very real threat of sudden storms, with winds exceeding one hundred miles per hour, that rise on Lake Baikal without warning, sometimes capsizing boats and drowning all aboard. The Siberians who live around Baikal have individual names for more than thirty different winds that disturb the lake's waters, and they have a healthy respect for the uncontrollable forces of nature that affect their daily lives.

None of my own imagined hopes or fears came to pass that day on Lake Baikal. Twenty minutes after the last breakdown, we were off again, moving at a slower pace and with the engine making a different, less reassuring sound than before. We made only one more stop in the water, north of Ol'khon Island, where the same motorboats that had met us the day before drew up alongside and offloaded onto the hydrofoil several big burlap bags full of fresh *omul'.* Some of the men from the motorboats also came aboard to purchase bottles of fruit juice and vodka, a jar of pickles, a can of powdered chocolate drink mix, boxes of tea, and a handful of chewing gum. After having spent five months in Siberia myself, I could well imagine what treasures those must have seemed to people living in that small, isolated settlement on the lake's northwest shore.

I had hoped to spend the remainder of the trip lazing on the deck, watching the sun sparkle off the water and the mountains change color as we moved slowly southward. But soon I was conversing with several passengers, including a German couple who worked at a geological institute in Irkutsk; Ivan, a polite young man from Severobaikal'sk, who had taught himself to speak American-accented English ("to keep my mind active," he said); and Viktor, an eccentric artist from St. Petersburg, who was restoring a small Russian Orthodox church near Severobaikal'sk.

Viktor was an icon painter who was also an amateur ethnographer. That day he was carrying with him a stack of old picture postcards that he had collected from people living around Lake Baikal. Most of the postcards dated from before World War I and had been sent from people living in Russia, Poland, Germany, China, and Japan. A Russian one, postmarked 1908, showed the interior of a traditional log house with a girl sitting at a Singer sewing machine next to an old Russian stove. Another, sent from Irkutsk in December, 1910, depicted Father Frost surrounded by Christmas decorations, giving pretzels as presents to small children.

When Viktor discovered my interest in ethnography, he began monopolizing my time on the boat, telling me in detail about the work he was doing around Lake Baikal. Ivan listened in on our conversation, occasionally translating when my Russian-language skills faltered. But after I told Viktor about my interest in old textile implements, his demeanor began to change from intellectual-artist-ethnographer to typical "New Russian" wheeler-dealer. "I have two warehouses full of such things in Moscow," he declared. "What do you want? I can get you anything you want!" By that time Ivan was surreptitiously signaling to me that Viktor was a bit crazy.

Wooden totem carved by an artist in
Bol'shaya Rechka near Lake Baikal.

As the day wore on, Viktor became more and more pushy, following me around the boat, asking for my name and address, and insisting that he come to my office in Irkutsk the next day to bring me an old spinning wheel. By that time Ivan had made it clear to me that we should all try to distance ourselves from Viktor. "There's something I don't like about that guy," Ivan remarked with a frown. "You shouldn't let him get too close to you."

By the end of our trip, however, Viktor had definitely decided that he and I were kindred spirits, despite my efforts to discourage any further discourse. Before he got off the boat, he insisted that I accept several gifts from him: two pre-Revolutionary postcards from his collection, an old black-and-white photograph of the ornate nineteenth-century Cathedral of the Kazan Icon of the Mother of God, in Irkutsk (a victim of Stalinist demolition in 1932), a copy of the New Testament in Russian, a bottle of champagne, a large bar of chocolate, and a color photo of an icon that he had recently restored. On the back of the icon photograph he wrote, "To Sharon Hudgins, in memory of our meeting on Lake Baikal. God protect you!"

As we neared Port Baikal that evening, the sun was already sinking behind the mountains on the western shore. To get home, we still had to travel for more than an hour on another hydrofoil down the Angara River back to Irkutsk. As I stood on the deck of that boat and watched the azure waters of Lake Baikal recede into the distance, I knew I would always remember that two-day trip as a highlight of my sojourn in Siberia. And, after finally traversing the entire length of that legendary lake, I had begun to understand why Baikal bewitches all who see it—and why Russians consider Lake Baikal to be "the Blue Heart of Siberia."

CHAPTER 6

~

Among the Buryats

Ten days after we first arrived in Irkutsk by train, Tom and I boarded the Trans-Siberian Railroad again, retracing the route eastward to Ulan-Ude, the capital of Russia's Buryat Republic. We had been invited to speak at a World Bank conference, held in the regional government's main office building, a ponderous, multistoried edifice that still displayed a bronze plaque identifying it as the headquarters of the "Buryat Autonomous Soviet Socialist Republic." In front of the building—and dominating Ulan-Ude's spacious, concrete-covered central square—was a monumental bronze head of Lenin, the largest of its kind in the world.

Tom's lectures on market economics were among the first presentations on that topic in a public forum in Ulan-Ude since Lenin and his Bolsheviks seized power in Russia more than seventy-five years before. Three hundred people from south-central Siberia attended the symposium, many of them ethnic Buryats from Ulan-Ude and the regions around Lake Baikal. At the buffet dinner that capped the first day of the conference, Tom and I found ourselves again in the company of these Asiatic people, with whom we had lively conversations about the changes occurring in post-Soviet Russia and about the future of the Siberian economy from the Buryats' point of view—encounters that piqued my interest in learning more about the Buryats themselves.

As the symposiasts stood patiently around the heavily laden buffet tables, waiting for the feast to begin, a tall, bulky Buryat man, straining the seams of his shiny gray-green suit, suddenly picked up a bottle of Russian champagne. Had I been making a movie about Genghis Khan, I would have immediately cast him in the leading role. In one swift move he tore the metal foil off the top of the bottle and untwisted the wire, releasing the plastic cork with such force that it struck and shattered a light fixture above the table. Laughing loudly, he began swilling champagne directly from the bottle, while the other guests—apparently unperturbed about the debris that had fallen into the food—took this as a cue to start filling their plates. Later in the evening, after most of the guests had left, I spotted Genghis Khan plundering the leftovers, stuffing sandwiches, fruits, and cold meats into the pockets of his tight-fitting suit.

I first became aware of the people known as Buryats on the journey from Vladivostok to Irkutsk in January, 1994. As the train neared Ulan-Ude, I noticed several old wooden signs with peeling paint that still bore the traces of words written in a cursive, exotic-looking alphabet that was certainly not Cyrillic. On the crowded station platform at least half the people were of Asian descent, most of them with high cheekbones, swarthy complexions, and jet-black hair. Having traveled in many other parts of Asia, I could tell only that they were a type of Asian different from the ones I had seen before.

I soon learned that many of them were local Buryats, residents of the Buryat Republic, a section of Siberia located just north of Mongolia and east of Lake Baikal. Occupying part of the area known as Transbaikalia in tsarist and early Soviet times, the Buryat-Mongol Autonomous Soviet Socialist Republic had been established in 1923 as one of several smaller political entities that made up the Russian Federated Soviet Socialist Republic of the Soviet Union. ("Mongol" was dropped from the Buryat Republic's name in 1958, in an effort to distance Soviet Buryats, politically, from their kin across the border in Mongolia.) Despite the nomenclature, however, such "autonomous republics" were neither truly autonomous nor on the same level as the fifteen socialist republics that made up the Soviet state. Autonomous republics and other areas designated as "autonomous" were subordinate territorial and administrative subdivisions created for certain ethnic minorities living in the Soviet Union.

In the 1990s the Buryat Republic had a population of more than one million, comprising sixty ethnic groups, of which the Buryats were the largest non-Russian group. During the Soviet era two other smaller Buryat "autonomous districts" had been also been created (within larger administrative regions), and these continued to exist in the new Russian federal structure established in 1992: the Ust'-Ordynskiy Buryat Autonomous District (within the Irkutsk Region), west of Lake Baikal and north of the city of Irkutsk; and the Aginskiy Buryat Autonomous District (within the Chita Region), east of Lake Baikal and the Buryat Republic.

Culturally and geographically, the Buryats are divided into two major subgroups: the Western Buryats, or Baikal Buryats, who live west and north of Lake Baikal and on Ol'khon Island in the lake; and the more numerous Eastern Buryats, or Transbaikal Buryats, who live in the areas east of the lake. Buryats are closely related to Mongolians, whom they resemble in language and appearance and with whom they share many customs. Some Buryats even claim their people are descendants of Genghis Khan, the legendary thirteenth-century Mongol warrior whose vast empire extended from northern China across most of Central Asia and southern Russia, and whose grandson, Batu Khan, led the Golden Horde that terrorized and subjugated much of Russia and Eastern Europe, ushering in 250 years of Mongol domination.

The Buryats were actually a separate Mongolic group, distantly related to Genghis Khan's clan, who lived in the lands just to the north of them. History tells us that conflicts between these two tribes eventually drove the Buryats farther north where, in the thirteenth and fourteenth centuries, they began to inhabit the area near the southern end of Lake Baikal. Buryat folklore, on the other hand, identifies the Buryats as originating on the shores of Lake Baikal itself. Whatever their place of origin, the Buryats no doubt mingled with the Mongol clans united under Genghis Khan and his descendants, as they swept through the Transbaikal region, producing a number of mixed Mongol-Buryat children, the ancestors of today's modern Buryats, many of whom proudly claim kinship with their warrior forebears.

Nomadic herders of cattle, horses, camels, sheep, and goats, the Buryats were well established in the areas around Lake Baikal when the first Russian Cossacks arrived in that region in the seventeenth century. Expert archers and horsemen, the Buryats initially resisted Russian rule and the forced payment of tribute, in the form of fur pelts, to their Cossack overlords. Only after a century of Buryat uprisings and guerrilla actions against the Russian invaders did these two Asiatic and European peoples reach an uneasy accord. Eventually the Russians and Buryats began to live together more peacefully, some of them intermarrying and producing children with mixed loyalties to their Russian and Buryat progenitors.

During the nineteenth century the Buryats became more Russified than their other native Siberian neighbors, the Yakuts and Evenks. Under pressure from the tsarist authorities, some Buryats even gave up their nomadic life, became farmers, and traded their portable felt-covered yurts for more stationary wooden yurts made of logs (although these wooden structures could still be disassembled and moved if necessary). Others served in Cossack regiments in the Transbaikal region. In the twentieth century Stalin's policy of forced collectivization drove even more Buryats into larger, permanent settlements on both sides of Lake Baikal. By the time I first encountered Buryats in the 1990s, most of them were settled members of modern society in the Russian Federation. The majority of them lived in rural areas, in small, single-family wooden houses in villages and towns in south-central Siberia, where they worked as farmers, fishermen, or stockmen. Others lived in the high-rise apartment blocks in major cities such as Irkutsk and Ulan-Ude, where they worked as industrial laborers and white-collar professionals.

Ulan-Ude was established by the Russians in 1648 as a fort near the confluence of the Selenga and Uda rivers. By the late twentieth century it had grown into one of the major cities in southern Siberia, with a population of four hundred thousand, of which approximately one-fifth were Buryats. Originally named Verkhneudinsk (Upper Udinsk, in Russian, because of its location on the Uda River), its name was changed to Ulan-Ude (Red Uda, in Mongolian) during the early Soviet era. An industrial city known for its large locomotive plant and railway repair workshops, Ulan-Ude was off-limits to most foreigners until the early 1990s, primarily because of its strategic location on the Trans-Siberian Railroad and its proximity to several military sites. Surrounded by typical Soviet-era high-rises, the center of the city in 1994 still retained a number of its old traditional wooden buildings trimmed with wooden fretwork. Ulan-Ude also boasted an opera house, a ballet company, two drama theaters, a large horse-racing track, interesting museums of fine arts and natural history, and a large, open-air, ethnographic museum, one of the best in Russia, where I spent an entire day wandering among the authentically restored wooden houses, looking at exhibits of daily life among the Russian Orthodox, Old Believer, and Buryat communities of the Transbaikal region in earlier times.

About twenty miles from Ulan-Ude is the Ivolginskiy Datsan (lamasery), the center of Tibetan Buddhism in Russia and a sacred place to many Buryats. Situated on a barren plain with a range of snow-capped mountains in the background, the Ivolginskiy Datsan looks like an exotic bird that somehow lost its way and alighted on the steppes of Siberia. Within its high-walled enclosure accessed by tall, ornately carved-and-painted wooden gates, the monastery complex comprises several houses, temples, prayer wheels, stat-

Buryat shrine overlooking Lake Baikal.

ues, stupas, and shrines, painted in a rainbow of bright colors accented with gold. In the center rises the main temple, a three-story brick edifice with curving roofs like a pagoda. Constructed in 1971, the main temple burned down only a few months after completion but was rebuilt within less than a year. Perhaps its initial fate was a reminder of the not-too-distant past when the Soviet government closed all the Buddhist monasteries in southern

Siberia, confiscated or destroyed most of the buildings, and sent thousands of lamas to the gulag. Only two lamaseries were reestablished after World War II, one of which was the Ivolginskiy Datsan, which has occupied this site since 1946. Today it serves as a center of Buddhist instruction and worship, a repository of rare manuscripts and valuable art, and a peaceful place of pilgrimage for believers and tourists alike.

Prior to the arrival of Buddhist lamas and Russian Orthodox priests in the Baikal region, the Buryats originally believed in a number of god-spirits who inhabited the earth, the water, and the sky. Beginning in the mid eighteenth century, however, many of the Buryats living east and south of Lake Baikal converted to Buddhism, whereas most of the Buryats living west and north of the lake tended to remain pagan or eventually converted, often only superficially, to Russian Orthodoxy. During my five months in Siberia, I asked several Buryats how many of their people were now practicing Buddhists, since Buddhism was experiencing a revival in post-Soviet Russia. The answer was often a sideways glance and the reply, in a quiet voice, "Some. But of course we have our own religion, shamanism."

Three months after our initial trip to Ulan-Ude, Tom and I were invited to speak at another World Bank conference, this one in Ust'-Orda, the capital of the small Ust'-Ordynskiy Buryat district west of Lake Baikal and about forty miles north of the city of Irkutsk. When I first visited this home of the Western Buryats, the winter snows had already melted, but spring had not yet arrived. Strong winds blew across arid landscapes reminiscent of west Texas or the high plains of Wyoming and Montana. Mineral salt deposits streaked the surface of the steppes like sweat marks on silk. In small villages, rows of unpainted wooden houses lined the narrow dirt streets. Everywhere I looked, the dominant color was brown.

Ust'-Orda, the largest town in the district, had a population of thirteen thousand, most of whom lived in traditional one-story, Russian-style wooden houses. Many were farmers and stockmen, for the Buryats are Siberia's cowboys (in fur hats instead of Stetsons). Cattle and horses wandered down the unpaved streets, and clouds of dust filled the air. Except for a couple of surfaced roads, a few Soviet-era multistory buildings, and a small central square with a statue of Lenin, Ust'-Orda looked much like it did when another American, Jeremiah Curtin, described his sojourn there a century ago, in an interesting account titled *A Journey in Southern Siberia: The Mongols, Their Religion and Their Myths.* Even in 1994, Ust'-Orda reminded me of sepia-toned photographs of small towns in the American West in the late 1800s.

After a morning session of the conference, I visited Ust'-Orda's ethnographic museum, in the company of two Buryat guides. Elizaveta (Liza)
Alekseyeva was an attractive single mother in her mid-thirties, a local teacher
of English who had honed her language skills at the regional pedagogical
institute. Terry Batagayev, an uncle of the chief government official of the
district, was a wiry, energetic, older former Communist who had learned
his English as a Soviet military translator in the Russian Far East more than
two decades earlier, monitoring radio transmissions by U.S. forces stationed
in Alaska, Korea, and Japan. Both he and Liza seemed delighted to have an
opportunity—rare in that part of Siberia—to actually converse in English
with native speakers while also showing them the sights of Ust'-Orda.

The local ethnographic museum contained interesting displays of old
Buryat folk art, iron agricultural implements, wooden kitchen utensils, ornately embroidered silk robes, and silver-and-coral jewelry. Liza explained
what the kitchen utensils were used for, how coral had been a medium of
exchange among Buryats in the past, and what symbols were sewn onto the
ceremonial clothing. At the end of our tour, past and present suddenly con-
verged in the form of a small television set showing a videotape of an annual
Buryat summer festival called *sur-kharban* ("straight shooting")—a combination country fair and sports competition, with archery contests, horse
racing, wrestling, singing, and dancing—that draws participants and onlookers
from all over the region. Although a few of the Buryats on screen were
dressed in colorful folk costumes, most of the crowd looked like modern
Asian Americans, in blue jeans, T-shirts, and baseball caps.

As we looked at the museum's reconstruction of an old Buryat kitchen, I
mentioned to Liza that I would like to learn more about traditional Buryat
cuisine. Reticent at first, she must have sensed my genuine interest in the
subject, because later she offered to arrange a meeting with her mother, a
seventy-two-year-old retired geography teacher with a longstanding interest in Buryat foods. Pleased at this chance to talk with a Buryat outside the
official context of the conference, I agreed to meet her mother, at her convenience, the following day.

A handsome woman of regal bearing, Liza's mother, Sofya Garankina,
arrived wearing a simple black dress, white crocheted shawl, white mink
hat, and a long necklace made of red coral. And, true to her daughter's
description, Sofya proved to be a knowledgeable source of information about
local foods and culinary customs. By the end of our long afternoon together, I had learned a new vocabulary of Buryat food terms and discovered how much Buryat cuisine differs from Russian cooking.

Sofya began by pointing out the importance of climate in influencing traditional Buryat cuisine, emphasizing that earlier nomadic Buryats lived off their livestock, whereas more settled ones in the modern era also ate fish and the kinds of vegetables that could be grown in southern Siberia. She went on to say that milk and meat—from horses, cows, sheep, and goats—are still the two major components of the Buryats' diet. And she emphasized that dishes made from milk "occupy first place in the 'national cuisine' of the Buryats"—including drinks such as "Buryat tea" (black tea flavored with butter, flour, salt, and cream or milk) and *tarasun*, known as "the Buryats' wine," a clear alcoholic beverage distilled from naturally soured milk. Milk also plays a symbolic role in Buryat life. For example, when guests arrive at a Buryat home, the hosts welcome them at the entrance with a bowl of milk or other milk products—such as sour cream or sweet cream—in the same way that Russians greet their guests with an offering of bread and salt.

Among the many Buryat meat dishes that Sofya described were meat-filled steamed dumplings similar to ones I had eaten in other parts of Asia, from Turkey to Japan. Far less appetizing (to me) was a Buryat specialty made from horse liver. Sofya told how several families in a Buryat village will join together to purchase a horse, which is given extra feed to fatten it for slaughter. The horse is killed in December—and among its meat products shared by the collective owners is a simple dish made by slicing the liver into very thin pieces, each topped with a thin layer of the best yellow-white horse fat. These slices of liver and fat are rolled up together into roulades and then put outside, in a place protected from hungry animals, to freeze solid in the Siberian winter. The Buryats cut the roulades crosswise into thin slices and eat them raw, garnished with chopped onion, garlic, and salt. Sofya said that one horse liver, prepared and preserved in this manner, was sufficient for the several families who had bought into the horse. According to her, these raw liver roulades, which stay frozen throughout the winter, are eaten mainly in the spring, by people who are anemic or who have bad eyesight. But I got the distinct impression that raw horse liver layered with fat was considered to be a tasty delicacy by many Buryats, including Sofya herself, regardless of their state of health.

The three-day World Bank conference in Ust'-Orda concluded with a banquet for fifty people in the dining hall of the district government—a room whose paneled walls were decorated with stylized horses and Buryat motifs made of wood and brushed metal. The meal, which began at half past noon, consisted of a jumble of courses, with heavy emphasis on meat dishes much like Sofya had described: first, an appetizer of sliced fresh tomatoes and Russian *kolbasa* sausage, followed by beef soup made with potatoes, onions, pickled red peppers, and paprika. Next came a large meat-ball accompanied by mashed potatoes, then a plate of stir-fried beef strips, onions, and pickled red peppers, garnished with pickled cabbage. Dessert was a flaky pastry made with lard, accompanied by a glass of milky tea. Before we could even finish dessert, however, the waitresses put plates of sliced fresh cucumbers on the table, then platters of sausage, followed by more stir-fried meat-and-onion strips, and yet another round of meatballs and mashed potatoes.

Every course was accompanied by tumblers of Russian champagne and seemingly innumerable toasts with small glasses of vodka. Before each Buryat knocked back a glass of vodka, he dipped the tip of the third finger of his right hand into the liquor and flicked a small amount of liquid into the air or shook a drop or two onto the table. One man always tapped his finger tip on the right-hand lapel of his suit coat. These were gestures that I had seen before, not only among Buryats but also among some of the ethnic Russians I knew in Irkutsk and Ulan-Ude. Russians had told me that the gesture was meant as an offering to "Burkhan," whom they identified as the god or spirit of Lake Baikal. But our Buryat hosts in Ust'-Orda said that many of their deities of earth, air, water, or fire could be honored in this manner.

Toast after toast, we all gulped down the vodka in the name of interna-tional friendship, personal goodwill, everyone's health, and future prosper-ity—always after making the requisite ritual offering to the various gods, whoever they were. As the meal wore on, toasts turned into speeches, which seemed to become more long-winded as each new speaker stood up to say his piece. Suddenly it was my turn. Fifty faces, most of them Buryat, looked expectantly at the head table where Tom and I were sitting with the other guests of honor, including the Buryat district chief. But after all that vodka and champagne, I had to concentrate on just standing up. Steadying myself by holding onto the edge of the table, I peered out at the group and won-dered what I could possibly say to a bunch of Buryat farmers, stockmen, factory managers, and local government officials in the outback of Siberia.

I took my cue from the physiognomy of the faces in front of me. After making the customary introductory remarks about how pleased I was to be there, I launched into an impromptu speech. "As you all know," I began, "most anthropologists think that the first people to inhabit America origi-nally came from Siberia more than ten thousand years ago." The listeners looked at each other in surprise, as if I had just told them that President Clinton was really a Russian. "They walked across the land bridge that used to connect northern Siberia with present-day Alaska," I continued, "and they eventually migrated farther down into what we now call North and South America. Those Siberians were the ancient ancestors of our so-called Indians, or Native Americans, today." The dinner guests continued to stare at me as if I were recounting some strange new fable. "And since some of my own ancestors were Native Americans," I went on, "that means way back in time we're all actually related to each other—you and I. And therefore we're all members of the same family!"

Those words brought the house down. After the loud applause finally subsided, an elderly, weathered-looking Buryat man stood up and said that he had never heard such a story before, but he would believe it because it was told to him by an honored American guest. And he added that since we were "family," he wanted to sing an old Buryat song to me. Everyone in the room became very quiet. Softly at first, then louder and louder, he began chanting in the Buryat language, his eyes closed and his face tilted toward the sky. The man seemed to be singing in a trance, enchanting his audience with secretly shared memories. In the midst of this unexpected performance, Tom and I looked at each other incredulously, both of us recognizing the strange familiarity of the song, which sounded just like Native American music we had heard as children in the American West. As the old Buryat continued to sing, louder and louder, with an intensity bordering on the ecstatic, the haunting sound sent chills down my spine, like a mystical melody from a long forgotten past.

When the singer finished, all the other Buryats cheered and clapped wildly. Then the old Buryat man asked Tom and me to reciprocate, to sing him a song from our own native land. We looked at each other apprehensively. Neither of us could sing our way out of a burlap bag if our life depended on it. But we had no choice: politeness required us to give it a try. "The Eyes of Texas?" I suggested to Tom. "I will if you will," he replied warily. Knowing that we were going to make fools of ourselves and embarrass our hosts, we stood up and proceeded to do just that. We sounded so terrible that both of us broke down laughing, long before we could finish the song—surely to the great relief of the audience, all of whom were laughing with us, acknowledging that we had at least made an effort, even if we couldn't carry a tune. "Now you know why we work as professors, not singers," Tom interjected between bouts of laughter, as we both gladly sank back into our seats, thankful that our social obligations had been fulfilled.

Our Russian colleagues from Irkutsk insisted that we leave the feast with them at 3:30 that afternoon, in order to get back to the city by nightfall, driving on a bad road ahead of a storm that was blowing in. Stuffed to the gills and barely able to stand on our feet, we bade farewell to our Buryat hosts. Some of them walked us to the door of the dining hall, all the while asking us—in halting French—how we, as Texans, might help them develop their livestock industry in the region. By that time Tom and I were so looped that we didn't think there was anything unusual about discussing ranching in French with a bunch of Buryat stockmen in Siberia. Meanwhile the other Buryats in the dining room were still going strong, singing songs in their native language, ordering more rounds of vodka, and asking why we were leaving so soon after the party had started. Later I learned that the banquet in Ust'-Orda had continued nonstop for another twelve hours, until 3:30 the next morning!

Two months after that official feast, I was pleasantly surprised when Liza Alekseyeva telephoned our university office in Irkutsk and left word that Tom and I were invited to Ust'-Orda on a certain day in June, for an opportunity to sample traditional Buryat foods. The message said only that someone would pick us up early in the morning in Irkutsk to drive us to Ust'-Orda—and that a full day was planned for us. The actual reason for the invitation, as well as the itinerary, remained a mystery to us.

Liza and a Buryat driver arrived by car in Irkutsk at 8:30 A.M. on the appointed day. During the hour-and-a-half trip to Ust'-Orda, Liza told me the story of her own Buryat family: how they had lost their house and lands during the forced collectivization of the 1930s; how some of the men had disappeared into the gulag; how her grandmother had managed to hide some of her jewelry when the Communists confiscated all their household goods and personal property. Liza's family, who lived in a rural area north of Irkutsk, had been forced, like so many others, to move from their own village into a designated town—in their case Ust'-Orda—during the "dekulakization" period in Siberia in the 1930s, when several thousand Buryat farmers and herders were displaced from their homes and an estimated ten thousand Buryats perished from starvation or at the hands of Stalin's henchmen. Without looking directly at me, Liza told the story quietly, dispassionately, as if such topics were matter-of-fact, daily fare. But she glanced at me occasionally as if to ascertain whether I really understood this hidden history now revealed, these events that people had dared not mention for decades, and which, even in the 1990s, some people still suppressed or denied. As I listened to her stories, I felt like we were traveling through time, across a landscape that had been ravaged by rulers from the Communist collectivizers of the twentieth century all the way back to the early Mongol khans.

The route to Ust'-Orda took us near the village where the log house of Liza's family had once been located, before they were driven off their land and the house sold to someone more acceptable to Stalin's regime. (The purchaser had dismantled the house and transported it elsewhere, to be reassembled.) We also passed a couple of old, dilapidated Russian Orthodox churches now being restored, a small Buddhist temple set back from the road, and—simplest yet most impressive of all—a pagan shrine, an *oboo*, consisting of two very tall wooden poles with a horse's tail attached to the top of each one. Also tied to the poles were hundreds of strips of colored cloth that fluttered in the wind above a jumble of small offerings placed at the shrine: pieces of sausage and bread, unsmoked cigarettes, a jar half full of homemade tomato sauce, even coins and paper money. Empty vodka bottles littered the ground all around. In fewer than forty miles, we had seen symbols of the four different belief systems—communism, Russian Orthodoxy, Buddhism, shamanism—that had vied for the Buryats' allegiance at various times over the centuries.

When I asked Liza why the shrine on the road to Ust'-Orda was situated in that particular, rather desolate and nondescript spot, she answered that a shaman had chosen the location. To her, that seemed to be explanation enough. I had seen similar but smaller shrines on the shores of Lake Baikal, deep in the Siberian forest, and on the steppes near Ulan-Ude. But, for

Three generations of a Buryat family in Ust'-Orda.

some reason, this particular *oboo* in western Buryatiya struck a primordial
chord in me. Each time that I passed it on the way to and from Ust'-Orda, I
felt the presence of something primitive pulling me toward it, as if I were
recalling memories formed centuries before I was born.

We arrived in Ust'-Orda at ten o'clock that morning and went directly to
the official government dining hall for breakfast. Although there were only
three of us—Liza, Tom and me—the table was set for a formal dinner for
twelve, with the best dishes, glasses, flatware, and linens available in that
part of Russia. As we dined on fresh tomatoes and cucumbers, hot yeast
buns made from Liza's own recipe, sliced cold sausages, raw *omul'*, milky
tea, and the inevitable vodka, Liza outlined our schedule for the day. She
felt obliged to advise us that in the afternoon something special was planned:
we could choose to be present for the event, or we could, of course, be
excused from watching it, whichever we wished. When Tom quietly asked
me what she was talking about, I whispered to him, "The Buryats are going
to kill a sheep for us, in their traditional manner. The sheep is going to die
whether we watch or not—so we might as well be present." Tom put down
his forkful of raw fish and reached for a swallow of vodka, while I told Liza
that we would be honored to attend all the events planned for us that day.

The first stop after breakfast was at the headquarters of the District Education Committee, where it finally became clear to me that our trip to Ust'-
Orda was at least partially sponsored by that organization, apparently in
gratitude for some assistance I had provided in obtaining English-language
educational materials for their schools. The chairman of the committee ush-
ered us into his office and made a formal speech welcoming us to Ust'-Orda,
then surprised us with unexpected gifts: for me, a set of traditional Buryat
jade-and-silver-filigree jewelry—earrings, necklace, and ring—and, for Tom,
a drinking cup made out of a cow's horn decorated with Buryat metalwork.
After such largesse we could not refuse the chairman's offer of something to
eat and drink: rich chocolate candies with cups of black coffee and glasses
of cognac. At eleven o'clock in the morning, however, that combination of
caffeine, sugar, and alcohol did not sit well on the raw fish and vodka we
had downed for breakfast only a short time before.

At the Education Committee's headquarters we were joined by Terry
Batagayev, the English-speaking Buryat who had accompanied us during
our first visit to Ust'-Orda in April. Together with Terry, Liza, and two drivers, we set off in two cars in the direction of a former Pioneer camp—similar
to our Scout camps—several miles beyond Ust'-Orda, where we were scheduled to eat a midday meal of typical Buryat foods. About halfway to our

destination, at a spot where I could see nothing but forest on either side of the road, both cars stopped. "This is 'Three Pines,'" said Terry, "a sacred place for Buryats. Buryat people always stop here when they pass this way." I looked around at the forest, but no three particular pines stood out from the hundreds of trees surrounding us. "Why is it called 'Three Pines,' and why is it sacred?" I asked. "Because the shaman said so," replied Terry, as if that explained everything.

Out came the vodka bottles. We clambered up a steep, muddy embankment, through dense, wet undergrowth, until we reached the edge of the forest. "This is it . . . I think," Terry said rather uncertainly. Nothing distinguished that spot from any other place I could see. Terry poured the vodka, and we all performed the ritual of dipping our third finger into the glass and sprinkling some of the alcohol into the air as an offering to the Buryat spirits. Then we stood around in a rather uncomfortable silence, wondering what was supposed to happen next, until Terry abruptly piped up, "Okay, time to go."

A few miles down the highway, both cars turned off onto a road so deep in mud that we had to get out and stand aside while the drivers made several attempts to move the vehicles onto firmer ground. Finally leaving one car behind, Liza, Terry, Tom, and I climbed into the second car and bumped down the rutted, muddy track for about half a mile until we bogged down once more. Just then, a spiffy, well-dressed Buryat woman in a tailored suit and high heels emerged from the forest and came walking toward us, struggling to maintain her balance in the squishy morass. She'd come from the Pioneer camp to tell us that the road was not passable beyond this point and the truck bringing the food supplies for our special Buryat meal had not been able to get through to the site.

Terry—who had apparently spent a lot of time arranging the noon meal for us—was obviously disappointed at this unexpected turn of events. Undaunted by the situation, however, we all got out of the car and slogged through the mud for the remaining half mile to the camp. Despite the remoteness of the location and the lack of special supplies, the camp's cook had managed to prepare a copious and delicious meal: fresh fish, stewed chicken, and fried potatoes; a salad of finely chopped red radishes, green onion tops, and wild garlic; plenty of yeasty Russian brown bread and a special fried bread made from a Kirghiz recipe; and commercial chocolates for dessert. Pitchers of Kool-Aid–colored *sok*—watery, artificially flavored "fruit" juice—were ignored in favor of bottles of warm Russian champagne. As we sat under two large hand-painted banners proclaiming PRIYATNOGO

APPETITA! (BON APPETIT! in Russian) and WELCOME (in English), our hosts
presented us with more unexpected gifts: a Russian wristwatch for me and
a decorative ceramic samovar for Tom—along with a bottle of champagne
and a bottle of vodka, which we promptly opened and passed around the
table, to the obvious delight of everyone there, including the cook, who
slipped out of her kitchen to join the festivities in the dining hall.

Barely able to stay awake after so much midday booze, we took a short
tour of the Pioneer camp, then boarded a large Russian four-wheel–drive
vehicle that managed to get us back through the oozing mud to the two cars
waiting at the highway. On the return trip to Ust'-Orda, we stopped again at
the sacred spot of the three pines to make the requisite offering to the gods
and consume another round of vodka. Fortunately for us, Terry didn't insist
that we climb the embankment that time. Apparently a roadside offering
was sufficient, especially at that stage of our fatigue and lightheadedness.

At four o'clock in the afternoon the car pulled up to a high wooden gate
at the home of the Tabikhanovs, a Buryat family who lived in Ust'-Orda. As
we started through the front door, Yekaterina Tabikhanova, the woman of
the house, warned us not to step on the threshold: to do so would bring bad
luck—a custom that Buryats share with Russians, Chinese, and Mongolians.
However, the Buryats were pleased that it was raining when we arrived, for
they considered it a good omen when guests brought wet weather with
them. After we had removed our shoes in the entry hall and changed into
slippers, Olya Tabikhanova, the grandmother, greeted us in the traditional
Buryat manner by presenting each of us with a bowl of *tarag*, a cool, re-
freshing, and (thankfully) nonalcoholic soured-milk drink similar to kefir
or cultured buttermilk. Under other circumstances I would have been better able to appreciate its taste and restorative properties. But soured milk
was not the best substance to add to a stomach already brimming with
vodka, cognac, and champagne.

The Tabikhanov family of husband, wife, five children, and one grandmother lived in a single-story wooden house, its exterior similar to farmhouses that I knew well from my childhood in Texas in the 1950s. The
interior had blue-washed plaster walls, middle-class Russian furniture, and
a graceful, Oriental-looking peaked archway leading into the kitchen. Although the house had electricity, there was no running water and indoor
plumbing; the toilet was located outdoors in a privy next to the barn. To my
surprise the Tabikhanovs had three cookstoves: a gas stove, hooked up to a
large orange gas cannister, in the entry hall; a modern Russian electric
range in the kitchen; and a traditional Russian brick-and-plaster stove, used

both for cooking and for heating the house, built into one wall of the kitchen itself.

As soon as we finished drinking the *tarag*, we all went outdoors to watch the slaughter of the sheep. The head of the family, Rodion Tabikhanov, led a ewe from his barn into the enclosed yard behind the house. He flipped the ewe on her back, knelt over her, and with a long knife swiftly made a deep incision in her breast. The he reached inside the animal with one hand to squeeze her heart until it stopped. This is the Buryats' traditional method of slaughter, the way that they and the Mongols have killed their livestock for centuries.

We watched as Rodion and his three sons butchered the sheep, first cutting off the forelegs and hind legs at the lowest joint, then gradually removing the sheepskin in one piece. The Buryats used a special knife—and only that one knife, which is reserved for this ritual—to make the initial incision and to butcher the animal. The method of slaughter ensured that little blood was lost and none of it touched the earth (for religious reasons, I was later told). An ax was used only once, with only one blow, to split the pelvic bone, as part of the ritualized process. And the carcass was then butchered in such a way as to preserve as much blood as possible, to be collected and used in making one of the specialties of the feast.

As the men proceeded to cut up the sheep, the women of the family worked on processing the innards at tables set up in the yard. When the sheep's liver was removed, fresh and steaming, from the carcass, the raw liver was cut into chunks and distributed among all of us as a special treat. I have to admit that I busied myself with taking photographs at that point, but Tom could not avoid the inevitable. He saved face for both of us by picking up a piece of raw liver, sprinkling it with salt, and managing to swallow it, all the while smiling and saying how good it tasted.

Rodion removed the sheep's heart, lungs, and trachea in one piece and hung them from a nail on the outside of the barn. The stomach and intestines were taken out and washed in cold water, while the muscle meat and the bones were thrown into an iron cauldron of boiling water, set over a wood fire. Soon the sheep's head—unskinned, with wool and eyeballs still intact—was placed next to the fire, to singe the wool a bit, before the head was also thrown into the pot. Occasionally Grandmother Tabikhanova tossed a tiny piece of raw meat or innards into the fire, as did two other Buryat men who showed up to help with the butchering. When I asked Terry why they were throwing those pieces of meat directly into the fire, he said they were making a gift to the gods—and that in earlier times people knew the prayers they were supposed to recite when making such offerings. I could see Grandmother Tabikhanova mumbling something each time she tossed a piece into the fire, and I suspected that she, of all the Buryats present, was the only one who really knew the appropriate words to utter.

I was curious about these offerings to particular deities worshiped by the Buryats. But when I pressed Terry for more information about these customs, he admitted that he didn't know much about such matters. A middle-aged former Communist, he was obviously one of the Buryats who, during the Soviet era, had consciously rejected many aspects of their own traditional culture in favor of the more modern, career-enhancing values of the dominant Soviet-Russian culture. Yet Terry was obviously enjoying all the Buryat rituals and foods that day, and I surmised that he—like many other indigenous Siberians—might seek solace in the symbols of his ancient past when confronted with the challenges of an uncertain future.

During all these activities outdoors, everybody drank mugs of *tarasun*, the potent clear liquor distilled from soured milk, which had the distinct and completely unappetizing aroma of a baby's wet diaper that needed changing long ago. When I asked Terry where our hosts had procured the *tarasun*, he just grinned and said that *tarasun* was something that couldn't be purchased in stores. Beyond that he was unable or unwilling to identify the owner of the illegal still that had produced the alcohol. But he hastened to assure me that it was first-rate *tarasun*, unlike the tainted home brews of vodka and other spirits that poisoned thousands of people in Russia every year.

The ritual associated with drinking *tarasun* was different from the vodka rituals I had seen before. When a Buryat was first given a mug of *tarasun*, he dipped the third finger of his right hand into the liquor and tossed some of it into the air or into the fire. Then he took one swallow from the mug and passed it someone else, who repeated the process. After that, the mug was returned to the first person, who could then drink the rest of its contents. All the Buryats were quaffing large quantities of this strong stuff as if it were water, and they just laughed when Tom and I were unable to match them mug for mug. Grandmother Tabikhanova was the hardiest drinker of all. While processing the bloody innards and eating raw liver, she downed huge amounts of *tarasun*, which didn't seem to affect her in the least.

When the meat was cooked, we all went indoors and crowded around a large dining table in the living room. By that time there were twelve adults in our party; the five children ate in the kitchen or carried plates of food back to the bedrooms. There were no napkins at the place settings, but the hostess ceremoniously draped a large towel across our laps, for Tom and me to share. Bottles of vodka, Russian champagne, and Bulgarian white wine stood at each end of the table.

Rodion Tabikhanov offered the first toast, welcoming us to his house and saying how honored his family was to prepare this feast for us. Then his wife passed around platters of appetizers to start the meal: slices of sausage, chunks of fresh raw *omul*, sliced fresh tomatoes and cucumbers, and thick pieces of dense, chewy white bread. These were followed by a soup course of hot mutton broth, which we drank from bowls. Before the broth was served, I noticed Grandmother Tabikhanova going outside to toss a small cup of it as an offering into the fire.

Vodka and wine glasses kept being refilled, as we toasted our hosts and they drank to our friendship. Then Tom and I, as the guests of honor, were served the most important part of the feast. The entire sheep's head, wet wool and sightless eyeballs still attached, was placed in front of Tom. Terry explained that it was traditional for the guest to sing a *töölei*, a special song about the sheep's head. But since Tom was not a Buryat and didn't know any sheep's head songs, we moved on to the next ritual. Rodion handed Tom a hunting knife and told him to cut off the sheep's left ear, to cut a cross on the top of its head, and to slice out a piece of the right cheek. Rodion then took the ear and cheek outside and threw them into the fire.

My turn was next. Placed in front of me was the sheep's stomach, which had been filled with a mixture of fresh cow's milk, fresh sheep's blood, garlic, and spring onions, then tied up with the sheep's intestines and boiled in the pot with the rest of the meat. I told myself that—despite all the food and alcohol I had already consumed that day—I was going to eat that repulsive blob without throwing up. I couldn't insult a group of people who had been so kind and generous to me. All the Buryats around the table waited expectantly for me to take the first bite. But I didn't know how or where to begin. Finally our hostess leaned over and sliced the top off the stomach. The contents had not been fully cooked and blood oozed out onto my plate. She took a large spoon, scooped out some of the semi-coagulated mass, and handed the spoonful to me. Trying to focus my mind on something else— anything else—far away, I swallowed the junketlike lump and forced a smile.

The other guests still waited for me to make the next move. Suddenly it occurred to me: pass the dish around. That's exactly what they wanted. The Buryats happily and hungrily scooped out and devoured big portions of the blood pudding, while Tom and I concentrated on the huge platter of boiled mutton in the middle of the table. More vodka. More toasts. Declarations of friendship. Buryat songs. More vodka. More wine. More champagne.

Buryats butchering a sheep for a feast in Ust'-Orda.

The Tabikhanovs presented me with a large purple paisley shawl and gave Tom a brown plaid shirt like those we had seen on Buryat cowboys near Ust'-Orda. Unprepared for all the gift-giving ceremonies of that special day, we had only a few small items to offer in return, including a box of Belgian chocolates that Grandmother Tabikhanova promptly opened and passed around the table before taking a piece for herself. The Buryats then gave me a bottle of wine and Tom a bottle of vodka, both of which we immediately opened and passed around the table, too. I was hoping the food and alcohol would soon run out, but there was still plenty of boiled mutton on the serving platters and a whole cauldron of steamy mutton broth simmering outside. When Tom and I protested that we couldn't eat another mouthful of their fine feast, the Buryats merely laughed, claiming that in the old days one sheep would not have been enough for twelve adults: at least three sheep would have been needed to feed such a gathering. Just at that moment, Grandmother Tabikhanova came out of the kitchen and set in front of us large bowls of *salamat*—a rich sour cream porridge, swimming in melted butter—which we were not allowed to eat until she had put an offering of *salamat* into the fire.

We had been at this feast for only five hours when Terry announced that it was time to leave for the *next* meal—at the home of Liza and her mother, Sofya Garankina. Sick from too much food and alcohol, Tom and I just

wanted to crawl away and hide somewhere. But we knew we couldn't dis-
appoint the Buryats still waiting for us. So at nine o'clock that evening, we
thanked the Tabikhanov family and bade them farewell, then climbed into
the car and bounced down the rutted, muddy streets of Ust'-Orda to Sofya's
house, all the while trying mightily to keep down the meal we had just
consumed.

The last feast of that long day remains only a pleasant blur in my memory.
I recall a beautifully set table in a cheerful kitchen, with white painted
cabinets, fresh flowers in a vase on the window sill, and a view of the garden
outside, luminous in the lingering Siberian twilight. I remember cups of
hot tea, fresh vegetables from Sofya's garden, rich mounds of homemade
clotted cream, tales of Buryat ancestors, a family photo album with pictures
of a man in military uniform and a beautiful Buryat woman adorned with
silver-and-coral jewelry—those fleeting images accompanied by a bottle of
sweet berry liqueur that proved to be an excellent digestif. I could have
spent days in that house in Ust'-Orda, looking at old photographs and listening to Sofya's stories about Buryat history, Buryat customs, and Buryat
cuisine. But all too soon it was time to go.

Liza, our companion for that entire unforgettable day, insisted on seeing
us safely home, even though it was a roundtrip journey of three hours, very
late at night. On the way back to Irkutsk we were all too tired for much
conversation. But I did learn that Liza would be taking a group of eighteen
school children from Ust'-Orda to London to study English for two weeks in
August. Her only other trip abroad had been to next-door Mongolia, and
none of the students had ever been outside of Russia at all. As we drove
across the steppes on that Siberian summer night, I tried to imagine what
the streets of London would look like to the children of Ust'-Orda—and
what they would think of the people, the foods, and the customs they encountered in such a strange and different land halfway around the globe.

Several months later, back in the United States, I happened to read
Jeremiah Curtin's account of his own visit to Ust'-Orda and the lands of the
Western Buryats in 1900. Only after having lived in Siberia could I truly
appreciate the conclusion to his narrative: "We left Usturdi [Ust'-Orda] September 13. I was glad to go from the Buriat country, where, though I had
gained considerable knowledge, we had endured many hardships." In 1900
Curtin arrived in Irkutsk after a two-day journey from Ust'-Orda, having
traveled the same route that took us only ninety minutes by car almost a
century later. Irkutsk must have indeed seemed like a welcome sanctuary
to him after two months of living with the Buryats, for he concluded:

That evening I dined with the governor of Irkutsk, and went with him to the opera. In this quick change from life among the Buriats to the refinements of civilized life in the capital of Siberia, I experienced the striking results of some centuries of social evolution—an evolution which through its effects upon humanity enables the man of cities to step back in a moment and with no mental effort from the wild, free life of fancy to the prescribed surroundings of material facts.

Thus did I leave the heroes of the past . . . and return to the no less valiant men of the present who, struggling with the evil forces of indifference and ignorance, are bringing to Siberia the prosperity that country so well deserves to call her own.

CHAPTER 7

The High-rise Village

When Tom and I were hired to teach in Russia, the University of Maryland administrators in College Park told us that the Russians would provide new, fully furnished apartments for all the American faculty working in Vladivostok and Irkutsk. Just before we left the United States, however, one of the American staff members casually mentioned that if the faculty apartments were not quite ready when we arrived in Russia, our local hosts would arrange temporary accommodations for all of us in a hotel. So, with visions of domestic comfort in mind, we blithely boarded the plane for Vladivostok.

On our way from the Vladivostok airport into the city, an administrator from Far Eastern State University (FESU) casually informed us that our promised apartments were not yet finished, so we would be staying somewhere else for a few days. Given what we had been told before we left for Russia, we all assumed that she meant a hotel. But we were soon disabused of that fantasy when we stopped in front of a dilapidated nine-story building that would have been classified as slum housing in the United States. It turned out to be one of the university's dormitories, with a special floor reserved for foreign students and foreign guests of FESU. As we climbed over the rubble near the entryway and stepped onto the unsteady wooden plank leading up to the front door, I began to suspect that Russian reality might not match up with previous promises. Wondering what was in store for us next, Tom and I hauled all of our baggage up two flights of dirty concrete stairs to the room that would be our first home in Russia—while our Russian escort kept assuring us that foreign guests of the university were assigned to the best accommodations available.

Our room measured ten by fifteen feet, with a large picture window over-looking the azure waters of Vladivostok's Amur Bay. But that view was the room's only redeeming virtue. The small space was crowded with flimsy furniture suitable for a monk's cell: two single beds, two small tables, and two straight-backed chairs. Just inside the front door, a tiny kitchen alcove contained a two-burner hot plate and a refrigerator, but no sink. Facing the kitchen area was a minuscule bathroom with a dirty toilet (no seat), a small sink, a permanently grungy bathtub, and a floor that looked like it hadn't been cleaned since the Bolshevik Revolution. But we soon adjusted to our new accommodations, making "toilet seats" from the only paper we had on hand—official announcements printed by the U.S. Consulate—and wedging empty beer cans between the metal window frames to keep them from squeaking all night in the winds that blew from the bay.

Whole families of Russian, Korean, and Chinese university students—some with small children and large dogs—lived in dormitory rooms the same size as ours. In the humid heat of that Vladivostok August, cooking aromas of cabbage, onions, garlic, and soy sauce mingled with the stench of stale sweat throughout the narrow corridors, attracting the roaches and rats that infested the building despite the numerous scrawny cats that roamed the dimly lighted hallways in search of food.

At first the weather in Vladivostok was so steamy that we hardly noticed the lack of hot water in our dormitory room. But a few days after we ar-rived, as I heated water in saucepans to launder all our dirty clothes by hand, I began to long for the luxury of hot water at the turn of a tap. In Russia you should always count your blessings, though. When the water in our building was cut off entirely for two days, we had to haul water in buckets and pans from an outdoor spigot a block away—up to our third-floor room—for all of our cooking, bathing, laundry, and toilet flushing. Under such conditions, it was not easy to appear refreshed and well-groomed each morning at the university, ready to embark on that day's round of classes, administrative meetings, and dinners welcoming the new American faculty. Finally our Russian hosts took pity on us and arranged for us to clean up one night at a bathhouse and sauna hidden away behind an un-marked door amidst a serpentine network of rusty pipes at a municipal waterworks station. Never in my wildest nightmares had I dreamed that my first hot bath in the Russian Far East would be in a setting from *Robocop*.

We and our three other American colleagues stayed in the FESU dormi-tory for two weeks, while the Russians kept assuring us every day that our apartments would be ready soon. Tired of living in cramped quarters and exasperated by the wait, we finally offered to help with whatever work was required to finish the apartments—painting, wallpapering, flooring, furniture assembly—explaining to the Russians that all of us could wield brushes and hammer nails as well as teach classes. But when our hosts seemed offended by that suggestion, we learned an early lesson in Russian-American cultural differences: By volunteering to do manual labor, we had not only stepped outside our official role as respected foreign professors, but had also implied, albeit unintentionally, that the Russians were incapable of completing the project themselves.

At last the new apartments were ready for us to move in. We dragged our luggage and boxes of books back down the dormitory stairs and loaded them into the university's Toyota van. After a forty-five-minute drive from the center of Vladivostok, where FESU was located, we arrived at a conglomeration of still-unfinished, prefabricated concrete high-rise buildings on an otherwise barren, windswept hill at the edge of the city. Our American colleagues looked in dismay at the bleak surroundings, as our Russian driver kicked open the battered metal entrance door on the ground floor and began bringing our baggage inside.

The elevator wasn't working, so Tom and I had to lug all our possessions up the concrete stairs to the fifth floor where our apartment was located. The other American professors had to trudge even farther, to quarters on the floors above us. As we hauled heavy boxes of books up the stairway, panting for breath, one of the Russians helping us with the baggage mentioned that Tom and I had been given "the preferred apartment" in that ten-story building. When I asked what he meant, he replied that the building had no fire escapes and Russian fire truck ladders could reach only to the sixth floor. "If you live higher than sixth floor and comes fire," he explained, "then you die."

That night Tom and I cooked a simple meal from our meager food supplies and toasted our new abode with cans of Lone Star beer he had miraculously managed to find at a local kiosk. And soon we were completely settled into the first of the three Russian apartments where we would live during the next sixteen months, in what I came to call "the high-rise village."

Only a few years earlier, in the Soviet Union, Americans would not have been allowed to live in a closed city such as Vladivostok, nor permitted to live in an apartment building side by side with ordinary Russians. Even in tsarist times, foreigners residing in Russia had often been confined to certain sections of Russian cities to segregate them from most of the local

Russian inhabitants. Under the more recent Soviet regime, we would have been required to live in a special "foreigners' compound," a single apartment building or group of buildings surrounding a courtyard, housing only foreigners and guarded by Russian militiamen placed there not only to monitor the occupants' movements but also to prevent access by other Russians. The only Russians allowed to enter these special buildings were those few who were officially permitted to interact with foreigners—housekeepers, chauffeurs, translators, tour guides, and government-sanctioned journalists—all of them previously vetted by, and most of them employed by, the Soviet state security organizations.

Soviet citizens, too, had been restricted as to where they could live. The government designated many cities—and even whole geographic areas—closed not only to foreigners but also to many Soviets as well. Some of those places were sensitive locations near the country's borders or in proximity to military sites. Others had military installations within their city limits or were secret military cities themselves—such as Krasnoyarsk-45 or Chelyabinsk-70 or Semipalatinsk-4—whose names and locations never appeared on maps. Still others were closed because they were near penal colonies or served as places of internal exile. And others—such as Moscow—were not off-limits to foreigners but were closed to many Soviet citizens because the government wanted to limit the size of those cities, or because there was insufficient housing for the number of people who wanted to live in those more desirable urban areas.

An internal passport system—initiated under the tsars, abolished after the Bolshevik Revolution, and revived by Stalin in 1932—controlled the mobility of Soviet citizens within their own country. Every person over the age of sixteen was required to have one of these documents, with a *propiska* (a residence registration permit) stamped inside. Only with such a permanent residence permit issued by the district militia of a particular city or town could a person legally live in that location. For decades during the Soviet era, collective-farm workers were not issued internal passports at all, hence keeping them tied to the farms like serfs in earlier times. And former criminals, political prisoners, and other "undesirables" were not given residence permits within 101 kilometers (63 miles) of most major cities in an attempt to isolate them from the majority of urban dwellers. Even ordinary Soviet citizens had to obtain a temporary residence permit if they planned to visit another city for more than three days, and the maximum stay allowed in certain closed cities, such as Moscow and Vladivostok, was only one month. The *propiska* system thus provided the mechanism by which the state controlled the migration of its people from rural to urban areas and from one city to another.

Soviet citizens inevitably found ways to circumvent this system of internal passports and residence registrations, which was never as effective at controlling the population as the government would have liked. The system was supposedly outlawed by the new Russian Federation constitution adopted in 1993, but in practice many of its features continued to exist. During the time that I lived in Russia, its citizens still had to obtain a residence permit to live in many cities, and some cities were still designated closed. In 1993 and 1994 my own foreigner's residence visa had to list not only the city I was working in, but also the names of any other Russian cities that I planned to visit—even though at the time I obtained the visa, I had no idea which places I might want to visit during the following year.

A joke broadcast on Radio Moscow in 1994 told about a rich American buying the Lenin Mausoleum in Moscow, transporting it to the United States, and installing it on top of a tall building in a major metropolis. After a while, Lenin woke up, looked around, and said, "Wow! This is just what I thought life would be like!" But if Lenin had been able to witness the urban development of his own country through seven decades of communism, his eyes would have beheld a very different landscape. The Soviet government controlled urban development to such an extent that Russian cities today look considerably different from those in the West. Moreover the centralized planning of the Soviets produced such uniform buildings that most Russian cities from Kursk to Khabarovsk are remarkably similar in appearance. What distinguishes one city from another is only the older pre-Revolutionary architecture (lacking in the new cities such as Akademgorodok and Severobaikal'sk in Siberia, which were built during the second half of the twentieth century), as well as a city's particular geographic location—next to rivers, as with Irkutsk, or on a series of hills and picturesque bays, as with Vladivostok.

Most major cities in the United States have a high center of tall, modern skyscrapers, surrounded by low suburbs of one- or two-story, single-family houses and scatterings of two- or three-story apartment buildings, all serviced by strip centers and shopping malls within or near the suburban areas. In contrast, most large Russian cities have relatively low central areas, composed of older buildings constructed prior to World War II, surrounded by newer, increasingly taller buildings farther away from the city center. Sprawling American-style suburbs, with their individual homes, crew-cut lawns, and paved, well-lighted streets were virtually unknown in Russia.

After the Bolshevik Revolution, the first major effort to provide housing for the Soviet Union's growing urban population occurred in the 1930s, with the construction of two- and three-story apartment buildings made of bricks covered with stucco. But in the middle of the twentieth century, World War II not only brought a halt to new residential construction throughout the country, it also resulted in the destruction of thousands of villages and towns, as well as whole sections of major cities in the western part of the Soviet Union, causing an even more acute housing shortage than before.

At the beginning of World War II, only one-third of the Soviet Union's citizens lived in urban areas; by the last decade of the twentieth century, three-quarters of the Russian Federation's population lived in cities. Throughout the 1950s, as the Soviet Union tried to recover economically and militarily from the war, most urban dwellers still lived in *kommunalki*—small, often crowded, communal apartments located in various kinds of multistory buildings, most of them constructed before World War II. A type of housing arrangement dating from the early Soviet period, these communal apartments often housed twenty or thirty people, or more, with individual families living in a single room that opened onto a central corridor used by all the other occupants, who also shared a single kitchen, toilet, and bath.

During the Khrushchev era of the late 1950s and early 1960s, the Soviets began to address the serious housing shortage in their country by constructing thousands of boxy, five-story, prefabricated concrete apartment buildings. Known as *khrushchevki*, these ugly, cheaply made buildings had small, low-ceilinged, twelve-square-meter apartments intended (theoretically, at least) for occupancy by only one family each. By the late 1960s the Soviets were putting up high-rise apartment buildings of nine, eleven, and fourteen stories—made of prefabricated, reinforced concrete slabs—in several major cities. Built with elevators that seldom worked, these high-rise structures contained hundreds of small apartments consisting of two or three rooms, plus kitchen, toilet, and bath, designed to house individual families.

Throughout the Brezhnev, Gorbachev, and Yeltsin eras, the Russians continued to build these huge high-rise apartment buildings, many of them sixteen to twenty-two stories tall, some of which housed fifteen hundred to two thousand people each. These massive, monotonous-looking, poorly constructed high-rises—similar in appearance to many low-income, public-housing projects in the United States—were built around the edges of Russian cities, where repetitive rows of identical apartment blocks, often surrounded by fields of mud, were grouped together into *mikrorayony*, municipal "microdistricts" of eight thousand to twelve thousand inhabitants. Tom and I used to joke about finding an appropriate term to describe the Soviet/ Russian architecture of these relentlessly boring buildings: Art Nogo. Art Dilap. Terminal Modernism. Slum Structuralism. Bau Louse.

Situated far from the city center—where most of the shopping and entertainment facilities were located—these microdistricts were designed, in theory, to have their own neighborhood shops, schools, sports facilities, and recreation areas. But theory and practice seldom coincided in Russia. Long after these urban agglomerations were built, many of them still lacked telephone service, retail stores, schools, parking spaces, sidewalks, playgrounds, landscaping, paved streets, or public transportation. Some of the worst did not even have the water and electricity connected when the residents moved in. And the people who in lived in these microdistricts often had to commute long distances on foot or by whatever minimal public transportation was available, not only to get to work or school each day, but even to shop for staples such as bread and milk.

Beyond these microdistricts of high-rise apartment blocks that ring every Russian city, the urban landscape became low and flat again, characterized by a seemingly haphazard scattering of single-story houses, old and new, some made of logs or planks, others little more than tar-paper–covered shacks, some well-maintained, others fallen into disrepair. Near the edge of the city, these were usually the homes of elderly, poor, or working-class people who lived in them year round. Farther away from the city limits, wooden houses ranging from romantic-looking, two-story, pre-Revolutionary edifices to small, modern A-frames were more likely to be dachas belonging to city dwellers who used them as weekend retreats and summer holiday homes. In the early 1990s a new type of house also began to appear in Russian cities, both inside the city and on the periphery, in seemingly random locations: detached, two- and three-story brick houses, which the Russians called *kottedzhi* (cottages), each built to house a single family of Russia's nouveaux riches, the only people who could afford to purchase such dwellings.

In both Irkutsk and Vladivostok, Tom and I lived in recently built microdistricts where our host universities had purchased or leased new apartments for the American faculty. As in other high-rise microdistricts—where the majority of Russia's urban population now lives—our neighbors came from all walks of life: blue-collar workers, white-collar professionals, elderly pensioners, young entrepreneurs, and members of the local *mafiya*. Some of them were recent immigrants from rural areas of the Russian Federation, whom our better-educated Russian friends often described as *"nekul'turnyy"* (uncultured, bad-mannered). Others were Chinese, Koreans, Georgians, and Chechens, all of whom were also considered to be *nekul'turnyy* and were looked down upon, socially, by their Slavic neighbors. This mix of social classes in a single apartment building was typical throughout the country, largely as a result of the low rents that the government, first the Soviet Union and then the Russian Federation, charged for housing. However, that situation was beginning to change in the mid-1990s, as Russians with more money sought to rent or purchase better living accommodations in the neighborhoods they deemed most desirable. And of course even the so-called classless Soviet Union always had certain areas within a city that were considered better places to live than others, where housing was available only to the political, intellectual, cultural, and military elites who had the necessary influence to acquire such accommodations.

Observers in both Russia and the West have described the crime, drunkenness, vandalism, juvenile delinquency, and high rates of divorce that often occur in these microdistricts of anonymous apartment blocks—social problems they attribute, in part, to the residents' lack of a sense of community. And indeed Russia's rapid industrialization and urbanization has certainly produced feelings of rootlessness and alienation among many of the people who have migrated from the country to the city. On the other hand, most urban Russians are only a couple of generations removed from their rural roots, and many have tried to maintain, or at least reestablish, a sense of community within their new surroundings. After living in these apartment blocks on the fringes of two major cities in Asian Russia, I came to the conclusion that this continuance of old ways in new housing has created a contemporary urban social environment that could be characterized as "the high-rise village."

In our own high-rise villages of Siberia and the Russian Far East, the external appearance of the modern microdistricts certainly had none of the rustic appeal of old Russian villages. In Vladivostok we lived in a typical ten-story building practically identical to the hundreds of other high-rises that crowded the hills around the city. Our nine-story building in Irkutsk was almost indistinguishable from the one in Vladivostok. From a distance the flat facades all looked as if they had been conceived by the same mind, designed by the same architect, and built by the same company. Close up, the exterior surroundings, the buildings themselves, and the interior stairwells rivaled the worst American tenement housing for squalor and decay.

Walking home from the bus stop nearest our apartment in Vladivostok, we had to trudge several blocks up a steep hill on a busy road with no sidewalks and no shoulders, while trying to avoid being splashed with water and mud from the cars and trucks barreling by at high speed. Halfway up the hill, pedestrians taking a shortcut to our microdistrict had worn a footpath through the dirt and rubble, wending its way over sharp rocks, electrical cables, and large pieces of scrap metal. At the top of the hill, a bumpy, wavy asphalt sidewalk—with steel rods sticking up out of it in several places—led the way to our apartment building. Although the sidewalk had only recently been poured, it was already covered with broken glass and littered with trash.

The small "yard" around our apartment building in Vladivostok had no grass, no flowers, no trees. Piles of trash burned near the building, next to the corroding chassis of a car that had been stripped clean. A few old shipping containers served as makeshift garages and temporary housing for workers still constructing the new neighborhood. At night, when fog enveloped those rusty metal hulks scattered around the hillside, the cold, diffused glare of a single mercury-vapor streetlight turned the scene into a setting from *Blade Runner*.

Inside the building's unprepossessing entryways, the five communal stairwells continued the visual, aural, and olfactory theme of dirt and deterioration. Crudely finished concrete stairs led to each landing. The elevator, which seldom functioned, was often wet with pools of urine, so we usually walked up the unlighted stairs to our apartment on the fifth floor, carrying a flashlight to guide us over the obstacles that sometimes littered the steps: animal feces, human vomit, rotting rubbish, broken bottles, smeared blood. During the dim light of day, we could see the graffiti that scarred the walls: "SEX" and "FUCK," in English; "SERGEY WAS HERE" and "DIMA LOVES SASHA," in Russian; "FUK YU," in the universal language of the limited adolescent mind.

On each landing an opening in the wall next to the elevator shaft provided access to a garbage chute where residents dumped their household refuse, which fell into a stinking metal bin on the ground floor. Far too small for the forty apartments they served in each stairwell, the trash bins overflowed onto the area near the entrances to the building, becoming an organic magnet for scavenging dogs, cats, and rats, as well as providing a continuous source of fuel for the bonfires set outdoors (and sometimes in the hallways) by children who lived in the neighborhood. Tom once saw a full-length fur coat mangled among the potato peels, orange skins, and vodka bottles that filled the trash bin; given Vladivostok's reputation for crime, he wondered for a moment if there might even be a dead body inside.

In Irkutsk the communal corridors in our apartment building were similar in appearance to those in Vladivostok but usually cleaner and somewhat safer. In both cities, however, I felt like a character in a film noir when I came home at night and had to make my way up those hazardous sets of stairs in the dark, not knowing what awaited me on the ascent. The lack of color recalled old black-and-white movies, as the roving beam from my flashlight met the knife-sharp shaft of light from someone's slightly opened apartment door before it was quickly pulled shut and bolted against unknown dangers from outside. Even the crude graffiti on the walls was painted in black or white—not surprisingly in a country where cans of colored spray paint were practically nonexistent and where even standard paint and brushes were hard to find.

Entrance to a high-rise village in Vladivostok.

Our apartment buildings in both cities were only a year old when we moved in, but the Russian propensity for producing instant urban decay had already turned their public areas into slums. Yet behind each apartment's steel doors, secured with multiple locks suitable for a medieval dungeon, the residents had managed to create their own personal, comfortable world, seemingly in defiance of the blight that lay only a few feet away, beyond their windows and within their halls. Whenever we visited the apartments of friends in Siberia and the Russian Far East, we were struck by this contrast between the exterior and interior worlds of the high-rise village. Even though the texture of daily life in Russia could be as prickly as coarse wool on the outside, it was often as soft and fuzzy as mohair on the inside.

During 1993 and 1994 we lived in three Russian apartments—one in Irkutsk and two in Vladivostok. All of them had an entry hall, small kitchen, living room, bedroom, bathroom large enough for only a tub and sink, and a separate tiny closet for the toilet; the apartments in Vladivostok also had a second bedroom, which we used as a study. The Vladivostok apartments measured approximately seven hundred square feet, not counting the balcony, compared to five hundred square feet in Irkutsk. Despite their small size in relation to most American apartments, our Russian quarters were large by local standards, almost an embarrassment of space compared to the crowded conditions under which most Russians lived. Many Russians worked their whole lives to obtain the kind of apartments that were provided to us because of our university position and foreign nationality. Before moving into our high-rise building in Vladivostok, one of our Russian neighbors had lived for several years with her husband and two children in a much smaller two-room apartment, along with three other members of her husband's family. But the worst situation among our closest circle of friends was that of a young, well-educated Siberian couple who were struggling to make ends meet in Russia's hyperinflated economy. They lived with their two small children and a friend from their hometown, all crowded into a one-room apartment measuring approximately ten by sixteen feet, with no hot water and no heat. At night the three adults slept on the floor and the two children slept on the divan.

The first semester in Vladivostok, the university provided our furnished apartment free of charge. The next semester we taught there, a year later, we paid 5,054 rubles (approximately $1.75) per month in rent for an identical apartment on a different floor of the same building. In Irkutsk, during the spring of 1994, we paid rent of 22,613 rubles (approximately $13) each month for a smaller furnished apartment. In both cities these rents were artificially low, reflecting the continued subsidization of rents by the state, a holdover from the Soviet era. In 1994 the average Russian household spent only 2 to 3 percent of its income on housing. And although a large number of Russians were now beginning to buy their own apartments, they were still not permitted to purchase the land on which those private dwellings sat.

Our apartments in Vladivostok were outfitted with the best new furniture that money could buy in the Russian Far East. Even so, the style was reminiscent of 1950s America, and the quality of workmanship left much to be desired. In the living room a brown, overstuffed, vinyl-covered couch and two vinyl armchairs faced a large, glass-fronted, wooden wall unit with a labyrinth of cabinets, drawers, and shelves, which occupied most of the longest wall. A Chinese-made brass-and-smoked-glass coffee table and matching television stand stood out among the stodgier Russian furniture. The study contained only two small desks, made of glossy lacquered wood veneer, with two short bookshelves mounted on the wall above them. Our Russian bedroom suite consisted of a small clothes armoire, a grandiose triple-mirror dresser, and a double bed that was so poorly constructed the slats broke soon after we moved in, sending us crashing to the floor one night, as also happened to our American colleagues in the apartments upstairs. After repeatedly catching and tearing her clothing on the badly made furniture, one of the American professors commented, "Have you ever seen anything manufactured in Russia that didn't look like a *reject?*"

Given the general Russian proclivity for clashing colors and mixed motifs in interior decoration, the walls and floors in our Vladivostok apartments showed remarkably understated taste: white ceilings, door frames, and window frames; wallpaper in muted, neutral colors; and a floral patterned carpet in shades of brown, beige, and soft yellow, which hid most of the dull brown linoleum floor. But the windows were covered with flamingo-printed translucent scrims shot through with gold lamé threads, overlaid by heavy drapes with a bold pattern of salmon-and-white flowers and mustard-brown leaves. And the bed covering would have been at home in a Japanese love hotel: a bright pink sateen bedspread with a triple ruffle around the edges and a huge ruffled heart in the center, surrounded by machine-embroidered roses. Two matching ruffled, rosed, and heart-centered pillow shams completed the gaudy ensemble.

Casement windows let in a large amount of light that was especially welcome during the long Russian winter. But the double-paned windows and floor-to-ceiling balcony doors in all of our Russian apartments were made of such wavy, poor-quality glass that if you walked past a closed window while peering at something outside, you could actually get motion sickness. Inset in the upper right- or left-hand side of each room's bank of larger windows was a much smaller window, a *fortochka*, that could be opened for ventilation without letting in undesirable elements, meteorological or criminal. Since none of the windows had screens, however, Russians sometimes nailed pieces of white synthetic scrim material, stretched taut, over some of their windows to keep out insects during the summer. One resourceful American professor improvised by stretching her old panty hose across a window. And in winter Nature delighted us by tracing lacy frost patterns on both the outer and inner panes of glass.

All three of our apartment kitchens were of similar size and basic appointments: approximately six by twelve feet, with a single porcelain sink, a few cheaply made pressboard-and-plastic-veneer cabinets, blue-green tile wainscoting in Vladivostok and painted plaster walls in Irkutsk. Underneath a small, white, plastic-topped kitchen table were four low, square stools, with hard seats and no backs. (A separate dining-room table and chairs with backs were furnishings that we could only dream about in Russia.) But the kitchens in Vladivostok were much better equipped than in Irkutsk. In Vladivostok we had a full-size, Korean Gold Star refrigerator, a Russian-made Pluton microwave oven, a French Leger combination food-processor-and-blender, and a Russian electric stove. Tom called our first one "the Stove from Hell" because none of the burners on top worked correctly, the oven blackened everything that was put into it regardless of the temperature setting, and if all the burners were turned on at the same time, the stove blew a fuse and knocked out the electricity in half the apartment. The kitchen cabinets were stocked with a Russian-made porcelain dinner set and tea set, a gaudily painted electric samovar that smelled of lacquer whenever it heated up, an enameled tea kettle and two saucepans from China, a Teflon frying pan from Algeria, a set of stainless steel flatware, a couple of covered casseroles from Czechoslovakia, and, most incongruous of all, six Donald Duck drinking glasses and two big Bart Simpson bath towels.

The apartment in Irkutsk represented a step down in our standard of living. What was most depressing was not the apartment's smaller size or its paucity of furniture—or even the bad taste in which it was decorated—but all the things we had to repair to make the place liveable. The toilet seat was broken (either you sat on the toilet or the seat did, but not both of you at the same time); the bathroom sink was falling off the wall; and the windows had to be sealed against the Siberian winter. In Vladivostok the university had sent someone to install weather stripping around all of our windows in late

September, before the first frost. But when we arrived in Irkutsk the following January, our new apartment felt like an ice cave. Nothing had been done to winterproof the double-glazed windows, which were so poorly made and badly installed that the biting wind blew right through them. A week after we moved in, the university logistics office tried to remedy the situation by sending us the materials for our first Siberian do-it-yourself project: putty, to daub into the cracks between the windows and walls, which had never been properly sealed when the building was constructed; strips of white paper that looked like adding-machine tape; and a large bar of crude brown soap. The last two items were a puzzle to us, until the deliveryman showed us how to wet the bar of soap, pull the strips of paper over it, then stick the paper over all the places where the wooden frames met the window sills and jambs. This provided a simple, if not particularly aesthetic, solution to the problem, even though we had to repeat the process frequently during the winter, whenever the strips of paper dried out and fluttered to the floor like autumn foliage.

The kitchen in Irkutsk was equipped with cheap cabinets that kept falling apart, a three-burner electric stove that never worked properly, and not much else except an apartment-size refrigerator. But at least we didn't have to keep our food cold on the balcony outside or hang it onto the exterior of the building in a cloth bag or small wooden box, as did so many urban Siberians who lacked the luxury of interior refrigeration. As in Vladivostok, however, the apartment in Irkutsk had no other modern appliances that would have been common in the United States—no dishwasher, garbage disposal, clothes dryer, coffeemaker, computer, or telephone. The Vladivostok apartments did come equipped with an electric vacuum cleaner, but for sweeping the uncarpeted floor in Irkutsk, we had only a bundle of straw tied together at the top, with no handle; for mopping the linoleum, we used two pieces of wood nailed together in the shape of a T, to push around a wet rag on the floor.

Each of our apartments had a large color television set in the living room. But the television in Vladivostok had a problem with the color adjustment: the only image we could get was in black-and-white with red accents, as if a political ghost from the past were trying to fight its way back into the electronic consciousness of the present. On screen the white-blue-and-red Russian flag always appeared as stripes of white, black, and red. In commercials for perfumes and candies, the only color was the shiny red of the models' luscious lips. News reports about the grain harvest looked like old black-and-white, Soviet-era documentaries with bright red tractors

hand-painted on the film. But most curious of all was the electronic relationship between the television set and our portable electric hair dryer:
whenever we switched off the hair dryer in the bedroom, it somehow acted
as a remote control that also turned off the television in the living room—
making us wonder what other electronic anomalies might be lurking elsewhere in that apartment.

Each apartment was also equipped with a small, portable, Russian-made
"semi-automatic" washing machine, with rubber hoses for hooking it up to
the water faucet in the bathroom sink and draining the wash water into the
bathtub. "Semi-automatic" was an unintentionally ironic term for these
machines, which required a fair amount of time and manual labor to do
each load of wash. Afterward we hung up the laundry to dry on wall-mounted
racks over the bathtub or on a clothesline outside on the balcony. When the
laundry on the balcony froze solid in the Siberian winter, we beat the ice
out of it by hand, then brought the clothes inside to finish drying on the
radiators. With such an inefficient system, it took an entire day to do a
week's laundry for just the two of us—not counting the drying time, which
added another three or four days to the whole process.

When one of my American colleagues in Vladivostok complained to the
university logistics coordinator that her washing machine didn't work—it
flooded the bathroom and hall with water whenever she tried to use it—the
official replied matter-of-factly, "Of course. That's because the machine is
new." The implication was that any appliance manufactured in Russia naturally had to be repaired soon after the purchasers brought it home. That
same shoddiness of workmanship extended to the construction of buildings
as well, a legacy of the old Soviet system that continued, with no sign of
abatement, in the new Russian Federation of the 1990s.

The interior finishing of high-rise apartment buildings was a case in point.
Doors and windows did not fit, floors were uneven, linoleum was loose,
walls were cracked, paint peeled off, wind blew through the electrical outlets, bathroom and kitchen fixtures were not properly installed—all of which
meant that the residents had to repair the new apartments as soon as they
moved in. The inefficiency of having to redo work that wasn't done correctly
in the first place was typical of the Russian system, but the poor construction
of these hastily built high-rises had potentially dangerous implications as
well. In Vladivostok I saw large multistory buildings whose prefab slabs had
been so precariously positioned on their foundations that a shift of less than
two inches would cause the entire edifice to collapse like a house of cards.
And since both Vladivostok and Irkutsk are located in major earthquake

zones, I always feared that a powerful temblor—like the one that later almost leveled the town of Neftegorsk on Sakhalin Island in 1995—would flatten these fragile cities in minutes.

Each apartment in these high-rise villages had a concrete balcony that added fifty to sixty square feet to the apartment's total floor space. Many residents enclosed their balconies with glass windows, thus turning this exterior area into another room of the apartment. Some balconies, like ours, were merely fitted with iron grilles to deter burglars but were otherwise left open to the weather. Whether open or enclosed, however, most balconies were used primarily as storage rooms, since few apartments had built-in pantries or closets.

The artifacts visible on these architectural appendages often provided clues to the occupants' hobbies, interests, skills, or professions. Many balconies exhibited big glass bottles of homemade sauerkraut next to smaller jars of jewel-toned jellies and jams. In autumn pale green cabbages were piled next to burlap bags of carrots and potatoes. Hanging to dry on clotheslines were whole yellow onions and ears of fresh corn, strings of brown mushrooms and bright red peppers, and rows of gutted fish, their silvery skins glistening in the golden light. In spring, behind the greenhouse glass of enclosed balconies, narrow wooden shelves held pots of tomato and cucumber seedlings, cradling the gardeners' hopes for a successful summer harvest.

Throughout the year blankets, pillows, Oriental rugs, and fur coats were hung on the balconies to air. On one balcony in Vladivostok, three rows of clotheslines were filled with women's tights—in several shades of lilac, purple, salmon, orange, and pink—fluttering in the breeze like a backdrop for an avant-garde stage set. And in the high-rise villages of Irkutsk, I occasionally saw rows of freshly skinned animal pelts—red fox, white arctic fox, brown mink, even bear skins—strung up on balcony clotheslines.

Old furniture served as makeshift storage closets on many balconies. In Vladivostok the wooden cabinet of an early television set, its innards removed, was mounted on a balcony rail and used as an outdoor refrigerator. Bicycles, bathtubs, sleds, and spare tires were suspended off the exteriors of balconies when there was no space for them inside. From one balcony protruded a homemade television antenna: four metal 35mm film reels, wired together and attached to the end of a pole. And on many of the balcony ledges cats of all colors paced back and forth across their limited turfs, sniffing the wind, swatting at seagulls, and basking in the warmth of the sun.

From my own balconies and windows in both cities, I watched an ever-changing kaleidoscope of high-rise village life. In the spaces between apartment buildings, residents brought their children to play, their dogs to run, their cats to scratch. Short, round *babushki*—made even rounder by their many layers of clothing—gathered on splintery wooden benches to swap gossip and soak up the pale winter sun. Preschool children played in sandboxes defined by rickety boards that separated these "recreation areas" from the identical dirt and sand that surrounded all the buildings. And kids climbed on rusty jungle gyms that looked much like the other pieces of old scrap metal littering the landscape nearby.

A *babushka* in short gray ankle socks and a printed head scarf tended a little blonde girl in a frilly dress, her hair tied up with a large purple organza bow attached to a Day-Glo plastic Slinky toy that hung down her back like a psychedelic ponytail. Teenage girls wearing the latest imported fashions paraded past pimply-faced adolescent boys slouching in consciously casual poses around the entrances to the building. Younger boys mimicked mountain goats as they scurried, seemingly without effort, up and the down the rock faces of the steep embankment just outside our door. At times they reminded me of miniature Druids, building bonfires in the dark out of the garbage and old tires that accumulated around the high-rises. Unsupervised by adults, these rowdy children also set fire to the weeds below our windows and threw flaming trash onto other kids, laughing as they tried to set their clothes ablaze. And once, as the acrid smoke of burning rubber drifted through our windows, the little pyromaniacs threw stoppered bottles into the fire, the glass exploding in tempo to the finale of Tchaikovsky's *1812 Overture*, which happened to be playing on our portable stereo inside.

In winter the thump-thump of people beating their Oriental carpets spread out on the snow mingled with the chunk-chunk of shovels chipping away at the ice near the building's entryways, all to the unrelenting rhythms of rock and rap music from teenagers' boom boxes. Parents pulled their children along on wooden or aluminum sleds. Other kids skidded around on sleds improvised from discarded metal milk-bottle cases or old automobile doors. And in Vladivostok, I once watched a group of small children build a huge snowball bigger than any of them, then attempt, unsuccessfully, to push it to the top of a steep hill. They looked like little Russian Sisyphuses as they struggled to inch the snowball upward, then retreated after gaining only a little ground, their efforts a visual metaphor for the many obstacles they would inevitably face as they grew into adults in the Russian Federation of the twenty-first century.

Peering out my windows, I often encountered unexpected sights: Huge, noisy snowplows lumbering by on treads, like tanks. Olive-drab American military vehicles, now owned by Russians, with "US ARMY" and their military identification numbers still stenciled on the doors. A big backhoe pulling up to our building in a cloud of dust and the driver getting out to deliver a large bouquet of fresh flowers to someone inside. A woman reaching down and putting a handful of snow into the mouth of an unresisting child. One Sunday morning, in broad daylight, I saw a well-dressed man stealing wood from the construction site nearby. On Sunday nights in the autumn, hundreds of potatoes were spread out to dry on the asphalt driveway, after people came back to the city from a weekend of digging in their dacha gardens.

Danger was never far away. Organized criminals, petty thieves, and casual muggers all preyed on the residents of the high-rise village. Below our back window in Vladivostok, the body of a man was found in a newly opened private parking lot that held 150 cars inside its chain-link fence, his corpse partially eaten by the guard dogs set loose in the lot every night. Twice outside our apartment building in Irkutsk, major explosions rattled the windows and shook the walls, the blasts so loud and percussive that they might have been caused by bombs. Another time in Irkutsk, a child was killed in the entrance of a nearby building, when he pulled the pin on a hand grenade he had found in the forest and brought home for a toy. The spot where he died soon became a small shrine, marked by sad offerings of flowers and little mementos left there by the residents.

The high-rise village was the setting for so many surrealistic scenes that I began to see them simply as a normal part of daily life in Russia: A parade of three jolly drunks in the middle of the afternoon—a man in a white sport coat and an Arabian headdress, followed by another fellow wearing a mixture of several different military uniforms, both happily reeling to the music of an old accordion played by an inebriated woman staggering along behind. Four pig's feet, carefully arranged on the ground next to a trash bin, with a pile of french fries perfectly placed in the middle of this arty installation. An empty bottle of Sudden Death vodka—its black-and-silver label showing a skull sporting a top hat—shining up from a pile of rotten potatoes. A frozen gray pigeon lying on its back in the snow, as a black cat gnawed on its innards, the bird's red blood the only bright color in the Siberian winterscape of black, white, and gray. Moonlight glittering on an icy patch of ground where a whirlwind gathered dozens of clear plastic bags into an urban ghost dance in the freshly fallen snow, a phantasmagoric trash storm of filmy plastic moving in a whispery spiral beneath the building's bleak facade.

Perhaps the most extraordinary sight was the herd of horses that came to graze on the weeds growing in the spaces between the apartment buildings in our microdistrict of Vladivostok. I spotted the first horses one evening in late August, 1994: an emaciated gray mare and her skeletal brown foal, searching for something green to eat in our blighted urban landscape. Surprised at seeing horses in such a setting, I wondered how long they could survive in the city before falling prey to starvation, traffic, or someone's hunger for free meat. As the horses continued to graze on the tufts of scraggly grass outside our window, I watched several children approach and try to feed them by hand. Occasionally the skittish mare would bolt for a few feet, scattering children along the roadside. Then a young couple strolled by, the man stopping to stroke the neck of the mare, who relaxed at his touch. Next a collie and a German shepherd raced past, spooking the foal but hardly disturbing the mare. But every time I looked out the window to check on the horses foraging in the lingering light, I feared seeing the little hooligans who lived in our building throwing stones at the forlorn pair of animals, just like they did at the stray cats and dogs that tried to eke out an existence in our high-rise village.

The next day I saw two scrawny brown mares and a hungry brown colt walking dazedly down a busy street nearby, as cars swerved left and right to dodge the disoriented animals. When two more horses showed up that evening to graze on the ridge outside our window, I asked my friend Alla, who lived in our building, where all of those horses had come from.

"Oh, it's awful," she sighed. "They come from the park below where we live."

That park was actually a fair distance downhill from our microdistrict.

"Why do they come from the park?" I persisted. "And why are they wandering around our neighborhood? They look pitiful. They're starving. I feel so sorry for them."

"So do I," Alla replied. "You see, they belong to the city park—for children to ride. At least that's the way it was before. But now there's no money to feed the horses, so they just let them out to find food wherever they can. It's terrible," she muttered, as if she were both saddened and embarrassed by the situation. "They're turned out of their stables during the day, and then they find their way home at night. It's terrible, terrible. . . ."

In early October I encountered the largest number of horses I had ever seen in Vladivostok. Coming home from work in the rush-hour traffic on

Patrice Lumumba Street, I suddenly spotted a man astride a bony mare, herding twenty-two horses down the road toward the park—the Russian version of an urban cowboy. Earlier I had watched a young woman on an Appaloosa round up three loose horses headed toward a murderous intersection that was almost gridlocked by angry traffic merging from several directions. A slim blonde wearing shiny jogging pants and a strapless Spandex top that barely covered her breasts, she was an excellent equestrienne, focusing on her work and keeping her cool in a situation that would have unnerved both a horse and a rider with less *sang-froid*.

During September and October, groups of grazing horses became such an accepted part of our urban environment that I expected to see them whenever I looked out my windows. In the golden evening light, kids skateboarded between the mares, and small children came up to pet the foals. Once I saw a young girl hugging a colt, then two other girls arrived with their hands full of wildflowers and proceeded to decorate the head of the little horse. The horses seemed to take all of this in stride, as if it were perfectly natural for them to be wandering around in a city, surrounded by tall buildings, noisy automobiles, yipping dogs, and little girls intent on dressing them in flowers.

As the horses continued to haunt our urban landscape that autumn, I happened to come across an observation by Eugenia Ginzburg in her classic account of life as a prisoner in a Soviet gulag, *Within the Whirlwind*. Describing the paradox of sharing the happiness of other prisoners inside the barbed wire of a penal camp in the Russian Far East, she wrote, "from my childhood days onward I had always noticed that people's faces light up when they are watching some little wild animal that has strayed into a built-up area. A hedgehog or a squirrel, say. . . . How their faces are transformed! A sort of childlike simplicity is visible behind their irritable, gloomy, city-dweller expressions. An astonishing glow lights up their faces, piercing through the malevolent mask." That same effect was evident on the faces of the high-rise villagers in Vladivostok whenever the horses appeared in our neighborhood, as if the animals' presence evoked memories of more pleasant places and times.

After the long Siberian winter, an inevitable aspect of springtime in the high-rise village was the hidden refuse and frozen filth that emerged from the melting snow: used condoms, rotted root vegetables, a solitary hat or shoe or glove, broken plastic toys, piles of dog feces, a child's hunting bow made from a birch branch tied with a piece of string. Especially grisly were the bodies of dogs and cats that had died or been killed during the winter and had lain there for several months, rigid under their shroud of snow. They reminded me of stories I heard about prisoners who had escaped from Siberian camps in the winter and then froze to death in the forest, only to be discovered in spring when the snow melted, exposing their corpses. Siberians called them *"podsnezhniki"* (literally, "under the snow"), the same term they use for the wildflowers (usually translated as "snowdrops") that are the first blossoms of spring to push their way up through the still snow-covered ground.

Several stray cats hung around our apartment building in Irkutsk, living off garbage and whatever scraps of food the occupants put out for them. But one day in March, most of the cats suddenly disappeared. I later learned that it was common practice at that time of year for the people employed as janitors in these high-rise buildings—phantom "concierges" whom we never saw—to poison any stray animals that survived the harsh winter. A few cats residing in the hallways on the top floor escaped this horrible fate, and one of them soon made her way to our apartment door on the eighth floor. A black-and-white kitten with huge golden eyes, she reminded us of our own cats that we had reluctantly left behind with friends when we came to Russia. Murlyka, as we named her, quickly moved into our hearts and into our home. Of course we had no choice: a Russian superstition says that if a new cat comes to your house, you should take it in because the cat will bring you good luck.

Many Russians kept house pets despite the difficulties of providing food and sanitation for them. In Irkutsk our Murlyka lived on Russian *kolbasa* sausage—"cat food in a tube," as Tom called it—and used a litter box filled with buckets of sand that Tom carried up eight flights of stairs from the construction site nearby. In Vladivostok large black Great Danes seemed to be one of the most popular pets in our microdistrict—many of them named Bagheera, after the inky-black panther in Kipling's *Jungle Book*. In our own building, one of these big Bagheeras shared a three-room apartment with our friends Sergey and Natasha, their two children, and Sergey's mother; somehow the dog seemed to take up more space than all of the human inhabitants combined. We knew other urban Russians, not far removed from their rural roots, who would have liked for their children to grow up with animals of their own but who lived in such tiny apartments that having pets was out of the question.

From our first days in Vladivostok, our neighbors Alla and Pëtr Brovko welcomed Tom and me into their home and into their lives. At family celebrations, at simple suppers, and on Russian holidays, through long con-

Microdistrict of new high-rise apartment buildings on the hills of Vladivostok.

versations around their kitchen table and over sumptuous dinners in their living room, we learned more than we had ever hoped to know about life in Russia, past and present. Alla herself was a can-do person—a rarity in Russia, in my experience. Whenever I suggested something that I would like to see or do or learn more about, Alla would immediately say, "Well, why not? Let's do it!" She was always the first person we asked our many questions about family relationships, Russian cuisine, shopping for food, and the seeming anomalies of Russian life. She and Pëtr also introduced us to other Russians who became our friends, all of whom welcomed us into the community of high-rise villagers in Vladivostok. In a country that worked almost entirely on the basis of personal connections, those friendships turned out to be a greater boon than we could ever have imagined.

But not all of our neighbors were so nice. During our first autumn in Vladivostok, the people who lived directly above us played loud rap, rock, and electronic music both day and night. When they had parties, the music was all too live: piano, accordion, and drunken, maudlin singing. One night, just as we went to bed, we heard a terrible crash over our bedroom ceiling, as if someone had dropped a refrigerator on the floor right above it. But the most irritating noises were the sounds of hammering, sawing, and drilling, so frequent that we felt like we were living below a carpentry shop.

Added to that was the pulse of pounding feet, like someone repeatedly jumping off the furniture onto the floor just over our heads—a sound so loud and forceful that it rattled our teacups in their saucers. We soon began referring to these neighbors as "the Remont Family" (*remont* is the Russian word for "repair"), after Tom came up with the theory that they wrecked their apartment every weekend with those rowdy parties, then spent the next week repairing the damage before the cycle started all over again.

When we moved to Irkutsk the next spring, our upstairs neighbors were so bad that we actually missed the Remont Family in Vladivostok. Often we heard a woman's voice letting loose with a high-volume, staccato barrage of venomous verbal abuse, like sustained machine-gun fire, followed by sounds of family violence—shouts, thunks, children crying, feet running across the floor (our ceiling)—all to the accompaniment of a radio blaring rap music. Seldom did we hear any sounds of joy from that apartment; more often, we felt like unwilling witnesses to a depressing drama that was all too real.

The noisy neighbor problem was even worse when we returned to Vladivostok the following fall. The Remont Family had apparently finished their work and moved on, replaced by another group who persisted in partying almost every night of the week, with the fun beginning around 11:00 P.M. and lasting until the early hours of the morning. Many nights we tried to sleep over the sounds of drunken male and female voices badly singing folk and rock songs to the accompaniment of taped music, while the revelers danced with their boots on, producing a rhythmic thudding that reverberated through our ceiling. Sometimes the fun was followed by arguments, shouting matches, screams, and fights. When the occupants of other apartments protested by banging on their radiators, they only succeeded in adding their own raucous racket to the general uproar.

The fights upstairs—with the shouts of the beating and the beaten, the crashes of overturned furniture, the angry voices in a language that was not Russian, the television turned up loud to cover the screams—made the verbal and physical abuse we had heard above us in Irkutsk seem like a simple soap opera compared to the drama of punch and pain in Vladivostok. After these altercations we sometimes saw fresh blood on the doors, walls, and floors in our stairwell. But whenever we heard the sounds of fights, or even strange noises in the hall, we knew better than to step outside to see what was happening. Like everyone else in that high-rise village, we stayed inside our own apartments, safely hidden behind our two multilocked, heavy steel doors.

Rowdy, violent, and suspicious neighbors were only one of the many problems of living in these multistory buildings. One of the greatest difficulties was the lack of dependable utilities, all of which were provided by the municipal governments. Electric power, hot and cold water, and steam heat for the radiators all came from a few huge plants located in various sections of each city. Residential customers had no control over these basic utilities, other than to turn on the light switch, the water faucet, or the radiator and hope that any or all of them functioned as they were supposed to. In return, residents paid artificially low prices for these subsidized utilities. In Vladivostok in the early autumn of 1994, we paid a monthly bill of 1,200 rubles (approximately 45 cents at the time) for electricity—which jumped to 6,000 rubles ($1.85 at the latest exchange rate) by the end of that year. Our December bills for other utilities totaled 14,512 rubles ($5.30) for heating, 4,011 rubles ($1.45) for hot water, and 1,782 rubles (65 cents) for cold water and sewage—at a time when the average monthly wage in Russia was less than $90. Earlier that year in Irkutsk, our average electric bill had been 1,700 rubles (about $1.00) per month. Irkutsk State University did not require us to pay for the other utilities in our apartment, but I was told that the average cost for a family of four in Irkutsk that spring was only 319 rubles (20 cents) per month *total* for central heating, hot water, cold water, and sewage.

Electricity was fairly dependable in Irkutsk, but in Vladivostok it was a major problem. Both times that we lived in the Russian Far East, the city of Vladivostok lacked sufficient coal and oil to fuel its electric power plants. Money from state subsidies was running out, and revenue from residential and industrial customers, many of whom didn't pay their bills at all, was not enough to pay the rising prices for fossil fuels, most of which had to be transported thousands of miles by train from Siberia. So the municipal authorities rationed the dwindling fuel supplies by cutting off electricity to various parts of the city at different times of the day and night.

The first power outages occurred in October and got progressively worse as winter came on. We usually returned home from work around 6:00 P.M., after the sky was already black and icy winds had driven the temperature below freezing. But often only five or ten minutes after we arrived at our apartment, the electricity went off—which meant that we had to prepare and eat our evening meal by the light of a single candle. (Candles were scarce in a city of 650,000 people where power outages were a daily occurrence.) Our first candlelight dinner in October, 1993, was typical of many meals we would have under similar circumstances during that autumn in Vladivostok: smoked salmon with sour cream, a cucumber-and-tomato salad, slices of cheese, whole wheat bread liberally spread with butter, a bottle of chilled Hungarian wine, and chocolates from the local candy factory. After dinner we read books and magazines, graded papers, wrote exams, prepared lectures, or played Scrabble—all by candlelight. It seemed rather appropriate to read nineteenth-century Russian novels by the same source of illumination under which they were written—but somewhat strange to be reading the *New Yorker* and the *Economist* by the flickering light of a candle in the last decade of the twentieth century.

The most frustrating aspect of these power outages was their apparent randomness. We never knew for certain when, or for how long, the electricity would be on or off. Sometimes it would be cut off in the morning, sometimes at night. Occasionally it was off for only a few minutes; other times we were without electricity for hours or even days. We became so accustomed to these power outages that once when we returned home to a unlighted apartment, we sat in the dark for several hours, wondering when the electricity would come back on, before we realized that we had just forgotten to flip on the light switches. Most disconcerting of all were the times when we forgot to turn *off* the light switches in the evening, after the electricity had been cut off, only to be flooded with bright light in the middle of the night, long after we had gone to sleep, when the electricity suddenly came back on again.

Central heating in both Vladivostok and Irkutsk was actually "centralized heating," controlled by Big Brother rather than the individual consumer. Instead of each apartment or building having its own heating system, steam produced at a few large municipal heating plants was pumped through huge pipes to the radiators in hundreds of buildings throughout the city. Most of these pipes were located above ground, looking like giant metal umbilical cords attached to the buildings. Not only were they an eyesore (and an inescapable aspect of the urban landscape), they were also badly insulated and poorly maintained, with clouds of steam escaping from cracks in the pipes before the heat could even reach its destination.

The local government, not the individual consumer, controlled the times when heating was provided and the temperature at which it was set. In Vladivostok, October 15 was the date on which the centralized heating was traditionally turned on for the winter, but the energy crisis in 1994 pushed that date back to October 30 for our apartment building. Heating was intermittent, however: whenever the electricity was cut off, the steam heat went off, too, causing all the radiators in the building to gurgle, ping, and clang as the steam condensed and water drained out of them. If the electricity was off for more than a day, we had to wear thermal underwear indoors to combat the cold. But when the power came back on and the radiators rattled back to life, the apartment became so hot and stuffy we had to open the windows wide to make the rooms comfortable again, thus adding to the inefficiency of an already highly inefficient heating system.

Running water, hot or cold, was always a problem, too. The water that flowed through our taps in both Vladivostok and Irkutsk ranged in color from clear to amber to orange to purple to black, with accompanying aromas of petroleum, sewer gas, ham, rotten eggs, or fish. Often it also left an oily, slimy sludge in the bathtub and sink. City officials in Irkutsk touted their tap water as being completely pure and safe, but a sanitation expert from the United States who came to Irkutsk on a fact-finding trip in 1994 informed us that the water was full of industrial and organic pollutants. In Vladivostok, however, municipal authorities were finally forced to admit there was a problem: when cholera bacteria and other dangerous microorganisms were found in the city's water supply, local radio, television, and newspapers carried official reports advising everyone to boil the water before using it.

Tom and I took no chances. From our first day in Russia we purified all the water we used for drinking, cooking, and tooth brushing, pumping the water by hand through a portable filtration device we had brought from the United States. Often we boiled the water first, a nightly ritual in Vladivostok whenever we had electricity. The next morning, Tom got up before I did, fixed breakfast, and pumped through the filter all the boiled water for use that day, storing it in eight 1.5-liter plastic bottles that originally held Del Monte fruit juices imported from Korea. We also kept a 10-liter plastic container full of filtered water in the kitchen, as an emergency supply for those many times when the water was cut off. Every day of our stay in Russia, Tom repeated this tedious task, often working by candlelight on dark winter mornings. As a result, we never suffered from digestive problems or other waterborne illnesses, as did some of our American colleagues who learned too late that purifying the water in Russia was just another necessary daily chore in the high-rise village.

But polluted water was better than none at all. Russians living in cities were accustomed to their hot water being cut off for one or two months during the summer, ostensibly for the pipes to be repaired, but sometimes even in the winter we went for weeks without any hot water (and no way to heat cold water on the stove when the electricity was cut off as well). At other times the cold water was cut off, and only scalding hot water flowed from the taps. That created its own problems, because we had to draw the hot water into buckets and the bathtub, then let it cool down before we could use it. Taking a shower in such scalding water was out of the question, and our clothes would shrink if washed at that temperature. Most difficult of all, however, was when the entire water supply was cut off. Living as we did on the fifth, sixth, and eighth floors of high-rise buildings, it was not easy to haul water by hand, from communal taps a few blocks away, up all those flights of stairs to our apartment. So we kept large buckets of water in reserve, in our kitchen, bathroom, and hall, for such basic necessities as toilet flushing and hand washing.

As with the electricity and heating, we never knew when the water would be cut off. Sometimes it happened when I was in the middle of taking a shower or washing my hair, leaving me no way to rinse off the soap or shampoo—a situation made even worse when I was showering in a cold bathroom by candlelight because the electricity had also been cut off. Sometimes it happened when the apartment was full of people for a party. Sometimes the water was cut off for only an hour; other times we were without any water at all for two or three days in a row.

But living in the high-rise village was most challenging when all of the utilities were cut off at the same time. Few people in the Western, industrialized world can imagine what it is like to live in a multistory apartment building that has no heat, no water, and no electricity, in the middle of the winter, with outdoor temperatures well below zero. In Vladivostok—where such a situation occurred frequently—Tom and I started the day by candlelight, fixing breakfast over a small, single-burner, gas-cannister camping stove that the university had bought for us when the energy crisis reached its height. Dressed in corduroy jeans and wool sweaters over thermal long underwear, we made tea with water rationed from our emergency supply and toasted pieces of bread by skewering them with a fork and holding them over the flame. Chunks of cheese and previously hard-boiled eggs completed the morning meal. After leaving the apartment for work at 8:00 A.M. every day, we returned at 6:00 P.M. to the same cold, dark abode—and another cold meal by the light of a single, scarce candle. By the time we left Russia, Tom had concluded that dinners by candlelight would never seem romantic to him again.

Life in Russia made us thankful for small favors. We became so accustomed to the lack of electricity, heating, and water that we were simply grateful when all three didn't go off simultaneously. But we also recognized that as the same attitude that had been engendered and fostered by the old Soviet system, where everything was planned, directed, and disbursed from above, by a small group of people who had plenty of heat, hot water, and light—while the great majority on the bottom had to take whatever was handed out to them, however meager the ration, just like the ragged beggars on the streets and in the churchyards of the new democratic Russia today.

Many urban Russians coped with life under such conditions by retreating, whenever possible, to their dachas or garden plots outside the city. From late spring to early fall—on weekends, during summer vacation periods, and on holidays—private automobiles and public transportation were filled with city dwellers, often toting their pets, heading toward their homes away from home. Other urbanites traveled to public places beyond the cities, where they could camp, hike, fish, swim, climb rocks, pick berries, hunt mushrooms. The dachas owned by most of our Russian friends living in Vladivostok were little more than small wooden cabins with no running water or electricity, built on plots of government-allotted ground measuring about one hundred to two hundred square feet. In Irkutsk, where some of our Russian friends were "better connected," the dachas belonging to them were larger and had more amenities but were still very basic by Western standards. More important than the buildings, however, were the gardens on the land surrounding these little dachas, where the Russians grew the fruits, vegetables, and flowers they proudly brought back to the city, to supplement what was available in local markets. But only the dachas and the foodstuffs grown there belonged to the owners; the land itself did not. Although Yeltsin had decreed that land could now be privately owned in Russia—and the constitution adopted in December, 1993, affirmed that, in principle—the concept of private ownership of land was still being disputed when we left Russia more than a year later.

Once in mid-October we spent a welcome weekend away from the city at the second home of friends who lived in a tiny apartment in Vladivostok. Transplanted Siberians who longed for village life, Larisa and Nikolay had purchased a small, twenty-two-year-old, two-bedroom wooden house in an agricultural village about halfway between Vladivostok and Khabarovsk. The whole family spent as much time as possible at their dacha, even during the winter holidays in January. The house had electricity but no running water; toilet facilities were in a wooden privy out back, and water had to be hauled in big metal cans from a communal pump two blocks away. Larisa cooked on a three-burner gas stove in the glass-enclosed verandah and also on a traditional, wood-burning, brick-and-stucco Russian stove that was built into the house itself, forming the entire wall between the kitchen and the front bedroom. Outside, the streets were paved (surprisingly, for a farm village) but bereft of traffic. Only a few cows and a gaggle of geese wandered by while we were there.

We arrived in the village at sunrise on a Saturday morning, surrounded by the gold and orange foliage of the autumnal forest, with deep purple mountains on the near horizon, feathery wisps of fog lingering in the valleys, and the border of China not far away. Larisa's neighbor, Yura, had dropped by earlier to stoke up the big Russian stove, so the house was already warm and inviting by the time we got there, as welcome as a cozy inn on a chilly day. Exhausted after the ten-hour trip from Vladivostok, we all went to bed and slept for a couple of hours, only to be wakened by the crowing of a raucous rooster next door.

Tom and I spent the weekend helping Larisa harvest the last vegetables from the large garden behind her house, shredding cabbage for sauerkraut, processing seeds for next year's planting, and preparing meals from her fresh produce: onions, bell peppers, tomato peppers, cauliflowers, parsley. When Larisa noticed Tom cleaning some dirt off a counter in her kitchen, she laughingly told him, "You don't have to do that. That's *country* dirt. I'm only afraid of *city* dirt. Country dirt won't hurt you." Later Larisa sent us back to Vladivostok with our rucksacks and tote bags full of her homegrown potatoes, beets, zucchini, white and red cabbages, melissa, and green onion tops.

We returned to Vladivostok by public transportation—an overnight trip on two buses, one train, and a tram—just in time to go directly to work at the university on Monday morning. Tired, hungry, and much in need of a hot bath, Tom and I finally got back to our own apartment at six o'clock that evening—only to discover on that coldest day of October there was no electricity, no heat, and no hot water. Only the cold water was still functioning. Fondly remembering the warmth of Larisa's wood-burning stove in the country, we lit a single candle and set about preparing yet another uncooked meal in our high-rise village apartment: canned sprats garnished with sour cream; a salad of canned garbanzos seasoned with chopped onions, garlic, and paprika; and a cucumber-and-tomato salad, all washed down with a bottle of Bulgarian white wine. Soon after we finished our cold, candlelit dinner, the lights came on again. Tom and I looked at each other and laughed, as we stacked the dirty dishes in the sink. There was no way we could clean up the kitchen that night, because when the electricity came back on, all the water was cut off. In the Russian high-rise village, seldom was anything given without something else being taken away.

CHAPTER 8

~

Feasts and Festivals

Russians love to party. They like to eat and drink and offer toasts and swap gossip and propound philosophy for hours on end around a table set with a bounteous spread of foods and beverages. And, despite the time, effort, and money required to obtain all the provisions for such a feast, they take every opportunity to get together and have fun. At these gatherings Russians let down their defenses and allow their natural warmth and humor to shine through their otherwise-often-dour countenances. After only a few shots of vodka, cognac, or champagne, the public facade disappears, and the Russian becomes your bosom friend—at least until the party's over.

Two days after Tom and I arrived in Russia, we were treated to the first of many feasts during our stay in Siberia and the Russian Far East. We were both still recovering from jet lag when the Russian dean of our university program told us that all the American faculty were invited to a special dinner that day, given in our honor, welcoming us to Vladivostok. Looking forward to an evening away from our tiny dormitory room, we were surprised when the dean hustled us all into a van shortly after noon and headed downtown for the meal.

Lesson One: When Russians say "dinner" in English, they really mean lunch.

We arrived at a restaurant located on a piece of prime real estate in the center of the city, on Vladivostok's main street facing the Golden Horn Bay. As soon as I walked through the door, I knew this was going to be no ordinary business lunch. The restaurant had been closed to other customers so we could have the entire place to ourselves. The focus of the dining room was a large table set with white linens and stemmed glasses. Seated at one end was the restaurant's owner, a big bearlike man who exuded the calm confidence of someone long accustomed to being in control. At the other end of the table was the lieutenant governor of Primorskiy Kray, Russia's Maritime Territory. And sitting across from us was the rector of Far Eastern State University, flanked by three other high-ranking university officials.

A stream of obsequious waiters brought platter after platter of *zakuski*, a medley of hors d'oeuvres that signal the start of every major Russian meal: mounds of red-orange salmon caviar, plump pink Kamchatka crab legs, delicate squid salad, beefy Russian potato salad, fresh cucumber-and-tomato salad, hard-boiled eggs, and thinly sliced ham. Second and third helpings of those tempting treats were followed by bowls of steaming-hot *borshch* with copious dollops of sour cream on top. And after the soup we were offered a choice of two main courses: Siberian *pel'meni*—bite-size dumplings of meat-filled pasta, shaped like Italian tortelloni—floating in beef broth or smothered in sour cream. Or we could have a dish called "the Captain's Meat," tender medallions of beef layered with thinly sliced potatoes and baked with cheese on top. Our host explained that "the Captain's Meat" was a Vladivostok specialty, a favorite of Russian seamen who returned home from long voyages with a craving for meat after subsisting on fish for so many months at sea. Toast followed toast, as our glasses kept being refilled with chilled vodka, warm Russian champagne, Moldovan white wine, and Georgian brandy—leaving us little room or inclination for the rather insipid ice cream served for dessert.

Lesson Two: At a Russian meal, never fill up on *zakuski*, because there's always more food to come.

As the meal progressed, however, the American faculty began to realize that Russian hospitality was not the primary purpose of that welcoming feast. Sitting around that private banquet table, eating the choicest foods that Vladivostok had to offer, we were not only the guests of honor but also the objects of a not-so-subtle Russian snow job, an attempt to impress upon us the power and prestige of our hosts. By the end of that lavish lunch, the Russians had made it very clear that our new university program was important to the political and business elites of the region—and that their support would be essential for the future success of the program. Mentioned only in passing, of course, was the fact that two of the students enrolled in our program were the sons of the men seated at opposite ends of the table: the lieutenant governor of the province and the owner of the restaurant—the latter an experienced entrepreneur with extensive business

interests in the region, who (we later heard) was also reputed to be well-
connected with the local *mafiya*.

Lesson Three: Always look a Russian gift horse in the mouth.

Russia was not the kind of place where you could say, "I don't feel like
cooking tonight"—and then go out to your choice of restaurants, have a
pizza delivered, or pick up some Chinese take-out food for dinner. Except
in Moscow and St. Petersburg—which have always been different from the
rest of the country—Russians had limited opportunities for dining in restaurants or for purchasing precooked foods to eat at home. Although many
people did eat meals away from home every day—mainly at school cafeterias or canteens connected with their workplace—there were few public
restaurants, even in major cities, of the sort we take for granted in the West.

Every city I visited in Asian Russia did have a scattering of small cafés
and cafeterias in the central shopping areas—although most of these were
dingy dives with unappetizing food and were open only during the middle
of the day. Kiosks located around town sold commercially packaged snack
foods, such as soft drinks, candy bars, and potato chips. And occasionally
street vendors near public transportation stops sold small, homemade fried
pies filled with meat, potatoes, mushrooms, or sauerkraut. But restaurants
were scarce, usually located far from the densely populated microdistricts,
and difficult to get into without reservations made well in advance. Even
when you could manage to get a table at such places, the menus were often
limited, the prices high, the service poor, and the quality of the food left
much to be desired. As in Soviet times, the food was not really the point:
when Russian families could afford it—perhaps only once or twice a year—
they went out to a restaurant as a form of entertainment, to celebrate a
birthday, a wedding, or another special event. Russians with high positions
in government or business—and hence with plenty of disposable income or
access to expense accounts—dined in restaurants more often, entertaining
official guests, business associates, and potential clients at the few upscale
eating establishments available, solidifying professional relationships over
generous servings of vodka and caviar. But on most occasions ordinary
Russians preferred to prepare even celebratory meals at home, where the
food was better and the amount of money spent on the feast went much
further than it would have at a restaurant.

Perhaps because it was a seaport, Vladivostok was a much better restaurant city than Irkutsk. Attracted by the city's location on the Pacific Rim,

investors from Canada, Japan, Korea, Australia, and the United States had opened restaurants in Vladivostok, most as joint ventures with local Russians. Other eating establishments were wholly Russian-owned, sometimes reputedly with *mafiya* backing. Some places were "cooperative" restaurants dating from the early days of Gorbachev's perestroika, when the first few small private enterprises were officially sanctioned within the Soviet state. And there was even a small vegetarian café in downtown Vladivostok run by the Hare Krishna religious sect.

When university officials took us to dinner in Vladivostok, we most often went to Nostal'giya (Nostalgia), an intimate eatery that seemed to appeal to their sense of sentimentalism about Russia's selectively remembered pre-Revolutionary past. Although the food at Nostal'giya was affordably priced and above average in quality, it was far less memorable than the schmaltzy decor, which looked like a provincial stage setting for a high-class San Francisco whorehouse of the 1890s. Victorian-style red-and-gold wallpaper rose above the dark wooden wainscoting behind banquettes with seats of padded brocade. A crimson-colored upright piano stood at one end of the dining room, the musical backdrop for singers of old Russian romantic ballads. Gold sconces with muted electric lights provided suitably subdued lighting. From one wall a portrait of Russia's last royal couple—Tsar Nikolay II and Tsarina Aleksandra—peered dimly across the room at individual portraits of Aleksandr Kolchak, Anton Denikin, and Pëtr Wrangel, White Army leaders whose actions during Russia's civil war would dampen the appetite of any diner with a decent sense of history.

When Tom and I were downtown at midday, we frequently ate at a small, Russian-operated café on Vladivostok's main street, whose specialty was round, individual-size savory pastries identified on the daily menu board as "pizzas." Made without tomatoes or tomato sauce, these Russian-style pizzas had perfectly baked crusts of thick, yeasty dough, topped with chunks of fresh brown mushrooms, cubes of fried pork, tangles of dark green fiddlehead ferns, or pools of creamy white cheese. The Russian patrons ate their pizzas by hand—not with a knife and fork as many Europeans do—often accompanied by glasses of thick white *smetana* (sour cream), which they slurped from a soupspoon between each bite of crusty pizza.

The dark, dingy decor of Vladivostok's pizza palace—with its grungy Formica tabletops, mismatched chrome-and-vinyl chairs, and seldom-swept floor—matched the Dostoyevskian appearance of many of its customers, down-and-out men of all ages, dirty and unshaven, dressed in layers of old clothes covered with two or three tattered overcoats, their hands in grimy gloves with the fingertips missing, their feet wrapped in filthy rags. Drinking bottles of cheap, watery beer, these representatives of Russia's underclass contrasted sharply with the café's other customers: stylish mothers with small children, sipping hot tea or spooning sour cream, sitting next to tables of rich Russian teenagers swilling cans of gin and tonic in the middle of the day. Oblivious to the chaos of the dining room, a tabby cat wandered around, scavenging scraps of food off the floor. And sometimes a small black-and-white kitten curled up on the chair next to me, while I watched middle-class matrons with bulging shopping bags eat part of their pizzas, then hurry away, leaving food on their plates, which was immediately scrounged up by the destitute drunks who always lingered over their own meals, slowly savoring each precious bite.

Our best culinary experiences were the home-cooked meals we made ourselves or ate at the apartments of Russian friends—the Russian and American holidays we celebrated with seasonal foods, the birthdays and wedding parties for which no expense was spared, and all the dinners given for no other reason than to enjoy each other's company while consuming whatever food and drink was available at the local market that day. Those small, personal get-togethers were often the finest form of entertainment in a land that offered little public night life, where they served to brighten up the drab surroundings of everyday existence and help dispel the inevitable doldrums of the deep Russian winter.

We met several good cooks during our stay in Russia, but the best was our neighbor Alla Brovko. Soon after we arrived in Vladivostok, Alla was the first Russian to invite us to her home, for an evening of getting-to-know-you conversation over a light dinner of savory meat pies. Upon entering the Brovkos' apartment, we immediately took off our shoes in the foyer and changed into *tapochki*—house slippers provided by the host—a custom observed in most Russian homes, Asian or European. Inside, the setting was typical of many meals we would eat in Russian apartments during the next sixteen months: hosts, guests, and children sat on mismatched chairs and backless stools crowded around a drop-leaf dining table temporarily set up in the middle of the living room, almost filling the small space. Crowded onto the table were plates and glasses of various sizes and patterns—whatever the family had been able to acquire during decades of Soviet scarcity—along with platters of home-cooked foods and bottles of Georgian brandy, Russian vodka and champagne, and imported fruit-juice drinks. Pëtr Brovko poured the first round of vodka and began instructing us in the etiquette of Russian toasts: the first toast from hosts to guests, the second from guests to hosts, and the third—customary in the port city of Vladivostok—to all sailors at sea and to absent family and friends. As we knocked back shots of vodka, sipped champagne, and devoured Alla's excellent meat pies, talk on many topics bounced around the group in a mixture of Russian and English, while Maksim, one of the Brovkos' sons, played background music on an upright piano nearby. At such a convivial meal, it was easy to understand why the Russians say, "A home is made by pies, not by walls."

Alla was a living link to Russia's pre-Revolutionary culinary past. Born three years after World War II, in Yakutsk in the far north of Siberia, she had moved to Sakhalin Island in the Russian Far East at the age of eight. Because of her parents' marital difficulties, however, Alla had been raised by her grandmother Polina, a Siberian born in a village near Krasnoyarsk in the 1890s. As a young woman, Polina had run away from an arranged marriage to her first husband, an older widower with three children of his own. Eventually she made her way to Irkutsk, where she found employment in the household of the last tsarist official to serve as governor-general of Eastern Siberia. For six years Polina worked in the basement kitchen of the governor's palatial residence in Irkutsk—first as a "market girl" sent to purchase fresh food supplies each day, and later as the cook herself during the last year before the Bolshevik Revolution broke out.

Polina, who had learned cooking from her own grandmother, honed her culinary skills in the governor's upper-class household in Irkutsk before revolution and civil war changed everyone's lives in Russia. Four decades and three husbands later, when Polina taught her granddaughter Alla how to cook, she was passing on knowledge that reached back to the mid-1800s, recipes and techniques transmitted from generation to generation over an entire century, regardless of wars and revolutions, purges and politics. And, indeed, many of the dishes prepared by Alla—a naturally talented cook herself—seemed like they came out of the pages of old Russian novels, not a tiny modern kitchen in a post-Soviet high-rise apartment building.

By November of our first semester in Russia, we had met so many people in Vladivostok—Russians and foreigners alike—that our weekends were often filled with dinner parties at homes all over the city. One of the most memorable was a sumptuous spread for eight prepared by our friends Larisa and Nikolay, a young Russian couple who lived in a minuscule apartment in one of those Khrushchev-era buildings. An edible mosaic of hot and cold dishes completely covered the gate-leg table that nearly filled their combination living-dining-sleeping room. Most of the ingredients came from their own dacha garden: finely shredded ruby-red beets, snow-white radishes, and bright-orange carrots; dark-green pickled cucumbers and jade-green tomatoes; "herring in a coat," a pink-and-white salad of salted herring filets, sliced boiled potatoes, and beets, all nestled beneath a mantle of mayonnaise and sour cream; Russian potato salad colored with carrots and peas; lecho, the Slavic rendition of French ratatouille; shredded red cabbage shiny with vinaigrette dressing; stewed chicken legs served on a bed of creamy mashed potatoes; and crispy croquettes of ground meat and rice browned in hot oil. After such a feast I barely had room for the chocolate candies and chocolate cake brought by the guests. But I was seduced by the plate of fresh yellow lemon slices that Larisa served with hot tea after dessert, luscious lemons so naturally sweet that I ate them like candy, peels and all. Not having seen any lemons since we arrived in Russia the summer before, I was even more impressed when I learned that Larisa's lemons came from a tree at their dacha more than 200 miles north of Vladivostok, in a region better known for Siberian tigers than for citrus fruits.

In early November, Tom and I hosted our first dinner party in Russia, a multicourse meal for ten people. In Europe or the United States we could have organized a dinner party of that size on a day's notice, but such a meal in Vladivostok required three weeks of planning, shopping, cleaning, and cooking—as well as making arrangements to borrow additional kitchenware and tableware and even a dining table and chairs. Wanting to prepare a dinner that would be both interesting and different for our Russian and American guests, we were limited by the dwindling food supplies at the local kiosks and open-air markets that autumn. Finally we decided upon an Alsatian-inspired meal based on some of the dishes we had often eaten in that region of France.

After acquiring the necessary ingredients, I still needed two large, heavy, covered casseroles to make the main course Bäckeoffe, a hearty dish of marinated pork and beef layered with potatoes and onions, braised in white wine. But I couldn't find any suitable pots in the sparsely stocked kitchenware sections of Vladivostok's stores. Calling on their network of contacts in the high-rise village, my neighbors Alla and Natasha finally came up with two well-used, much-chipped, enameled cast-iron casseroles, like antique versions of French Le Creuset. Early on the afternoon of the party, I climbed the six flights of stairs to Alla's apartment (the elevators, as usual, weren't working) and loaded up several old shopping bags full of her china, crystal, and flatware, along with Alla's only tablecloth, vinyl-plastic printed with a pastel "Lovely Rabbit" children's design. Later Tom trudged back up to

Alla's, carrying one of the heavy casseroles to bake in her oven, because our stove was too small for both. And an hour before dinner Alla's teenage son Danilo and several of his friends showed up at our door to deliver her dining table and four extra kitchen stools, which we needed for our party of ten. Without the assistance of so many people in our apartment building, it would have been difficult, if not impossible, to give the kind of dinner party in Russia that we took for granted in the West.

Our guests arrived that chilly November night bearing gifts of Russian champagne and caviar, Bulgarian white wine, German chocolates, and—most exotic of all—a plastic bag of American baking powder, a product almost impossible to find in Asian Russia. After a champagne aperitif, we sat down to a four-course French meal, with different wines for each course—a meal that approximated, as closely as we could, the kind of dinner that might be offered in an Alsatian country restaurant.

The first course of mixed cold hors d'oeuvres included a salad of shredded red cabbage tossed with small cubes of pistachio-studded mortadella-type sausage; another salad of shredded carrots, diced apples, and raisins, its oil-and-vinegar dressing flavored with honey and ginger; green peas marinated in a mustard vinaigrette with plenty of fresh garlic; halves of hard-boiled eggs garnished with garlic mayonnaise; pieces of Danish salami and Chinese canned ham; and a few slices of fresh tomatoes and cucumbers.

The main course was a surprise to everyone. In the center of the table I placed the two covered casseroles, their lids hermetically sealed with a ring of flour-and-water dough that had baked to a hard crust as the *Bäckeoffe* cooked. When I cracked open the crust and lifted the lids, heady aromas of onions, garlic, and wine wafted around the room, as the guests oohed and aahed over the dramatic presentation.

In France this substantial main dish would usually be followed by a light salad of fresh greens with a simple Dijon-mustard dressing. But we had not seen a single fresh green since arriving in Russia three months before. So we moved on to the cheese course, featuring the two kinds of cheeses that were available in Vladivostok at that time, accompanied by a French red table wine and a basket of Russian white bread. Dessert was a compote of mandarin orange slices, morello cherries, and raisins macerated in a mixture of Russian spiced rum and sweet Azerbaijani wine, each serving of fruit surrounded by a pool of *crème anglaise* scented with vanilla and lemon peel. And as a "taste of home" for the American guests, I had also baked a batch of Snickerdoodle cookies, a crunchy counterpoint to the fruit-and-custard finale.

Everyone seemed to enjoy the whole evening immensely, and all the Americans claimed they had never eaten so well during their entire time in Russia. But minor cultural differences surfaced during the party. The Russians commented on the novelty of eating a meal where the individual plates were served and decorated in the kitchen, then brought to the table in separate, distinct courses. And throughout the meal they looked longingly at the bottles of wine and liquor lined up on our coffee table, which we served separately with the different courses. This custom seemed strange to the Russians who, at their own dinner parties, would have placed bottles of vodka, brandy, champagne, red and white wines, fruit juices, mineral water, sweet liqueurs, and bitter digestifs all on the dinner table at the same time, to be drunk—seemingly indiscriminately—throughout the meal. And after dessert, when we offered our guests coffee with brandy and liqueurs, as would have been customary in France, all the Russians requested hot tea instead.

That first year in Vladivostok I discovered that, for people who like to party, Russia may well be one of the best places in the world to spend the winter holidays. In Russia we could celebrate two Christmas Eves, two Christmas Days, two New Year's Eves, and two New Year's Days, all in a three-week period, thanks to historically different ways of calculating the calendar. "European Christmas," as the Russians in Asia called it, occurred on December 25 but was an occasion observed only by non-Orthodox Christians. The official beginning of the winter holidays was New Year, on January 1, the most important secular holiday on the Russian calendar. Then Eastern Orthodox Christmas was observed by the Russian Orthodox Church on January 7, followed by "Old" New Year on January 14, the last day of the winter holiday season.

On the evening of December 23, an office assistant from the university delivered a large evergreen tree to our apartment—a holiday gift from the Russian dean of our program. Outside, a blowing snowstorm had begun to blanket Vladivostok. But the next day my dreams of a Russian white Christmas melted under the winter sun, as the temperature on our balcony reached sixty-seven degrees in the afternoon. That evening Tom put together a light Christmas Eve dinner for just the two of us: salmon caviar and smoked salmon with buttered brown bread, cold boiled shrimp, and sauteed scallops garnished with garlic mayonnaise and shredded crab, all accompanied by a dry Colli Verde Spumante from Italy. We dined by candlelight on the glass coffee table in the living room, with German Christmas music playing in the background. Afterward we ate carrot cake leftover from Tom's birthday earlier that month, then quaffed several cans of Hamm's beer while making decorations for our bare evergreen tree still propped up in one corner of the room.

On Christmas morning Tom set out to find something we could use for a Christmas tree stand, so we could finally put up the tree and decorate it before "European Christmas" was already over. But Russia was not the kind of country where you could just drive down to the local Wal-Mart and buy a tree stand. Tom had lived long enough in Vladivostok to know that the best source of materials for a makeshift stand would be the piles of garbage outside our apartment building. After foraging in the neighborhood for a fairly long time, he finally returned with a look of impish triumph on his face. "See what I found in the trash!" he exulted, as he held up a dented, nickel-plated electric samovar that someone had discarded. While I wondered how such a piece of junk could ever be used as a tree stand, Tom disappeared into the kitchen with his Leatherman Tool and proceeded to bang away on the samovar for fifteen minutes. Once it was disassembled, washed, and polished, he turned it upside down and stuck the base of the tree into a hole in the bottom. But the tree still wobbled too much, so he braced it firmly by ramming five empty beer cans into the extra space inside the inverted samovar. Voilà! A shiny and elegant, if somewhat unorthodox, stand for our first Christmas tree in the Russian Far East.

We spent the day listening to radio broadcasts of Christmas music on the BBC, VOA, and Radio Moscow World Service while preparing food for a large party the following day, draping swags of tinsel around the doors and windows, and finally decorating the tree. Only a few seasonal ornaments were for sale in Vladivostok that year—most of them inexpensive, Chinese-made plastic baubles too gaudy for our tastes—so we made our own simple decorations from whatever materials we could find: paper snowflakes cut from squares of heavy white toilet paper, animals cut out from a colorful set of children's Cyrillic alphabet cards. Also adorning the branches were a few striped candy canes given to us by an American friend and several translucent red and green glass icicles that we bought for only 12 rubles (1 cent) each. Alla loaned us a string of multicolored lights shaped like miniature versions of old-fashioned coach lanterns. And topping the tree was an ornament especially appropriate for Vladivostok: a big orange starfish from the nearby sea, attached with a length of insulated wire that Tom had salvaged from a pile of trash outside.

The day after "European Christmas," Tom and I hosted a potluck dinner at our apartment, continuing a holiday tradition we had begun several years before while living in Germany. All of our Russian university colleagues were invited, as well as a number of Russians and foreigners we had met during our first four months in Vladivostok. Word of the forthcoming party spread throughout the local American Peace Corps community, too; a couple of Peace Corps volunteers even traveled several hundred miles from sites north of Vladivostok to attend.

Twenty-eight people crowded into our apartment that afternoon, bringing an array of home-cooked dishes and commercial products that reflected the wide range of shopping ingenuity, culinary skills, disposable incomes, and cultural backgrounds of Russians and Americans living in Vladivostok at that time: curried pasta salad with walnuts and sultanas; fruit salad made with expensive imported ingredients, fresh and canned; American chocolate bars, candy canes, gum drops, and Tootsie Rolls; Korean fried apple pies; Russian fiddlehead ferns, home-grown fruit preserves, and an exotic dish made with sea slugs, a costly delicacy in the Russian Far East. The guests arrived to find two makeshift buffet tables in our living room already set with our own favorite party dishes: Tom's Russian potato salad shaped into a large dome on a serving platter, covered with crab aioli and decorated with a large red-orange "crab" fashioned out of salmon caviar; a big pot of spicy Texas chili and another filled with homemade sauerkraut cooked with ham, onions, and white wine; trays of chocolate brownies and carrot cakes; and a selection of drinks for every taste—Russian champagne, Italian Spumante, Russian vodka (straight and flavored with hot peppers), Bulgarian white wine, Azerbaijani "Port," Georgian brandy, Russian berry liqueur, Del Monte fruit-juice drinks from Korea, American coffee, and Indian tea. It had taken us two weeks just to find all the foods and drinks for our own part of the buffet.

But Alla's dishes were the star of the show. She and Pëtr arrived bearing two big platters of food fit for a tsar. One displayed a large fish that had been skinned and deboned, whole, so that the skin remained in one piece with the head intact. The skin had then been filled with a fish mousseline, formed back into its original shape as a fish, and baked in the oven. The other platter held a large, whole, deboned chicken stuffed with a baroque concoction comprising several layers of herbed chicken flesh, pork, and veal, accented with prunes and pine nuts. Following an old Russian custom, Alla had also inserted a small coin into the stuffing before baking the chicken; the lucky guest who found the coin in his serving would supposedly have good fortune throughout the following year.

At first the Russians and Americans didn't mingle very much, standing

apart in their own little groups. But as the afternoon turned into evening—
and the food and drink had their effect—the social and cultural barriers
dissolved, with the Russians and Americans singing holiday songs in both
languages around the Christmas tree and taking sides against each other in
a lively game of *Menedzher* (Manager), a sort of Russian version of Mo-
nopoly. And no one seemed to mind that all twenty-eight people had to
ration the reserve buckets of water to flush the toilet that day, because the
cold water was cut off the entire time. The party started at one o'clock in the
afternoon and was such a success that it didn't break up until ten o'clock
that night, a late hour for social functions in Vladivostok, where most residents preferred to avoid the city's mean streets after dark.

The next two evenings found us at gala receptions given by local and
foreign dignitaries at Dom Peregovorov, the Negotiations Hall, a modern
marble-and-glass cube located several miles outside the city in the upscale
Sanatornaya district. Nestled in the heavily wooded area were a number of
stately dachas previously owned by pre-Revolutionary merchants and Communist elites, and currently occupied by local bigwigs. The Negotiations
Hall, which belonged to the Primorskiy Kray administration, served as a
locus not only for government meetings, but also for parties given by the
top stratum of local and regional officialdom, past and present, communist
or capitalist. Just inside the glass entrance doors, the focus of the spacious
reception area was a mosaic-encrusted pool with a fountain in the center.
The rooms on either side of the foyer included a large, red-carpeted, wood-
paneled banquet hall and a smaller chamber-music room with a vermil-
lion-lacquered grand piano of the sort that Liberace might have played on
a flashy Las Vegas stage. Outdoors, the full moon glistened off the snow that
had sifted over the city that day, while the VIPs' chauffeurs waited patiently
inside their cars and vans, smoking cigarettes and eating plates of food
sneaked out to them by the catering staff—just like the droshky drivers of
earlier times, who used to wait outside in the cold with their horse-drawn
carriages while their aristocratic masters partied the night away.

The first party at the Negotiations Hall, on December 27, was given by
the International Office of Far Eastern State University. As we entered the
grand foyer, we were greeted by girls in Russian folk costumes, one holding
a bright silver Star of Bethlehem wrapped in aluminum foil and attached to
a long pole. A massive evergreen tree stood in the middle of the mosaic
pool, decorated with hundreds of multicolored lights and glass balls, garlands of silver tinsel, sparkling silver icicles, and wads of cotton "snow."
Champagne coupes in hand, the crowd of formally dressed students, fac-

ulty, and staff listened to an introductory speech by V. I. Kurilov, the rector of the university, clad in full academic regalia, followed by an eclectic entertainment program: an amateur ballet performance on the theme of *The Four Seasons;* a Russian choral group singing a medley of modern music; Japanese students singing Japanese and Russian folk songs; a young, Spanish-looking man playing "Recuerdos de la Alhambra" on an acoustic guitar; a Japanese jazz band composed of trumpet, saxophone, sousaphone, and battery-powered electric guitar, belting out a Dixieland version of "Jingle Bells."

Then the doors to the banquet room were opened, revealing the most magnificent buffet I had ever seen in Russia. Rows of long tables covered with crisp white tablecloths held silver platters filled with the finest foods to be found in Vladivostok that winter: bright pink prawns and rosy-red Kamchatka crabs; scallop shells filled with crab-and-pineapple salad; hard-boiled eggs garnished with glistening salmon caviar; assorted cold meats (ham, beef, and sausages) and cold fish (poached salmon, steamed crab, sprats in oil, herring with vinaigrette sauce); large whole squid stuffed with seasoned rice; baked stuffed salmon; squid-and-carrot salad; an Oriental shredded cabbage salad with green onion tops and fresh ginger; soy-sauced chicken chunks; fried white fish filets; buttered bread with caviar; champagne, vodka, and mineral water. Before the feast began, two Russians costumed as Ded Moroz (Grandfather Frost, the Russian equivalent of Saint Nicholas or Santa Claus) and his helper Snegurochka (Snow Maiden) entered the banquet hall. After Ded Moroz had entertained the assembled guests with a high-spirited Cossack dance, he and Snegurochka passed out small presents to everyone in the crowd, offering the first gift from his bag—a decorated pine cone—to me.

The following night we returned to the Negotiations Hall for a formal party hosted by the United States consul general in Vladivostok. In many ways the affair was almost a repeat of the previous evening's university party but with a different set of guests. Crowded into the large reception hall were most of the Americans we had met in Vladivostok that autumn and winter—government officials, Peace Corps workers, businessmen—as well as members of the local Russian business community (legitimate and otherwise) and the international business community from Australia, Korea, and Japan. Most prominent of all, however, were the Russian political elites from Vladivostok and Primorskiy Kray. Shortly after I entered the reception hall, I was greeted heartily by the rector of the university, who steered me across the room to meet the mayor of Vladivostok and the governor of Primorskiy

Kray—long time foes who, in classic Russian style, managed to smile with their mouths but not with their eyes as they reluctantly stood side by side surveying the crowd for enemies and allies. Afterward, as I headed toward the bar to get a glass of champagne, I was joined by a savvy young American businessman who spoke Russian fluently and had traveled extensively in the Russian Far East. Gazing slowly around the gaily dressed gathering, he smiled sardonically, then casually whispered to me, "If someone set off a bomb in here right now, it would wipe out the entire *mafiya* leadership of Vladivostok."

The last week of December was a frenzy of activity in the city, as shoppers scrambled to purchase foods, gifts, and ornaments for the upcoming New Year's holiday. Vladivostok's stores were suddenly stocked with a larger quantity and greater variety of goods than I had seen during the past four months combined. Despite the subfreezing temperatures and streets slick with ice, the stores and open-air markets were packed with last-minute shoppers handing over their hard-earned rubles for fuzzy mohair sweaters, hand-knit shawls, warm flannel nightwear, winter boots, brightly colored woolen scarves, cheap-looking fur coats, gaudy plastic flowers, new calendars, children's toys, and boxes full of fancily decorated cakes for the special New Year's meal.

Russians also thronged to the special open-air markets in Vladivostok where pine, fir, and spruce trees were being sold off the backs of trucks. The normally overcrowded buses, trolleys, and trams were jammed even tighter with commuters taking the prickly trees home, while other people trudged along on foot, carrying tall trees shrouded in sheets or burlap bags, and cars raced past with evergreens tied to their roofs. Others who wanted to avoid the annual hassle and expense of buying a fresh tree purchased artificial ones, although many Russians considered these to be a poor substitute for the real thing. And I was told that in the villages some people still observe an old custom of planting an evergreen in the yard when their first child is born, then decorating the tree every New Year season.

In Russia, the *yëlka*—the evergreen tree that adorns almost every home, office, factory, and school, as well as many public parks and squares—is erected for the January 1 New Year celebrations, a week after our "European Christmas." A yuletide custom originally adopted from Germany in the mid nineteenth century, the Russian Christmas *yëlka* shifted stance to become a New Year's tree (with a red star on top) under the antireligious Soviets, when New Year became the major secular holiday replacing the religious observance of Christmas. But during part of Stalin's regime even

Ice cream vendor at Maslenitsa festival in Irkutsk.

the New Year's *yëlka* was not permitted. Some of my Russian friends born in the 1940s still remembered when decorated evergreen trees were prohibited because of their possible religious significance, and neighbors informed on people who surreptitiously set up trees in their own homes. At other times, however, the capricious Stalin allowed the custom to be observed. One Stalin-era propaganda film, shown on television during the

New Year's season in Vladivostok in 1993, portrayed a smiling, grandfatherly
Josef Stalin welcoming young children to the Kremlin to sing and dance
around a tall, ornately decorated *yëlka*, glistening under the twinkling chandeliers of the St. George Hall.

In the post-Stalin era, the custom of having a *yëlka* at New Year's time
had become firmly entrenched. Almost every apartment balcony in
Vladivostok sported a freshly cut tree waiting to be taken inside and decorated on New Year's Eve. On the exterior walls of high-rise buildings without balconies, trees were suspended upside down from window ledges to
keep them cold and fresh, looking like uprooted evergreens blown there by
the wind. But Alla fretted that she and Pëtr wouldn't even be able to afford
a New Year's tree that season. "Two years ago, trees cost 10 to 30 rubles,
depending on the size," said Alla. "Last year the price was 1,000 to 1,500
rubles ($2.50 to $3.50), but this year a small one costs 10,000 rubles ($8),
and you have to pay 15,000 to 20,000 rubles ($12 to $16) for a good sized
one, 1½ meters or so."

The Brovkos had invited us to celebrate New Year's Eve at their apartment—"just a small family dinner with us and our sons," said Alla. Knowing
that additional food would always be welcome, Tom and I hurried to the
nearest open-air market on the morning of December 31 to shop for something to contribute to the meal. After spending four hours outdoors in the
twenty-degree temperature, with a wind chill well below zero, we both felt
frozen to the bone by the time we returned home early that afternoon. Still
bundled up against the cold, I trudged up the six flights of frigid stairs to
Alla's apartment to ask what time she wanted us to arrive for dinner that
night. "Come around ten," she said, casually adding that she didn't know
when dinner would actually be ready, because the electricity had already
gone off three times that day—and was still off, as was all the hot water and
heat.

"*Why?*" asked I, thinking of all the cakes that were falling in ovens
throughout Vladivostok, all the meats not roasting, all the vegetables not
boiling. "God doesn't know," she sighed, pointing heavenward. "Well, surely
the water and electricity will be turned back on *sometime* this afternoon,"
I ventured, with typical American optimism. "After all, this is New Year's
Eve! We can't lose all of our utilities on *New Year's Eve!*" Alla just smiled
wearily, as if I still had a lot to learn about life in Russia.

When I returned to our apartment, it was so cold that I had to put on a
second layer of thermal long underwear. There was no way to warm up
with even a cup of hot tea, so Tom and I tried to distract ourselves from the

cold by reading, first by sunlight through the frosted windows, later by candle-light after dark, all the time expecting that the electricity, heating, and hot water would surely be restored before the big New Year's Eve dinner began in thousands of homes throughout the city. Until the utilities were turned back on, we had no way to bathe, no way to wash our hair, no way to cook all the dishes we had planned to take to Alla's that night.

At seven o'clock Tom and I began bumping around the dark apartment, flashlights in hand, getting dressed for the party and trying to figure out what kind of cold foods we could prepare for that evening. Looking out the living room window, I saw several kids from our building gathering garbage to start a big bonfire. For once I welcomed the sight of trash burning be-neath our windows, and for a moment I even entertained the thought of taking potatoes and carrots down to roast in the fire. As the flames flickered against the snow, casting shadows of children in rabbit-fur hats dancing gaily in a circle and throwing firecrackers into the blaze, I understood their primitive desire to defy the darkness, with whatever means at hand, during the depths of that frigid Russian winter.

At 7:30 that evening, the heat began trickling back into the radiators, and a short while later hot water sputtered through the pipes in the kitchen and the bathroom. At 8:30, just as we started putting together our platters of cold food, the return of electricity was greeted with a loud collective cheer from all the apartments in our building. Taking advantage of the situation, we quickly peeled potatoes and zapped them in the microwave, to make a Russian potato salad. A few minutes later, Tom put a bowl of diced fresh carrots into the microwave, touched the timer, and the electricity went out again. But we had already cooked enough ingredients to make the po-tato salad, so—by the light of a solitary candle—we composed our dishes for the party: Tom's signature dish, a big mound of Russian potato salad cov-ered with crab aioli, decorated with strips of pickled red peppers and a large "crab" made of salmon caviar; smoked salmon garnished with pickled green tomatoes; canned green peas marinated in wine vinegar with fresh garlic; a platter of sliced pickled red tomatoes and bright green cucumbers; salmon caviar with butter and bread; half of a leftover carrot cake and a large plate of day-old brownies; champagne chilled on our balcony and the remnants of a bottle of Chinese vodka that another Russian neighbor had shared with us earlier in the day.

Russians customarily dress up in their party best for New Year's Eve, but I dressed for the weather instead: black slacks and a black sweater over my thermal long underwear, with an amber necklace that I hoped would catch the candlelight in the darkened apartment. Food and drink in hand, we arrived at Alla and Pëtr's place at the appointed hour, delighted to discover that the electricity in their part of the building had been turned on. But just as we walked through the door, all the lights went off again.

"We have a chicken singing in the oven," trilled Alla, as she cheerfully arranged platters of cold food on the table in her living room, while explaining that the chicken she planned to serve for the main course was still uncooked. The table for six had been set with Alla's "Lovely Rabbit" vinyl tablecloth, her best faceted crystal wineglasses from Moldova, cloth napkins, an assortment of porcelain plates of different sizes and patterns, and flatware with handles of ivory-colored plastic. The only light in the room came from three tapers in a baroque-style ceramic candelabrum in the center of the table and a single candle on the upright piano nearby. Next to the dinner table stood a large New Year's tree, Pëtr's surprise to Alla, festooned with shimmering pink, blue, and silver icicles, garlands of silver tinsel, glass ball ornaments, tufts of cotton "snow," and a string of multicolored lights waiting, like the rest of us, for the electricity to come back on.

Alla placed all the foods on the table together—even the desserts—crowding them onto every inch of available space. In addition to the dishes we had brought, Alla put out her own version of Russian potato salad, a platter of sliced sausages, the most expensive kind of smoked salmon sold in Vladivostok, a plate of canned red peppers from China, a bowl of cold beet salad decorated with walnuts on top, a box of chocolates, and bottles of Russian champagne, Rasputin vodka, and mandarin orange liqueur. Despite the lack of electricity, hot water, and heat, we had succeeded in assembling a formidable feast to welcome in the New Year, a candlelit array of colorful foods that seemed symbolic of Russian resilience in the face of adversity.

Many Russians start their New Year's meal only after the clock has struck twelve, after the guests have shaken hands (instead of kissing), and after everyone has drunk a champagne toast, saying "*S novym godom!*" (the Russian version of "Happy New Year!"). But our meal began at 11:00 P.M., with a toast from Pëtr the geographer, who happily pointed out that we could celebrate the New Year every hour throughout the night, as midnight crept across Russia's many time zones. When the magic hour approached in Vladivostok, I was eager to go out on the balcony to watch the Chinese-made fireworks I had seen people buying at the open-air markets during the weeks leading up to New Year's Eve. But Alla and Pëtr were completely uninterested in my suggestion. "Why do you want to stand out in the cold when the clock strikes twelve?" they asked. Finally, at two minutes after midnight, I persuaded all of the Brovkos to join Tom and me on the freezing balcony. What a sight we beheld! From top to bottom of every high-rise we could see, people were shooting off red, green, and white Roman candles, while others lighted red fusees that seemed to envelop the buildings in flames. It was like watching a naval battle among stationary warships, with fireballs continuously being hurled from one gray hulk to another.

Vladivostok was ablaze with fireworks. "It's like a civil war!" exclaimed Alla, adding, without a hint of irony, "The Chinese are guilty of this." As we all watched in awe, the battle of tricolored lights was waged in every direction, while high above the city red, white, and green signal flares, fired from ships in the harbor, floated in the sky. Twice we heard salvos from battleships in the bay, the percussive sounds shaking the walls of our ten-story building. But otherwise all we could hear was the constant whoosh-whoosh of Roman candles, as they leapt from balconies into the frigid night air, like anti-aircraft tracer fire over the city.

Pëtr surprised us by setting off three rounds of fireworks himself, before we all went back inside, shivering from the cold and laughing like children at the pyrotechnic display. Alla said she had never seen anything like it in her life. "Didn't you always have fireworks on New Year's Eve?" I asked, remembering all the brilliant displays I had seen in Europe at that time of year. "No," replied Alla, "Vladivostok was a closed city before, and this is the first year that the Chinese have been able to come in and sell fireworks like that."

At 12:30 A.M., just after we stepped indoors, the electricity came on again. "Now we have a chicken singing and *dancing* in the oven!" laughed Alla, hoping that the power would stay on long enough for the bird to finally roast. I thought the party would soon be winding down, but the fun had actually just begun. A few minutes before 1:00 A.M. all six of us—bottles of booze and platters of leftover food in hand—headed for the next stairwell in our building, for *another* dinner at the apartment of our neighbors Sergey and Natasha. Together with them, their two children, Sergey's mother, and Bagheera, the big black dog, we all squeezed around a table set with many of the same kinds of cold foods that Alla had served—not surprisingly, given the ingredients available in Vladivostok and the erratic nature of the electricity that day. And in the center of the table a large crystal vase held a bunch of just-budding pussy willow branches, the first harbinger of spring and a symbol of hope for the coming year.

Gathered around that congenial table, we all nibbled on leftovers, drank champagne, and toasted the New Year with vodka every hour as the calendar changed to 1994 in the next time zones across Russia. Beside the table, Sergey and Natasha's artificial evergreen sparkled with colored lights, while the adjacent television blared out a flashy New Year's program from Moscow—a Russian variety review with singers, dancers, and comics, including excellent impersonators of Lenin, Brezhnev, and Yeltsin, like a Russian version of "Saturday Night Live." But Natasha, who was both serious and superstitious, thought it was a very bad omen that the electricity had been off when the New Year arrived in Vladivostok. She believed, as many Russians do, that your own state of mind, the circumstances of your immediate environment, and the way you see the New Year in—just at the stroke of midnight—all foreshadow the year to come. I tried to lighten her mood by suggesting that we look at the positive signs of that special evening: despite the lack of electricity, we were all happy and healthy, we had watched a fantastic fireworks display, and we had feasted well in the company of friends. "What more could we ask for?" I concluded, while silently conceding to myself that I certainly wouldn't relish spending the next year in Vladivostok without electricity, if that was what the darkness at midnight had truly foretold.

It was still dark outside when Tom and I stumbled home at 5:45 that morning, after having capped the night's revelry with several cups of strong sweet tea at Alla's place. On the way home we passed other merrymakers dressed in evening clothes, straggling back to their apartments from New Year's parties elsewhere in the city. And when I crawled into bed fifteen minutes later, a few Roman candles and strings of firecrackers were still sputtering below our windows. At that very moment the Remont Family upstairs started playing hard rock at full volume, loud enough to vibrate the concrete walls of our bedroom. Punch-drunk from eight hours of partying, I felt like I was falling to sleep in a disco, as our other neighbors began banging in protest on the radiators, adding their own live percussion track to the beat of the Remonts' recorded racket.

I awoke at noon on January 1 to discover that all the apartments in our stairwell were still without electricity, which remained cut off for the rest of the day. Alla—who now had electrical power in her part of the building—sent her younger son Maksim to deliver a thermos of hot water so Tom and I could fix tea for breakfast. Maksim also brought an invitation for dinner at their home that night, to eat the (finally) cooked food that Alla had originally planned to serve on New Year's Eve.

We arrived at 7:30 P.M., happy to be back in an apartment that had lights. Tom began the party by introducing Alla to all-American orange-juice-and-vodka screwdrivers—a "healthy" drink, by Russian standards—which he contended the cook could consume while toiling in the kitchen without getting drunk. Pëtr, in turn, introduced us to Russian "Aurora cocktails," a potent combination of vodka and champagne. By the time Sergey and Natasha showed up, Tom was concocting his own "Vlad Mai Tai's," a festive mixture of imported Korean orange-and pineapple-juice drinks spiked with Russian spiced rum. These fruity aperitifs sustained us throughout the early evening, while Alla put the finishing touches on the meal and Pëtr showed color slides of his scientific expeditions to Sakhalin Island, the Kamchatka Peninsula, and the Indian Ocean.

By nine o'clock Alla had laid out a feast fit for starting the new year on a solid culinary footing: individual portions of beef tongue enrobed in aspic, decorated with canned green peas and fancily cut carrots; a platter of pickled cucumber rounds and whole pickled red, green, and yellow tomatoes; smoked salmon garnished with red peppers and onions; shredded carrot-and-cabbage salad; paprika-seasoned red beans that we had brought over to cook on her stove earlier in the day; a huge tray of "the Captain's Meat"; and Alla's stuffed chicken (with a good-luck coin baked inside), the same fowl that had been singing and dancing in the oven on New Year's Eve while the electricity went on and off. Natasha had made a rich chocolate-walnut torte for dessert, and Alla put out a big pitcher of brine from the pickled cucumbers and tomatoes, the classic Russian hangover cure for the alcoholic excesses of the night before.

Two hours later, when all the diners felt so full they couldn't take another bite, Alla announced that it was time to go into the kitchen to make *pel'meni* together! Tom and I thought she was joking, until Alla explained that Siberian *pel'meni* were a traditional Russian food for New Year's Day, and that we had to start making them before January 1 ended at midnight. Alla had prepared the dumpling dough in advance, as well as the filling of mixed ground beef, pork, and onions. Working together in her small kitchen, Alla and Natasha and I rolled out the dough, cut it into two-inch circles with a crystal wineglass, and formed it into bite-size, meat-filled pockets of pasta. Then Alla put a large pot of water on the stove to boil, tossed in some spices, and told us to leave the kitchen so the men could come do their part.

The three of us retired to the living room, where we sat around drinking goblets of Bulgarian white wine, watching the movie *My Fair Lady* on television, and listening to the men singing lusty songs in the kitchen as they rolled, filled, and formed their own portions of *pel'meni*. After Pëtr, Sergey, and Tom had cooked all the *pel'meni* that both groups had made, they served the dumplings with a choice of garnishes: butter, sour cream, Russian hot mustard, soy sauce, and Russian ketchup (which looked and tasted like British bottled brown sauce). While the men knocked back shots of vodka, Alla showed Tom and me the proper way to eat *pel'meni* by popping each one whole into our mouths, as she emphasized that Russians consider it uncouth to cut their *pel'meni* into pieces.

In Russia, January 1 is only the start of the winter holiday season. During the following week, the city of Vladivostok sponsored a variety of public activities for children and adults to welcome in the New Year, which the local *Vladivostok News* described as "a resurrection of seasonal songs, rites, magic tricks, and other traditions from pre-Soviet Russia." Dancers, singers, and clowns entertained on the central square, beneath a massive New Year's tree decorated with multicolored plastic balls, big boxes wrapped liked gifts, and a huge lighted star on top. Grandfather Frost and Snow Maiden made daily appearances, the Moscow Circus gave a performance, and a special "New Year's train" wound through the downtown area and carried passengers out to local amusement parks.

On January 7, Tom and I attended the Orthodox Christmas service at the onion-domed Church of St. Nikolay (the patron saint of seamen), the only functioning Russian Orthodox church in Vladivostok at that time. Constructed in memory of the Russian sailors who died during the Russo-Japanese War of 1904–1905, the small church's art nouveau interior was decorated for the Christmas season with unadorned evergreen trees and boughs, red and white carnations, and a large red candle set in a silver star-shaped sconce. Outside the church several beggars wrapped in rags shivered in the snow and held out their hands for alms, as worshipers entered and left during the lengthy service. The congregation comprised several social classes, from mink-coated matrons to poor people in threadbare woolen coats and cheap Chinese anoraks, some of the women with string bags full of groceries in hand. But all were united in the warmth of the yuletide service: the brilliant icons, the flickering candlelight, the aroma of incense, the bowing by believers as they bobbed up and down, making the sign of the cross—all to the accompaniment of the liturgy sung by a nervous young man dressed in black and an off-key choir that sounded as if they were merely rehearsing for a performance yet to be polished.

Our last big feast of that holiday season in Vladivostok was a dinner for ten people—children and adults—at the Brovkos' apartment, on "Old New

Year's Eve," January 13. Tom and I brought an array of appetizers to contribute to the meal, and Alla put out several staples of the Russian winter table, along with her homemade *belyashi*, savory fried pies made of yeast dough stuffed with seasoned ground pork. After we had eaten our fill of these hot and cold *zakuski*, Alla surprised us with her main course: a tray of ten large fresh herring, each whole fish baked with a stuffing of onions, garlic, and herring roe, with an additional flourish of herring roe on top. The fish were accompanied by baked potatoes still in their skins, split open and slathered with creamy unsalted butter. Alla explained that it was customary to eat both the herring and potatoes only with one's fingers—a messy procedure that we all agreed to try, even though the foods were steamy hot. As we sucked on our burning, buttery fingers, we complimented Alla on the rich flavor of the fish and happily quaffed glasses of an excellent French *vin mousseux* that Pëtr had somehow managed to find. Thinking I was too full to eat anything else, I changed my mind when Natasha brought out the dessert: a serving plate stacked high with lacy *blinchiki*—like the best French crepes I had ever eaten—accompanied by her own homemade strawberry jam and a bottle of Russian champagne.

That evening was traditionally the season's last opportunity for fortune-telling, a New Year's custom that Russians have practiced for centuries. Every group of female friends seemed to have one who was recognized for her ability to predict the future by reading tea leaves, dealing cards, or casting hot candle wax into a plate of cold water, to make shapes whose meanings could be interpreted only by the seer. In earlier times, maidens sought to learn whom they might marry in the coming year, but modern Russians seemed to be more interested in how much money they were likely to make during the next twelve months.

After dinner Alla turned off the lights, lit three candles on the table, and assembled the materials for telling our fortunes with molten wax. In the kitchen she heated half a cup of candle wax in a small pan on the stove and filled another small shallow pan with cold water. Then she brought both pans out to the youngest person at the table—Sergey and Natasha's eight-year-old daughter, Dasha—who poured the hot wax into the water. Alla asked Dasha to describe what the wax figure in the water looked like. Then the rest of us were allowed to add our own comments, as we deciphered this Russian Rorschach test for ourselves. Dasha thought the wax was shaped like a mandarin duck, which Alla interpreted to mean that she would grow up to be as pretty as a mandarin duck—a prediction that greatly pleased the wide-eyed Dasha, who already exhibited the physical features of an unusual beauty.

The game continued around the table, clockwise, as each of us cast hot wax into the pan of cold water to predict our own future. Whenever Pëtr looked at other people's wax figures, he saw the map of some country or region, not surprisingly for a professional geographer. Tom's wax image did indeed look like a map of Eastern Siberia, where we were planning to move only four days hence. And everyone agreed that my wax casting looked like a standing bear, which foretold that I would be staying in Russia for another year—an uncannily accurate prediction, even though on that "Old New Year's Eve" in January, 1994, I had no plans to stay in Russia beyond the following June!

On our way home from the party, just before midnight, we had to dodge the discarded New Year's trees blowing around the building like giant green tumbleweeds, their scraggly remnants of tinsel shimmering sadly in the cold moonlight. Just as the clock struck twelve, flares and Roman candles illuminated the neighborhood again—not as many as on the night of official New Year, two weeks earlier, but still a fifteen-minute display that indicated we weren't the only people in Vladivostok celebrating this second New Year's Eve. And the next morning we awoke to snow falling on a blazing bonfire of New Year's trees beneath our window—a fitting end to the winter holiday season in Vladivostok.

Our social life in Irkutsk that winter seemed circumscribed in comparison to the livelier scene in more cosmopolitan Vladivostok—partly because we had no Russian friends such as Alla living nearby. So we and our three new American colleagues who lived in apartments just below us amused ourselves on the long winter nights by cooking meals for each other, playing Trivial Pursuit together, and occasionally going out to restaurants for a change of scenery, in a usually futile search for meals that might add some variety to our culinary routine.

Any occasion became the excuse for a party: birthdays, anniversaries, Groundhog Day, Valentine's Day, St. Patrick's Day (on which we greedily ate a huge green salad made with the first lettuce I had seen since arriving in Russia seven months earlier). For a Mardi Gras party at the apartment of a faculty couple from New Orleans, we dressed up in homemade costumes and chowed down on chicken gumbo, red beans and rice, cherry cobbler, and all the Bulgarian wine we could find in the market that day. Winning the prize for best costume was the fellow who came as Neptune, clad in his blue thermal long underwear and draped in a toga made from his bedroom curtains, sporting a beard and bushy eyebrows fashioned out of cotton balls gleaned from medicine bottles, and brandishing a trident salvaged from a nearby garbage dump.

Late one weeknight in March, Tom and I were reading in our living room when someone knocked loudly on the door. Thinking that it was probably just a drunken guest from the noisy party in full swing in the adjacent apartment, we tried to disregard the persistent knocking. But when the rap-rap-rap continued without letting up, I finally went to the door to see who was making all the racket. Standing outside were two pleasant-looking, well-dressed Russian women carrying an unopened bottle of expensive vodka. The two strangers introduced themselves, held up the bottle, and asked if they could come in. When I hesitated, they explained that they merely wanted to get away from the party next door. Neither of them seemed drunk, so I decided to take the risk. They headed straight for our kitchen, plopped the vodka bottle down on the table, and started looking in the cabinets for glasses.

The four of us sat on stools around the kitchen table, knocking back shots of vodka and getting better acquainted as the night wore on. One of the women was tall and plump, with an attractive face and a jovial personality. The other was very thin, with dyed blonde hair, a mouth full of gold teeth, and a serious demeanor. "I'm a forensics expert for the city," she told us. "It's a horrible job, horrible," she kept repeating, as she pantomimed different ways of cutting up dead bodies. "We're friends of Anna," the jolly one added, nodding toward the apartment next door. "She's celebrating her thirty-third birthday tonight. We've known her for fifteen years. We were all in college together. We're all thirty-three years old."

The conversation was similar to many that I'd had with other Russians, focusing on innocuous topics limited by languages and social conventions: families, professions, hobbies, why Tom and I had come to Russia, how long we had been there, what parts of the country we had visited. But when the two women learned that I would soon be forty-eight years old, they asked me to repeat the number again. Incredulous that I could be that "old," they pointed to their own faces and then to mine, to their own figures and then back to me. "But you look the same age as us!" they exclaimed, as I mentally noted that it would have been more accurate to say they both appeared closer in age to me. Then they laughed and declared that of course I didn't look my age, because I came from America where life was easier, where good cosmetics were available, and where women kept their figures by getting massages. I agreed that life in the United States was certainly easier than in Russia—but out of courtesy I refrained from mentioning that I hadn't lived in America for the past thirteen years, I used cosmetics sparingly, and I had never had a massage in my life.

A knock on the door interrupted our small talk. "No, no, don't answer it," they both said. "Let whoever it is go away." But the knocking became so insistent that we could ignore it no longer. "Come back to the party! Come back!" slurred a happily drunken fellow, as he motioned for all of us to follow him through an open door down the hall. Inside our neighbor's apartment, seventeen people were crammed into a living room considerably smaller than ours, but much better furnished. Taking up half the space was a dining table set with the best porcelain dinnerware and stemmed crystal glasses I had ever seen in a Russian apartment, the entire surface of the table covered with the remnants of Anna's birthday feast, including several half-empty bottles of crystal-clear vodka and psychedelic-colored Dolce Vita sweet liqueurs.

Anna insisted that we join the meal, as she brought out fresh food from the kitchen and introduced us to some of the other guests: another forensics expert, a lawyer, a bank employee, two public prosecutors (which was Anna's profession, too), her husband (a construction foreman), her three children, and the family *babushka*, the only member of the group whom I had met before. But conversation with this party of soused Siberian young professionals was almost impossible over the sounds of 1960s Beatles' ballads and 1970s heavy-metal rock blaring from a boom box in the claustrophobic room. After several rounds of inebriated toasts, some of the women got up and started to dance, motioning for us to join them. By that time Tom was the only man still able to stand on his feet; all the others were sprawled out on their chairs, in various stages of drunken stupor. Amid this congenial chaos Anna disappeared into the kitchen to make tea for her guests, while the old *babushka* and I continued dancing the Twist together to a scratchy Chubby Checker tape. When the clock struck 2:00 A.M. and Anna hadn't yet reappeared, Tom and I decided it was time for us to go. We went into the kitchen to say good-bye—only to find Anna sitting on the floor, slumped against the wall, passed out cold. "I pity the poor souls who have to face these prosecutors in court this morning," I whispered to Tom, as we quietly closed the door behind us, trying not to wake the other guests, who were now snoring loudly, like an asthmatic, out-of-tune calliope, in the stuffy living room.

March was also the month of *Maslenitsa* that year, the seven-day "Butter Week" festival that immediately precedes the seven-week Lenten fast lead-

Grilling shashlik at an outdoor festival in Irkutsk.

ing up to Easter. *Maslenitsa* itself is a secular festival—equivalent to Shrovetide in Britain, Fasching in Germanic countries, and Carnival and Mardi Gras in many Latin countries. All these festivals date from pagan times, when people gathered during the spring equinox to chase away the evil spirits of winter, make offerings to the sun, celebrate the regeneration of life, and welcome the return of spring. In the Christian era, Russian *Maslenitsa* evolved into a period of last-minute merrymaking the week before Lent, a culinary orgy during which people devoured huge quantities of circular *bliny*—yeast-raised pancakes, golden rounds symbolizing the sun, drenched in melted butter or smothered in sour cream. The name of the festival comes from *maslo*, the Russian word for butter, in reference to the richest food consumed during the time just before the Great Fast of Lent, when believers abstain from eating meat, fish, eggs, animal fats, and dairy products for seven long weeks.

On the last Sunday before Lent, Tom and I headed to downtown Irkutsk to see how the Siberians were celebrating this spring festival, which had only recently been revived after the collapse of communism in Russia. Outdoor activities had been organized at several places around the city. Municipal parks were decorated with images of the sun, shining from atop tall poles, and with brightly painted plywood murals depicting sun symbols, birds and flowers, Carnival characters and religious references. In the winter playgrounds children bundled up in parkas and snow boots shrieked in delight as they whooshed down slides made of ice, while their parents watched from the sidelines, licking ice cream cones in the frigid air. Handsome horses decked out in fancy trappings, with brass bells on their harnesses, provided rides for the kids and pulled sleighs full of revelers. And women wrapped in floral-printed shawls sold sweet and savory pastries, small rolls and buns, cookies and cakes, all stacked on folding tables set up in the snow.

Throngs of people filled the square in front of the sports stadium downtown, where the main events of *Maslenitsa* were being held. An outdoor stage had been set up, topped by a row of huge animal masks made of red-painted papier-mâché. Folk dancers in colorful costumes from different parts of Eastern Siberia performed to live and recorded music, while jesters and clowns worked the crowd. Gaily decorated food stalls offered fried meatballs and grilled shashlik, stacks of freshly cooked *bliny* served with jam or sour cream, and the largest variety of baked goods I had ever seen in Irkutsk. And towering over the crowd was a giant effigy of *Maslenitsa*—the Old Witch of Winter—constructed of paper, cloth, and wood, her grotesque form covered with long red ribbons and straw streamers that rustled like whispered warnings in the chilly wind.

At one side of the square, a high pole had been erected, made from the trunk of a tall tree stripped of its branches and bark, sanded smooth, and slicked with grease. As the aromas of buttery *bliny* and grilled meat wafted through the air, we watched a succession of shirtless men and boys try to climb the pole and grab the prizes attached to the top: an electric samovar, a fringed paisley shawl, a mystery prize inside a plastic bag. Suddenly at 2:30 in the afternoon, a big bonfire was set alight at the foot of the *Maslenitsa* witch, and five minutes later the frightening figure was nothing but a pile of harmless ashes. All day the sky had been gray and cloudy, the weather cold and windy—but just after the effigy burned to the ground, the clouds suddenly broke, the sun came out, and the snow began to melt, as if right on cue. March 13, that *Maslenitsa* Sunday, was the first day the temperature rose above freezing in Irkutsk that year. Surely there must be some truth to those ancient Siberian superstitions!

During Lent that spring, two of our Russian colleagues, Gennadiy Konstantinov and Nataliya Mikhalkovskaya, took us to a service at the Church of the Icon of the Virgin of the Sign (*Znameniye*), located within the walls of the Znamenskiy Convent, where they had been married a few years before. Ornately decorated by master woodcarvers, icon painters, and fresco artists, the stone church built in 1762 ranks among the surviving treasures of Russian ecclesiastical architecture in Eastern Siberia. In the small, tree-shaded churchyard were the graves of several Russian historical figures, including Grigoriy Shelikhov, the eighteenth-century merchant-explorer known as "the Russian Columbus," who established the first Russian settlements in North America and became the first governor-general of Alaska. Also buried near the church were a number of Decembrists and their families, among them Countess Yekaterina Trubetskaya and three of her children.

Bishop Vadim of Irkutsk conducted the service that day, assisted by eleven other bearded priests and deacons, all clad in black-and-silver brocaded chasubles embellished with silver embroidery, the colors symbolic of mourning. The soprano voices of a women's choir rang out from one side of the church, followed by the lower notes of a men's choir on the other side, providing the only melodies for a liturgy traditionally devoid of instrumental music. At one point in the service, a priest swinging a censer from a silver chain circled the interior of the church, filling the air with the heavy aroma of incense. Later all twelve of the clergymen, with the bishop in the center, followed the same path around the inner walls of the church, past jeweled and gilded icons illuminated by candles burning beneath them, while members of the congregation made the sign of the cross, the right hand touching the forehead, then the breast, then the right shoulder and finally the left, in a slow, majestic sequence of arcs, like the silent pealing of a single bell.

On the evening before Orthodox Palm Sunday, Tom and I gave a dinner party for eleven people, including our American colleagues, three Russian administrators from our university program, and the Russians' wives, two of whom were also members of our faculty. For such an occasion we wanted to serve a meal composed of dishes that none of the guests was likely to have eaten before. Given the ingredients available in Irkutsk at that time of year, we decided on a Spanish menu, featuring a range of regional dishes, ending with a Russian Easter specialty for dessert, in honor of the season.

As each couple arrived that evening, I presented them with two postcards that I had purchased at an art gallery in downtown Irkutsk: a reproduction of a nineteenth-century Russian painting showing a happy bourgeois couple in front of a formally set table covered with an array of traditional Russian Easter foods, and another depicting a 1926 painting of a gold-domed Russian Orthodox church with a pyramid-shaped *paskha*—a Russian Easter sweet—in the foreground. On the back of the first postcard I had written the dinner menu in Spanish. On the back of the other was the recipe for the *paskha* I had made for dessert that evening.

Lacking a Spanish sherry for the aperitif, we began the meal with Russian champagne and Bulgarian dry white wine, to accompany a selection of hot and cold Spanish tapas: slices of Spanish chorizo sausage and Russian cheese; mushrooms sauteed with garlic and ham; Galician-style squid seasoned with onions, sweet red peppers, paprika, and olive oil; white fish with onions, lemon, and cilantro; a pseudo-*romesco* sauce richly flavored with chipotle peppers that we had brought from Texas; and *ensalada rusa*, the Spanish version of Russian potato salad, bound with garlic mayonnaise. After these tapas I ladled out bowls of cold Andalusian gazpacho, showing the guests how to sprinkle the top of their soup with herb-seasoned croutons and finely chopped cucumbers, peppers, and onions.

The main course was Catalan *pollo con vino tinto*—chicken leg quarters braised in red wine with onions, garlic, bacon, and mushrooms—accompanied by Valencian-style rice cooked with raisins, dried apricots, and walnuts. With this course we served a red-wine sangria, redolent of oranges, lemons, and brandy, which turned out to be a special treat for the Siberians, who all said they had never tasted anything like it before.

But dessert was the biggest surprise of all. The day before, I had made a traditional Russian Easter *paskha*, a kind of uncooked cheesecake, chock full of ingredients forbidden during Lent: *tvorog* (fresh white farmer cheese), butter, egg yolks, and sour cream, the rich mixture sweetened with sugar and enhanced with vanilla, grated lemon peel, candied orange peel, and raisins soaked in brandy. A *paskha* is usually formed in a tall, four-sided wooden or plastic mold, shaped like a truncated pyramid, or simply in a ceramic flower pot if a special *paskha* mold is unavailable. But I had to make do with the only thing I could find, a three-liter cylindrical plastic bucket, in the bottom of which I poked holes to let the *paskha's* liquid drain off while it chilled in the refrigerator overnight. On the day of the party, I inverted the *paskha* onto a serving plate, carefully slipped off the plastic mold, and decorated the cylinder of cheesecake with dark raisins, golden sultanas, and toasted almonds, forming flowers on one side of the *paskha* and the Cyrillic letters "XB"—for "*Khristos voskrese*" ("Christ is risen")—on the other.

To a chorus of delighted exclamations from the guests, I placed the *paskha* in the center of the table, for everyone to see before I cut it into servings. But it was my turn to be surprised: none of the Russians knew what it was. When I explained that *paskha* was a traditional Russian Easter dessert, dating back centuries into Russian history, they all looked at me with blank faces. I went on to say that *paskha* is normally served with *kulich*—a tall, cylindrical, saffron-scented bread with white icing drizzled over its dome-like top. But only three of the Russians were even vaguely aware of what a *kulich* was, even though several bakeries in Irkutsk were selling *kulichi* that spring. Sizing up the situation, I decided not to mention that I had been making *paskha* and *kulich* at Easter for many years. But after the meal, as we all sat around sipping glasses of Spanish brandy, I couldn't help noting to myself the irony of an American from Texas introducing these sophisticated, highly educated Russians to the Easter foods that had once been well known to their Christian ancestors.

The next evening we attended a Palm Sunday service at the Znamenskiy Convent church. Before the service began, a group of several women holding pussy willow branches gathered in a side chapel, where a priest blessed the branches and sprinkled them with holy water. Behind the candles burning below an icon on the side wall were a few jam jars filled with raw rice—the grains symbolizing death and resurrection, the deceased rising again like planted seeds. A coffin draped with purple-and-black satin sat on a bier near the choir, and an icon of Christ with his crown of thorns stood in the center front of the church.

The congregation that Sunday comprised people of all ages, including old *babushki* with kerchief-covered heads and young men in military uniforms—all standing on the cold church floor, since Russian Orthodox churches do not have pews. Among the worshipers were a large number of children holding pussy willow branches, many of whom followed their parents to the front of the church, first to kiss the coffin, then to the kiss the icon, before lighting a white candle in the circular, several-tiered brass candelabra situated on either side of the holy image. Adding to this continual movement during the service was the motion of heads bowing, hands making the sign of the cross, people kneeling and touching their heads to the floor, others making the sign of the cross with their right hand while standing up, then bending down and touching their right thumb to the floor, while all around the sound of somber choral music contributed to the solemn spectacle. Afterward snowflakes fluttered around us as we walked through the quiet churchyard, where small offerings had been left on the tombstone of the Trubetskoy children: a cracker, a slice of cake, some pieces of wrapped candy, an apple, a few flowers, a small plastic toy.

A week later, on the following Saturday night, Tom and I squeezed into Gennadiy and Nataliya's small car, alongside Yuliya, their teenage daughter, and Estée Lauder, their big black poodle, to drive to the Znamenskiy Convent church for the Easter midnight service. The most important festival on the religious calendar, Easter is celebrated at Orthodox churches all over Russia with a magnificent Divine Liturgy lasting several hours, culminating in the annual revelation of Christ's resurrection. And afterward, at the homes of millions of believers, no expense has been spared for the special Easter feast that breaks the long Lenten fast—actually or only symbolically—a holiday meal unequaled during the rest of the year.

When we arrived at the Znamenskiy Convent that Easter eve, the parking lot and surrounding grounds were already full of cars. Within the convent walls, the churchyard was filling with the faithful, as a single bell summoned them to the special service. The church itself was packed with people who had arrived early enough to find a place inside. But the continual coming and going of the worshipers provided the opportunity for me to inch my way forward until I could watch the pageant of priests and parishioners unfold under the glare of halogen lights illuminating the event for broadcast on national television.

The clergy's somber Lenten vestments of black and silver had been changed to white and silver, white and gold, for the joyful Easter service. The coffin on its bier was now covered with white lilies, and flanking the central door of the gilded iconostasis were rose-red light bulbs, initially unlit, forming the Cyrillic letters "X" on the left side, "B" on the right. In a small anteroom adjacent to the sanctuary, long boards set up on sawhorses and covered with white cloths served as temporary tables for the *kulichi* and baskets of eggs that had been brought to the church to be blessed. Fifty or sixty *kulichi* of several sizes filled the tables, with more *kulichi* sitting in the deep window recesses of the room's thick stone walls. Some of the *kulichi* were baked in the traditional tall cylindrical shape, but most were wider and shorter, made in fluted brioche pans. Their rounded tops were decorated in a variety of ways: one was crowned with a cross made out of dough; another had "XB" traced on it with colored sugar granules; and many had white icing drizzled over the domes. Each had a tall, pencil-thin taper stuck into the top, the cumulative candlelight casting flickering shadows like fitful spirits against the plain plaster walls. Easter eggs surrounded many of the *kulichi,* and more eggs were displayed separately on plates and in glass jars. Most of the eggs were medium brown, their color imparted by onion skins; only a few had been dyed with commercials colors—a yellow one here, a turquoise one there, standing out from the others like painted ladies at a prayer meeting. I was surprised there were no *paskhi,* however, because in many parts of Russia *paskhi* are brought to the church, along with the *kulichi* and dyed eggs, to be blessed before the Easter feast.

Just inside the church's front door, a beggar held out his cloth cap for coins. When someone placed an Easter egg into it, the beggar crossed himself, bowed his head, and muttered something unintelligible above the chanting of the priests and the low murmur of the crowd. The congregation that night was different and more varied than I had seen previously at the Znamenskiy church: many people in their twenties and thirties, at least as many men as women, and a large number of people who looked like they came from the countries of the Caucasus. All the women had their heads covered with scarves or shawls, and some of the middle-aged and older men were wearing Russian military uniforms. Standing out from the crowd were the Cossacks in uniforms representing their different regiments. Many were dressed in dark blue pants with a yellow stripe down the side, tucked into shiny leather riding boots (just like old U.S. Cavalry uniforms), topped with loose brown tunics cinched at the waist with narrow leather belts. One was decked out in a flashy uniform of medium blue and silver, with a satin sash; another wore all brown and carried a braided leather quirt. Some had on billed caps; others sported classic Cossack *papakhi*, tall hats made of curly astrakhan. Several of the men were bearded, and a few even had tsarist-era military medals pinned proudly on their tunics.

As midnight approached, a feeling of expectancy filled the crowded church. Several of the Cossacks gently began clearing a path through the congregation. At the stroke of twelve, in a reenactment of the Gospel story, the bishop approached the coffin, raised the shroud, and saw that Christ was no longer in the sepulcher. Holding a large white candle in his hand, the bishop lighted his own candle from one burning on the altar, then passed the flame to the worshiper standing nearest him—each also holding a single white taper—who in turn passed the flame to others with unlit candles, and so on, throughout the church and into the mass of people assembled outside in the dark.

As hundreds of candles flickered to life, the bishop began the *Krestnyy Khod*, the Procession of the Cross, the most dramatic segment of the Easter service. Holding an ornate golden cross high in front of him, the bishop was followed by all the other priests, deacons, and acolytes, carrying candles, crosses, and intricately embroidered banners richly decorated with silver and gold. I was standing in the deep archway just inside the church doors when the procession passed by, the crosses and banners tilted to fit through the low-ceilinged space. As the holy men exited the church, the crowd of believers behind them began pressing through the archway like a sudden rush of wind. The looks of intense devotion on the faces of the priests and old women were like those in a painting from long ago, which had suddenly come to life and was swiftly moving past me. I couldn't understand the words of Old Church Slavonic intoned at the Easter service—but the choral music and bells, the incense and candlelight, the icons and frescoes, the gold and silver, and the collective faith of the congregation all combined to strike a primitive chord in my soul.

I let myself be carried outside by the crush of the crowd, where I watched the priestly procession set off to circle the church, like the doubtful Disciples, in a symbolic search for the vanished body of Christ. After the priests and a large following of parishioners had completed one circuit—and found no trace of Christ—the bishop mounted the steps of the church and proclaimed to the multitude, "*Khristos voskrese!*" ("Christ is risen!")—to which the faithful responded, "*Voistinu voskrese!*" (Truly, He is risen!"). Bells pealed joyfully from the steeple, as people in the crowd turned to those standing next to them, repeating the jubilant greeting and response, "*Khristos voskrese!*" "*Voistinu voskrese!*"—then exchanged three kisses in succession on alternate cheeks, the triple kiss of the Holy Trinity. The priests continued to chant and swing their censers, sending clouds of incense floating over the crowd, as church bells chimed throughout the city, proving the power of bells to evoke deep human emotions from the sonority of molded metal in motion.

A sea of tiny candle flames flickered in the light breeze, as Tom and I followed the procession of priests back into the church. Joyful singing filled the air, and the rose-red light bulbs forming the letters "X" and "B" now glowed from the gilded iconostasis. I could have stayed in that sacred spot until the service ended several hours later, but Gennadiy and Nataliya were ready to leave. As we carried our lighted candles out of the church and across the convent grounds, I noticed that several candles had been placed on the graves of the Trubetskoys. My own candle and Tom's stayed lighted until we passed through the arched gate in the convent walls—a good omen!—at which time we blew out the flames and headed for the car in the dark.

Gennadiy and Nataliya had invited us and our three American colleagues to have Easter dinner with them the next day. When we arrived at their small apartment in a high-rise village similar to ours, I was pleasantly surprised as I walked through the front door. Most of the Russian apartments I had seen were filled with frumpy furnishings in a clashing mixture of patterns, colors, and styles—sometimes a reflection of the owner's personal taste, more often merely the only goods that had been available for purchase in the skewed socialist economy of the past. But Gennadiy and Nataliya's home was so strikingly stylish in decor that it could have been located in northern Europe instead of southern Siberia. Boldly colored modern art hung on the white walls, some of the paintings done by Gennadiy himself. The tiny living room was almost filled by a divan and matching chair covered with a black-and-white zebra-striped cotton fabric. A black, upright, Jugendstil-era German piano stood at one end of the room, and the remaining space was taken up with two tables pushed together to accommodate the eight of us gathered for the Easter feast. On a small serving cart in the corner, a bundt-shaped Ukrainian Easter bread, decorated with white icing and colored sugar sprinkles, sat on a cake plate covered with bright green paper cut to resemble grass, surrounded by several dyed Easter eggs. Three small candles stuck into the bread symbolized the Holy Trinity, and one large candle in the center signified the Resurrection.

Never had I seen a Russian dinner table set so beautifully. Dainty white cloths had been spread over the surface. Pretty pink-and-silver Japanese porcelain plates defined each place setting, along with silver-plated flatware, pastel paper napkins, and the most extensive array of stemmed wine glasses I had encountered in a Russian home: heavy cut-crystal sherry glasses, modern balloon-shaped red-wine glasses, and black-stemmed champagnes flutes. (Nataliya was the only Russian I knew who served champagne in flutes.) Handmade, tulip-shaped place cards—cut from bright green, orange, and pink paper—indicated where each guest should sit. A crystal vase of silk daffodils graced the center of the table—the first time I had seen any flowers, real or silk, on a dinner table in a Russian home. And a basket of five hand-painted wooden eggs—each one a gift for a guest—completed the artistic table setting.

Competing for space on that elegant Easter table were bottles of Russian champagne, imported white wine, and vodka, both domestic and foreign, as well as the first-course *zakuski* that Nataliya brought out from the kitchen. Gennadiy formally began the festive midday meal with a champagne toast, after which we slowly drank the bubbly brew on our empty stomachs as we savored the sunshine streaming through the picture window, warming our skin while the wine worked its wonders within. Next came sherry glasses topped up with locally produced Baikalskaya vodka, the smoothest vodka I had ever tasted. Already giddy from these potent aperitifs, none of us refused a glass of imported lemon-flavored vodka, which we all proclaimed to be the best fruit-flavored vodka we had ever drunk. By then Nataliya was insisting that we serve ourselves some of the *zakuski* set out on the table: a large salmon, baked whole, garnished with pickled green peppers and swimming in *lecho* sauce; "herring in a coat," its pinkish color especially appropriate for springtime; and a platter piled with individual rounds of flat pastry, each topped with mushrooms and red kidney beans in a thick garlic-walnut sauce—a Georgian specialty baked by Siberian Gennadiy and one of the most delectable *zakuski* that I ate during our entire stay in Irkutsk.

Soon after we began nibbling on those hors d'oeuvres, Gennadiy and Nataliya suggested that we all drink a round of Bloody Marys, Russianstyle. They filled each balloon glass halfway with tomato juice, sprinkled in some salt and pepper, then placed a dinner knife at a 45-degree angle into the glass and slowly poured vodka down the knife blade until the clear liquor floated in a half-inch layer on top of the tomato juice. We all sipped this concoction as if it were another of the cold foods among the *zakuski* spread, as we complemented our hosts on their culinary accomplishments. Perhaps we were too effusive in our praise, because Gennadiy insisted that— purely for purposes of comparison—we drink another round of Bloody Marys, this time "Maryland-style." None of the University of Maryland professors at the table knew what he was talking about. But who were we to refuse balloon glasses half-filled with a mixture of vodka and tomato juice, with chopped fresh cilantro on top? (*Cilantro?* The style in *Maryland?*) By that point none of us was sober enough to dispute Gennadiy's assertion that these gargantuan cocktails had to be drunk in one draw, Russian-style. Once again Russian reality had outpaced my expectations: never had I envisioned starting an Easter dinner chug-a-lugging Bloody Marys in Siberia.

Tom and I knew that all those delicious dishes on the table were merely a prelude to the main course. But our American colleagues—who had never been invited to a Russian home for such a feast—ate and drank their fill of all the *zakuski*, with no notion of what was to come. So they were genuinely surprised when Nataliya brought out the next course: German-style beef *Rouladen*, accompanied somewhat incongruously by commercial shrimp chips from Vietnam and crunchy potato sticks, like crinkle-cut French fries, from Korea. That multicourse Easter meal might well have prefigured the urban Siberian cuisine of the future: a fusion of East and West, Asia and Europe, the old and the new, as forgotten recipes are resurrected, as a wider range of foodstuffs is imported into Russia, and as more Russians become acquainted with the cooking of other countries.

After so much food and alcohol, all of us were so sleepy we could hardly sit up. So Gennadiy wisely suggested that he and the guests take Estée Lauder for a walk down to the nearby Angara River before we tackled dessert. The fresh, crisply cold air revived us as we strolled along the banks of the river, still frozen in many places on that first day of May, the sun only a distant white orb in the hazy Siberian sky.

By the time we returned to the apartment, Nataliya had completely changed the table settings, once again demonstrating her flair for design. Modern black, white, and gold porcelain chargers supported dessert plates dished up with light pink gelatin topped with banana slices and a slabs of rich Russian vanilla ice cream. As if this bounty were not sufficient to celebrate the resurrection of Christ, Nataliya also passed around the platter with her own sweet Ukrainian Easter bread, as well as three desserts baked by Gennadiy's mother: a traditional Russian *kulich*, crowned with raspberries; light, fluffy meringue cookies; and a large, rectangular, blackberry pie, with lattice-work pastry on top. Gennadiy offered us snifters of Remy Martin cognac to complete the meal, but none of us was willing to waste such a treasure on our overloaded palates. So—six hours after we had arrived for that midday feast—we all sat around and finished off the champagne and white wine, as the sky darkened outside and Nataliya lighted the candles in the brass sconces on the piano and Yuliya entertained us with selections from Borodin and Bach, ending with a rousing rendition of a Scott Joplin rag.

After a summer break that took us to England and the United States, Tom and I returned to Vladivostok the following August. Just before leaving Texas on our way back to Russia, we stocked up on personal and professional supplies for the coming semester, stuffing all the remaining spaces in our suitcases with packages of corn tortillas, the one food product we had sorely missed in Siberia. I feared that the tortillas would be confiscated at the border, but when we arrived back in Russia, the airport customs officials were completely incurious about all those plastic bags full of Mexican flatbread filling our luggage.

Tom and I hosted several dinner parties, large and small, in Vladivostok that autumn, but the most memorable was in mid-November, when we decided to prepare a Tex-Mex meal for some of our foreign friends. We invited Alla and Pëtr and two other couples—the Siberians Larisa and Nikolay, and a Yugoslav couple, Igor and Slavitsa—all of whom were good cooks themselves and who seemed adventuresome about trying new foods. So we felt completely confident that our guests would appreciate and enjoy of the variety of Tex-Mex and Mexican-inspired dishes on the menu that evening.

210 210 210 210 210 210 210 210 210 210 210 210 210 210 210 210 210 210 210 210 210 210 210 210 210 210 210 210 210 210 210 210 210 210 210 210 210 210 210 210 210 210 210 210 210 210 210 210 210 210 210 210 210 210 210 210 210 210 210 210 210 210 210 210 210 210 210 210 210 210 210 210 210 210 210 210 210 210
Eight of us gathered around the dining table we had once again borrowed from Alla and set up in our small living room. Arrayed in the center was a selection of predinner snacks: a large bowl of cold garbanzo salad with chopped black olives, seasoned with sauteed onions, green peppers, and plenty of garlic; two platters of the Russian version of Ritz crackers, our not-too-satisfactory substitute for tortilla chips (which were unheard of in Vladivostok); and several bowls of dips, including homemade green-tomato-and-chile dip, mild and hot *pico de gallo*, cheese-and-sour-cream dip seasoned with Texas chili powder, and smoky black bean dip. For drinks we offered cold beer, imported from Western Europe, and Bulgarian red wine.

Tom, as host, proposed the first toast, hoisting his glass of beer and welcoming our friends to that special Tex-Mex dinner showcasing the kinds of foods that we often ate back home. But none of the guests knew how or where to begin. We had to demonstrate how to use the crackers to scoop up the dips, while explaining that these foods were typical of the snacks that Texans would nibble on before the main meal was served. Pëtr and the Yugoslav couple didn't have much trouble with this culinary concept, but everyone else just dunked a cracker or two, out of courtesy, then stopped. The garbanzo salad seemed slightly more acceptable to them, although the Russians had never seen black olives before and thought the shiny slivers were some kind of mushrooms.

The guests chatted in the living room while Tom and I dished up the main course in the kitchen, filling each diner's plate with two turkey *mole* enchiladas garnished on top with sour cream, chopped onions, and black olives, accompanied by side servings of ranch-style pinto beans and Spanish rice. Tom was especially proud of his *mole*, the rich dark-brown sauce made with a combination of dried ingredients we had carried to Russia and fresh ingredients found in the local markets: onions, pumpkin seeds, garlic, chicken stock, crushed dried chiles, Texas chili powder, cocoa powder, cinnamon, allspice, and pumpkin-pie spice. To accompany his *pièce de résistance* (and sop up the thick sauce), he also put out a platter of steamy-hot corn tortillas, the last of our precious supply brought from Texas three months earlier and stored in the freezer.

The guests looked at their plates, then at each other, in complete silence. "What is it?" Alla finally asked, pointing to the enchiladas. "I recognize beans," said Slavitsa, the Serbian, who knew them from her own country's cuisine. "Why is the rice that color?" Pëtr asked hesitantly, as everyone just sat there without even lifting a fork.

Alla ventured the first bite, but only after I had explained that the enchiladas were a kind of Mexican *blinchiki*, made from corn and filled with turkey cooked in a special sauce. Following Alla's lead, the other guests started picking at the food on their plates, but without much enthusiasm. When Pëtr asked if we had any bread, I explained that tortillas are the flatbread that Mexicans customarily eat with their meals. But when I passed the platter of tortillas around the table, Tom and I were the only ones who took any.

The guests continued to push the food around on their plates, taking only an occasional bite. The looks on their faces reminded me of a matter-of-fact statement that one of my Russian students had once written in an essay: "When you are cooking, you can make some mistakes. When you will eat it, you will find them." Alla commented that she had never eaten anything like those enchiladas before, adding that she could taste cinnamon in the sauce, although she couldn't imagine combining cinnamon with meat. Thinking that such a good cook as Alla would want to know what else was in the *mole*, I proceeded to name the other ingredients. That was my blunder. When I got to "cocoa powder," all the guests put down their forks and stared at their plates. "You put *chocolate* in the meat sauce?" asked Alla incredulously, as if I had just admitted to adding insects to a salad. After that, no one ate much else except for a few bites of rice or beans, just to be polite.

Dessert was no more of a success. I thought surely the Russians would like my sweet-potato pudding, a baked blend of mashed sweet potatoes, butter, sugar, and eggs, flavored with orange juice, cinnamon, nutmeg, and raisins macerated in rum, each portion of golden-orange pudding garnished with chopped pineapple soaked in spiced rum. But that dish seemed as strange to them as the enchiladas had. "I've never eaten such a thing for dessert," Alla said wonderingly, as she took a second small bite in a kindly attempt not to offend me. "These things come from Africa, don't they?" asked Pëtr, referring to the sweet potatoes, as he tried to find something—anything—to say about the peculiar pudding sitting in front of him.

Later that night, after the guests had left, Tom and I speculated about what had gone wrong with the meal. During the previous fifteen months, we had successfully entertained friends in Russia at a variety of dinner parties with menus ranging from French to Spanish to Italian—but that Tex-Mex dinner in Vladivostok had been a real disaster. As we scraped all the uneaten food off the plates and into the trash, we concluded that the meal had seemed strange to our Slavic guests for several reasons: the tastes were too alien even for those adventuresome people's palates; we didn't serve any bread, the staple expected at every meal in Russia (tortillas didn't count); and we didn't serve any vodka. Reflecting on the fact that this was the only time in our lives we had given a dinner party that was a such a flop, all we could do was laugh, chalk it up to experience, and recall a line that Nikolay had said the first time we went to dinner at his apartment in Vladivostok: "It's always better to have banquets than to have battles."

~~

CHAPTER 9

The Market Economy

The American slogan "Shop till you drop" took on an entirely different meaning in Russia. Although the country was moving rapidly toward a market economy, shopping in Russia was a time-consuming chore, a constant quest for the necessities and niceties of daily life—food, toilet paper, candles, laundry soap—because retail marketing was still firmly mired in the past. In Asian Russia of the mid-1990s, there were no supermarkets or department stores where you could simply take a basket, load it with products taken from the shelves yourself, and do most of your shopping under one roof. There wasn't even the equivalent of a neighborhood 7-Eleven. Instead we had to go to a number of stores, open-air markets, and kiosks all over the city, in the hope of eventually finding the items we needed. After living in Russia for several months, Tom concluded that "You know you've been here too long if a pretty girl walks by on the street and instead of looking at *her*, you peek at her shopping bag to see what kinds of vegetables are in it and wonder where she bought them."

But hunting for particular products was only half the process. Once the product was found, we still had to stand in three different lines to make each purchase at a store. First we stood in a line leading up to the merchandise counter in that section of the store—dairy products, dry goods, whatever—where one or more usually surly shop girls listlessly waited on the customers, one at a time. Since all the products sold in that section were displayed on the shelves behind the counter, we had to ask the shop girl for each item we wanted. She scooped the rice or beans or flour out of a wooden barrel or burlap bag and weighed them on a scale, or measured out lengths of fabrics, or stacked up the requested boxes of detergent and rolls of toilet paper—then added up the total price on an abacus and handed us a scrap of paper with the price of each item, plus the total, penciled on it. At that point we went to another part of the store and stood in line at the cashier's booth to pay for the products in cash. After the cashier had totaled up the items once more on an abacus, she took our money and handed back the change with a receipt marked "paid." Then we returned to the merchandise counter and stood in line once more, to exchange the receipt for the products them-selves—which we put into our own shopping bags because the stores pro-vided neither plastic nor paper bags for their customers. In larger stores we had to repeat that three-stage process several times, once for each separate section of the store that had an item we wanted to buy. Finally Tom and I lugged the purchases home on the crowded and dirty public transportation system, or we walked for miles—often in fog, rain, or snow—whenever the buses and trams weren't working. The experience of shopping in Russia convinced me that if enough of the Soviet populace had seen an American supermarket thirty years ago, communism would have died a much earlier death.

Shopping was not only time-consuming, but also often frustrating—especially when there were shortages of staples such as sugar, flour, eggs, and soap, which might disappear from the shelves for several weeks. Some stores had what I called "Potëmkin displays," empty boxes or single samples of goods that were not actually available, put on the shelves or in the win-dows just to fill up the space. Others did have the products they displayed but would not sell more than one or two of any particular item to a cus-tomer even if the store had dozens in stock. When one of my American friends tried to buy a large quantity of dried noodle soup mixes, the Russian shop girl refused, saying, "If I sold you that many packages, there wouldn't be any left to sell to anyone else."

Pricing was also problematic in Russia's inflationary economy. Once at a major food store in downtown Vladivostok, I stood in line to purchase a box of tea, received my payment slip from the girl behind the merchan-dise counter, then stood in line at the cashier's booth, paid the amount penciled on the slip of paper, and got my receipt from the cashier. But by the time I returned from the cashier and stood in line to collect my pur-chase, the price of tea had increased 100 rubles (4 cents). Since my cashier's receipt was now 100 rubles short, the shop girl refused to give me the tea, and I had to repeat the whole three-stage purchasing process all over again.

Although Yevgeniy Nazdratenko, the governor of Primorskiy Kray, referred disparagingly to "middle men with their self-serving markups," not all Russians had a backward attitude toward commercial transactions. A Peace Corps administrator in Vladivostok recounted the story of an official Peace Corps van that was broadsided by a small Russian car at a busy intersection in the city. While the drivers of both vehicles waited thirty minutes for the police to arrive at the scene of the accident, two private automobiles, with local license plates, pulled up alongside. The owners got out, opened up their trunks, and took out a selection of replacement bumpers to sell to the Russian fellow who had plowed into the Peace Corps van.

Welcome to Russia's new market economy.

When Tom and I first went to Moscow in June, 1993, the currency exchange rate was around 1,000 rubles to the dollar. By the time we left Vladivostok at the end of December, 1994, one dollar would buy almost 4,000 rubles. According to Goskomstat, the Russian government statistics agency, between January, 1993, and December, 1994, the average wage in Russia rose from around forty dollars a month to almost ninety dollars a month, an increase of 125 percent. But inflation ate up those gains, causing the Russians' real incomes to decline significantly. The *Vladivostok News* reported that prices for goods sold in Primorskiy Kray rose 900 percent in 1993, prices for services increased 2,300 percent, and during that year Vladivostok was second only to Magadan as Russia's most expensive city. In December, 1993, the "market basket index" of prices for nineteen staple foods in Vladivostok was almost double the Russian national average. By November, 1994, Vladivostok was a few notches lower on the list of Russia's most expensive cities, but the cost of living there had still doubled during the first three quarters of the year.

During that early period in post-Soviet Russia, the economic situation was simultaneously better and worse than imagined by people living in the highly developed market economies of the West. An increasing number and variety of imported consumer goods became available for sale, from Chinese anoraks to Japanese automobiles, from French wines to Uncle Ben's Rice. But the emerging market economy was still skewed in several ways. Despite privatization of many state-owned enterprises—from major industries to small stores—land could not be privately owned, and much of the agricultural sector was still controlled by the government. Millions of people who worked in the public sector—schoolteachers, firefighters, soldiers, policemen—saw their purchasing power erode precipitously as salaries stag-nated while prices inflated. Old-age pensioners on small fixed incomes suffered the most, especially those who lacked families that could provide additional support. And hyperinflation in the early 1990s had wiped out the savings of many people who had hoarded their hard-earned rubles during the decades before.

Moreover, many people working in both the public and private sectors were not paid their salaries for weeks or months at a time. Some went on strike to protest the situation. Others accepted payment in goods ranging from vodka to tampons, which they then bartered or sold for whatever they could get on the open market. Many subsisted on foods grown in their dacha gardens and canned at home. Even when they weren't being paid, however, most Russians still showed up at their official place of work, at least for a few hours each day. Otherwise, they would lose all the medical, educational, housing, old-age pension, and other benefits—however mea-ger—provided by their primary employers.

For Russians born and bred in a "full-employment" socialist economy, with cradle-to-grave social services guaranteed by the government, unem-ployment became a frightening fact of life in the new market economy, as more and more people lost their jobs when inefficient factories went out of business and state-owned stores closed their doors. Others who were fortu-nate enough to keep their often low-paying jobs took on second or third jobs in an effort to earn sufficient money for themselves and their families. They were able to make ends meet—and even purchase many of the new consumer goods coming onto the market—because their rent and utilities were still highly subsidized by the state. But those workers also divided their time among different places of employment each day, a practice that increased their incomes while decreasing the amount of time actually spent on any one of their jobs, thus adding another dimension of inefficiency to an already highly inefficient economy.

Other Russians prospered in the new market economy, where they profited from a range of business activities large and small, legal and illegal. The most successful of these were the "New Russians," the emergent entrepre-neurial class, people with the kinds of skills and personal connections that enabled them to amass large sums of money in a short time, particularly during the period when Russia was just beginning to make the transition from a controlled economy to a more open one. On our first day in the Russian Far East, one of our Russian students summed up the situation in a single sentence: "When the Soviet Union ended, the Communist thieves took state property, privatized it to themselves, sold off the assets for hard currency, and deposited the money in their foreign bank accounts." And in Vladivostok we soon saw for ourselves the lifestyle that such newly acquired wealth could buy: expensive foreign cars, fancy clothes and jewelry, new apartments, big dachas, trips abroad to Europe and the United States, private education for the children. As the *Vladivostok News* reported in December, 1993, "Rapid stratification of society into 'haves and have-nots' is a striking feature of Primorye's post-Soviet economic landscape."

Organized crime, money laundering, racketeering, tax evasion, pyramid schemes, lack of clear and enforceable commercial laws, graft and corruption, an unstable currency, inflation, high interest rates, bank collapses, and the illegal transfer of billions of dollars out of the country—all took their toll on Russia's economy. But the rapid loosening of government economic controls also provided the opportunity for many Russians to improve their lot in life, whether by purchasing their first car or acquiring a better apartment or starting up their own business. And although there were numerous reports about the extent to which the *mafiya* influenced or controlled commerce throughout the Russian Federation, most consumers were directly affected in the day-to-day marketplace mainly by such practices as price fixing by *mafiya* suppliers or by higher retail prices to cover the shop owners' protection-money payments to local thugs.

Many of the new businesses in Russia's emerging market economy were small retail stores that had been privatized from previously state-owned outlets. Although the Soviet Union had always lacked the kind of clean, bright, colorful shops and department stores so common in the West, maps of Vladivostok and Irkutsk dating from the late 1980s showed the locations of dozens of retail stores all over those cities—from bakeries to fabric shops to furniture stores—although far fewer than in Western cities of the same size. Many of these Soviet-era stores were hidden away in dingy courtyards, or up flights of dirty back stairs, their dusty displays of inferior goods secreted behind unmarked doors. Others were located on main thoroughfares in the center of the cities, the signs on front nothing more than a single word naming the product sold—BREAD, MEAT, MILK—without any other embellishments to entice the customers. Under the old system supply was so limited and demand so great that no one had to make much effort to sell whatever products were available, regardless of their quality.

That system was just beginning to change when I lived in Siberia and the Russian Far East. Although a large number of retail stores had already been privatized by the time I arrived there, many of them continued to perpetuate the practices of the Soviet past: sparse and unreliable stocks of goods, unappealing displays, sullen shop girls, and the time-consuming, three-line purchasing process. By the time I left Russia, however, Western marketing techniques were just starting to appear in a few of the smaller stores. But self-service shopping was still a concept that had not yet caught on.

Retail outlets in Vladivostok and Irkutsk ranged from each city's single, multistory department store in the center of town to individual street vendors sitting behind small folding tables, with a wide variety (although not a great number) of stores, shops, and kiosks in between. Russians shopped at the department stores for housewares, fabrics, and clothing; at food stores that sold several kinds of products or specialized in only one category, such as bread, poultry, or fish; at book stores, record shops, florists, and a few furniture stores (one in Irkutsk sold furniture made only by convicts); at "factory outlets" for products such as liquor or fish, sold at a markup of 10 percent over cost; at kiosks that offered small items such as cigarettes, liquor, snack foods, and costume jewelry; at large open-air markets with a jumble of products, from fresh produce and meat to hardware and clothing; at small, temporary street stalls set up by individual vendors who had only one or two items to sell (smoked fish, a few fuzzy hand-knitted shawls, some packages of soap); and at their place of work—office, school, or factory. In our dean's office at Far Eastern State University, we purchased flour scooped out of a big linen bag, Chinese apples, Russian cheese, bulk sugar, and fresh meat, all weighed out on a handheld scale by the departmental secretary.

As cities located on major transportation routes, both Vladivostok and Irkutsk were better supplied with consumer goods than were towns not near the Trans-Siberian Railroad tracks. But as Russia's primary port on the Pacific Ocean, Vladivostok had a definite advantage over Irkutsk, with better stocked stores and a wider variety of products available. The largest store in Vladivostok—still known by its Soviet name of GUM (Gosudarstvennyy Universal'nyy Magazin—State Department Store)—was located downtown, on the city's main street. Originally constructed in 1885 for the German-owned firm of Kunst and Albers, it was described by a visitor at the time as "an encyclopedic store" where customers could purchase everything from a needle to a live tiger. Nationalized during the Soviet era, it continued to offer a range of products, although much more limited than before the Bolsheviks came to power. More than a century after it was founded, GUM still sold the widest selection of goods in Vladivostok—although, from my own perspective, it looked more like a small department store in the American Midwest of the 1940s than a modern retail emporium of the 1990s.

Perhaps most surprising to my Western eyes was the product mix found in Russian retail outlets. Even though GUM was divided into separate departments, the same items might be sold in several sections of the store: for example, Teflon skillets in kitchenware, hardware, stationery, and shoes. Smaller shops sold anything they could get from suppliers. At one shop a porcelain toilet was displayed next to cans of Coca Cola and a stack of ladies' gloves; at another a locked glass display case held costume jewelry, small screwdrivers, cheap plastic cigarette lighters, and bulbs for Christmas tree lights. At street kiosks packages of tea and individual Snickers bars sat side by side on the shelf with Toyota and Nissan oil filters, and boxes of Tampax vied for space with bottles of vodka and lacy brassieres.

Purchases at most of these places were tallied up on wooden abacuses— those early calculating devices first brought to Russia by the Mongols during the late Middle Ages. Even if the store had a modern handheld electronic calculator or a large old-fashioned cash register, the sums were still double-checked by abacus. At the largest jewelry store in Vladivostok, a wooden abacus sat behind the counter, next to an unplugged electric cash register designed for printing out receipts on a roll of adding-machine tape. Beside the cash register, a computer console and keyboard both gathered dust. All the financial calculations were made by abacus, the transactions registered by hand by a cashier who penciled them into a cheap paper notebook like the kind that kids used at school. Meanwhile the drawer to the cash register remained open all the time so she could make change—just like using a cigar box to hold all the money at a flea market or garage sale.

Despite the large number of consumer goods coming into Russia's new market economy, friends had warned us in advance about the continuing scarcity of many products there. So we brought from the United States boxes full of spices, plastic bags, kitchen utensils, over-the-counter and prescription medicines, personal hygiene products, office supplies, a portable compact-disk player with several CDs, a laptop computer, all the clothing we needed, and enough recreational reading, in English, from British murder mysteries to classics of Russian literature, to last us for a year. But even though our Russian apartments were supposedly furnished, we soon developed a long list of additional items still needed for daily living: kitchen towels, cutting boards, mixing bowls, potholders, skillets, saucepans, a colander, cake pans, wastebaskets, candle holders, and much more. Few of those household items were available in the sparsely stocked stores, however, and some we never found during our entire stay in Russia.

When I think about the amount of time we spent searching just for toilet paper, I wonder how we ever accomplished anything else. But when a sought-after item was not available at all, we learned to improvise with whatever materials we could find. In the autumn of 1993, none of the stores in Vladivostok sold such products as cling wrap, wax paper, aluminum foil, paper towels, or plastic bags. Instead we used old student homework assignments for paper towels in the kitchen. We saved all the thin aluminum foil from inside the wrappers of imported German chocolate bars, which we carefully washed, dried, smoothed flat, and pieced together to make larger sheets of foil to use for wrapping leftover foods. We washed, dried, and reused for months every one of our own precious plastic bags in which we carried home bloody cuts of unwrapped meat, dirty vegetables, and leaky liquids from the markets several times each week. We rinsed and reused every plastic bottle and glass jar that came filled with food. I rolled out pastry dough with a champagne bottle because I could never find a simple wooden rolling pin. I darned socks stretched over a light bulb. One American colleague turned her metal dish draining rack into a roasting rack for chickens in the oven. Another improvised a filter coffeemaker from a tea strainer lined with tough Russian toilet paper. And another constructed a more elaborate coffeemaker out of a plastic detergent dispenser and HandiWipes, both of which she had brought from the United States, the whole contraption supported by an inverted kitchen stool.

The scarcity of so many ordinary household products also created in Tom and me an inescapable urge to scrounge. We never walked past a rubbish bin or pile of garbage without at least glancing to see if something useful might be lurking there—a hammer, a few nails, some screws, a piece of wire, a handle for our broom (only the bottoms of brooms were sold in stores), a plastic bucket (we had hunted for months to find one for sale), a metal milk-bottle carrier (maybe we could make it into an outdoor grill). Although we never succumbed to taking food from the trash, we couldn't help but notice a box of sprouted onions (greens!), a pile of potatoes (why were they thrown out?), three juicy-looking beets (what were they doing in the garbage?). In Russia it was almost impossible not to develop this attitude toward trash, because so many items, even basic ones, were often unavailable or so hard to find in the markets and stores.

During the spring in Irkutsk, Tom won our "All-Russia Dumpster-Diver Award for Best Treasure Found in the Trash" when he came home one day with a true hunting trophy: a large, full-size, stuffed Arctic owl, mounted on a birch branch. This excellent example of the taxidermist's art had sat atop a huge mound of rubbish outside our apartment building for two days,

Vendors at an open-air market in Ussuriysk,
Russian Far East.

unmolested by children, uneaten by dogs, and unclaimed by anyone else. Even though we weren't the sort of people who decorated our house with stuffed wildlife, Tom couldn't resist rescuing that handsome owl from the garbage. We took it to the university, named it Minerva (after the Roman goddess of wisdom), and kept it in the faculty office where it became the unofficial mascot of our education program in Siberia.

Since our housing costs were subsidized by the universities, most of the money we earned in Russia was spent on food. Not long after we first moved to Vladivostok—while we were still basking in the warmth of an unexpected Indian summer—I was suddenly overcome by a strong feeling that we ought to lay in a large stock of provisions for the winter. Perhaps it was some ancestral memory of all the famine fears of my farmer forebears. Despite temperatures that rose into the eighties during September and October, I possessed a peasant's pessimism about the mild weather. That Indian summer of 1993 lasted so long that I expected to wake up any morning and find the mud puddles from last night's rain turned into sheets of ice as autumn suddenly froze into winter. And I knew that as the months went by, finding food was only going to get worse, not better.

Alla became our guide to savvy shopping in Vladivostok, taking us to open-air markets and *gastronomy* (food stores) that we would never have found on our own. With Alla's help, Tom and I soon learned our way around the city, shopping several times each week at farmers' markets for fresh produce; at indoor food stores for bread, dairy products, flour, grains, and canned goods; and at kiosks and street stands for anything useful they might have, from candles to toilet paper.

We shared Alla's attitude that shopping was a treasure hunt, a quest primarily to find a product worth buying, at a price we were willing to pay. And, like Russians all across the country, we never went anywhere without a shopping bag, just in case we happened upon something good for sale. Even if we didn't need that particular product at that time, we bought it anyway, as a hedge against future shortages (or merely against nasty weather, which always made shopping much more of a chore).

Almost all the indoor food stores—formerly state-owned, but now most of them privatized—were dull, drab, and dirty by Western standards. Sometimes customers standing in line had to step over a derelict drunk passed out on the floor. Shop cats wandered around behind the counters and curled up to sleep on the shelves. Once at a bakery Tom spotted a small cake decorated all over with raisins—but when he started to buy it, he saw one of the raisins move and realized the cake was actually covered with flies stuck to the frosting. A friend from Yugoslavia said she had lost fifteen pounds after she moved from Belgrade to Vladivostok, because of her nausea at the sights and smells of the local food stores: insects crawling on the unwrapped butter, cheese, and meat; the aroma of rotting produce; the grunge and grime on counters and floors. Two stores in Vladivostok did have more visual appeal than most others, however: the city's main *gastronom* downtown, with an authentic art nouveau interior featuring mirrored walls, marble counter tops, sinuous painted tiles, and ornate brass lighting fixtures; and *Dary Taigi* (Gifts of the Forest), whose walls were covered with colorful murals made of hand-painted ceramic tiles depicting wild animals native to the Russian Far East. But many of the foods in these architecturally interesting stores were unappetizingly displayed in large, shallow, white enameled metal pans that looked just like old hospital bedpans.

Much of our food came instead from the two types of farmers' markets located in sections of Vladivostok miles from the city center. The permanent markets had an open-air section of weathered wooden stalls, long wooden trestle tables, and folding metal tables where vendors displayed their wares, as well as smaller indoor areas—usually in concrete-slab buildings like little warehouses—with designated sections for meat, dairy products, vegetables, and so on, or simply with counters where vendors offered a limited variety of foodstuffs, domestic and imported. Around the edges of most of these markets a few small kiosks and wooden buildings—most of them nothing more than flimsy shacks—served as shops selling bread, pastries, soft drinks, alcoholic beverages, and a hodgepodge of the newer food products now being imported into Russia. Movable markets, on the other hand, were set up temporarily on a public square or patch of ground where we stood in line, even in subfreezing temperatures, to buy food off the backs of trucks, sold directly from the producer to the consumer: one line for beets, another for onions, another for potatoes, another for cabbages, the damp earth still clinging to them from the farm.

The vendors ranged from weathered farmers with rough, gnarled hands, to raw-boned country women, their heads covered with kerchiefs, their ruddy faces recalling the heroic countenances on old propaganda posters touting the triumphs of Soviet agriculture; from fresh-faced young farm girls in flouncy short skirts, like American cheerleaders of the 1950s, to middle-aged Koreans with deadpan expressions and sharp eyes, to stolid, heavily made-up Russian matrons sitting behind stacks of imported canned vegetables. Urban peasant women in thick rubber boots scrambled over a small mountain of muddy carrots offloaded by a dump truck, rooting out the best in the pile. Cats darted between the stalls in search of scraps. A bored-looking vendor with a table full of frozen fish heads munched on a fish tail as if it were a potato chip. Another vendor opened a bottle of ketchup, stuck her finger in, licked it off, then recapped the bottle and set it out on the table to sell.

In the early autumn fresh tomatoes and cucumbers could be found in Vladivostok's markets, along with shiny purple eggplants, white squash, green cabbages, bright orange pumpkins and persimmons, crimson pomegranates, and a variety of fresh peppers—red, green, and yellow, mild, medium, and hot. But as the supplies of fresh produce steadily declined and prices quadrupled during October and November of 1993, we switched to buying canned red peppers from Bulgaria and big jars of Russian pickled green and red tomatoes, sometimes packed with cucumbers and seasoned with long hot red peppers, whole cloves of garlic, and a sprig or two of dill. The best we ever found was a three-liter jar of tomatoes and cucumbers sold by a private vendor with only a few items displayed on the hood of her car. Home-preserved over a wood fire, her pickled vegetables had a subtle smoky flavor that evoked scenes from nineteenth-century Russian novels, where strong-willed women supervised the preservation of summer's bounty at country estates surrounded by dense forests of birch and pine.

Fresh fruits and berries also added their jewel tones to the colors of Vladivostok's markets: imported oranges, apples, bananas, and kiwis; purple wild grapes from Primorskiy Kray; small red *limonnik* berries, big celadon-colored gooseberries, and jade-green *kishmish* (the term for seedless raisins in the rest of Russia, but the name of a rather rectangular-shaped fruit in the Russian Far East that tasted like a cross between a kiwi and a guava). Smoke-dried cherries were for sale in the autumn, and fresh lemons suddenly became available in December. But by winter most fruits and berries were so highly priced that we chose to forgo such luxuries and spend our money on less costly foods instead.

Thirty percent of all the honey produced in Russia came from Primorskiy Kray, so it was not surprising that two stores in Vladivostok, as well as individual sellers at the farmers' markets, offered a wide variety of honeys, some flavored naturally by the particular pollen the bees had fed on, others infused with herbal extracts made from birch leaves, honeysuckle, sweet clover, camomile, valerian, and St. John's wort. But Russian sugar was of such poor quality that it always posed problems in the kitchen, especially for baking. Except for the one time that Tom found a five-pound bag of extra-fine granulated sugar imported from the United States, all the sugar we purchased in Russia was the type known as *pesok* ("sand") because the granules were shaped like big grains of sand, which were difficult to dissolve in liquids or batters. Worse yet, this Russian sugar always had to be sifted before using, to sort out the impurities, and sometimes it was so damp that I had to dry it in the oven before I could decide whether it was even usable at all. Likewise, flour and other grains always had to be sifted thoroughly to remove the dirt, rocks, hairs, insect parts, and clumps of unidentifiable matter that infested every bag. Sometimes I became so disgusted that I threw out the entire lot of rice or flour or buckwheat groats—and just hoped that the next bag I bought would be somewhat less adulterated.

Spices were a real rarity in Asian Russia. After searching for months in Vladivostok, I managed to find only paprika, salt, bay leaves, anise, and black peppercorns. Only once did I see a single bottle of Tabasco sauce for sale (at a high price), although Cholimex brand "chilli sauce" was beginning to be imported from Vietnam. On the other hand, hot-spicy Russian mustard was a pleasant discovery, as was *adzhiga*, a type of homemade salsa containing sweet peppers, hot peppers, tomatoes, and garlic, several versions of which were sold by *babushki* at the farmers' markets. Hottest of all, however, was home-preserved horseradish root. One enterprising vendor described his product's pungency by quickly lifting his fur hat straight up from the top of his head—the perfect pantomime of "It's so strong it'll blow your head off!" He was right: Tom bought the single jar of horseradish he had for sale, and we laughed at the memory of his gesture every time that horseradish scorched our tongues and seared our sinuses.

We were continually surprised by the high quality of fresh red meat available in Vladivostok. But shopping for meat in Russia was not for the squeamish. Fresh meat was sold out of the trunks of cars or on tables set up in the farmers' markets—directly from the animal to the customer. The severed, bloody head of the cow or pig was displayed on the table or the hood of the car, the animal's lifeless eyes seeming to stare reproachfully at the customer for purchasing pieces of its butchered body, while skinny cats slithered along on the ground below in search of scraps. Behind the counter or beside the car sat a big tree trunk on which the butcher chopped the carcass into pieces with an ax. The result was not so much a "cut" of meat as a "whack." Our favorite "whacks" were T-bone roasts, about two or three inches thick (with an ax, steaks were out of the question). These prime whacks of meat cost only about a dollar a pound in the autumn of 1993, and when roasted properly, they always turned out to be more tender and flavorful than their method of slaughter and sale would ever suggest.

Poultry was less reliable. Locally raised chickens were so stringy and gamy that Tom referred to them as "Russian roadrunners." And even imported chickens were sometimes suspect. In November, 1993, the *Vladivostok News* reported that a shipment of chickens frozen in Argentina in 1986 had come into Vladivostok seven years later, where local sellers were attempting to peddle the poultry that had been stored far too long to meet Russian food safety standards (which were actually lax compared to those in the West). But frozen chicken leg quarters imported from the United States were quite another matter. Large, fleshy, and tender, they were the chicken of choice for any Russian who could afford them at the price equivalent of about one dollar per pound. Tom and I jokingly called these topless chickens "yuppie leftovers," because the majority of chicken products sold in the United States were white-meat products (chicken breasts, tenders, wings) favored by health-conscious and convenience-oriented customers, whereas much of the darker meat was exported to countries such as Russia and China, where the fact of having any chicken at all was more important than food fads. But we had difficulty explaining the concept of "yuppie leftovers" to Alla, who had never been to the United States and who, like any Russian, was merely happy to find a good piece of poultry to purchase, white meat or dark. Alla, in turn, told us that Russians nicknamed these imported American leg quarters "*gorbushki*," because the Russian-American trade agreement for importing this product was signed when Mikhail Gorbachev and George H. W. Bush were both in office.

Fish and other seafood were much easier to find in Vladivostok. Salmon was sold fresh, frozen, and canned, although the supply of all of these was irregular. Best of all was smoked salmon locally made by a fisherman or his wife, who skewered the whole fish on green twigs and smoked them over open fires made of birch logs. Canned squid was sometimes sold in the stores, and once we bought fresh squid directly from a fisherman on Reyneke Island. Scallops and shrimp were also occasionally available, and once I even found a whole sturgeon for sale at a *gastronom* downtown. Cans of crab (the size of tuna fish cans in the United States) cost 3,500 rubles ($2.80) each, and a 140-gram can of salmon caviar cost the same.

Salmon caviar was so abundant in Vladivostok that we almost took it for granted—if not as a staple, at least as a garnish as common as parsley in the United States. Glistening red-orange eggs of fresh salmon caviar were sold in half-liter and one-liter jars by *babushki* in the farmers' markets and in bulk at some of the fish stores, where you brought your own jars for the caviar to be ladled into. Once when Alla and Tom were standing in line to purchase frozen whole salmon off the back of a truck, Alla suddenly pointed to one and exclaimed, "Tom, you want *that* salmon!" "Why that particular one?" asked Tom, who thought that Alla's choice looked exactly like the hundreds of other fish stacked in the truck. "It's a female," she explained, "and it's still full of eggs. Make sure the seller gives you *that* one." Never one to dismiss Alla's advice, Tom brought the salmon home, where we cut it open and processed the red-orange roe according to the directions in an old edition of *Joy of Cooking*, the cookbook we always carry with us wherever we live. We ended up with so much fresh caviar that it was difficult to eat all of it before it spoiled. For the next three days, we spread gobs of salmon caviar on buttered bread, spooned it onto halves of hard-boiled eggs, mixed it with scrambled eggs for breakfast each morning, and even carried it to school for lunch.

Supplies of fresh red meat and scrawny local chickens suddenly increased in late autumn, as farmers began slaughtering their animals before the onset of winter. But dead chickens don't lay eggs. As eggs became increasingly scarce in Vladivostok—and sometimes disappeared entirely from the markets for a week or two—the price rose from 250 rubles (25 cents) for ten eggs in late September, 1993, to 3,500 rubles ($2.80) for ten eggs in early January, 1994—a tremendous price increase in a period of less than four months.

Prices for dairy products rose, too, but we continued to purchase them because most Russian dairy products were of such good quality that we considered them indispensable in our kitchen: milk sold in old-fashioned half-liter and one-liter returnable bottles made of thick greenish-blue glass, or in flimsy plastic bags that often broke open on the way home; kefir, a cultured milk product similar in taste to cultured buttermilk; pure sour cream with 15 to 20 percent butterfat; creamy unsalted butter (and an unusual chocolate-flavored butter that was sometimes available); and several kinds of cheeses, including *tvorog* (fresh white farmer cheese, plain or sweetened), processed beige-colored "*kolbasa*" cheese pressed into sausage skins, yellow semihard cheeses like Tilsit and more-aged ones like Cheddar, and even a grating cheese that tasted surprisingly like real Italian Parmesan. Seldom did we find more than one kind of cheese at any particular store, however, and sometimes there was only one type of cheese available throughout the entire city of Vladivostok. But despite eating so many fat-laden foods—butter, milk, eggs, cheese, sour cream, and red meats—during our entire stay in Russia, Tom and I both lost twenty pounds without even trying, and our cholesterol levels remained normal. After we returned to the United States, the doctor who did our blood tests attributed our svelte figures to the "Siberian spa" regime of rigorous daily exercise—walking for miles and climbing several flights of stairs each day—in the calorie-burning cold climate.

Bread remained the staff of life for Russians, for whom a meal was not complete without plenty of fresh bread to accompany every dish but dessert. In both Vladivostok and Irkutsk, the most common type was light-colored, whole-wheat bread, with a moderately dense texture, sold in blocky 500-gram loaves, unsliced and unwrapped. Bakery shops in Vladivostok sometimes also offered *bubliki*, small, crunchy rings of bread dough, and *kalachi*, large ring-shaped loaves of yeasty white bread that we indelicately called "toilet seat bread" because of their shape and size (a truly Western cultural reference in a country where toilet seats were as rare as French *baguettes*). Occasionally a bakery store, or a bread truck at the farmers' markets, would offer oblong loaves of white bread for sale. And once in Vladivostok we found large rounds of chewy flatbread, stamped on top with repeated motifs of a ring encircling a star, like *naan* from Central Asia. But we looked in vain for the heavy, dark rye bread for which Russia was famous. When I asked several of my Russian friends why there was no traditional Russian black bread to be found in Vladivostok, they all replied that black bread had disappeared from the bakeries two to three years earlier, as the country was just beginning to make the transition away from a socialist economy. Further inquiries were fruitless. No one seemed to know *why* black bread was no longer available—nor did anyone really seem to care.

Alcohol was another staple of the Russian diet, especially the ubiquitous vodka, most of which was distilled from potatoes, rye, or wheat. But newspaper and radio reports warned about bottles of vodka contaminated with high concentrations of poisonous fusel oil, shipped to the Russian Far East from China and from other parts of Russia. The brother of one of our Russian colleagues had even died from drinking tainted vodka—as did hundreds of other Russians each year, who imbibed poisonous products either from commercial distilleries or illegal stills at home.

Beer imported from Europe, Australia, Japan, and the United States was far superior to the Russian and Chinese brews that often left me with a horrible headache, even after only one bottle. Russian beer was also relatively tasteless. "Before I came to Russia, I thought *American* beer was watery," said Tom, who referred to Russian brews as "bulldog piddle." And our Russian students advised us not to buy any of the local brews sold on tap at little wooden PIVO (beer) stands in the city. "You might find a mouse—or something worse—floating in it," they warned.

To my surprise, however, Russian champagne was far better than I expected. On earlier trips to Eastern Europe, I had suffered through several bottles of sickly sweet Soviet champagne, which always left me wishing I had chosen anything else to drink. But most of the Russian champagne we

bought in Asian Russia was dry enough for our tastes, and it was often the
best deal, in price and quality, of any of the other alcoholic beverages available there. We ended up consuming more champagne during our time in
Russia than the total amount we had drunk during the rest of our lives.
Although supplies were irregular in Vladivostok, we could also buy red and
white wines, of varying quality, from France, Spain, Bulgaria, Moldova, and
Azerbaijan. And we always kept a bottle of *spirt*—180-proof Russian white
lightning—around the house, not for drinking, as Russians do, but for use as
an all-purpose cleaning agent, paint remover, and disinfectant for cuts and
scratches.

Occasionally we shopped for supplies at the local "Chinese market" in
Vladivostok, an open-air market on a plot of land designated by the municipal authorities, where vendors peddled a jumble of bargain-priced goods
piled on flimsy folding tables or laid on sheets of newspaper spread out on
the ground: clothing, towels, handkerchiefs, housewares, plastic toys, toilet
paper, prescription medicines in Russian packages (this was Harry Lime
country), fireworks, car batteries, "Kennedy" brand cigarettes with an American flag on the pack. Russians didn't hesitate to state their opinions of these
Chinese traders with their bulging bundles of cheap consumer goods, whose
wares the Russians simultaneously coveted and despised. Well-educated
Russians told me that the Chinese were bringing diseases into Russia in
their textile products and that school children in Vladivostok were suffering
from an outbreak of ringworm contracted from Chinese-manufactured clothing. But when I asked these same Russians why they simply didn't wash the
Chinese clothes before wearing them, they looked at me in silence, puzzled
by my question. Meanwhile radio and newspaper reports warned about
adulterated Chinese food products that threatened the health of the Russian populace. And several of my Russian friends claimed that commercially grown, pesticide-polluted produce was exported from China to Russia, where "those clever Chinese" got old Russian women to sell the tainted
fruits and vegetables in the farmers' markets, fooling Russian customers
into thinking they were buying organically grown foods from someone's
small dacha garden.

Russians also complained about the poor quality of Chinese goods—new
clothes that soon came apart at the seams, toys that broke easily—while overlooking the shoddy workmanship of most of their own Russian-made goods.
Whatever sense of quality Russian manufacturers might once have had, it
was almost entirely lost, stifled, or snuffed out under the Soviet system—
which also failed to provide many of the products that Russian consumers

needed or desired. So, despite their prejudices against the Chinese, ordinary Russians in Vladivostok's new market economy thronged to the local Chinese market, where they could purchase inexpensive products not available to them only a few years before.

I thought the open-air markets in Vladivostok looked primitive until I saw the one in Ussuriysk, a city located seventy miles north of Vladivostok, not far from the Chinese border. To the peal of bells from the adjacent Russian Orthodox church, I stepped out of a new Toyota van into the sights, smells, and sounds of a medieval marketplace. Only the people's attire, and a few of the manufactured goods, gave any clue that I was still in the twentieth century. The crowded market teemed with Russians, Chinese, Koreans, Gypsies, Georgians, and Armenians. At the entrance a middle-aged woman hawked her homemade *pirozhki*, each small savory pie wrapped in a page torn from a Russian chemistry book. Long parallel rows of crude wooden tables held an assortment of goods for sale: clothing and hardware on the smaller side of the market, foods on the larger side of the fence-enclosed field. Behind the tables sat old Russian women in fringed shawls, selling autumn vegetables and herbs, dried beans, and homemade sauerkraut. Swarthy Georgians and Armenians offered fresh fruits, berries, and walnuts, while young Korean girls sold several kinds of hot-spicy *kimchi* and Chinese men peddled track suits, mohair sweaters, and fur hats.

Inside a big barnlike building, more rows of vendors displayed their wares on rough wooden tables. Soft shafts of sunlight filtered through the structure's dusty windows, set high in the walls, the only illumination in the dim interior. Butchers whacked away at cattle carcasses thrown across massive tree-trunk chopping blocks at least a meter wide. At one stall a cheap, shiny, red-and-gold brocade tablecloth, with heavy gold fringe, was draped over half a pig still waiting to be cut into parts, its fresh blood stains mingling with the designs in the cloth. Another vendor offered a few pieces of smoked pork, next to a fellow selling two plump whole chickens. Honey was for sale on another aisle—four or five kinds, from light yellow to dark amber, the sweet nectar dripping from the honeycombs at each stall. On the opposite side of the barn, several rosy-cheeked women with kerchiefs on their heads were selling soft white farmer cheese and ivory-colored sour cream, fresh from their farms, brought to the market in big enameled buckets. Each of them offered me a taste of her wares. The nutty-flavored sour cream was so thick and buttery that wooden spoons stuck into it stood upright. Although the prices for these homemade dairy products were two to three times higher than commercially made fresh cheese and sour cream in

Vladivostok, I couldn't resist. After tasting several samples, I settled on the sour cream sold by a handsome blonde woman, who smiled as she ladled the rich cream into the glass jar I held out to her, then reduced the price by 20 percent when she discovered that I was an American.

When we arrived in Irkutsk in January, 1994, I was surprised to see that far fewer consumer goods were available than in Vladivostok. Although both cities were similar in size of population, Irkutsk did not have nearly as many food stores as Vladivostok, and the "Chinese market" that eventually opened in Irkutsk was much smaller than the one in Vladivostok. The majority of our purchases in Irkutsk came from just a few stores in the center of the city, at least an hour away from our appartment by public transportation. Most of the time, we shopped for food at the large Tsentral'nyy Rynok (Central Market), with its open-air section and enclosed market hall, plus a row of kiosks and street vendors just outside the market gates. And we purchased household products at the three-story department store called Torgovyy Kompleks (Commercial Complex), a Soviet-modern building that was sparsely stocked in comparison to Vladivostok's GUM.

My Russian friends in Vladivostok had often muttered, "The Chinese, they are not our friends," and referred sarcastically to "our friends from the Caucasus" (meaning Georgians, Armenians, Chechens, Azeris)—all of whom they both envied and disliked for their business acumen and economic successes in Russia's new market economy. In Irkutsk, the Central Asian and Caucasian food sellers at the downtown market were the focus of a similar jealousy. One of my Siberian colleagues advised me to purchase fresh produce only at state stores, where prices were lower and where you could count on the quality of the products. "At the Central Market," she warned, "those Georgians and Uzbeks can't be trusted. They inject dyes into the tomatoes and oranges, and they use chemicals on their produce." But the Central Market in Irkutsk offered the best variety and largest selection of foods to be found in the city, and it was often the only place where we could buy certain products, such as fresh tomatoes, in the winter.

Our weekly shopping trip to the Central Market in Irkutsk was always an adventure, because we never knew what we might find. During that winter and spring, Russian vendors offered fresh and roasted pine nuts, dried sunflower seeds, and jars of amber-hued honey; bunches of golden sea-buckthorn berries and crimson-colored jams made from whortleber-ries and currants; home-preserved sauerkraut and pickled garlic cloves;

butter, cheese, and sour cream; a hodgepodge of packaged imported goods from Turkish olive oil and Danish ham to Italian pasta and Swiss chocolates; and irregular-shaped pieces of a strange-looking, dark brown substance, larch-tree sap (I was told), boiled down to form a solid mass, which Siberians chewed as a kind of gum supposedly good for cleaning the teeth. Merchants from Central Asia and the Caucasus erected enticing displays of pomegranates, persimmons, pears, and plums; apples, oranges, cherries, and melons; eggplants, peppers, red radishes, and ripe tomatoes; peanuts and walnuts; raisins, sultanas, prunes, and dried apricots—although many of these products were priced considerably higher than an equivalent amount of fresh meat. Vendors in kiosks and small vans sold large rectangles of yeasty flatbread, chewy and flavorful, which everyone called *"lavash,"* even though the bread was actually more like Italian *focaccia* and Central Asian *naan* than the paper-thin flatbread from Armenia known as *lavash.* Buryats purveyed a few cuts of beef, and *babushki* peddled bunches of parsley and dill in winter, wild garlic and green onion tops in the spring, like wishful little bouquets, often the only fresh greens we saw in the market for weeks at a time.

Russian men in well-worn dark suits, with dingy shirts and no ties, hung around the edges of the market, smoking cigarettes, eating sunflower seeds, and swapping stories. On the sidewalks wizened old women sat patiently behind rickety folding tables with their meager displays of wares: a loaf or two of unwrapped whole-wheat bread next to a few jars of homemade jam, a couple of ladies' girdles, some sticks of Hollywood chewing gum, and a well-used socket wrench, gunky with oil. An Uzbek woman wrapped in a brightly colored, shimmery shawl sold raisins and nuts in small paper cones made out of official forms from the Irkutsk Municipal Water Department. People with puppies or kittens to sell stood with the little animals tucked into their woolen coats, the frightened furry heads peeking out above the topmost buttons. In one part of the market, a pretty teenage girl, wearing a garish, flower-printed dress and a thousand-yard stare, held a handful of peacock feathers and sipped a can of Dr Pepper, while in another section two older women, both drunk, tried to punch each other out in a fist fight.

In winter, nervous little chickadees hopped around on the wooden crates of unwrapped frozen meat, pecking at the blocks of beef, pork, chicken, and fish piled on top of each other without danger of their contents thawing in the frigid air. Customers couldn't select a certain cut of this frozen fare. You merely told the vendor the amount you wanted to purchase, and he either chopped off a chunk from the icy block with an ax or dropped the solid mass of meat onto the ground to break it up into smaller pieces. But the

Siberian winter was harder on other perishables. Eggs purchased indoors at the market sometimes froze and cracked before we could get them home on the long ride by trolley and tram. A small, precious head of Romaine lettuce that Tom found at the Central Market in March froze in transit to our apartment, then wilted into limp, lifeless leaves as it thawed. We ate it anyway: that was the first lettuce we had seen since arriving in Russia seven months before—and it turned out to be the last we would taste until the end of June that year.

In Irkutsk, milk was still marketed in a manner dating from far in the past. Fresh milk, straight from the cow, was poured into one- or three-liter buckets and set outside to freeze in the Siberian winter. As the milk froze, a thick wooden dowel or small tree branch was stuck upright into the middle of each pail. When the milk had frozen solid, it was removed from the pails in the form of large, white, truncated cones, like giant Popsicles, which were taken to the market and stacked for sale on tables outdoors. We carried the milk home, using the stick as a handle, and it never melted in transit, even on the trolleys and trams. After the milk had thawed overnight in a bucket in our kitchen, I boiled it to kill the germs and strained it through cheesecloth before using it. This farm-fresh frozen milk smelled strongly of the barnyard as it heated on the stove, but the boiled milk tasted fine, and we reveled in the rich cream that floated on the top.

Business of all sorts was being conducted in the new market economy in Irkutsk—from the single vendor with a cardboard suitcase just outside the Central Market gate, selling unwashed Karakul fleece from Kazakhstan, to the Russian friend of ours who purchased an armored railroad car from the Russian military, built for transporting missiles, which he used for shipping Japanese automobiles to customers all across Siberia. Former state-owned stores were slowly being turned into private enterprises, and new small shops were springing up like mushrooms. As in Vladivostok, most of these small stores sold a strange mix of products: wedding dresses and boom boxes, cosmetics and German wrenches, Pyrex casseroles and brass earrings shaped like the international symbol for "radiation," Turkish-made clothing and "Hollywood Star" dolls that were cheap copies of Barbie and Ken. A dingy store located far from downtown offered a limited but eclectic selection of Russian radios and televisions, car parts, children's toys, and phonograph records. Displayed side by side were an album by the Sex Pistols, music of the Russian Orthodox Church, and a probably pirated version of the Beatles' 1967 "Sgt. Pepper" album, its cover a faded photocopy of the real thing.

The small art galleries and folk craft shops that were opening their doors every month had more specialized stocks and a better sense of product display. They often exhibited the works of talented local painters, as well as selling traditional Russian lacquerware and Siberian crafts: handcarved wooden items, from nutcrackers to saltcellars; intricate birch-bark boxes and simple terra-cotta figurines; copies of icons and handmade silver jewelry set with semiprecious stones found around Lake Baikal. More basic Siberian products were available, too. One of our students kept pestering us to buy sable pelts for 200,000 rubles (120 dollars) each, a bobcat skin for 300 dollars, and a bear skin for 1,000 dollars (far too high a price, since bear skins were going for 800,000 rubles [470 dollars] in downtown Irkutsk that spring). And local newspapers published advertisements for more unusual items such as mammoth tusks, reindeer antlers, and bear bile.

By the time we returned to Vladivostok the next August, the selection of goods available in the stores was noticeably larger than only seven months before: Krystal and Tide detergents, contraceptives, Chinese brooms that actually had handles on them, molded plastic ceilings that needed only four screws to install, a new plastic Rus' brand 8mm movie projector (already outdated in the age of video). Imported Asian products—and along with them, foreign Asian styles—had invaded the Russian Far East with a bright and gaudy vengeance, almost as if shouting, "Hey, look how colorful a capitalist economy can be!" The fabric section of Vladivostok's GUM department store had changed its stock completely, from dull, drab, 1950s-style prints on heavy polyester knits, to slinky Asian synthetic "silks" dyed in strong, currently fashionable colors and abstract designs. Track suits and miniskirts, women's scarves and men's neckties, placemats and table napkins—all came in a palette of colors seldom seen on Russian fabrics. The counters of GUM were stacked with a plentitude of perfumes, bath soaps, aftershave lotions, and occasionally even toothbrushes. And the housewares section offered well-designed stainless-steel utensils, enameled cookware, and glass casseroles, all in stark contrast to the Russian products of lesser quality sold there only a few months before.

A big sign on Vladivostok's main thoroughfare advertised Barbie dolls for sale. Nearby, a bookstore displayed children's books and pornographic magazines side by side on the same counter. A new Russian Orthodox Church boutique, staffed by nuns in black habits, offered religious books, small copies of icons, votive candles, and other related paraphernalia. Down the street

Russian vendor at the Central Market in downtown Irkutsk.

a bagpiper in a kilt paraded in front of an Australian-funded food store to promote its products. And on a side street, a gun shop named "Sniper" sold high-powered rifles with scopes, single- and double-barreled shotguns, and gas pellet pistols. A guard at the door collected a 1,000-ruble (38 cent) entry fee to the store, which he waived for me, apparently because he was so surprised that a woman wanted to go inside. I wondered why: several of the women I knew in Siberia and the Russian Far East hunted with rifles and shotguns, and some were trained to use military firearms, from handguns to heavier weapons.

As the weather became colder, the GUM department store, smaller shops, and open-air markets began to offer a wide range of fur coat and fur hats, from less expensive rabbit and dog to more costly sable and mink. By December a new kind of Christmas card had made its appearance: musical cards that played "Jingle Bells" or "White Christmas" when opened, much to the delight of Russians, who had never seen anything like them before. These large, glitzy, gold-rimmed cards all had colorful covers depicting an old-fashioned Christmas tree or nineteenth-century European winter scene— but the greetings on the front were printed in both Russian and Chinese, or English and Chinese, or Spanish and Chinese, with the inside wording in Chinese only. Customers carried home these new treasures in plastic shopping bags printed with images that would have been banned only a few years before in the Soviet Union: a yellow bag with a reproduction of a Renaissance engraving of Christ and his disciples at the Last Supper; the double-headed Russian imperial eagle superimposed over the white-blue-red stripes of the Russian Federation flag; a red-white-and-blue bag with the American eagle and the words "Made in USA" and "In God We Trust" printed in English; another bag proclaiming, in English, "Nature Food Centre. Please Don't Litter."—a sardonic statement in urban Russia, where litter seemed to be a natural feature of the landscape.

Television and newspaper ads touted Black & Decker tools, Daewoo and Samsung electronic gear, Finnish furniture, Sony stereos, French perfumes, Gillette razors, Old Spice aftershave lotion, German toothpaste, Italian leather boots, Maggi bouillon cubes, Ilion exercise equipment, Whiskas cat food, and BASF videotapes. But—as so often in Russia—image often outstripped reality. Tom and I still had to spend an inordinate amount of time shopping several days each week just for basic supplies, and most of the new products I saw advertised in the media never actually appeared in any of Vladivostok's stores.

Food markets, on the other hand, displayed the bounty of the late-summer harvest and the contents of container ships from countries all around the Pacific Rim. At the farmers' markets that autumn of 1994, I found the best quality of fresh produce I had ever seen in Russia: green, red, and yellow tomatoes; purple and orange eggplants; dark green cucumbers, golden ears of sweet corn, and even a few green beans; big white onions, slender green onion tops, and thick leeks; bunches of garlic, shallots, and radishes; leafy green sorrel, Swiss chard, bok choy, and three kinds of lettuce; six different types of peppers; red and green cabbages; pumpkins, pumpkin seeds, and white squash; potatoes, carrots, turnips, and beets; cilantro, mint, and two types of parsley; apples, oranges, bananas, pears, watermelons, and honeydew melons; and wild mushrooms of so many colors and types that I had to ask Alla to identify them for me. A host of brightly packaged foreign food products was also rapidly displacing the drab displays of Russian goods: Australian ginger marmalade, Chinese chocolates, American Pop Tarts, papaya juice, peanut butter, Quaker Granola Bars, Velveeta cheese, TetraPaks of UHT milk (white and chocolate), American potato chips, Korean crab-and-shrimp-flavored chips, German tea cakes, Dove Bars, Del Monte canned corn, and wines from Italy, Spain, and the United States. But not all of these products were available every time we went to the markets—and as the weather turned colder, the supply of both fresh produce and imported processed foods dropped sharply, leaving most of the tables, stalls, and shelves stocked mainly with those standbys of the Russian winter: root vegetables, grains, and bottled green tomatoes.

Early in the autumn fresh crawfish, shrimp, carp, and crab legs sometimes turned up in the markets, but I noticed a definite decline in the overall availability of fresh and canned Russian fish products—salmon, sprats, crab, squid, salmon caviar—compared to the year before. Russian friends said that prior to perestroika, there had always been more than ample supplies of fresh and canned fish in Vladivostok, but now these products were being exported abroad for hard currency, causing shortages on the shelves at home. On the other hand, I was surprised to see so much more beef, pork, and poultry for sale in Vladivostok's open-air markets: vans filled with fresh and frozen beef hearts, livers, and tongues, looking like Arctic charnel houses; slabs of smoked pork and small whole piglets; chicken parts and ground turkey. Big truck loads of inexpensive meat suddenly appeared in the markets during late September and early October, but Alla warned us not to buy any. "It's from farms that were flooded in Primorskiy Kray," she explained. "The meat is no good. It's from livestock that drowned." A few days later I asked her if the price of potatoes would be going up, since so many potato fields were also wiped out in the floods—but I was puzzled by her reply. "Yes, the prices will be higher because more potatoes will be for sale at the market," she claimed, exhibiting no concept of the normal relationship between supply and demand.

Alla was a much better guide to the actual products for sale than to the economics of the marketplace. In early November she enticed me away from the office with news of a "special fish market" that afternoon on a quay downtown. By the time we arrived, a long line of people had already formed on the concrete pier, waiting to purchase giant Kamchatka crabs from the crew of a large commercial fishing boat, the *Kievka*, a ship so rusty that it looked like it might crumble apart and sink before the cargo could be unloaded. Live crabs were selling for 20,000 rubles ($6.50), 25,000 rubles ($8), or 30,000 rubles (less than $10) for an entire Kamchatka crab, depending on the size of the crustacean. A sailor on the gangplank took the customer's money and handed it to someone on board, then another crewman tossed the live crab from the boat down onto the pier. Alla and I couldn't pass up such a bargain. We each purchased a crab, then struggled to get the large, spiky, wriggling creatures back to our apartments. Tom and I had a pot barely big enough to cook ours in, but—in a situation all too reminiscent of the famous lobster scene in Woody Allen's *Annie Hall*—we finally managed to stuff the whole crab into a boiling-water bath. Lacking any proper crab-eating utensils, we cracked open the shell with Tom's Leatherman Tool and pulled out the flesh with toothpicks. And for the next two days we gorged on the freshest, most flavorful crab we'd ever eaten, sprinkled with lemon juice or garnished with garlic mayonnaise.

Our ability to "cook from scratch"—and our willingness to process caviar and crab meat directly from the animal instead of just opening a can—gave Tom and me a culinary advantage over some of our American colleagues in Russia, who were not accustomed to cooking for themselves every day and who sorely missed American fast-food chains and commercially prepared products. Other than a limited selection of canned and bottled goods, Russia produced few of the kinds of "convenience foods" so common in the United States. Prior to the importation of Oriental dried noodle soups, American packaged mixes, and Australian frozen foods in the mid-1990s, "convenience foods" in the Russian Far East consisted of pickled vegetable salads from the local *gastronomy*, big blobs of yeasty *testo* (fresh bread dough) sold by some bakeries, and plastic bags of homemade *pel'meni* sometimes sold by street vendors or at farmers' markets.

Meanwhile American-style supermarket shopping was a gleam in the eyes of several foreign entrepreneurs. In the 1990s Dick Schindler, a retired American grocery executive, spent several years and millions of dollars trying to open his dream store, the 91,000-square-foot Giant Vladivostok, a project that ultimately never materialized. Only a couple of much smaller, relatively modern food outlets, backed by foreign investors, had opened by late 1994, including an Australian store on the ground floor of GUM and a small food store owned by the American Globus Corporation (a company that also distributed food products elsewhere in the Russian Far East), which was inconveniently located several miles out of town in a sparsely populated area. Globus sold an array of imported food products new to Russian consumers, including Newman's Own salad dressings, American baby foods, Chi-Chi's Chunky Restaurant Salsa, Francesco Rinaldi Spaghetti Sauce, Kraft Non-Dairy Creamer, and Dinty Moore Beef Stew.

But as an increasing number of these new foreign food products came into Russia, customers often puzzled over how to use them, particularly when the directions were printed only in a foreign language. A locally produced television commercial showed Russian viewers how to mix American powdered milk with cold water in a big plastic punch bowl. A handwritten sign in a small store in downtown Vladivostok explained to shoppers that cans of Paramount Beef Tamales with Sauce, imported from the United

States, were actually *"Bliny c myasom"* (pancakes with meat). And the editor of *Anna*, the largest-circulation women's journal in the Russian Far East, asked me to write an article for her readers, telling them how to prepare and use many of these new, imported convenience foods, including canned soup concentrates, bottled spaghetti sauce, packaged dry cake mixes, and peanut butter.

Foreigners living in Russia encountered similar problems with local food products. At many of the grocery stores, dry products such as flour, sugar, salt, semolina, buckwheat groats, macaroni, millet, and a variety of other grains were sold in plain, clear-plastic bags weighing 500 grams or 1 kilogram, with no labels identifying the contents. Russians could recognize these basic foodstuffs, but most Americans—accustomed to clearly labeled products in distinctive, brand-name packages—could not always distinguish salt from sugar, flour from cornstarch. A more dangerous example was Russian white vinegar—not 5 percent acid, like American white vinegar, but industrial-strength acetic acid that had to be diluted 20-to-1 with water before it was safe to ingest. But unless you could read the small-print directions in Russian, you had no way of knowing that the clear liquid was so lethally concentrated.

Despite the move toward more modern marketing, many Russian products continued to be sold in bulk, each customer's request individually weighed on a big, old-fashioned, metal scale, while the other customers stood patiently in line waiting their turn. Given Russians' sense of generosity in their personal lives, I was always surprised to see the obsessive precision with which every shop girl weighed each order to the exact gram. Typical was the scene I witnessed at a bakery in Ussuriysk, where the saleswoman was weighing a kilogram of gingerbread cookies for a customer. The last cookie pushed the scale to just slightly over a kilo, so the girl took one of the cookies, broke it in half, and weighed each half separately with the remaining cookies on the scale, to find which half produced a total closer to 1 kilogram. When she dumped the cookies into the customer's shopping bag and handed him a few rubles (worth less than 5 cents) in change, he looked at her disgustedly and shook his head in disbelief, as if to say, "Why didn't you just give me the other half of the cookie and keep the paltry change?"

By October, 1994, the value of the ruble had declined so much that few people even bothered handing back small change to a customer. Between September 1 and October 10, the value of the ruble fell 29 percent against the dollar, and on October 11 it plummeted another 22 percent, to almost

4,000 rubles to the dollar, the largest single-day decline in its history. After a slight recovery, the ruble's value continued to slip downward during the remaining months of that year. With the collapse of the Russian currency, the prices of consumer goods rose accordingly. People began paying for products—and getting their change in return—with stacks of banded bank notes, totaling 10, 20, and 50 thousand rubles each. Few people bothered with individual notes of 100- or 200-ruble denomination, because they were now worth so little. As we loaded stacks of rubles into our shopping bag before going out to purchase food that October, we were reminded of those documentary films about hyperinflation during the Weimar Republic in Germany seventy years before, when people took a wheelbarrow full of reichsmarks to the store just to buy a loaf of bread. In 1994 the Russian economy never reached that point. But buying modern merchandise with stacks of banded rubles always reminded us that living in Russia's new market economy was like living simultaneously in several different layers of time.

In the midst of this monetary turmoil, Tom was teaching principles of macroeconomics to Russian students at the university in Vladivostok. And some of their written responses on quizzes and exams provided a welcome bit of levity as he graded papers by candlelight in our chilly apartment that autumn. In answer to the question, "What is economics?" one student replied, "The subject that helps people not to get lost in the world of money." Another defined economics as "a science which predicts some events in an economy and then tries to explain why they did not take place." When asked, "What are the three most important economic problems facing Russia today?" one student wrote, "Inflation, insecurity, and economists." To the question, "What can be done about Russia's economic problems?" another replied, "There is no 'safe and sound' way to manage the economy. Any economy is balanced on the edge of a blade." And on a major examination one student kept using the term "laissez-failure economics" (instead of laissez-faire), which may well have been an unintentionally appropriate description of the situation in Russia during the early stages of that country's transition to a market economy.

CHAPTER 10

~

School Days

Earning our living as university professors in post-Soviet Russia was a learning experience for all the American faculty in Irkutsk and Vladivostok. The duties were the same as for professors in any country: preparing lectures, teaching classes, advising students, and grading homework, research papers, and exams. But the Russian education system, cultural differences in the classroom, and the way in which we were paid for our work—all differed considerably from our previous experiences in the West.

Faculty members sent to Russia by University of Maryland University College (UMUC) earned a salary paid in American dollars, which was deposited by the university in banks in the United States. We also earned a monthly stipend, paid in rubles, from the Russian universities where we taught. When Tom and I first arrived in Vladivostok in 1993, the stipend in September was 95,000 rubles (95 dollars) each; in October, it increased to 130,000 rubles (108 dollars). This ruble stipend was supposed to be sufficient to pay for basic foodstuffs and household supplies, but we usually had to dip into our own cash reserves—dollars brought to Russia in money belts and carry-on luggage—to pay for beer, wine, souvenirs, and gifts, as well as all entertainment, restaurant meals, and travel expenses.

All the professors at our two Russian universities—Russians and foreigners alike—were paid their salaries every month in cash, with rubles transported by car or van from the central administration building to the various university departments scattered around the city. Often the pay was late—sometimes a few days, sometimes much longer—causing the Russian faculty to threaten going on strike. When the money finally did arrive, each professor was summoned to his or her departmental office to sign a pay receipt in return for bundles of cash. As inflation increased and the value of the ruble declined, many of the Russian professors were paid only a portion of their salaries, and often they had to wait two or three months to be paid at all. But the American faculty in our program always received their ruble stipends—even if a few days late—probably because the Russian administration did not want to lose face with UMUC.

When we arrived in Irkutsk in early 1994, the monthly ruble stipend (which included a new 30,000-ruble "regional cost-of-living adjustment") increased to 250,000 rubles (160 dollars)—which was our take-home pay after Russian income tax and mandatory Russian pension-fund contributions totaling 64,000 rubles (41 dollars) had been deducted. In early April we were pleasantly surprised to learn that our stipends had risen to 250,000 rubles *plus* a separate cost-of-living adjustment of 125,000 rubles, making a net salary of 375,000 rubles (220 dollars) for each of us that month. And we were even more surprised to hear that the new, additional cost-of-living adjustment would also be paid retroactively for March.

Toward the end of April, however, we began to suspect the new salary figures were nothing more than empty promises, as the Russian dean of our program continued to apologize for our not yet receiving that month's pay. "The university will have the money any day now," he kept saying, as we dipped further and further into our own dollar reserves. Finally I received a message to report to the departmental accountant's office, a few doors down the hall from our faculty office. When I walked through the door, her face was beaming. "The money has arrived!" she announced in Russian. "Please sign these two receipts—one for you and one for Tom. Then you can take the money for both of you."

I couldn't believe the figures in front of me on those slips of paper. With the inclusion of the retroactive cost-of-living adjustment for March, each of us was receiving 500,000 rubles (280 dollars) that month! Still surprised that the Russians had really managed to come up with that amount of money, I signed the receipts for both of us. "Where are your shopping bags?" asked the accountant. I had no idea why she'd suddenly changed the subject from salaries to shopping. Thinking I'd misunderstood her question, I asked her to repeat it. "You'll need a shopping bag," she said, pointing across the room to a desk piled high with banded stacks of rubles. Our combined stipend of one million rubles that month was being paid to us in thousands of bank notes of 100-ruble, 200-ruble, and 500-ruble denomination.

Since the weather was warm that day, I was wearing a skirt and a long, loosely fitted, crinkle-cotton overblouse. I looked at the accountant and laughed, as I reached for the front hem of my blouse and held out the material to form a makeshift container for the money. Chuckling at the situation, she carefully stacked the bundles of rubles onto the flimsy cotton material. I gathered it around the cash, exposing more of my midriff and brassiere than propriety allowed, and hurried back down the hall to my office. Later that day, Tom and I toted all the money home in a shopping bag he'd brought to school. And that evening we celebrated our good fortune with a bottle of Russian champagne, toasting the pile of rubles on our kitchen table and laughing as we joked that this was the first time in our lives—and surely the last—that we would ever "make a million" as college professors.

In August, 1993, the first group of seven professors from University of Maryland University College arrived in Russia to begin teaching in what was called "the American curriculum" of the joint Russian-American undergraduate degree program there. The program had been established two years earlier, at Far Eastern State University (FESU) in Vladivostok and Irkutsk State University (ISU) in Irkutsk, to prepare Russian students for future positions as business managers in the emerging market economy of the Russian Federation.

During their first two years in the program, students took courses solely in the Russian part of the curriculum, taught in the Russian language by local Russian professors. They also had several hours of intensive English-language training each week, taught mainly by Russian instructors. At the end of their second year of study, those students who demonstrated sufficient English-language skills were admitted to the upper-division (third- and fourth-year) American part of the curriculum, which was taught entirely in English by faculty sent to Russia by UMUC, using textbooks and course materials shipped from the United States. Upon successfully finishing this four-year program, the Russian students received a bachelor's degree from University of Maryland University College. They could then spend a fifth year completing the requirements for a *diplom*—a degree halfway between the American bachelor's and master's degrees—from their Russian universities, which usually included serving an internship with a Russian company and writing a thesis on a topic concerning Russian business or the Russian economy.

Enrollments at both universities were limited to fifty students entering the program each year, with a maximum of 250 students (total) eventually enrolled in all five levels at each location. Unlike in Russian state-supported universities, however—where education was provided free—students in the Russian-American program had to pay tuition of several thousand dollars, in a combination of Russian and U.S. currencies. Some of the students came from families wealthy enough to finance their education privately, but most of them were sponsored by Russian businesses or regional governments, which paid the tuition in return for the students' working for their sponsors during summer vacations and for two to five years after graduation.

Just as in other departments of Russian universities, first-year students were admitted to the program through competitive entrance examinations taken after they had completed their last year of high school. Unlike in the United States, students in Russia could apply to, and take entrance examinations for, only one university and only one department within it. And since the examinations were given just once a year, students who failed them had to wait another twelve months before trying again. In a country where admission to a university—and the particular university you were accepted by—was a prime determinant of your career, your prospects for advancement, and your social status, those entrance examinations were a major milestone in a young Russian's life. Moreover, in the new market economy of the 1990s, our Russian-American program was one of the most highly desirable departments to enter, despite the steep tuition costs. At both ISU and FESU, nine times more students applied for the program than were admitted to the fifty places available at each location every year.

Applicants to enter the program as first-year students took Russian university entrance examinations in three fields: English, mathematics, and Russian. But several of the students at FESU bragged about how easy it was to bribe the local examiners to give them a passing grade. In the autumn of 1993, one of my students told me that the current price for passing the Russian composition entrance examination was a one-hundred-dollar bill placed inside a blank testing notebook, which the student handed back to the Russian professor after sitting for an appropriate period of time in the testing room. And, as in the old Soviet system, it was tacitly assumed that the "gilded youth"—the children of important and influential people—would be given preferential treatment in determining who was accepted for admission to the university. To its credit, the Russian administration in Irkutsk publicly tried to dispel this commonly held belief: at a meeting with parents and sponsors of prospective first-year students, one father stood up and asked to be told the exact amount of money he would be expected to pay as a bribe to get his son into the program. Vladimir Saunin—a vice president of the university, director of the Russian-American program at ISU, and a man of integrity—immediately replied, with great dignity, that this was a new program in the new Russia, and students would be admitted to it only on the basis of proven merit, not bribes.

The first group of seven UMUC professors was sent to Russia in 1993 with the goal of merging the American and Russian education systems into a successful "joint venture" within our departments at both FESU and ISU. Tom had been hired to teach economics to third-year students. I was selected to serve as Maryland's on-site program coordinator that year, the first semester in Vladivostok and the next in Irkutsk. But my primary job was to teach study skills—time management, test taking, cross-cultural communications, all in English—to second-year students still in the Russian segment of the curriculum, to prepare them for making the transition to the American part of the program, where all their courses would be taught in English and where teaching styles, classroom discipline, homework assignments, examinations, and grading were all very different from the students' previous experience in their Russian schools.

All the UMUC professors were expected to re-create an American classroom environment at the two Russian universities, to the extent possible. But the first time I walked into a Russian university classroom, all twenty-five students stood up at attention. Not even my students at German universities had done that, much less the ones in American classrooms. The Russians remained standing, looking straight ahead in silence, until I asked them please to sit down. Most of them were dressed in their finest clothes: suits and ties on the young men, fancy sweaters and skirts—and even cocktail dresses—on the young women. When I read the roll out loud, each student stood up again as his or her name was called. And whenever I asked one of them a question, that student stood up to give the answer. In those first few minutes in my new Russian classroom, I had already encountered some of the many cultural differences that would continue to crop up throughout the three semesters that I taught there.

Initially none of the Maryland professors sent to Russia were fully aware of the considerable differences between the American and Russian education systems. For a start, all of us were surprised to see that the students sitting in our classes were two years younger than their counterparts in the United States. Prior to Russia's educational reforms in the early 1990s, Russian students spent a total of only ten years in their primary and secondary schools, graduating from high school at the end of the tenth grade when most of them were seventeen or even sixteen years old. More accustomed to teaching upper-division college students in their twenties, we were not really prepared for the level of immaturity of some of our Russian students, especially the younger ones. But their adolescent attitudes and lack of experience in the wider world were more than matched by the quality of their education up to that time, and, for some, by a certain amount of cynicism, intellectual detachment, or plain old street smarts that belied their youth.

On the other hand, our Russian students were surprised to discover that we expected them to attend class regularly, to take extensive notes, to do so much reading, and—in many courses—to do so much homework each week. They were also surprised to learn that their final grades in each course would be based on a series of written homework assignments, quizzes, and examinations given throughout the semester—instead of little or no written homework and only one oral examination, at the end of each term, as in the Russian system. The longer some of our professors taught in Russia and talked with their students about the courses in the Russian curriculum, the more convinced they became that, from the American point of view, Russian oral final examinations were seldom as rigorous as American written final exams. These oral exams also provided much opportunity for cheating or mere "muddling through" (often with the help of the professor giving the exam, who didn't want to sully his or her own reputation by flunking any students). Yet all of us also recognized that most of the admittedly highly selected students we taught at ISU and FESU were fairly well educated by the time they entered the American part of the program, despite our own perceived problems with the Russian education system.

Both the Russian students and their university administrators had difficulty understanding that students in the American part of the curriculum could choose to enroll in any section of a course offered during the semester—and could drop out of a course for personal or academic reasons, or even fail a course, then repeat it at a later time. Students in the Russian education system were accustomed to going through each school year—and in most cases, even their entire university careers—with the same cohort of approximately twenty-five to forty students. They were assigned to that group by the departmental administration when they first entered the university, and from then on they attended all their classes together. The Russian administration, not the individual student, determined which courses a student would take each semester and what time of day he or she would be sitting in any particular class.

These cohorts of students progressed together from one class to the next, from one semester to another, with very few failures among the group. In the Russian university, a student who failed even one course, any semester, was usually kicked out of school. So the university had an unwritten but expected "pass-along" policy, which tended to blame academic failure on any number of reasons external to the students themselves, including "inadequate" or "unsupportive" teachers. No wonder the Russian universities had so few failures: Anna Khamatova, the dean of our program in Vladivostok, told me that 90 percent of the students admitted to FESU went on to graduate from the university. In contrast, only 50 percent of entering students completed a four-year degree in the United States at that time.

My own experience of teaching in Russia led me to conclude that although the joint Russian-American program was considered to be an elite department at both universities, the one in Irkutsk was indeed an education program for intellectually elite Siberian students, whereas the one in Vladivostok could be better described as a program for the children of social, political, education, and business elites of the Russian Far East. In Irkutsk, the students at ISU were well prepared for university-level work, and almost all of them had a serious attitude toward successfully completing their studies. For that reason a larger percentage of students entering the program at ISU actually graduated from it five years later, compared to the number who completed the program at FESU. The students in Vladivostok were more like those at any mid-ranking state university in the United States, ranging in academic performance from excellent to average to well below average—although the top students we taught in Vladivostok were certainly as good as the best ones in Irkutsk.

At both universities, the American faculty were particularly impressed with the mathematical skills of our Russian students, who were far better educated in that field than most Americans of the same age. The Russians also possessed a level of English that enabled them to take two years of upper-division, American-oriented, academic courses taught entirely in English. (In comparison, very few U.S. university students have the foreign language skills necessary to take all their junior- and senior-level courses at a Russian university.) I later learned that in the Soviet and Russian school systems, more students took English (the British version) than any other foreign language, followed by French and German—despite the Soviet Union's longstanding animosity toward the governments of most English-speaking countries.

Most of our students at ISU and FESU had taken English for six years prior to entering the university, but their general consensus was that English-language instruction in the lower grades had been almost worthless, and they attributed most of their language skills to the Russian professors of English who had instructed them during their first two years of higher education. However, I should note that some of the best English-speaking adults I met in Siberia (including some of our students) were graduates of a special English-language, primary-secondary school that I visited in the city of Angarsk, where students were taught English from the first grade, and where many of their other academic subjects, such as geography and natural sciences, were also taught in English. In Irkutsk I also visited the special, elite Irkutsk Experimental School No. 47, where primary- and secondary-school students were given higher levels of instruction in such languages as English, German, French, Spanish, Japanese, and Korean.

All of our university students belonged to the generation that straddled the old and the new, the Soviet Union and the Russian Federation. Born when Brezhnev was still in office, most of them were only ten years old when Gorbachev came to power. They had grown up in a society, and a school system, in transition, where the social sciences were mere handmaidens of the state, and where the history books had recently been removed from the shelves to be rewritten once again. And as products of the Soviet education system, many of our Russian students lacked the intellectual openness and curiosity that we took for granted among our best students in the United States. They came from a school system that still relied primarily on rote memorization and recitation and that emphasized conformity of thought—a system where the teacher ruled the classroom, and where independent thinking and initiative were discouraged. Hence they were not accustomed to critical thinking, to discussing an idea from several different viewpoints, to asking questions or challenging the teacher in class. As one of my American colleagues in Vladivostok observed, "These students have incredible memories—if they've read it, they can regurgitate it, but they don't know how to apply [it]. . . . They can't synthesize—they're only three years away from seventy years of repression when individual thinking was punished. They can't deal with 'what if' questions—they don't know 'what is.'"

But such generalizations, while accurate in the aggregate, failed to account for those outstanding students who were innately curious and questioning and for whom critical thinking seemed to come naturally. And in certain ways, many of our Russian students were less "provincial" than their counterparts in the United States, despite the limitations of the Soviet system that had educated them. Not only did they speak at least one foreign language, many of them also had traveled to several parts of the former

Soviet Empire, from the Baltic countries, Eastern Europe, and Ukraine, to the Caucasus and Central Asia. Others had visited China, Japan, England, and the United States.

But I also discovered that when traveling abroad, few of my students felt comfortable dining in foreign restaurants, because they'd had so little experience eating in restaurants at all. As part of the cross-cultural communication segment of my study skills course, I took dishes and flatware to class, displayed various kinds of table settings, and showed the different ways of handling knives and forks in Europe and the United States. I described the sequencing of multicourse meals in countries such as France and explained which pieces of flatware to use with each course. I demonstrated the proper use of chopsticks in different Asian countries and how to eat with only the fingers of the right hand in other countries—all for the practical purpose of teaching my students how to behave correctly at business meals, whatever part of the world they were in. They loved those cross-cultural classroom sessions, and some of my best students were thrilled when I loaned them my copy of *Tiffany's Table Manners for Teenagers*, which they read as avidly as the latest issue of *Playboy* or *Cosmopolitan*.

A surprising set of cultural differences surfaced one day when I asked a Peace Corps volunteer to be a guest speaker in one of my classes for second-year students in Vladivostok. Mark was a Philippine American from California—an attractive, extroverted, personable young man with dark hair, olive skin, and a gentle demeanor. He was also an accomplished ballroom dancer who had participated in several competitions in the Russian Far East. But when he walked into my classroom, the Russian students visibly recoiled at his presence.

I had asked Mark to explain the U.S. Peace Corps mission in the Russian Far East, then describe his specific role in setting up a local business center to provide information for Russians in Vladivostok who wanted to start small businesses of their own. After that he could answer any questions posed by the students. A good public speaker, at ease in front of strangers, Mark introduced himself, then began his presentation by standing close to the first row of students. I don't know if he noticed their reaction, but I certainly did: the students glanced around uncomfortably, then shifted in their seats, partially turning away from him, while some of the others in the back of the room began to snicker.

During the entire class session there was a palpable feeling of unease in the room. Mark's presentation was lively, interesting, and informative, and he tried several good techniques for drawing the students out of their shells.

But only one or two of them ventured to ask him a question. And when Mark turned to the blackboard to write something on it with his left hand, some of the students laughed out loud, while a low murmur of voices rose up from the group.

At the end of class, after Mark had left, a group of students gathered in front of my desk, standing around in an embarrassed silence until I finally asked, "What's wrong? Is something the matter?"

"We've never seen a black man before," one of them volunteered.

"But Mark *isn't* black," I replied, caught by surprise by their assumption, since Mark would never have been mistaken for a black person in the United States. "He's a Philippine American," I explained. "His parents came originally from the Philippine Islands in the Pacific Ocean."

"He's not *black?*" chimed in several of them at the same time.

"No," I reiterated. "Just because a person's skin is a little darker than yours or mine, that doesn't mean the person is 'black.' Black people or their ancestors originally came from Africa. And those who live in the United States are called 'African Americans.' Mark's family came from the Philippines, on the other side of the globe. He's not 'black' at all."

They stopped to think about this for a few moments. Then a young woman, the best student in the class, added, "But he's also one of 'those'. . ."—as all the other students started to giggle again.

"I don't know what you're talking about," I responded, as it began to dawn on me that they perceived Mark as gay. "What do you mean 'one of *those*'?" I persisted.

"*You* know . . . ," she replied with a grin, although neither she nor any of the others was willing to elaborate on her assertion. I looked at them neutrally, letting the silence grow. Then suddenly another student blurted out, "And he's left-handed, *too!*"

Without realizing it I had invited a guest speaker whose color of skin, manner of speaking, body language, and writing hand had all directly confronted Russian prejudices regarding racial stereotypes, images of masculinity, and natural left-handedness (which Russians consider an inferior trait). Yet when I told those students that I thought Mark was a nice guy, they seemed to accept my opinion, at the same time indicating their own surprise that someone so "different" could also appear to be so nice.

In his presentation to the class, Mark had invited the students to visit the business center that he'd recently set up in a room at our university. Two weeks later, several of those students came up to me in the hall with American business textbooks in their arms and big smiles on their faces. "We've just come from the business center," they announced. "Mark has loaned us all these books, and he's letting us use his reference books there, and he's even letting us use his computers and software!" they enthused, their words tumbling over each other. "You were right. He's a *wonderful* person!"

And *you* have learned a valuable lesson, I thought.

During each semester in Russia, I gave questionnaires, to be answered anonymously, to all the students in our program, asking their opinions about several Russian political figures, as well as their own perceptions of the economic and social problems confronting post-Soviet Russia. Only a few of them had much to say about specific economic and social issues—but almost all of them were very articulate about Russian political leaders, past and present. After evaluating more than two hundred questionnaires, I reached the conclusion that most of our Russian students considered Lenin to have been a cruel genius, a great leader, "a man for his time," but one who made grave errors in the direction he took Russia after the Bolshevik Revolution. Stalin was viewed more negatively, as the worst leader Russia had had, a brutal dictator responsible for the deaths of millions of innocent people. Contrary to the opinions of their parents and grandparents, however, our students had a much more positive attitude toward Gorbachev, whom they credited for his innovative policies of glasnost and perestroika and for taking the first steps toward democratization of Russia, as well as his role in ending the Cold War. But they also felt that Gorbachev never realized his own potential—either because he was fundamentally a weak leader, despite his personal attractiveness and articulateness, or because he was unable to rise above his Communist roots. In the same year (1993) that Yeltsin was reelected president of the Russian Federation, more than 90 percent of our students thought that Yeltsin was a tired alcoholic buffoon, not competent for the role of president and not trustworthy to lead Russia into the twenty-first century. But they reserved their greatest criticism for Zhirinovsky, whom almost all of them viewed as "a second Stalin," "a Russian fascist," a madman hungry for personal power, all the more dangerous because he "speaks to the hopes and fears of many people who don't like to think about things too deeply."

Despite the credit all the American professors gave our Russian students for their intellectual abilities and their determination to succeed in a new, very different American education program within their own rapidly changing society, there were still certain cultural chasms we never completely bridged. All the UMUC teachers were continually displeased by the Russians' propensity to talk with each other in class while the professor was lecturing or while another student had the floor during class discussions or presentations. This seemed to be a learned behavior that was characteristic of the culture, from the concert hall to the classroom. During my time in Siberia and the Russian Far East, I had the opportunity to visit classes at several different kinds of schools—from primary schools to vocational-technical colleges to polytechnic institutes—and this constant chatter occurred in all of them. Some of the American faculty eventually came to accept that our students were not intentionally being disrespectful or disruptive. But the Russians never seemed to fully understand why their American professors placed such a high value on paying attention in class and listening to only one speaker at a time.

Cheating was a far more serious problem. Our Russian students were masters of the classic methods of cheating, which they considered to be just another study skill or merely a game to be played to get through the course, not an ethical transgression at all. They copied each other's homework, word for word. They came to tests with answers written on the palms of their hands and on crib sheets hidden in their pockets or slipped up their sleeves. They whispered answers to each other during exams and passed notes back and forth concealed in Russian-English dictionaries. After finishing a test, they revealed all the questions to the students waiting in the hall to take the exam during the next class period. And at the end of the course, some even copied each other's course-evaluation comments, word for word, providing further proof of the persistence of the cheating mentality.

As part of a lesson about writing research papers, I introduced the concept of plagiarism to my students in Vladivostok. After explaining why plagiarism was morally and intellectually wrong, I gave examples of how allegations of plagiarism had tainted the reputations of American public figures such as Sen. Joseph Biden and Dr. Martin Luther King. But my Russian students had difficulty understanding why stealing someone else's words or ideas would be a problem for anyone. One of my best students—a young woman who always sat on the first row of the class and who never openly engaged in cheating—looked at me incredulously and said, "You've got to be kidding! You're not really *serious* about that?" No wonder the Maryland professors who assigned research papers complained every semester that most of the Russian students copied information directly from their textbooks and from library sources, without any citations whatsoever, stringing the plagiarized paragraphs together without even any thoughts, ideas, or analysis of their own. But for students who had grown up in a system that never fostered independent thinking, that seemed a perfectly acceptable way to write a "research" paper.

The American faculty—who placed a high value on individual initiative and achievement—had to work constantly to overcome what we euphemistically called "the Russian students' collectivist approach toward doing homework and taking tests." Some of the students tried to get us to see the situation from their point of view. "A Russian proverb says, 'One head is good, but two are better,'" a student in Vladivostok pointed out to me. Others with a well-developed sense of humor satirized the situation in a very Russian sort of way. On an assignment asking students to apply four specific problem-solving strategies to a problem of their own choosing, one of my top students in Vladivostok explained how to use these strategies to cheat successfully on my tests. When our English professor in Irkutsk asked his students in a technical-writing course to select a task and write a detailed description of how to perform it, one student produced an excellent essay on various methods of cheating in class.

Such attitudes were not surprising in a country where the concept of collectivism long predated the twentieth-century Soviet regime and in a society that had for decades considered "individualism" to be a dirty word. "The tallest blade of grass is the first to be cut down," says an old Russian proverb. And, indeed, many of our modern-day students seemed far more comfortable conforming to their own group than calling attention to themselves by taking the initiative in class or taking responsibility for their own answers on exams. The "collectivist spirit" was so strong that even the best students helped others to cheat. In both Vladivostok and Irkutsk, it was not unusual for the best student in a class to sit next to the worst one—so the poor student could copy the correct answers from the one who'd actually studied the material and understood it. The Russians justified this behavior on the basis of expected collective spirit within their cohort. And they seemed genuinely surprised whenever their American professors caught them cheating and automatically gave them a failing grade—on that exam or for the entire course—even though that policy was stated on the course syllabi and reiterated frequently by the American faculty throughout each semester.

Business professors from UMUC found that Russian students given hypothetical problems to solve in business ethics often did not understand the problems at all. Although many Russians had a strong sense of personal morality in their dealings with family and friends, they often seemed to have a different code of behavior for interacting with people outside their own immediate group. One Maryland professor in Vladivostok noted that his Russian students believed that a business should hire family members over better-qualified outsiders, simply *because* they were members of the

Sharon and Tom Hudgins at the Siberian-American
Faculty of Management in Irkutsk.

family; there was nothing wrong with a business person doing insider trading; and it was necessary to cheat in order to make a profit. Such attitudes were not unusual in a country where the *mafiya* controlled so many businesses and where cheating was endemic from the classroom to the boardroom, from the shop floor to the centers of political power. At an informal gathering of several high-ranking Russian university administrators, the chairman of another department at Irkutsk State University even bragged to us about how he had cheated all the way through school, including his graduate study for the Russian equivalent of a Ph.D.

Classroom conditions themselves were conducive to cheating. Students sat side by side at long rows of parallel tables rigidly ranked across the room, or they sat together in pairs, at desks made for two, on hard wooden benches bolted to the floor—seating arrangements that made for cozy quarters in class. In Vladivostok, even though the building had been constructed in the 1980s, I often felt like I was teaching in a time warp, in classrooms that dated from the 1930s. Many of the blackboards (which were actually milk-chocolate brown) looked like the sides of old weathered wooden buildings, with surfaces so cracked and uneven they were nearly impossible to write on. Chalk and erasers were practically nonexistent; we had to bring our own chalk from the United States and use filthy wet rags to clean off the boards. Most of the students wrote with pencils or fountain pens on the same kind of low-grade-paper notebooks, lined like graph paper, that Russian primary-school students used. Some even turned in their homework on several sheets of paper sewn together in one corner with white thread or held together with a straight pin, since staples and paper clips were not available. A few of the richer students in Vladivostok subtly flaunted their wealth by coming to class with colorful spiral notebooks, yellow highlighter pens, and sticks of white correction fluid, all purchased in the West—although most of the other students had never even seen such school supplies as three-ring clip binder notebooks and 3-by-5 cards.

In Vladivostok we never knew what to expect when we came to school each day. Since the elevators didn't work, we had to walk up six or seven flights of stairs to our office and classrooms. Electricity was erratic, causing multiple problems throughout the building because the heating and water systems were also electrically controlled. Classrooms were sometimes vandalized, and once a stall in the men's restroom was set on fire. Signs on the restroom doors warned, in Russian, "NO SMOKING, NO LITTERING," admonitions that were ignored by almost everyone. The toilets themselves were filthy and had no seats; often only one or two toilets functioned on each floor of the FESU building. "Toilet paper"—when there was any at all—consisted of pages from Soviet-era history and government textbooks, cut in half and wedged between the wall and the exposed water pipe behind the toilet. One semester, all the faucet handles were stolen from the women's restrooms, making it impossible for us to wash our hands—a problem never fixed during the remainder of the term. Yet the Russians were offended when we returned from the restrooms and washed our hands with the rusty-looking hot water from the samovar in our faculty office. One day in October, we came to school and found that *all* the restroom doors were locked because the water had been cut off when the university didn't pay its bill. That situation lasted for several uncomfortable days, while the Russian staff speculated, only half in jest, about whether the university would have to erect outhouses behind the seven-story building.

In winter, icy winds blew through the cracks around the closed windows in our FESU classrooms, forcing the students to wear their fur coats and fur hats indoors. Broken window panes were repaired by merely sliding an unevenly shaped piece of glass over the broken-out part, overlapping any jagged pieces of glass still stuck in the frame. Sometimes it was so cold we could see our breath in the room. On the worst days, students huddled together at the desks on the side of the room farthest from the windows, blowing on their fingers to warm them up enough to take notes. When FESU could not afford to pay its heating bill in 1994, three of the Russian professors went on strike and dismissed their classes, claiming the rooms were too cold for any learning to occur.

In the midst of this wintry weather, the university suddenly decided to paint all of our classrooms, without informing us in advance, forcing us to find other places to hold class, while we wondered why the rooms had not been painted during the summer vacation instead. Such unexpected disruptions also caused us to lose valuable class time—an issue that the Russian administration never seemed to understand. Coming from University of Maryland University College, where we were required to make up any missed class sessions, we were surprised to discover that the Russians canceled classes for any number of reasons (in addition to national holidays): bad weather, burst water pipes, flooded hallways, visits to the department by university administrators or other VIPs, local conferences, and—in the very recent past—helping with the potato harvest in the autumn. In the Russian system, students and faculty could easily miss two weeks of a sixteen-week semester, because of "normal" cancellations—without having to make up any of the lost class time at all.

After suffering through a semester of academic and logistics problems, large and small, an American colleague in Vladivostok bluntly told me his opinion of the Russians who continued to plod along in their jobs and in their lives, even when their classrooms were freezing, their working conditions were miserable, and their living conditions at home were so bad. "My attitude constantly vacillates between admiration and contempt," he said, "admiration for their ability to put up with so much, yet contempt for their docile willingness to do so."

Working conditions were better in Irkutsk, however, where the facilities were more modern, the building cleaner, the heating system sufficient for the Siberian winter, and the blackboards more usable (although supplies of chalk and erasers were still problematic). But all the American faculty were shocked when the Russian staff cut out squares of white paper and pasted them over every graph, chart, and picture on classroom materials we had asked them to photocopy. At first we suspected that this "censorship" was a holdover from the Soviet era, when information was restricted and the use of copy machines tightly controlled. But when questioned about it, the Russians replied that they were just trying to reduce the amount of toner used by the copy machine. When I offered to purchase the necessary toner myself, however, the Russians refused to let me buy it—but also, probably to save face, they reluctantly agreed to quit blanking out all the illustrations on our handouts for students.

In Irkutsk, as in Vladivostok, office supplies were minimal. The ISU staff member who cut huge rolls of white paper by hand into smaller sheets for the photocopy machine told me that the office had only one pair of scissors. The department's single stapler sat on the secretary's desk and was seldom used, mainly because staples were so scarce; at the end of each day she locked the precious gadget away in her safe. And every evening the doors on the department's safes—as well as the doors to the computer laboratories, the library, and any other rooms containing valuable property—were all "secured" with pieces of heavy string stretched across a point where the door fitted into the frame, the twine held in place with circles of red sealing wax.

At both universities, Tom and I had good relationships with our Russian colleagues, who were seriously interested in education and who were working hard to make our joint-degree program a success (even if they were also trying to make ends meet, financially, by also holding down one or two other jobs somewhere else). But all the Maryland professors were continually caught up short by the differences between Russian and American work habits. In Vladivostok, far more people were listed on the padded payroll than were necessary to get the work done—perpetuating a practice from the Soviet era satirized in the old joke: "The Soviet definition of a job is five people not doing the job of one." In the low-wage societies of both the Soviet Union and the new Russian Federation, workers adhered to the principle that "they pretend to pay us, and we pretend to work." Secretaries in offices sat around sipping tea, swapping gossip, and reading romance novels, while photocopy requests, materials to be typed, and letters to be answered stacked up on their desks. In comparison, Russian faculty members seemed genuinely surprised at the amount of work the Americans accomplished each day. And when they saw the American professors taking home piles of homework assignments and exams to correct almost every night, the Russians became defensive about how little paper-grading they themselves did.

In a country where the language has no word for "efficiency," there was little expectation of efficiency in the workplace. Many Russians either spent a lot of time doing very little at their jobs or expended inordinate effort on a single activity that yielded few results. And in a land that had glorified central planning for at least seventy years, they seemed to avoid any planning ahead at all. Many postponed doing even the simplest tasks until they could put them off no longer, then knocked themselves out to accomplish the job, exerting far more effort than would have been the case if they had not procrastinated in the first place. But as a Russian proverb says, "Until the thunder claps, the peasant won't cross himself."

The "can't do" attitude of many Russians was a particular source of frustration for the American faculty. With the notable exception of the top administrators of our programs at ISU and FESU—and our friend Alla, who handled many logistics matters for the Maryland faculty in Vladivostok—often a Russian staff member's first response to a request by an American professor was, "Oh, we can't do that," or "It can't be done." When we asked why, some of the Russians were taken aback by the question. Others retreated into answers such as, "It's never been done before," or "That's not our responsibility. You'll have to ask someone else." As a Texas oilman who had worked in Russia once told me, "Nobody's really in charge. You've got to get everybody's okay to do anything—and then it all changes tomorrow anyway."

In a country where social stratification was more highly developed than in the United States and where job hierarchies were rigidly observed, bureaucratic buck-passing was a well-honed skill, with obsequious deference to authority often a necessity for getting anything done. So in such a rank-consciousness society, I was always surprised to see students, teachers, and administrators doing custodial work at school. Once I found a departmental secretary washing windows while another ironed curtains on her desk, spitting mouthfuls of water onto the material to dampen the cloth. Another time, late one Friday afternoon, I opened the door to our dean's office in Vladivostok and found her down on her hands and knees, with a bucket of water and a rag, scrubbing the floor. When I asked why she was working like a cleaning woman, she explained that our department's Russian staff rotated such chores because they couldn't trust the regular custodians with all the valuable equipment in the dean's office.

Despite the unexpected cultural differences we all encountered, the Russian and American faculty and staff generally got along well together, both on the job and outside the university. During the first year of the American program in Vladivostok, the Russian administrators held parties at the office to celebrate Russian and American holidays and faculty and staff birthdays. They arranged Russian-American group outings by van and boat to places of interest outside the city, and they took us to dinner several times at Vladivostok's best restaurants. In contrast, the administration in Irkutsk was extremely reticent about spending any money to entertain the American faculty outside the workplace, an attitude that contributed significantly to the sense of social isolation many of the Maryland professors felt in Siberia. But the Russians in Irkutsk were gracious hosts on the job, inviting us to participate in office parties held on holidays such as Russian Army Day (February 23) and International Women's Day (March 8), as well as personal milestones such as birthdays, which we celebrated in the faculty lounge with a few glasses of vodka, brandy, or champagne, a box of chocolate candies, and a platter of small cakes.

In both Vladivostok and Irkutsk, we took our Russian colleagues out to dinner at good restaurants and invited them to parties at our own apartments. But by the second year of the program, even the more hospitable Russians in Vladivostok had greatly reduced the social activities they invited the Americans to. I think they were understandably tired of spending so much time and money on the American professors, who did not have any long-term stake in the program and most of whom considered teaching in Russia merely an adventuresome and remunerative job for a semester or two before they moved on to another position somewhere else in the world. And surely the novelty of the American presence in Russia had worn off by that time, too.

But the Russians never lost sight of the importance of making a good impression on their own superiors. In Siberia, for instance, visits to our university department by the mayor of Irkutsk, the governor of Irkutsk Oblast', the rector of the university, and officials from the Ministry of Education in Moscow—all with their accompanying political and media entourages in shiny black cars—were always an occasion for bringing out the vodka bottles and toasting the success of our joint Russian-American program. The most memorable of these events at ISU was a meeting at our department attended by the top administrators of our program, the Russian and American faculty, sixteen deans and department chairmen from elsewhere in the university, and the parents of prospective students. After a two-hour presentation about the goals and requirements of the program, including a candid question-and-answer session with the parents, eleven members of the ISU top brass and all the American faculty retired to a private conference room adorned with an American flag that had flown over the Capitol in Washington, D.C., and a Russian flag that had flown over the Russian Federation parliament building in Moscow.

For the next five hours, we all sat in oversized, overstuffed chairs, arranged in a large circle, while the departmental staff plied us with plenty of vodka, cognac, and champagne. Occasionally they also brought in plates with a few slices of pickles, sausage, bread, and chocolate cake, which helped slow down the effects of the alcohol. And sometimes a cup of coffee or tea was suddenly set in front of us, apparently to keep us awake. Each new round of drinks required a toast. The dignified director of our program at ISU raised his glass and quoted a few succinct lines from a poem by Osip Mandelstam. Our personable dean, a mathematician, stood up and recited long stanzas of Pushkin's poetry, then placed his hand on his breast and announced that "every Russian carries Pushkin in his heart." Grinning broadly, he then balanced a glass of vodka on his elbow and proceeded to drink all of it without spilling a drop. Conversational topics swirled around the room, mingling with the heavy cigarette smoke, while the liquor glasses kept being topped up and our brains reeled from all that alcohol. Having endured many of these drinking bouts with Russians before, I knew how to pace myself. But the rest of the American professors were out of their league. Seven hours after arriving at the university that afternoon—for what we thought was going to be just a short, routine, faculty-staff meeting—the five Americans staggered home single-file in the snow, holding on to each other for support, with me (the most sober) walking in front, shining a small flashlight to guide us through the dark Siberian night.

The trust and good will established between the Americans and Russians did not always extend beyond the walls of our university department, however, and the breaches of that trust sometimes affected our education program, too. In August, 1993, the night before I left for Russia, I received a telephone call from an old friend of mine in Washington, D.C., who held a high position in the American intelligence community. He wanted to warn me that any notes I wrote about my experiences in Russia might be confiscated by the authorities there. By way of example, he told me about a fully-accredited American journalist who had recently traveled in the Russian Federation for two months on assignment. The Russians were very helpful, letting her go wherever she wanted and see whatever she requested. But the night before she left Russia, all her notes were stolen from her hotel room—and nothing else was taken.

I got the message. After I moved to Russia, I didn't conceal the fact that I'd previously worked as an author and journalist—but I also didn't reveal that I was keeping notes about my experiences and observations there, either. When Russians wondered why I was asking so many questions about my surroundings, I simply explained that in addition to being a teacher, I was also a food writer. Therefore, I was naturally interested in Russian agriculture, food markets, bakeries, home kitchens, recipes, and related aspects of daily life.

At first I didn't take any special precautions to conceal the notes that I was writing about life in Russia. But I knew better than to leave them sitting out on my desks at the office or at home, so I carried them in my purse at work or stashed them in the back of a cabinet, behind stacks of student papers, in our Vladivostok apartment. Then, two months after we arrived in Russia, I came home from work one day and even before I turned on the light, I knew that something was wrong. Someone else had been in the apartment.

Far Eastern State University had hired a housekeeper to clean the quarters of all the American professors there, despite our objections that student tuition money should not be spent on such a luxury. But FESU officials had become very defensive about the matter, insisting that we had to have a housekeeper "for security reasons"—as a deterrent to daytime thieves, they said, since there had already been so many break-ins in our apartment building. So the Russian housekeeper continued to clean the faculty apartments twice a week while we were all at work.

That day in October—when I sensed so strongly that someone else had been inside our apartment—was not like the other days when I had come home from work after the housekeeper had been there. This time something was wrong. I searched the apartment, but couldn't find anything missing or even disturbed. Our valuables were still where we had hidden them, and my notes had not been moved. Yes, the woman had cleaned the apartment that day. No, there was nothing amiss. But all my intuition told me that something had changed.

The same thing happened the next week. I came home from work and had a strong feeling that my privacy had somehow been invaded. I checked the papers on my desk and the notes hidden in the cabinet. Nothing seemed wrong. I'm not by nature a paranoid person, but I am what could be called "an intuitive realist." I *knew* that something wasn't right.

So I set a simple trap. I aligned the edges of my personal notebooks inside the cabinet in such a way that they looked perfectly normal but I could tell if anyone moved them. The next time I came home and sensed that someone else had been in the apartment, I immediately went to the cabinet and checked my notebooks. The trap had been sprung. I realigned the edges of the notebooks and checked them a few days later. They had been tampered with again. After that, I left the notebooks in the same place, but made notes using more abbreviations and oblique references, omitting the names of people whom I was writing about, and using cue words coded to jog my memory when I expanded the notes at some future time and safer place.

Proof that my notes were being read by someone else came about a month after I had begun to suspect that the apartment was not secure. The first major snowstorm of the season hit Vladivostok in mid-November, causing power outages, disrupting public and private transportation, and bringing the city to a standstill. We were at the university when the first snow flurries began around noon, and by 3:30 the administration decided to close the school and send everyone home before the blizzard trapped them in town. Thirteen of us, Russians and Americans, crowded into the university van to head home in the storm. An hour and a half later, we had not even reached the central square downtown, a trip that would have taken no more than ten minutes on a normal day.

As we inched through the worst traffic jam I had ever seen in Russia, the snow reducing visibility to only a few feet, one of the secretaries from our office said, in Russian, to the other Russians in the van, "Look at this snowstorm! I wonder if she's going to put *this* in the book she's writing about us?" The other Russians laughed, including two secretaries, a professor from our department, and the chairman of another department. Their subsequent comments, referring to what the first secretary had said, all indicated that they thought I was writing a book about Russia.

I was dumbfounded. But now I also had proof that my notes not only were being read by someone else, their contents were being shared with the Russians I worked with—the people who, from that moment onward, I never completely trusted again.

In another sense I was almost relieved to have my suspicions confirmed, because now I could do something to protect my notes without feeling paranoid. And the secretary's statement in the van had an effect that I'm sure she never intended. I'd already discovered that Russians felt safe in speaking their language in front of me, because the Russian I had learned in America twenty-five years earlier was rusty indeed. But they didn't know that although I spoke the language badly, I could understand it much better. That incident in the blizzard taught me a valuable lesson: by keeping my ears open and my mouth shut, I could learn a lot more about the Russian world that I lived in.

Some of the Americans who worked in our program came to Russia assuming that their apartments would be bugged. During conversations over dinner, they would voice their frustrations about life in Russia, then look up at the light fixtures and shout, "Got it, guys?!" On the other hand—even given my own knowledge about Russian history and politics—I wondered why anyone in post-Soviet Russia would consider us important enough to bug. What useful information could they expect to glean from the domestic chatter of a few college professors? But after my personal notes were tampered with in Vladivostok, I became more cautious. When I casually mentioned the possibility of such surveillance to officials at the U.S. Consulate in Vladivostok, however, I heard conflicting responses. One high-ranking diplomat blandly dismissed my statement, saying with an air of bored certainty, "All those things are in the past." But another warned me very seriously, "The KGB mentality is still in place and don't ever forget it."

Information security was much more of a problem at work. Twice we found the office secretaries in Vladivostok listening in on our supposedly confidential telephone calls to UMUC administrators in the United States (which prompted Tom to quip, "The Party isn't over, it's still on the line"). All faxes—the best way of sending or receiving official documents during the first semester in Vladivostok (other than using an ancient Telex machine)—had to go through FESU's International Office, where the faxes could be read by anyone who worked there. Incoming faxes took five or six days to be delivered to us—and one was delayed for three weeks—even though the International Office was located right next door to the American faculty office. I soon learned that the only way I could send outgoing faxes somewhat confidentially was to take them to the International Office myself, sit there while the secretary tried to transmit them over the undependable Russian phone lines, and attempt to distract her by chatting about trivial subjects so she couldn't read the faxes at the same time. Of course that still didn't prevent our faxes from being copied and read somewhere else down the line.

When Tom and I moved to Irkutsk the next semester, an entirely new group of American professors joined us there, people who had never been to Russia before but who were sensitive to information security, having previously worked in positions connected with the U.S. military. Our department had a recently installed an E-mail hookup at our university building in Irkutsk—although I had been told by Americans who worked there the previous semester that Yevgeniy, the Russian fellow who set up the connection, was using the old KGB phone lines to make possible this miracle of modern communications deep in the heartland of Siberia. So I warned my new colleagues that anything they sent or received by E-mail was very likely to be read by someone else in Irkutsk or even in Moscow.

Our first inkling of surveillance occurred when the new American professors began complaining about the Russians' unwillingness to confront certain logistics problems we were having at the university. We were all tired of trying to get the Russian staff to improve the situation, but we had not made any progress toward solving the problems. Two of the Americans sent long E-mail messages to their families in the United States, venting their frustrations about working with the Russians and the difficulty of getting them to provide the promised logistical support. Two days later, the Russian dean of our program came to our office, clothed in his friendliest manner, and asked what he could do to help us with problems A and B—which just happened to be the same problems that my colleagues had complained about in their E-mails back home. Soon we were joking that the most effective way to communicate with the Russian administration was through E-mail messages to the United States.

Real proof of E-mail surveillance came about two months after we arrived in Irkutsk. In February the director of the UMUC's Asian Division came from Tokyo to visit our program in Siberia. Later I needed to contact her in Japan, but I didn't have her E-mail address. So I sent a short E-mail message to our university headquarters in Maryland, asking how to reach her. My message never made it that far. The next day a note was waiting in my electronic mailbox: "The Asian Director's E-mail address is office_director%umad@umuc.umd.edu. Sincerely, Yevgeniy." This Yevgeniy was the same Russian who had established E-mail connections for us in Irkutsk and whose company we paid for the service each month. All of our messages went from the university to the node at Yevgeniy's office in another district of the city, before being transmitted elsewhere on those reli-

Banner of Siberian-American Faculty of Management at Irkutsk State University.

able KGB lines. Tom suggested that perhaps Yevgeniy, who seemed like a nice guy (and who had once done a business internship in Maryland), was just trying to be helpful—and perhaps also let us know that our E-mail was indeed being monitored.

The longer we lived in Russia, the more we came to realize that it was a society that placed little value on truth—perhaps because its people had been lied to for so long by their government and other institutions that

266 ~ THE OTHER SIDE OF RUSSIA

affected their daily lives: schools, clubs, the medical system, the mass media. Especially disheartening to the American professors was the apparent dishonesty of some of our Russian colleagues who seemed to care very little for facts. Often when we asked a question of our Russian coworkers, they would make up an answer—any answer, even a blatant lie—just to have a reply to give us. Whenever we challenged their answer, questioning it ourselves, they would just shrug and come up with another answer. So many of the Russians we dealt with daily seemed to disregard facts to such a degree that one of the American professors remarked, "Ask ten Russians the same question, and you'll get twenty different answers." And indeed, the Russians themselves have long recognized this aspect of their character. An old Russian saying notes, "Two Russians—three points of view." A Russian proverb points out, "The bigger the lie, the easier it is to believe." And a joke broadcast on Radio Moscow when I was in Irkutsk went, "There is a slogan from the Communist era: 'We say the Party and we mean Lenin. We say Lenin and we mean the Party.' For seventy years we've been saying one thing and meaning another."

Administrators at both universities attracted students to the program by promising that part of their tuition money would be used to fund business internships for them in the United States or Japan—a provision that had never been part of UMUC's official agreement with the Russian universities. At ISU, important, confidential administrative files that had been left in the faculty office for me by the outgoing American program coordinator "disappeared" before I arrived the next semester and remained "lost" for two months before they were suddenly "found" by the Russians and finally handed over to me. And on the students' Russian transcripts Russian administrators at both universities "cooked the books" in regard to grades. At FESU, students who earned grades of D or F in UMUC courses actually had grades of C or D recorded for those courses on their Russian transcripts; at ISU, grades of D or F were boosted by the Russians to C-minus or D, respectively—thus giving some students a higher grade-point average on their Russian transcripts than on their UMUC records. No wonder many researchers in the West considered the term "Russian statistics" to be an oxymoron.

The Russians never seemed to understand why the Americans were so offended by these falsehoods, which the Russians merely viewed as *vran'yë*—not really lies, as such, but just a sort of double-talk, deliberate deceits, fudging of the facts, for any number of reasons from lack of knowledge to expediency to face-saving. This led me to nickname one of the most persistent prevaricators "Uncle Vran'yë"—a Soviet-style *apparatchik* who tried to block access to public information to both his superiors and his students; who denied that certain events, even matters of public record, had ever occurred; who, when questioned about something, might give one answer on one day and a completely contradictory answer on the next; and who used UMUC as the scapegoat for unpopular (and sometimes unethical) decisions that he himself had unilaterally made.

These Russian attempts to control or distort information—even information of the most innocuous sort—extended from the highest to the lowest levels of society. While many Russians often seemed to have a casual attitude toward facts, they also stockpiled, hoarded, or restricted real information until they had an opportunity to use that information by selling it or bartering it or dispensing it as largesse. For many people in this obsessively secretive society, information was power—and only those privileged to receive it from a more powerful person were allowed to do so. Without the right personal connections, it was exceedingly difficult for us to get information on even such mundane matters as airline schedules, train fares, bus routes, population statistics, the year a public building had been constructed, or the date an election was to be held. When I described an "open-stack" library to my students in Vladivostok—a library where readers could browse the shelves, freely select their own books, and check them out to take home—they couldn't believe that such a thing really existed. And even with more openness and better communications systems in the post-Soviet era, serious scholars in Russia still sometimes showed great gaps in their knowledge about specific information pertaining to their own fields of study. This lack of easily accessible and accurate information in so many areas of Russian life led me to conclude that Russia of the mid-1990s was still a "low-information society." As the *Economist* reported in December, 1995, "There is freedom of speech and the press in Russia (tempered by an occasional assassination of a journalist), but it is not matched by much serious freedom of information." Or, as Tom put it, "Russia is the super-chuckhole on the information super-highway."

Of course not all Russians shaped or distorted information for their own purposes—and many scholars in that country were appalled and embarrassed by such practices on the part of their colleagues. When I asked an open-minded and well-informed Russian professor at FESU if she knew the actual number of closed cities in Russia, she replied, "That information would never be published—and if it were, could you really believe the numbers cited?" Moreover, not all of the Russians we worked with at ISU and FESU fudged the facts: some of the best teachers and administrators associated with our program were both honest and straightforward in their dealings with the Russian students and the American faculty, thus gaining the respect of all of us.

But there were still attempts to control public information on the job and to access private information at home. The worst involved people tampering with our computer files. In both Irkutsk and Vladivostok, we kept our own laptop computer and disks at home, not in the office, hidden under furniture in the bedroom—a precaution designed to deter casual thieves, not professionals. And in Irkutsk, until the last month we lived there, I never had the feeling that anyone had entered our apartment while we were away. But in June, when Tom and I came back from our two-day boat trip on Lake Baikal, I wondered if anyone had taken advantage of our absence to search the apartment. After the incidents in Vladivostok the previous autumn and the E-mail intercepts in Irkutsk that spring, I wouldn't have been surprised at anything. I checked the apartment thoroughly, but nothing seemed amiss.

Later that month, when Tom and I returned home at midnight from our long day of feasting with the Buryats in Ust'-Orda, I had the distinct feeling that someone had been in the apartment while we were gone. I checked the entire place, but everything was exactly as I had left it. The following week, we packed and sealed several boxes of winter clothing, books, lecture notes, and office supplies—including computer disks—which the Russians had agreed to ship from Irkutsk back to Vladivostok, where we were scheduled to teach the next semester. The morning we left Irkutsk, our dean helped us load all the boxes into the van and take them to the university office, where they would remain until the Russians sent them to Vladivostok later in the summer. Then Tom and I boarded a Trans-Siberian train for the first leg of our summer vacation—and put all thoughts about the boxes and their contents out of our minds.

Somewhat to our surprise—given the large amount of theft in the Russian postal and shipping systems—all the boxes were waiting for us when we arrived back in Vladivostok that August. They were still sealed—and when we opened them we found all the contents intact, exactly as we had packed them. But in September, when I needed to access some information in a computer file that I had made in Irkutsk, I couldn't get into that file—or into any other files on that disk, all of which dealt with university business pertaining to the program in Irkutsk. Tom tried various ways on the computer to correct the problem, but was unsuccessful. Finally, he tried to reformat the disk, but that, too, was impossible. The entire disk had been electronically destroyed.

I didn't mention this at first to my new American colleagues in Vladivostok because I didn't want to add to the negative opinions that some of them were already forming about life in Russia. I did warn them that their personal papers and mail might not be secure in their apartments and certainly wouldn't be safe at the office. But one day in mid-semester Ann Snodgrass, one of our English teachers, asked if she could talk with me about a problem. "Have you ever had any trouble with people tampering with things in your apartment?" she asked. "I don't mean the maid who comes in and tries on my clothes and puts them back on the hangers the wrong way. Although I'm getting ticked off at her trying on my jewelry and leaving it scattered on the dresser." I was aghast. Nothing like that had happened to me in our apartments, as far as I knew. "I mean fooling around with your computer disks," she continued. "Has anyone tampered with your disks?"

I told her about the destroyed disk from Irkutsk, although I couldn't be certain whether it had happened in Irkutsk or Vladivostok, since the boxes had been in the care of Russians at both locations. And I added that I hadn't been too upset about it—first, because I'd already learned not to completely trust our Russian hosts, and second, because I had sent hard-copy back-ups of all the important information on that disk back to the United States by courier before I ever left the disks behind in Russian hands.

"You know I'm writing a mystery novel," Ann went on. "It doesn't have anything to do with Russia, but when I got out the disk to work on it last night, I couldn't access any of the files. I thought I was just screwing up somehow, so I put in another disk, and I couldn't get it to work either."

"Did you get Jim to check it out?" I asked. Her husband Jim was a business professor in our program, a former employee of IBM, and our resident computer guru. "He couldn't get them to work, either," she said. "The disks had been destroyed."

"What was on that second disk?" I asked, halfway expecting to know the answer already. "All my letters home," she replied.

I wasn't surprised. Fortunately, Ann did have a copy of her mystery novel draft, but I advised her to make back-up copies of all her other disks, label them something innocuous like "cooking files and recipes," and keep that set of disks in her purse or well hidden in the apartment. I also suggested that she make hard copies of any important material she wanted to save and send them to her home address whenever she could find an American leaving Russia, someone who was willing to carry a large envelope back to the United States and drop it in the nearest mailbox. I had been sending mail out of the country that way for over a year, ever since I realized that none of my personal papers were safe in Russia.

The story didn't end when we left Russia. A month after we returned to the United States, Tom needed some information from a computer disk whose files he'd created and used only in Irkutsk. The disk contained the syllabus, study guides, homework assignments, quizzes, and examinations for an economics course that he had taught only in Irkutsk. But when he tried to retrieve that information, he discovered that the disk had been completely destroyed, electronically.

Later we learned that our colleagues Ann and Jim—who had gone back to America in December, 1994, for their Christmas vacation—were unable to return to Russia the following semester. All of their personal belongings, including their laptop computer and disks, had been left in Vladivostok because they had planned to return there after the Christmas holidays. They themselves had put their personal computer and disks into the safe in the dean's office at FESU. When the Russians finally shipped Ann and Jim's personal belongings back to them three months later, the laptop computer battery (which had a shelf life of only about three weeks) was fully charged; a number of files on the hard drive had timestamps of January and February, 1995; several of their computer disks had also been redated; and some of their files had been destroyed. The files that had been read or destroyed were their course examinations, personal correspondence, and fiction-writing drafts.

Experiences such as those—along with the difficulties of everyday life in Russia—contributed to the relatively high turnover of American faculty during the first two years of the program. From August, 1993, through May, 1995, University of Maryland University College sent a total of nineteen faculty members to Russia. Almost half of them stayed for only one semester, and few remained for more than two semesters. In subsequent years the situation improved somewhat, with a handful of Maryland professors teaching in Russia for longer periods of time. But not all those early problems were attributable to the Russian side of the program. Poor communications with the university administration in Maryland sometimes caused misunderstandings between faculty in the field and the staff back home. And both communication and transportation difficulties often resulted in a lack of even basic logistical support—from textbooks and test banks that didn't arrive until the semester was almost over, to new water filters and hearing-aid batteries that the faculty couldn't obtain in Russia. Speaking through an especially bad telephone connection between Vladivostok and College Park, one of our professors asked UMUC to send him twenty-two plastic transparencies to use with the overhead-projector in his classroom. Three months later, he received twenty-two clear plastic, accordion-pleated, ladies' rain-hats. At times like that, some of the American faculty felt like they were characters working for John Cleese in the British television comedy "Fawlty Towers"— East. At other times, when setbacks occurred, we joked that we were doing our own version of a famous Russian folk dance, the Lenin Three-Step: one step forward, two steps back.

Despite such problems with the program, Tom and I still enjoyed our three semesters of teaching in Russia. The unexpected cultural differences we encountered daily in the classroom gave both us and our students better insight into the very different societies from which we came. And we admired our Russian students for their determination in pursuing a university degree in a new kind of learning environment and in a language not their own. In turn, most of them responded favorably to our teaching methods and our attitude toward them as responsible young adults whom we expected to meet our academic standards. At the end of each semester in Vladivostok and Irkutsk, the deans of our department informed Tom that the Russian students had selected him "Best Professor in the American Program." And when we left, the Russian administrators, faculty, students, and staff said good-bye to us with gifts of champagne, poetry, flowers, and Russian cookbooks.

Likewise, for many of the other UMUC faculty who taught in the program, their positive experiences in the classroom—as well as the friendship and hospitality of Russian students and colleagues at both universities— more than compensated for the difficulties they encountered there. George Morgan, a retired naval officer whose career spanned the Cold War from the building of the Berlin Wall to its fall, taught business courses for ISU. Morgan later wrote of his experiences in Siberia: "For me, as an old cold warrior, it was an exciting adventure that I will always remember. The best part was the eagerness of the students to learn and their interest in me as a retired military officer. . . . Life was not always easy, but the enthusiasm and commitment of the students made it worthwhile." And Maggie Smith, an American professor who taught in the program for two years, described her experiences as "a great way to make an exciting contribution to global business—and certainly an opportunity to walk on the side of change as history takes place."

But it was the students themselves who spoke most eloquently about the education they received through this new Russian-American program, in the many letters and E-mail messages they sent to Tom and me after we left Russia. Some of our students came to the United States for graduate school or for business internships. Many of the others, after completing their fifth year in the program in Russia, found good jobs with major businesses, both Russian and foreign, or accepted positions in local or regional governments in Siberia and the Russian Far East. And a few even went on to become university professors themselves.

Two years after we returned to the United States, Oleg Mamayev, an outstanding student in the FESU program in Vladivostok, wrote to us: "Yes, today there are many economic and managerial departments that try to teach a new generation of businessmen, but who are the teachers? Professors who, ten years ago, taught the basics of Marxist-Leninist theory! Now they read lectures on the market economy, an economic system they have never been exposed to. On the other hand, the Russian-American Department at Far Eastern State University gave us a tremendous amount of knowledge that we could never have gotten anywhere else. I believe that no other program in the Russian Far East could give such a deep knowledge in the fields of market economics, marketing, management, international accounting, and other disciplines related to the field of business. Moreover all the lectures are given in English, which gives tremendous advantage to the students—learning business subjects at the same time they are mastering English. Today, after four years in the program, I feel confident that I will be able to excel in business and succeed in my future career. Good education, plus eagerness and hard work, will do their job."

CHAPTER 11

~

Farewell to Russia

Our last month in Russia was a flurry of activity—finishing up the school term, grading final examinations, sharing farewell dinners with friends, packing for the move back to the United States—all carried out within the inevitable constraints of the Russian winter. December, 1994, began with a blizzard in Vladivostok, concealing some of the city's more salient blemishes under a camouflage of snow. But the weather also put an added strain on the already undependable municipal utilities. As daylight decreased in advance of the winter solstice, the supply of electricity became even more erratic, with brownouts and power outages occurring three or four times a day. To make matters worse, our next-door neighbor drilled a hole in his bedroom wall and accidentally severed one of our electrical cables, cutting off the power to half our apartment, leaving our own bedroom, bathroom, and study without lights for a week before we could get anyone to fix the problem. When the university finally sent out an electrician, we returned home from work that day to find a note saying, "The electricity has been repaired, but now the heating does not work. We will try to send someone to repair it in a few days." Meanwhile some of the residents of our high-rise village had started setting off fireworks from their balconies every time the electricity went off, as if they were determined to bring a little light and excitement into an otherwise dark and dull daily existence.

Amid these vicissitudes of everyday life in Russia, Tom celebrated his fiftieth birthday that December, noting that he was glad to be leaving Russia soon, since the average life expectancy for males in Vladivostok was only fifty-five (two years less than the average for Russia as a whole). On the night of Tom's birthday, our Russian dean hosted a festive dinner party for him at an upscale restaurant downtown. Seated in comfortable upholstered chairs around a large dining table set with crisp white linens and vases of vibrantly colored silk flowers, we perused the Russian menu and tried to decipher the English translations typed under each entry: "Trepang scraping. Hot with cheese Salad. Shell, mayonnaise dressing. Kaluga smoked. Muscles with spices adding. Furn stewed with vegetables. Trepang stewed." Instead of the twice-touted trepang (sea slugs), Tom and I selected several other assorted hot and cold seafood appetizers, followed by main courses of seafood au gratin and *pel'meni* swimming in a spicy broth. But just as the first course was being served, the electricity went off. So we ate the rest of his birthday dinner in the now all-too-familiar, no-longer-romantic, Vladivostok fashion—by candlelight.

The following morning—Saint Nicholas Day on the Christian calendar in the West—Tom and I went to the St. Nikolay Russian Orthodox Church, where priests in shimmering blue-and-silver vestments were celebrating a special liturgy for Aleksandr Nevsky, the thirteenth-century Russian leader revered as a statesman, warrior, and saint, defender of the Orthodox faith against invaders from both Europe and Asia. Later that week we attended a different sort of celebration held in honor of a modern-day group of warriors: the fifty-fifth anniversary concert of the Song and Dance Ensemble of the Russian (formerly Soviet) Pacific Fleet. The formal invitation to the affair had apparently been printed sometime in the 1980s, as a generic invitation to performances by this group. Featured on the front were silhouettes of a submarine, a battleship, and a two fighter planes. Inside, a quotation from Lenin proclaimed: "Art belongs to the people." And the remainder of the text boldly stated: "For our Soviet Motherland! By command, the artistic soviet of the Song and Dance Ensemble of the Red Banner Pacific Fleet invites you to a concert to take place at . . ."—with blanks to be filled in for the date, time, and location of the show.

That year's concert was held at the Pacific Fleet's Officers Club in downtown Vladivostok, a facility surprisingly similar in appearance to U.S. military officers clubs built in the 1940s. As soon as I walked into the familiar-looking foyer, I felt like I had stepped back half a century in time. Reinforcing that initial impression was the musical performance that followed, which reminded me of old movies of those rousing USO shows for American troops during World War II. Authentic versions of Glenn Miller–style big-band numbers were played by an excellent instrumental ensemble seated on staggered risers arrayed across the back of the stage. Above the band sparkled the large numerals "55"—cut out of cardboard and covered with pieces of crinkled aluminum foil just like the shiny stuff I always salvaged from candy-bar wrappers at home. Muscular, acrobatic young men bounded onto the stage to perform complicated Cossack dances, dizzying displays of fast-moving contortions set to music. Men's and women's vocal ensembles belted out Russian folk songs and patriotic tunes. Athletic young women in short, military-style costumes danced numbers that would have made Mary Martin proud in *South Pacific*. High-ranking naval officers ceremoniously accepted the flowers and gifts presented to them by members of the ensemble: a ship's model, a framed oil painting, a giant papier-mâché hamburger. And emceeing the whole affair was a superb baritone singer with a fine sense of comic timing, who looked exactly like a young Milton Berle. At any moment I expected Bob Hope to come out on stage and start cracking jokes.

The next Monday, December 12, was a new national holiday in Russia, Constitution Day, held in honor of the adoption on that date in 1993 of the Russian Federation's first constitution since the end of the Soviet era. Ironically, only a few hours before the observance of the new holiday, the Russian government had sent troops and tanks into the breakaway republic of Chechnya, escalating a longstanding conflict that would soon develop into a bitter and protracted war in that region. I spent that day at home, baking cakes and cookies for an upcoming Christmas party, but I was nearly driven batty by the incessant pop-pop-pop of loud fireworks just below my kitchen window. Released from school for the holiday, the neighborhood ragamuffins amused themselves by throwing firecrackers into a big bonfire of burning trash gathered from around the building. The din lasted all day. I am usually a rather laid-back person, but by late afternoon my nerves were on edge, making me flinch every time a firecracker exploded outside. For a change of pace, I went over to Alla's apartment to visit for an hour, only to discover upon returning home that vandals had ripped out both of my doorbells while I was gone.

After a dinner whose menu had to be changed three times because of intermittent power outages, Tom and I turned on the television news only to see pictures of Russian tanks rolling into Chechnya, grinding down the road to Grozny, the capital, while the announcer blandly read official government statements assuring viewers that the rebellion would quickly be put down. Hoping to counter the cumulative disruptions of that day, we turned off the television and put on a CD of Gregorian chants by the Spanish monks of the Abbey of Santo Domingo de Silos. But the soothing voices of the monks were soon drowned out by the thump-thump-thump of our neighbor's stereo blasting out raucous electronic rock music next door. In our high-rise village, Russia's new Constitution Day was just another opportunity for drunken revelry, malicious mischief, and the metronomics of mindless music.

During that last December in Russia, a colleague from the university, Maria Lebedko, took us on a tour of some of the historical sites that we had not yet seen in Vladivostok. Maria was one of the Russians I most admired for her honesty, straightforwardness, and serious sense of scholarship. She was also particularly knowledgeable about the city, having written a detailed guide to the historical buildings and monuments of Vladivostok. Of all the landmarks we visited, the most impressive was Vladivostok's large Naval Cemetery, situated on a windswept hill overlooking the sea. Some of the city's most prominent citizens had been interred there: explorers, sea captains, scientists, authors, professors, an international chess champion, local Communist Party leaders, *mafiya* bosses, and veterans of conflicts from the Russo-Japanese War to Afghanistan. There were also several graves of Britons, Canadians, Czechs, and Americans who had died in Vladivostok during Russia's civil war, as well as those of Japanese prisoners who had perished in that region of Russia after World War II. Many of the gravesites consisted of stone-slab memorials facing small stone tables with stationary seats or benches on the sides, all enclosed within a low iron fence, where Russian families came on special days to eat picnics and honor their dead. And many of the headstones had their own tragic story to tell: a Russian family—father, mother, son—who had succumbed within four days of each other; a naval captain and all his crew, who had gone down together with their ship at sea; a young man from an "influential" family, who had recently been killed in his expensive automobile, his untimely demise commemorated on the massive black marble tombstone by an action-cartoon-style engraving of a prized sport-utility vehicle seeming to roar out of the polished marble as if in defiance of death at such an early age.

Maria also took us to Pokrovskiy Memorial Park—the new name of Vladivostok's old City Park—where Vladivostok's largest Russian Orthodox cathedral had once stood. Completed in 1902, the Cathedral of the Intercession of the Holy Virgin had been built to hold one thousand people beneath its five large domes crowned with gilded crosses. But in concert with Soviet campaigns against religion in Russia during the 1920s and 1930s, the Communist government of Vladivostok decided to blow up the cathedral on Easter Sunday, 1935. Although the first attempt failed, the cathedral was later destroyed and a statue of Lenin erected on the site of the former altar. The adjacent cemetery was also obliterated, and an amusement park with an outdoor concrete dance floor was built over the bones of the people buried there. Standing in that still-melancholy spot, I was reminded of other places in the world where I had seen the results of such anger produced by hate: Muslim graveyards in Bosnia and Jewish ones in Central Europe, which had been similarly desecrated for political reasons during the twentieth century. And I told Maria the story of how, only two years before, I had finally found the Protestant cemetery in a town in present-day Poland where my Prussian ancestors had been buried since the early 1800s. Near the end of World War II, most of the cemetery had been demolished by Polish "People's Army" troops as they advanced toward the Oder River, pushing the German forces back into Germany; later a Polish-Soviet war memorial had been constructed over the graves of many of the town's ethnic-German Lutherans and official records of their existence destroyed. Maria—whose sense of scholarly objectivity transcended the personal interpretation that many Russians would have put on this story—comprehended both my understanding of why the Poles would have reacted that way toward ethnic Germans in their country in 1945, as well as my sadness that once again, as so often in history, people were judged according to their racial, ethnic, linguistic, or religious group rather than their own individual characters.

But such stories were now just another part of the fading past. In Vladivostok, the municipal authorities had finally returned part of the city park to the Russian Orthodox Church in 1993, and a new church was slated to be built there whenever enough money could be raised. Meanwhile, during my last December in the city, Vladivostok was dressing up like never before in preparation for the winter holiday season. Major stores, small shops, tiny kiosks, and open-air markets offered far more Christmas decorations and imported products than had been available only a year before: Christmas cards and colored lights; Ded Moroz (Father Frost) and Snegurochka (Snow Maiden) dolls made of wood, plastic, or papier-mâché; and children's masks (much like our Halloween masks) for the Christmas and New Year's mummery that has been a long-established tradition among Slavic people. Stores and restaurants were adorned with swags of shiny tinsel and strands of colored lights. One big display window of the GUM department store even held a large nativity scene, with characters standing almost two feet tall. Local television reported that this was the first time such a Christian crèche had been displayed at GUM since the beginning of the Soviet era more than seventy years before. Prominent red and white letters on the window glass spelled out "MERRY CHRISTMAS"—in English. And

suspended over the nativity scene was a beautiful Advent wreath made of
evergreen boughs, like those I knew from churches in my childhood. The
crowds who gathered to gawk at this unusual sight at GUM could also walk
a few blocks along the same street down to the city's central square, where
special holiday market stalls had been set up, children's amusement-park
rides erected, and ice slides constructed—all towered over by the largest
New Year's tree ever put up in Vladivostok, which had been transported to
the square and lowered into place by a helicopter.

But not everyone in Vladivostok was benefiting from the new market
economy, and many people on fixed incomes were feeling the pinch of high
inflation and the recently devalued ruble, as they tried to find ways to finance the expected family celebrations for New Year's Eve. One evening
Alla came to our apartment "to ask us about something," she said in an
uncharacteristically vague and nervous manner. Sitting stiffly on the divan
in our living room, she refused our offers of food and drink. Finally she
came to the point, pulling out a small, gold-encrusted icon from her shopping bag and offering to sell it to us for twelve hundred dollars. When we
hesitated, not knowing what to say, Alla added that she also had several
Tsarist-era gold coins for sale. Tom and I were embarrassed by the situation: during the entire time we had known her, Alla had never tried to take
advantage of our friendship for her own gain. She seemed uncomfortable
in this new role, making me wonder who had put her up to it, and even
whether Tom and I were being set up for engaging in an illegal financial
transaction. When I gently explained that we weren't really interested in
icons and gold coins—and would have trouble taking them out of the country, anyway—Alla suddenly relaxed, as if she had been relieved of an odious
burden. She accepted Tom's offer of a stiff screwdriver to drink and stayed
to chat with us, just like the old Alla we knew, finally confessing that someone else had asked her to approach us about the illegal sale of these Russian treasures, and that her husband Pëtr had opposed it, accusing her of
trying to sell off Russia's heritage.

The week before Christmas, we put up two artificial evergreen trees borrowed from Russian friends, which we decorated with sea urchin shells and
sand dollars, tiny Russian wooden dolls, and homemade paper cutouts of
snowflakes, angels, and animals. For "icicles" we hung on the tree long,
thin, bright red peppers that we had dried in our kitchen. The living room
was also adorned with swags of multicolored tinsel, large paper snowflakes,
Christmas cards from friends abroad, a big silver star fashioned from salvaged aluminum foil, and a shiny gold garland made from the foil wrapping

found inside a giant Cadbury's chocolate bar. A few nights later, Tom and I were sitting in the living room surrounded by these cheerful decorations, listening to Bach on our CD player and enjoying a warm sense of serenity that seemed to fit the holiday season. Suddenly I smelled something burning. After checking each room in the apartment, we followed our noses out into the communal stairwell, where we finally located the source of the smoke: someone had set fire to all the paper snowflakes I had pasted on the front door as winter decorations. Tom and I stood in the dark and dirty hallway, among the dog feces and the cement dust from construction projects, breathing the acrid smoke of burning paint and paper while two homeless cats rubbed up against our legs. Looking around at that desolate sixth-floor landing, Tom remarked with a sigh, "Daily life in Russia always impresses me with how hard it is to create or build anything—and how easy it is for things to be destroyed."

The two stray cats—a big black-and-white male and a smaller orange tabby—had shown up in our stairwell a few days earlier. Both were very tame, and I suspected they had recently been abandoned by someone who had moved away from our building. We and one of our neighbors began putting out bowls of water and food for the homeless cats on the landing, but the orange tabby disappeared a couple days after our door was vandalized. The other cat stuck around, and we soon named him "Gollandskiy," after the Russian word for "Dutch," since he reminded us so much of black-and-white cats we had known in the Netherlands. Every day Gollandskiy tried to follow us into our apartment, but we resisted letting him in. We were leaving Russia in just over a week, and we knew we couldn't take him with us. But one morning as we departed for the university, we noticed that powdered yellow-green poison had been spread along the base of all the walls in the stairwell. Poor Gollandskiy was hunkered down in a corner, on the cold concrete floor, looking miserable. We quickly picked him up and carried him inside, leaving him with a hastily contrived sandbox, a bowl of water, and some food—hoping that he would still be alive when we got back home from school that night.

It took a few days for Gollandskiy to get the poison out of his system, but he lived happily with us for that week before we reluctantly had to leave him behind. During that time we tried desperately to find him another home. But most of our American friends had already gone back to the United States for Christmas, and our Russian friends already had pets of their own. Alla said that if she didn't already have a cat, she would take Gollandskiy herself, but she didn't want her own female cat to get pregnant and produce a litter of kittens. Russia was a country where pets were not neutered, and unwanted kittens and puppies were summarily killed, a practice that Alla abhorred as much as we did. (Earlier that year, when an American friend of mine in Vladivostok had adopted a homeless female cat and wanted to get her spayed, she had to persuade a regular gynecologist to perform the operation, because no veterinarian would do it.)

Finally I suggested to Alla that we go to a veterinarian's office and ask if the doctor would take Gollandskiy and find him a good home. Alla was doubtful. "There are only two veterinarian clinics in Vladivostok," she said, "and one other place where, if you take him there, he will be used for medical experiments." When I insisted that we seek help, she reluctantly took me to one vet's office, such a depressing place that I wanted to turn and run out the moment I walked through the door. The doctor was no better: she spoke to me contemptuously, berating me for bothering her about trying to find a home for the cat. That wasn't her job, she said, yelling something else in Russian that I couldn't understand. As I turned away in tears, Alla put her arm around my shoulders and told me not to cry, promising that she would take care of Gollandskiy herself and see that everything came out all right. By that time I had no choice but to trust that Alla would keep her word.

Two days later, on the morning of December 24, Tom and I attended the special Christmas service held by the Lutheran community of Vladivostok. The first Lutheran church in Russia had been established in the European part of the country in the late sixteenth century, and the number of Lutherans in Russia had waxed and waned during the following four hundred years. Many of them were Germans and Balts who had settled in Russia, in major cities or along the Volga River, or who had been dispersed by choice or circumstance throughout the vast territories of the country. The first Lutheran church in Vladivostok was constructed in the 1870s, and in 1908 the congregation's original wooden edifice was replaced by a handsome red-brick building with a graceful steeple, which looked as if it had been transported intact from some Hanseatic city near the Baltic Sea. Used as a church until 1930, St. Paul's Lutheran Church in Vladivostok was eventually turned into a club for naval petty officers in 1935 and converted into a Soviet naval museum in 1950. When I lived in Vladivostok in the mid-1990s, the building was still being used as a military museum, complete with heavy artillery from several eras displayed around the exterior walls. Despite a decree by Yeltsin in 1992 that all religious buildings in Russia would be returned to their original owners, at the end of 1994 the Lutheran community of Vladivostok was still trying to get its beautiful building back from the state.

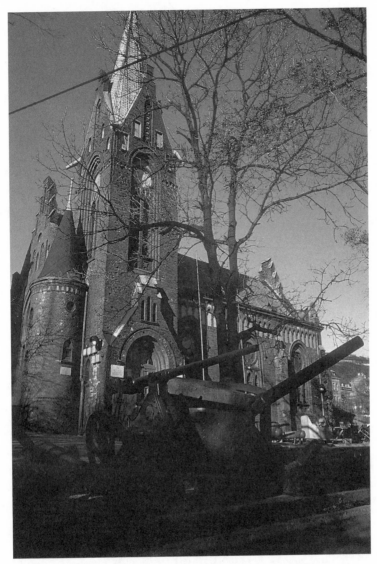

*St. Paul's Lutheran Church when it was still
a naval museum in Vladivostok.*

The leader of the Lutheran church in Vladivostok was Pastor Manfred Brockmann, a German who had come to the Russian Far East in 1992. Brockmann was assisted by a local Russian psychology professor who translated the minister's sermons into Russian for the church services that were conducted each week, half in Russian, half in German, at a meeting hall near the center of the city. Pastor Brockmann told me that a total of three hundred people in Vladivostok considered themselves members of the church, with fifty or sixty people in attendance at most services, including a number of Jews, atheists, and nondenominational intellectuals who were attracted to the gatherings by the pastor's open-mindedness, the topics addressed in his sermons, and the high quality of the music performed there. When Brockmann first arrived in Vladivostok, however, he initially had difficulty even locating any Lutherans in the city. After the former KGB rejected his request for a list of religious dissidents in the area—and the local Russian Orthodox leader refused to help at all, stating categorically that, "In Russia, there can be only Russian Orthodoxy!"—Brockmann was almost ready to give up and go back to Germany. But one evening at a classical music concert, he happened to meet a Catholic priest who was also working in Vladivostok, a man who graciously helped him find the addresses of several Lutherans living there. And so the congregation of St. Paul's Lutheran Church was reestablished after a hiatus of more than sixty years.

The Lutheran Christmas service in 1994, held at the city's modern Palace of Culture, was a delightful mixture of Russian and German Yuletide traditions. The cavernous assembly hall had been decorated with a large Christmas tree, a nativity scene, and several posters handpainted with German Christmas symbols so familiar to me from the many years I lived in that country. Most of the members of the congregation were dressed in their finest clothes, but one cute little Russian girl showed up in a whimsical snow-leopard costume. Each line of the liturgy was spoken by Brockmann in German, then translated into Russian, and the worshipers sang old Lutheran hymns in both languages. After the service, the congregation shared a pot-luck meal in the assembly hall, followed by a special Christmas program. The children reenacted the nativity story, a folk-dancing group in colorful costumes performed traditional Russian dances, and an accomplished string quartet, of which Pastor Brockmann was a member, played several pieces by Mozart, while nature supplied a backdrop of softly falling snow outside.

The next morning, December 25, we attended Christmas Mass at Vladivostok's only Roman Catholic church. The service was conducted in Latin, English, and Russian by Father Myron Effing, an American from Indiana who had moved to Vladivostok in early 1992 to become pastor of the Most Holy Mother of God Roman Catholic Parish. A few days before Christmas, Father Effing had given me a tour of the historic church, a red-brick building originally begun in 1909 by Vladivostok's Polish Catholic community to replace an earlier wooden structure destroyed by fire. The church was still under construction when Vladivostok's Catholic parish was closed in 1922 after the Bolsheviks came to power. In 1935 the Soviet government confiscated all Catholic church buildings in the Russian Far East, and a few years later the church in Vladivostok was converted into a government archive. After the building was returned to the Catholic church in 1993, Father Effing celebrated the first mass conducted there in more than seventy years. But when I visited the church in late 1994, services were being held in the basement, because the remainder of the building still needed many costly repairs.

Like the Lutheran church, the Catholic church had been functioning in Russia for several centuries. After the official reopening of the Vladivostok parish in 1992, the local congregation had grown to approximately 350 members, many of whom were attending mass that Christmas Day. Among the large gathering, I spotted Russian students and friends of ours, a number of Asians, and several people from the local American community. In that small basement sanctuary, with its white plastered walls, red seats, and blue-painted pillars, we all listened to the familiar Christmas service accompanied by carols sung in English and Russian. As a children's choir gathered around the crèche at the front of the church and began singing "Away in a Manger," Tom and I looked at each other with tears in our eyes, recalling so many other Christmases past—particularly those of our childhood, when we had sung in similar choirs, off-key and nervous at performing in front of our elders. And we also realized that our feelings of nostalgia were magnified that day by the significance of celebrating Christmas in Vladivostok, on the edge of Asian Russia, so far from the places of our many other holiday memories.

Tom and I spent our last few days in Russia packing up our belongings, giving away most of our books to Russian friends, and wrapping small New Year's gifts to leave for colleagues and staff at the university. On our last night in the Russian Far East, Alla prepared a special farewell dinner for us: a copious *zakuski* spread of beet-and-potato salad, home-preserved cucumbers and mushrooms, pickled yellow tomatoes from her dacha garden, slices of sausage and ham, herring in mustard sauce, sliced apples with horseradish, and hard-boiled eggs topped with salmon caviar—followed by a main course of homemade *pel'meni* with a selection of garnishes. Sitting around the table with Alla and Pëtr and their two sons, Tom and I raised our glasses to them and proposed our final toast, complimenting Alla on her excellent cooking and thanking the Brovko family for their friendship and the many fine meals they had shared with us in their home. Alla sat for a long moment without speaking, her head bowed, then looked up at us with a mixture of pride and weariness on her face as she replied, "I wanted you to see that even in the midst of everything that is happening in Russia, people can still have a normal life."

That night we went to bed early, letting Gollandskiy the cat sleep curled up on the covers beside us. At five o'clock the next morning, Alla and Igor, the driver of our university van, knocked on the apartment door. While I gathered up our last few belongings, Tom helped Alla and Igor take most of the luggage downstairs in the elevator, which was actually functioning for a change. I thought Alla would return to "sit the house" with us, as she had done when we left Vladivostok the first time, almost a year before. But Tom came back up to the apartment alone. So he and I observed the old Russian custom by ourselves, going into our living room and sitting quietly together side by side on the divan, one last time. After a few minutes of silence, we both knew that we should go. But neither of us wanted to be the first to stand up and make the final break with the life we had lived in Russia. Our reluctance also had roots that went even deeper: we had not lived in the United States since 1981, and now our longest overseas adventure was coming to an end. The past stretched behind us as a succession of fond memories from forty countries on three continents—but the future was something we weren't quite ready to confront.

While we were still sitting there in silence, Gollandskiy walked into the living room and jumped into Tom's lap. The cat stayed there for a few minutes, purring profusely, then moved over to my lap where he continued to purr, making the only sound in the room. As I stroked his sleek fur, I knew that Tom and I were both remembering the cats we had left behind with friends when we moved to Russia, as well as our little Siberian Murlyka that we had given away in Irkutsk only six months before. And we both wondered what would be Gollandskiy's fate after we left Vladivostok. But there was little time for us to ponder those bittersweet memories or to dwell on thoughts of the uncertain future. Suddenly, just as abruptly as he had entered the room, Gollandskiy jumped off my lap and ambled into the kitchen to his food bowl—signaling to us in his own way that it was now truly time for us to leave.

Without saying a word, Tom and I picked up our last two bags sitting in the foyer. On the way out of the apartment, we stopped at the kitchen door to look at Gollandskiy once more. He was hungrily chowing down on breakfast as we both reached down to pet him for the last time. Then, through a haze of tears, we stepped out into the cold, dark stairwell. I pressed the button for the elevator. As it slowly creaked up to our landing, we both looked back toward the apartment door, and Tom sighed, "It sure doesn't take them long to get into your heart."

The drive to the Vladivostok airport took almost two hours through the heavy snow on that coldest day of December. Our first stop in the terminal was at the Russian customs inspection station, where a sour old biddy in a stiff wool coat with a moth-eaten fur collar insisted that I open up several of my suitcases, making me cut all the heavy twine and strapping tape that I had so carefully secured them with. When she found that I was actually trying to smuggle Russian newspapers out of the country, she became unduly upset. Upon making this momentous discovery, she called out loudly to another customs inspector who seemed to be her superior. After the two women conferred animatedly for several minutes, the second official finally decided that it would be permissible for me to leave Russia with a few public periodicals that I'd purchased at local newsstands. But I was charged a 100-percent "export tax" on a small oil painting that I'd bought in Vladivostok for the ruble equivalent of ten dollars—which meant that I had to spend another half hour in a different office at the airport to pay the ten-dollar tax and get a sheaf of official papers filled out and properly stamped.

Our next stop in the terminal was at the Alaska Airlines check-in counter, where the local representative informed us that we would have to pay several hundred dollars for all of our excess baggage. We were already prepared for this contingency, because we had far more luggage than our tickets allowed. Money in hand, we stood at the check-in counter for an inordinately long time, while the Russian employee of Alaska Airlines went off to find someone with the authority to process the necessary paperwork and take our dollars. At last she returned and told us to give all the luggage to the baggage handler. "Go to passport section and waiting room," the Russian woman said in halting English. But when we tried to hand her the money for the extra luggage, she shook her head solemnly and replied, "I am sorry, but Alaska Airlines does not want to take your money."

Farewell to Absurdistan.

Only twenty-four passengers were leaving Vladivostok on Alaska Airlines that day, several of them people whose faces I recognized from previous flights. Sitting next to us in the frigid waiting room was another American, a courier for a New York bank, who had arrived at the airport very early that morning and heard that the weather was so cold the pilot couldn't get the plane to start. While we sat contemplating that unwelcome but not-too-surprising bit of news, we were all suddenly summoned to board a rusty, rickety old bus, which took us out onto the tarmac and up to the plane.

Once aboard, I had planned to peel off several layers of winter clothes and slip out of my snow boots, but the cabin felt almost as frigid as the outdoors. Just after take-off, when everyone was hoping for a cup of hot coffee or tea, the pilot announced that no hot drinks would be served because the water system on the plane had frozen up. As the passengers let out a collective groan, the pilot added that the lack of water would also affect the toilets, except for the chemical flush system which was fortunately still working. But he assured us that he hoped to get the problem fixed during the next scheduled stop at Khabarovsk.

The water problem apparently affected the plane's heating system, too, because the cabin was so cold the passengers had to put on additional clothing and huddle under blankets to keep warm. At Khabarovsk, we picked up a few more passengers, but the frozen water system remained unrepaired. At our next scheduled stop, in Magadan, the Russian ground crew changed a tire on the plane, and a few more people came aboard while the wings were being de-iced. But the plane's water system remained frozen. So for the entire ten-hour flight to Alaska, we all stayed wrapped up in blankets, drinking cold drinks and eating cold meals. "This Russian route is a killer," one of the stewardesses told another passenger. "Why?" he asked. "Because you fly ten hours and come in on Wednesday," she replied, "then turn around and go back on Thursday morning." She paused, then added, "Also because of the language problem. And also because something always goes wrong!"

Despite our discomfort, the winter scenery below us was so spectacular that I looked out the window most of the way from Vladivostok to Magadan and some unknown point beyond: the snow-covered mountains, the bluish glaciers, the frozen rivers, the occasional isolated settlement of log houses, the pack ice on the sea. But as I marveled once more at the beauty of the Russian winter landscape, I could not help remembering the countless numbers of innocent people who had been sent to the gulags located in that remote region of Russia, to live out wretched lives and die horrible deaths in those frigid northern lands slowly slipping away from my view, thirty thousand feet below the plane.

After darkness descended, I tried to distract myself from such thoughts by flipping through the Alaska Airlines in-flight magazine. A feature article titled "Night Lights"—about the aurora borealis—caught my eye. About the

The Naval Cemetery in Vladivostok.

same time, the pilot announced that we had left Russia and entered American air space. A few minutes later, while I was still reading about arctic atmospheric conditions, the man seated in front of me turned around and said, "Look out the window." There, on the left side of the plane, somewhere between us and the North Pole, was a folding, waving, constantly changing curtain of eerie green light shimmering in the night sky, the luminous bands of phosphorescence stretching heavenward for miles, extending as far as I could see. I watched in wonder as brilliant streaks of bright light shot through the coldly burning sky, like celestial beacons searching for some mysterious meaning in the vastness of the universe. And as I gazed in awe upon my first sight of the northern lights, I suddenly felt an ineffable sense of joy, as if the whole display had been specially staged to greet us upon our return from Russia.

Welcome home.

Postscript

Since leaving Russia, I have traveled to many other places on the globe, but not yet back to the lands "east of the sun." Given my longtime interest in Russia, however, I have tried to keep abreast of subsequent developments there, through personal contacts and published materials. All of these sources agree that significant changes have occurred in the Russian Federation since 1995, although the pace of change in places such as Siberia and the Russian Far East has been slower than in Moscow, which has modernized at a much more rapid rate than the rest of the country. Meanwhile the Western news media continue to focus their reporting primarily on Moscow and European Russia, even though Asian Russia is now much more accessible to outsiders than it was only a few years ago.

When Vladimir Putin became president of the Russian Federation in 2000, he reconfigured the previously unofficial macroregions of the country into seven federal districts (South, Central, North-West, Volga, Urals, Siberia, Far East), each overseen by a governor-general appointed by Putin and answerable directly to him. At all levels of government, from the Kremlin to the village, Russian officials at the beginning of the twenty-first century still faced a host of problems stemming from the past: environmental pollution; organized crime; the flight of capital out of the country; decaying roads, bridges, and infrastructure; the breakdown of public utilities; an increase in health problems and a decline in medical care; lowered life expectancy; and a declining birth rate. Ten years ago, the population of the new Russian Federation was 148 million. Today it is estimated to be 145 million—and expected to decline further during the next decade.

Vladivostok continues to be a city of contrasts. Friends report that "certain parts of the city are now blossoming," with the construction of elegant new apartment buildings and the renovation of existing structures. St. Paul's Lutheran Church has finally been returned to the local Lutheran congregation, and the red-brick neogothic building is now undergoing restoration. In 1999, for the centennial of the founding of the Russian Far East's first institution of higher education, the rector of Far Eastern State University spruced up parts of the urban campus, improving both the interiors and exteriors of some of the buildings, as well as the landscaping around them. On the other hand, some of Vladivostok's architectural heritage is also being destroyed, as older edifices in the city are razed to make room for new, very expensive apartment buildings, many of which are characterized by the kind of ostentatious design favored by Russia's nouveaux riches. And development within the city remains uneven, with the infrastructure still decaying and with many older buildings and neighborhoods still badly in need of repair.

Meanwhile public utilities remain a major problem in Vladivostok, with power outages and heating cutoffs becoming even worse than when I lived there. Residents of Vladivostok suffered especially during the record-breaking cold in the winters of 2000–01 and 2001–02, sometimes taking to the streets to protest the lack of electricity and heat in their homes. Officials attribute the problems to fuel shortages resulting from the high cost of coal and oil for the city's power plants and heating stations, along with a dearth of funds to purchase fuel because so many customers—including some state institutions and major industries—have defaulted on their utility bills. One of my friends observed that during a particularly bad spell of cold weather, many homes, hospitals, and day-care centers were without heat or electricity, while the villas of local elites had plenty of lights shining in their windows. She surmised that while Vladivostok's public utility problems were indeed a result of fuel and revenue shortages, another dimension was the selective distribution of electricity to powerful politicians and their cronies in the city.

Politics has always played a role in the problems plaguing Vladivostok. After almost a decade in office, Yevgeniy Nazdratenko, the controversial and reputedly corrupt governor of Primorskiy Kray, was finally forced by the Kremlin to resign in February, 2001. However, Nazdratenko—always one to land on his feet—was then appointed to a high position in Moscow as chairman of the State Fisheries Committee, a ministerial-level post. And his archrival Viktor Cherepkov, the former mayor of Vladivostok, also moved upstairs, becoming a deputy in the state Duma in Moscow.

Transportation within Vladivostok appears to have improved, with Cherepkov getting credit for having constructed several new thoroughfares in the city. Visitors to Vladivostok report that municipal buses, trolleys, and trams are still very inexpensive to ride, yet less crowded than before (except at rush hours), primarily because several private companies now operate vans that follow the bus routes. These privately owned van lines charge more per ride than public transportation, but are popular with local residents because they run more frequently and are a more efficient way to get around the city.

Alaska Airlines no longer flies to Vladivostok, having terminated its entire Russian Far East route after the Russian financial crisis in 1998 reduced business travel between the United States and Asian Russia. Another factor was Alaska Airlines' inability to compete with Aeroflot's lower ticket prices, which were a function of lower fuel costs and labor costs in Russia. Today Aeroflot is the only remaining airline that flies directly from the United States to the Russian Far East, although travelers can also reach Vladivostok and other destinations in the Russian Far East on flights by Korean Air Lines via Seoul, Japan Air Lines via Tokyo, and Russian airlines via Moscow.

After the collapse of the Soviet Union, most Russian citizens were no longer restricted from traveling to foreign countries without permission from their own government—although, until 1998, only those who possessed a *propiska*, an official residence permit for a city or town within Russia, were eligible for a passport enabling them to travel abroad. Despite that restriction, thousands of Russians have taken the opportunity to visit parts of the world that only ten years ago seemed as distant to them as the moon. But the devaluation of the ruble in 1998, coupled with much higher long-distance transportation costs in Russia itself, have resulted in fewer Russians being able to afford travel either within their own country or abroad. One friend of mine who has traveled to Asian Russia almost every year since 1992 observed that, since 1999, "The airports are almost empty. Only the trains are still busy and even they are operating on reduced schedules. Ordinary people have no money to travel—and the rich have private means."

Colleagues of mine teaching in Irkutsk, students at the university there, and frequent travelers to southern Siberia have all described many changes in the city of Irkutsk during the years after I left. A former director of the University of Maryland's Russian-American program, who worked for two years in Irkutsk and still keeps in touch with several Russians there, told me that housing conditions are basically the same as in the mid-1990s, although "suburbs" are also sprouting up on the periphery of the city. He described the houses in these suburbs as newly constructed, single-family dwellings that are still referred to as dachas, although they are actually larger, sturdier structures built of bricks, with electricity and indoor plumbing, which people now live in year-round.

Several colleagues in Irkutsk also report that the transportation system is much improved, with fleets of private vans operating on the same routes as city buses, providing more frequent and more comfortable service, although at three times the cost of public transportation. With these vans it now takes only thirty minutes to reach the center of the city from the microdistrict where I used to live, instead of the one to one-and-a-half hours (including waiting time) by bus that was standard when I was there in 1994.

William Craft Brumfield, an expert on Russian architecture, reports that the revival of religion in the Russian Federation has resulted in the restoration of many historic churches in Irkutsk, as elsewhere throughout the country. New churches are being built as well. In Irkutsk, the nineteenth-century neogothic Catholic church had been confiscated by local authorities during the Stalin era and turned into a concert hall. When the Polish Catholic community of Irkutsk was unable to get their church back from the municipal government in the 1990s, they constructed a new, ultramodern house of worship, the Cathedral of the Immaculate Heart of the Virgin, in another section of the city. Brumfield notes that "the multiconfessional ambience of life in Siberia is very much in evidence in Irkutsk," a city with several Russian Orthodox churches, both old and new, as well as the Roman Catholic cathedral, a synagogue, and a mosque. During 2002, however, several foreign Catholic priests assigned to dioceses in Eastern Siberia and the Russian Far East were denied entry into Russia, despite holding valid visas.

Changes in the market economy are evident in Irkutsk and Vladivostok, with many more private businesses opening up in both cities than when I was there. Friends now report that shopping for food and other essentials is easier than in 1993–94. In the microdistrict of my former high-rise village in Irkutsk, kiosks surrounding the apartment complex sell basic supplies such as alcoholic beverages, cigarettes, snack foods, and toilet paper, and several new stores located near the microdistrict sell meat, cheese, bread, and other food products. A wholesale market was established about two miles from our high-rise village, where customers can now purchase entire crates of food and other goods (such as a crate containing sixty packets of dried noodles or several dozen cans of peas). Another fairly large market specializes in basic hardware, with individual vendors selling screws, nails, lightbulbs, and plumbing supplies from big bins—sort of like a Russian version of Home Depot. Downtown, the Central Market in Irkutsk was completely renovated in the spring of 1998, with a spacious new building constructed alongside the old one. Still primarily a food market—where individual vendors sell whatever fifty or sixty food items they happen to have that day, the new market also has stalls for the sale of clothing, household goods, makeup, and appliances. It is also reputed to be cleaner, more modern, and better organized than the old Central Market where I shopped on a weekly basis in 1994.

Visitors to Vladivostok say that now you can buy almost anything you want in the city. Although there are still no large, American-style supermarkets, the First River and Second River indoor-outdoor markets offer a wide variety of foodstuffs and other consumer goods, as do other privately owned stores in the city. An American who has spent considerable time in Vladivostok told me that a few stores still adhere to a form of the old, inefficient, three-step purchasing process, but many others do not. "There are fewer self-service stores than here [in the United States]," she added, "but at the same time the European system of 'specialty stores' for different kinds of foodstuffs persists, and although this can be time-consuming, there is an old-fashioned charm in asking the salesperson for the specific goods. Often one can then pay directly to that person, and this is similar to how the [farmers'] markets work." Another frequent traveler to Asian Russia says that a sense of customer service has also developed during the past few years, a change from the old Soviet stance of "take what we give you" to a more capitalist attitude of "we want to keep you as a customer." Meanwhile most retail business is still conducted on a cash basis, because personal checking accounts and credit cards are still not common in the Russian Federation.

The problem for many Russians, however, is that they do not have the cash to buy the consumer goods now available in Russia's market economy. Salaries of most employees in the public sector—doctors, nurses, teachers, soldiers, policemen, firemen—have not kept pace with inflation, and many people still are not paid for weeks or months after their meager wages are due. In Vladivostok, workers have gone on strike and staged mass demonstrations, blocking major highways, to protest low wages and delayed payments. Yet in a country where the average wage is approximately one hundred dollars a month, a small middle class of business entrepreneurs and private-sector employees is slowing emerging, although there is still a very wide gap between the haves and have-nots in the Russian Federation, where a few people have amassed huge fortunes and millions of others live in poverty.

Many Russians were badly hurt by the financial crisis of August, 1998, when the country defaulted on its debts, banks collapsed, and the ruble was steeply devalued. Living standards, which had been rising in many urban areas, declined sharply, and most Russians were no longer able to afford the imported goods that constituted a large segment of the consumer market. However, one consequence of higher prices for imports is that domestic production has been stimulated—especially in the areas as food production, processing, and packaging—so that Russians are now able to purchase certain good-quality, low-cost, Russian-made versions of products that were previously available only as more expensive brands imported from abroad.

The financial crisis of 1998 also had a major effect on the University of Maryland's Russian-American education programs in Vladivostok and Irkutsk. Those programs continued to exist in the form described in chapter 10, through the end of the 1998–99 academic year. By that time, nearly four hundred students had earned bachelor of science degrees from UMUC in Russia. But the steep devaluation of the ruble in 1998 ultimately made it impossible for the two Russian universities to continue paying the high costs of American faculty sent to teach in Russia annually. Beginning with the 1999–2000 academic year, half the courses in the third and fourth years of the program were taught by local professors in Russia, most of whom were Russians hired by their respective universities. The other half were taught by UMUC professors located in other countries, through distance education programs in which the Russian students and UMUC faculty communicated by computer. The educational experiment of creating an American academic department and an American classroom environment within two Russian universities had come to an end because of economic factors beyond the control of the Russians and Americans who had had the foresight and initiative to establish that unique program during the waning years of the Soviet Union.

Despite these changes, the Russian-American departments at Irkutsk State University and Far Eastern National University continue to attract students to their programs. And those who successfully complete their four years of undergraduate education still earn bachelor's degrees from University of Maryland University College. Many of these graduates have now started firms of their own or have been hired for high-level management positions with international businesses such as Panasonic, British Petroleum, and Procter & Gamble. Others have gone into public administration at the local and regional levels, including one of our top students from 1994 who has recently become the vice-governor of Irkutsk Oblast'.

Ever since the Russian Federation was established, after the collapse of the Soviet Union, it has suffered a "brain drain" of bright, well-educated people who sought better economic opportunities in Europe, Israel, Canada, and the United States. Many of our students from Irkutsk and Vladivostok, who later came to the United States on fellowships to study for advanced degrees, initially found ways to remain in this country, where jobs in their professions pay well and living standards are much higher than in Russia. But most people with whom I have spoken recently believe that 2001 was a turning point for the Russian Federation. The economy is growing again, living standards are slowly improving, and people seem to be more upbeat, more positive, more accepting of change, more hopeful about the future. A new generation is growing up that has no experience of the old Soviet system. And many well-educated younger Russians, including many of our former students, have decided to remain in their homeland, or to return there from abroad, because they want to use their talents and skills to help build a better Russia for themselves and their descendants.

I have included this postscript to update some of the information in this book and to put the past, as I observed it seven years ago, into the context of the present. My descriptions of present-day Vladivostok and Irkutsk are based on a variety of sources, including the reports of several people who have lived and traveled in Asian Russia during the time after I left. As with any secondhand account, however, this information has been filtered through the eyes of other observers. Ultimately one's own view of Russia is dependent on who you are, where you come from, what you read, where you look, what you see, whom you listen to, and how you interpret it. And regardless of your own perspective, there will always be some people who see Russia's glass of vodka half empty and others who see it half full.

~

BIBLIOGRAPHIC ESSAY
AND NOTES

GENERAL SOURCES

In addition to using the material that I gathered directly while living in Russia, I also consulted a number of books about Russia while I was writing this personal memoir. Three of the best contemporary books about the history of Siberia and the Russian Far East are W. Bruce Lincoln's *The Conquest of a Continent: Siberia and the Russians* (New York: Random House, 1994); John J. Stephan's *The Russian Far East: A History* (Stanford: Stanford University Press, 1994); and Benson Bobrick's *East of the Sun: The Epic Conquest and Tragic History of Siberia* (New York: Poseidon Press, 1992), all of which are well written and well documented. Two other highly useful books are *Siberia: Worlds Apart*, by Victor L. Mote (Boulder, Colorado: Westview Press, 1998), and *The History of Siberia: From Russian Conquest to Revolution*, edited and introduced by Alan Wood (New York: Routledge, 1991). I relied on all these sources for much of the general historical and geographic information that I included in the introduction and in chapters 2 through 6.

Other books that provided especially valuable information about Asian Russia were *Rediscovering Russia in Asia: Siberia and the Russian Far East*, edited by Stephen Kotkin and David Wolff (Armonk, New York: M. E. Sharpe, 1995), and *The Development of Siberia: People and Resources*, edited by Alan Wood and R. A. French (New York: St. Martin's Press, 1989). Additional background information about the geography, economy, and people of this part of Russia during the Soviet period came from *Soviet Union: A Country Study*, second edition, edited by Raymond E. Zickel (Washington, D.C.: Federal Research Division, Library of Congress, 1991); *Siberia Today and Tomorrow: A Study of Economic Resources, Problems and Achievements*, by Violet Conolly (New York: Taplinger Publishing Company, 1976); and *Russian Land, Soviet People: A Geographical Approach to the U.S.S.R.*, by James S. Gregory (New York: Pegasus, 1968). A useful source for more recent information about the new Russian Federation was *Russia: A Country Study*, edited by Glenn E. Curtis (Washington, D.C.: Federal Research Division, Library of Congress, 1998). For geographic information I also consulted two post-Soviet maps: *Rossiyskaya federatsiya politiko-administrativnaya karta* [Russian Federation Political-Administrative Map] (Moscow: Federal'naya sluzhba geodezii i kartografii rossii, 1993), and *Russia and the Newly Independent Nations of the Former Soviet Union* (Washington, D.C.: National Geographic Society, 1993).

Before writing my own memoir of post-Soviet Russia, I also read the tales of many travelers who had gone before me, including three classics from the nineteenth century: Astolphe, marquis de Custine's *Empire of the Czar: A Journey through Eternal Russia*, reproduction of text of 1843 Longman edition (New York: Doubleday, 1989), and George Kennan's two fascinating accounts of his journeys in Asian Russia, *Tent Life in Siberia*, reprint of original edition published in 1871 (Salt Lake City: Peregrine Smith Books, 1986), and *Siberia and the Exile System*, volumes 1 and 2 (New York: Century, 1891). From the same era are two other interesting personal memoirs written by Westerners who traveled through the Asian part of Russia: Henry Lansdell's *Through Siberia*, originally published by Houghton Mifflin in 1882 (New York: Arno Press, 1970), and John Foster Fraser's *The Real Siberia: Together with an Account of a Dash through Manchuria* (London: Cassell, 1902).

During most of the twentieth century, relatively few travel narratives were published in English about Soviet Siberia and the Soviet Far East, primarily because so much of Asian Russia was inaccessible to foreigners, especially those from the West. Books that date from the Soviet period vary greatly in tone and quality, depending on the specific geographic areas that Western authors were allowed to see and the people they were permitted to meet, as well as the authors' own attitudes toward Russians in general and Siberians in particular (and, in the case of Soviet authors, the political constraints under which they were working and the political points they wanted to make). For a wide variety of travel accounts by Western authors, see Douglas Botting's *One Chilly Siberian Morning* (New York: Macmillan, 1965); Gaia Servadio's *A Siberian Encounter* (New York: Farrar, Straus & Giroux, 1971); Hugo Portisch's *I Saw Siberia*, translated from the 1967 German edition by Henry Fox and Ewald Osers (London: George G. Harrap, 1972); Farley Mowat's *The Siberians* (New York: Penguin Books, 1972); Stan Grossfeld's *The Whisper of Stars* (Chester, Conn.: Globe Pequot Press, 1988); and Frederick Kempe's *Siberian Odyssey: A Voyage into the Russian Soul* (New York: G. P. Putnam's Sons, 1992).

Even fewer books by Soviet authors about Asian Russia were published for English-language readers. Those I've read were almost always written from a "politically correct" (that is, Soviet) point of view. *Glimpses of Siberia*, compiled by Nikolai Yanovsky (Moscow: Progress Publishers, 1972), an English-language edition of *Rasskazy o sibiri*, comprises a series of essays "specially prepared for the foreign reader by the staff of *Sibirskiye Ogni* (*Siberian Lights*) magazine," a group of Soviet authors writing during the Brezhnev era. Despite the book's shortcomings, there are gems of information about Siberia to be mined from it. Leonid Shinkarev's *The Land beyond the Mountains: Siberia and Its People Today* (New York: Macmillan, 1973), which identifies itself as "Prepared by the Novosti Press Agency Publishing House, Moscow," is chock-full of information about Siberia filtered through the thick lenses of Soviet propaganda.

One of the most interesting recent books about this part of Russia—written by a native Siberian and translated into English—is Valentin Rasputin's *Siberia, Siberia* (Evanston, Ill.: Northwestern University Press, 1996; translated from the Russian and with an introduction by Margaret Winchell and Gerald Mikkelson; originally published as *Sibir', Sibir'* [Moscow: Molodaya gvardiya, 1991]). In their introduction the translators note that "With the possible exception of Aleksandr Solzhenitsyn . . . Valentin Rasputin was the most gifted and influential Russian prose writer of the last thirty years of the Soviet era." In this major nonfiction work, he writes passionately about Siberia past and present, from the perspective of a native Siberian who holds strong opinions about that part of Russia, the people who inhabit it, and the problems facing Siberia in the twenty-first century.

During the post–World War II era, several books about life and travel in the Soviet Union—primarily the European part—were also written by Western journalists, many of them with a keen eye for their surroundings and a good ear for the stories they heard while there. As a child, I avidly read John Gunther's *Inside Russia Today* (New York: Harper & Brothers, 1957), Irving R. Levine's *Main Street U.S.S.R.* (Garden City, N.Y.: Doubleday, 1959), and Wright Miller's *Russians as People* (New York: E. P. Dutton, 1961). When I reread these same books in the 1990s, I was struck by the fact that daily life in Russia had changed so little during the decades since they were published. Living conditions, food markets, street scenes, finding a telephone book, dealing with bureaucrats, getting stamps at the post office, buying an airplane ticket—all seemed nearly the same in the Soviet Union of the 1950s and the Russian Federation of the 1990s.

Subsequent accounts of life in the Soviet Union were written by a number of journalists from the West, most of whom lived in Moscow and could travel only to those parts of the country that the Soviet authorities allowed them to see (at least until the Gorbachev era, when foreigners began being permitted to visit certain areas that had previously been off-limits). Despite those restrictions, many fine books published from the 1970s to the 1990s provided Western readers with a sense of what life was like in a country that most of them would never have an opportunity to visit. Notable among these books are Hedrick Smith's best-seller, *The Russians* (New York: Quadrangle/New York Times Book Company, 1976), and his sequel, *The New Russians* (New York: Random House, 1990); Robert G. Kaiser's *Russia: The People and the Power* (New York: Atheneum, 1976); Michael Binyon's *Life in Russia* (New York: Pantheon Books, 1983); David K. Shipler's *Russia: Broken Idols, Solemn Dreams* (New York: Times Books, 1983; revised edition, 1989); David K.

Willis's *Klass: How Russians Really Live* (New York: St. Martin's Press, 1985); and David Remnick's Pulitzer Prize–winning *Lenin's Tomb: The Last Days of the Soviet Empire* (New York: Random House, 1993). Although all of these books focus mainly on European Russia, they provide a wealth of information and valuable insights about many aspects of Soviet life: housing conditions, the economy, health, education, the workplace, religion, the arts, leisure activities, crime, social class, and issues of "nationality," all within the political context of the time that each book was written.

During the Soviet era few women from the West went to live in the Soviet Union, and even fewer wrote about their experiences afterward—but those who did have produced some interesting books that describe life in that country often from a more personal perspective than accounts by journalists sent to report about Russia for Western newspapers or magazines. Margaret Wettlin's *Fifty Russian Winters: An American Woman's Life in the Soviet Union* (New York: Pharos Books, 1992) is the story of an American who went to Russia in 1932, married a Russian theater director, and subsequently lived in several locations in the Soviet Empire—from Moscow to Mongolia, from the Volga to the Caucasus to Siberia—during the darkest days of the Stalin era and World War II. *Sixteen Years in Siberia: Memoirs of Rachel and Israel Rachlin*, translated from the 1982 Danish edition (Tuscaloosa and London: University of Alabama Press, 1988) is a first-person account of the lives of a Jewish couple and their family who were deported from Lithuania to Siberia in 1941 and lived in exile there until 1957. Their story documents the details of daily life in Siberian transit camps and exile villages, as experienced by two remarkable people who survived the Soviet political persecutions of the mid-twentieth century. Told with honesty, dignity, and humanity, it should be read by anyone interested in the realities of life in Siberia during that time.

More contemporary accounts by Western women include Andrea Lee's *Russian Journal* (New York: Random House, 1981), an entertaining and perceptive memoir written by an American who lived for almost a year in Moscow and Leningrad in the late 1970s, when her husband was a university exchange student there. Another very personal story—which centers on Moscow, but also ranges afield to Baku, Stavropol', Dagestan, and Novosibirsk—is Susan Richards's *Epics of Everyday Life: Encounters in a Changing Russia* (Hammondsworth, Middlesex, U.K.: Penguin Books, 1990). And one of the best books about life in early post-Soviet Russia—focusing primarily on Moscow and European Russia—is *Waking the Tempests: Ordinary Life in the New Russia* (New York: Simon & Schuster, 1996), by Eleanor Randolph, who worked there as a reporter for the *Washington Post* from 1991 to 1993.

A handy reference book that I carried to Russia was Genevra Gerhart's *The Russians' World: Life and Language* (New York: Harcourt Brace Jovanovich, 1974), which explains Russian terms and concepts associated with different aspects of daily life (clothing, animals, numbers, housing, education, holidays, the correct forms of Russian names). A second, updated edition was published by Holt, Rinehart, and Winston in 1995. Two other books especially helpful in explaining the cultural differences that I observed between Russians and Americans are Victor Ripp's *Pizza in Pushkin Square: What Russians Think about America and the American Way of Life* (New York: Simon & Schuster, 1990), and Yale Richmond's *From Nyet to Da: Understanding the Russians* (Yarmouth, Me.: Intercultural Press, 1992; revised and updated, 1996). I recommend these two slim volumes as background reading for anyone planning to live or work in the Russian Federation.

Additional sources that I consulted when writing specific chapters are listed below.

INTRODUCTION

For a good description of travel restrictions in the Soviet Union, see *Open Lands: Travels through Russia's Once Forbidden Places*, by Mark Taplin (South Royalton, Vt.: Steerforth Press, 1998), pp. 3–12. The quotation on page xxiv is from Anton Chekhov's *Ostrov Sakhalin* [Sakhalin Island], quoted in James Forsyth's *A History of the Peoples of Siberia: Russia's North Asian Colony, 1581–1990* (Cambridge: Cambridge University Press, 1992), p. 198. The two quotations from Michael Binyon, on pages xxv and xxvi, are from his book, *Life in Russia* (New York: Pantheon), p. 13 and p. 3. And the quotation on page xxvi is from Birgitta Ingemanson's newspaper article "In the Soviet Union, Nothing Is What It First Appears," *Idahonian/Daily News*, June 9–10, 1990, p. 2C.

CHAPTER 1. THE ROAD TO RUSSIA

Among the many books I read before going to Russia, two autobiographies published almost half a century apart held a special interest to me because of my slight connection to their authors: Alexander Barmine's *One Who Survived: The Life Story of a Russian under the Soviets* (New York: G. P. Putnam's Sons, 1945), and Andrei Sakharov's *Memoirs / Andrei Sakharov* (New York: Alfred A. Knopf, 1990), both written by men who achieved high positions within the Soviet system before becoming outspoken critics of it.

CHAPTER 2. VLADIVOSTOK:
CAPITAL OF RUSSIA'S WILD EAST

Several sources provided background information on the city of Vladivostok, both historical and contemporary. In addition to the works by Lincoln, Stephan, Bobrick, and Kotkin and Wolff, cited in "General Sources," I also consulted the following papers by Birgitta Ingemanson: "Cosmopolitan Vladivostok: Swedish Glimpses, 1908–1923," *Scando-Slavica*, Tomus 42 (1996): 36–57; "Vladivostok, Window to the East: Stories of a City," lecture delivered at Washington State University, October 28, 1991; and "Vladivostok, Window to the East: The End of the Line and a New Beginning," paper presented at the conference of the American Association for the Advancement of Slavic Studies, 1992.

Two sources were particularly informative about the architecture and urban history of Vladivostok: William Richardson's "Vladivostok, city of three eras," *Planning Perspectives* 10 (1995): 43–65, and Maria Lebedko's "Vladivostok Downtown: A Historic Walking Tour," an unpublished manuscript given to me in 1994 by the author, a professor at Far Eastern State University, who also took me on several guided tours of different sections of the city. Lebedko's manuscript was published on the Internet in 1999, edited and with an introduction and photographs by Birgitta Ingemanson and others, with Web editor Donna McCool *(www.wsulibs.wsu.edu/vladivostok)*.

While living in Vladivostok, I also acquired several books written about the city by Russian authors. *Staryy Vladivostok"* [Old Vladivostok] (Vladivostok: Utro Rossii, 1992) is a coffee-table book, with text in Russian and English, amply illustrated with very interesting historical photographs of the city's buildings, landmarks, streets, and inhabitants. *Zhemchuzhina Zolotoga Roga* [The Golden Horn Pearl], by N. Ayushin (Vladivostok: Ussuri Publishing, 1992) focuses on the contemporary city and its environs; the Russian-English text is illustrated with dozens of color photographs of Vladivostok in the modern era. Another bilingual publication is *Vladivostok*, by G. Oleynikova (Vladivostok: Ussuri Publishing, 1992), a paperback guidebook to the city, illustrated with color photographs from the early 1990s.

The biweekly English-language edition of Vladivostok's major newspaper, *Vladivostok News* (May 21, 1993–December 16, 1994), provided useful information about population figures, criminal activities and crime statistics, pollution problems, public health issues, and important local events during the time that I lived in the city. Information about Vladivostok's having the highest crime rate of any urban area in the country during the late Soviet era comes from "Urbanization and Crime: The Soviet Experience," by Louise I. Shelley, in *The Contemporary Soviet City*, edited by Henry W. Morton and Robert C. Stuart (Armonk, N.Y.: M. E. Sharpe, 1984). For a good description of the problems of crime in the Russian Federation after the breakup of the Soviet Union, see Steven Handelman's *Comrade Criminal: Russia's New Mafiya* (New Haven: Yale University Press, 1995). Handelmann (pp. 21–22, 381–82) points out that *mafiya* is a Russian term that has been in use since the 1970s, applied to various groups depending on the time period and the speaker's point of view: corrupt bureaucrats, the KGB, black-marketeers, con men, gangsters, smugglers, anyone who made money and flaunted it. According to Handelman, "By 1992, it carried an additional meaning, describing the groups of criminal entrepreneurs and corrupt officials who came to prominence in the post-Soviet era" (p. 382). In this book, I have used the term *mafiya* to denote members of organized crime groups in the Russian Federation.

For a good explanation of the United States's role in Siberia and the Russian Far East during the Russian civil war, see George F. Kennan's *Soviet-American Relations, 1917–1920*, volume 2: *The Decision to Intervene* (Princeton, N.J.: Princeton University Press, 1958). The quotation from Konstantin Kharsky, on page 18, describing Vladivostok in 1919 during the civil war period, is from Stephan's *The Russian Far East*, p. 126.

For several decades Vladivostok was the site of transit camps where thousands of prisoners were held before being sent by ship to the notorious penal colonies and labor camps to the north, in the regions of Sakhalin, Kamchatka, and Magadan. The best-known books in the West about the Soviet penal system are Aleksandr Solzhenitsyn's classics, *One Day in the Life of Ivan Denisovich*, translated by Max Hayward and Ronald Hingley (New York: Praeger, 1963), and *The Gulag Archipelago, 1918–1956: An Experiment in Literary Investigation*, volumes 1–7, translated by Thomas P. Whitney (New York: Harper & Row, 1974–78). Another survivor of Stalin's camps in the Russian Far East, Eugenia Ginzburg, wrote two moving accounts of her experiences: *Journey into the Whirlwind* (New York: Harcourt Brace Jovanovich, 1967), and *Within the Whirlwind* (New York: Harcourt Brace Jovanovich, 1981).

CHAPTER 3. RIDING THE RAILS:
THE TRANS-SIBERIAN RAILROAD

Guide to the Great Siberian Railway (1900), edited by A. I. Dmitriev-Mamonov and A. F. Zdziarski, English translation by L. Kukol-Yasnopolsky, revised by John Marshall (St. Petersburg: Ministry of Ways and Communication, 1900), is a massive, detailed, and fascinating book about the history, geography, architecture, and populations of the regions traversed by the Trans-Siberian Railroad up to that time, as well as a history of the construction of the railroad itself. I found it to be an interesting source of information not only about the railroad, but also about Vladivostok, Irkutsk, and Lake Baikal in the late nineteenth century.

The Trans-Siberian Railroad has attracted writers throughout the twentieth century. Among the best books in English are Harmon Tupper's history of the world's longest railroad, *To the Great Ocean: Siberia and the Trans-Siberian Railway* (Boston: Little, Brown, 1965), and Eric Newby's entertaining travel account, *The Big Red Train Ride* (New York: St. Martin's Press, 1978). Other travelers' tales include Laurens van der Post's *Journey into Russia* (New York: Penguin Books, 1964), which contains sections on the Trans-Siberian Railroad and Siberia; Elizabeth Pond's *From the Yaroslavsky Station: Russia Perceived*, revised edition (New York: Universe Books, 1984); Herbert Lieberman's *The Green Train* (New York: Avon Books, 1986); Mary Morris's *Wall to Wall: From Beijing to Berlin by Rail* (New York: Doubleday, 1991); and Fen Montaigne's "Russia's Iron Road," *National Geographic*, June, 1998, pp. 2–33. In a category all its own is Lesley Blanch's haunting personal story, *Journey into the Mind's Eye: Fragments of an Autobiography* (London: William Collins & Sons, 1968). For a scholarly "biography" of the Trans-Siberian Railroad and its effects on the economic development of Russia, see Steven G. Marks's *Road to Power: The Trans-Siberian Railroad and the Colonization of Asian Russia, 1850–1917* (Ithaca, N.Y.: Cornell University Press, 1991).

On my own railroad trips in Russia, I carried along Robert Strauss's *Trans-Siberian Rail Guide*, second edition (Chalfont St Peter, Bucks, U.K.: Brandt Publications, 1991). An even better traveling companion would have been Bryn Thomas's

Trans-Siberian Handbook, third edition (Hindhead, Surrey, U.K.: Trailblazer Publications, 1994), which I later consulted for more detailed information about the railroad and its routes. I also gleaned further information about Primorskiy Kray, the Russian Far East, and Siberia from a number of sources that dealt with the areas traversed by the Trans-Siberian tracks: *Primorsky Region* (Vladivostok: Ussuri Publishing, 1993); *Glimpses of Flora and Fauna of Primorye (Legends and Facts)*, by Maria Lebedko, given to me as an unpublished manuscript by the author in 1992 (Vladivostok: Dalpress, 1995); *Pocket Handbook of the Russian Far East: A Reference Guide*, by Elisa Miller and Alexander Karp (Seattle: Russian Far East Update, 1994); and *Khabarovsk-Irkutsk by Train: Siberia and Far East* (Khabarovsk: Intourist Khabarovsk, n.d.), a Russian railroad map with a separate supplement (in English) containing historical, geographical, and railroad information.

During the 1990s a number of articles documented the plight of endangered Siberian tigers in the Russian Far East. See "Poachers Pursue Siberian Tigers to Extinction," by Michael Specter, *International Herald Tribune*, September 7, 1995, p. 2; "Tiger in the Snow," by Peter Matthiessen, *New Yorker*, January 6, 1997, pp. 58–65; "Siberian Tigers," by Maurice Hornocker, *National Geographic*, February, 1997, pp. 100–109; "Making Room for Wild Tigers," by Geoffrey C. Ward, *National Geographic*, December, 1997, pp. 2–35; and "Whose Environment? A Case Study of Forestry Policy in Russia's Maritime Province," by Elizabeth Wishnick, in Kotkin and Wolff, editors, *Rediscovering Russia in Asia*, pp. 256–68. For an update on the plight of the Siberian tigers, see Peter Matthiessen's *Tigers in the Snow*, with an introduction and photographs by Maurice Hornocker (New York: North Point Press, 2000).

In regard to the Decembrists, I have cited 100 as the approximate number of men condemned to imprisonment, hard labor, and exile in Siberia after the abortive uprising against the tsar in December, 1825. Historians disagree on the exact number, citing figures ranging from 90 to 121.

Scholars also disagree about the etymology of the word "*Sibir,*'" from which we derive the English term "Siberia." Several possible origins include (a) *sibir*, a Tatar word for "sleeping land"; (b) *Sibir*, the name of a western Tatar settlement; (c) *siber*, a Mongolian word for "pure," "beautiful," "wonderful"; (d) *sever*, the Russian word for "north"; and (e) elements of the name of an ancient people who once inhabited the Itrysh River area.

CHAPTER 4. IRKUTSK: THE PARIS OF SIBERIA

When I lived in Irkutsk, the best short guidebook, in English, about the history, architecture, and famous inhabitants of the city was Mark Sergeyev's *Irkutsk and Lake Baikal*, translated from the Russian by Jan Butler, revised edition (Moscow: Planeta Publishers, 1990). A quite different and more detailed source of information, in Russian, was *300 Irkutsku-gorodu* [The City of Irkutsk: 300 Years] (Moscow: Glavnoye upravleniye geodezii i kartografii pri sovete ministrov sssr, 1987), a report issued in connection with the 300th anniversary of the city of Irkutsk.

Christine Sutherland's *The Princess of Siberia: The Story of Maria Volkonsky and the Decembrist Exiles* (New York: Farrar Straus Giroux, 1984) is a very readable account of the lives of those remarkable people, many of whom contributed significantly to the intellectual and material development of nineteenth-century Siberia. The Volkonsky's wooden house is one of two Decembrist-family homes now preserved as museums in Irkutsk. When I visited there in 1994, Sutherland's book was prominently displayed in a glass case along with other works about the Decembrists that had been published in Russian and French.

Readers interested in learning more about the contemporary Siberian writer Valentin Rasputin should see Margaret Winchell and Gerald Mikkelson's introduction to their translation of Rasputin's major nonfiction work, *Siberia, Siberia* (Evanston, Ill.: Northwestern University Press, 1996), which provides a good overview of the writer's background, outlook, and works, both fiction and nonfiction.

CHAPTER 5. LAKE BAIKAL:
THE SACRED SEA OF SIBERIA

Most of the facts and figures cited about Lake Baikal in this chapter come directly from sources whom I met at the Limnological Institute of the Siberian Branch of the Russian Academy of Sciences, located in the village of Listvyanka near the point at which the Angara River flows out of the lake. I visited the Limnological Institute in the spring of 1994, interviewed officials there, and toured the institute's exhibits of the geology, hydrology, flora, and fauna of the Lake Baikal region.

Although many of the books written about Siberia contain a section on Lake Baikal, fewer focus solely on this subject. Among the ones I consulted are Peter Matthiesson's *Baikal: Sacred Sea of Siberia*, with photographs by Boyd Norton (San Francisco: Sierra Books, 1992); O. K. Gusev's *Svyashchennyy baykal: zapovedniye zemli baykala* [Sacred Baikal: Baikal Nature Reserve Areas], with text in Russian and picture captions in both Russian and English (Moscow: Agropromizdat, 1986); and Mark Sergeyev's *Baykal / Baikal*, with an introduction by Valentin Rasputin and with text in both Russian and English (Moscow: Planeta Publishers, 1990). See also "The World's Great Lake: Russia's Lake Baikal," by Don Belt, *National Geographic*, June, 1992, pp. 2–36.

Lake Baikal is known by a number of secondary names in addition to the four mentioned in my text. These include "the Holy Sea," "the Holy Lake," "the Glorious Sea," "the Eye of Siberia," "the Bright Eye of the Earth," "the Sacred Lake," "the Sacred Water," "the Gem of Siberia," "the Blue Jewel of Siberia," and "the Inland Sea."

Sources disagree about several "facts" regarding Lake Baikal, including the number of islands in it (27, 29, or 30) and the number of tributaries flowing into it. In *Siberia, Siberia* (p. 135), Valentin Rasputin says that citing 336 tributaries is a commonly repeated mistake. Other sources say "more than 200" tributaries or "more than 300" flow into Baikal, without being more specific. Sources at the Limnological

Institute told me that more than 1,000 rivers, streams, rivulets, and runoffs flow into the lake, depending on the time of year, but that 336 of them flow into it year round, of which only five are large, the largest being the Selenga River that originates in Mongolia.

A useful report on ecological issues concerning the Baikal region, with text in Russian and English, is *Lake Baikal Region in the Twenty-first Century: A Model of Sustainable Development or Continued Degradation? A Comprehensive Program of Land Use Policies for the Russian Portion of the Lake Baikal Region* (Center for Citizen Initiatives-USA; Center for Socio-Ecological Issues of the Baikal Region; Davis Associates; and Russian Academy of Sciences, March, 1993).

Baykal'skiy tsellyulozno-bumazhnyy kombinat [Baikal'sk Pulp-and-Paper Mills] is a full-color publication by the pulp-and-paper company (no date), with text in Russian and English, which I acquired at the paper mill in March, 1994. In form and content it closely resembles the annual reports that Western companies send to their shareholders.

CHAPTER 6. AMONG THE BURYATS

Rossiyskaya federatsiya politiko-administrativnaya karta [Russian Federation Political-Administrative Map], 1993, identifies the Buryat "administrative territories" as Respublika Buryatiya [Buryat Republic], Ust'-Ordynskiy Buryatskiy Avtonomnyy Okrug [Ust'-Ordynskiy Buryat Autonomous District], and Aginskiy Buryatskiy Avtonomnyy Okrug [Aginskiy Buryat Autonomous District] respectively, whereas *National Geographic*'s 1993 map, *Russia and the Newly Independent Nations of the Former Soviet Union*, identifies them as Buryatia, Ust' Orda Buryat Autonomous Okrug, and Aga Buryat Autonomous Okrug. Some maps (both Russian and American) identify the capital of the Ust'-Ordynskiy Autonomous District also as Ust'-Ordynskiy. When I was there in 1994, the city limit sign identified the town itself as Ust'-Orda. A local government official confirmed to me that the name of the town is Ust'-Orda, whereas the name of the district is Ust'-Ordynskiy. At the time, the district contained 79 "nationalities" (ethnic groups), with 36 percent of the population classified as Buryat. Source: *Ust'-Ordynskiy buryatskiy avtonomnyy okrug* [Ust'-Ordynskiy Buryat Autonomous District], pamphlet published by the district government (no date), given to me by the district governor in April, 1994. I also consulted *Buryatiya: unikal'nye ob"ekty prirody* [Buryatia: A Unique Object of Nature], a Russian map with historical, cultural, and geographic information about Buryatia (no publisher or publication date indicated), as well as *Burat's* [sic] *Origin*, an unpublished manuscript, translated from Russian into English, author unidentified, which was given to me in Irkutsk in May, 1994.

Jeremiah Curtin, an accomplished linguist with a degree from Harvard, was secretary of legation of the United States in Russia from 1864 to 1870. In 1900 he traveled to Siberia, to the land of the Western Buryats, to study the Buryat language and Buryat customs. His interesting account, *A Journey in Southern Siberia: The*

Mongols, Their Religion and Their Myths, originally published by Little, Brown in 1909 (New York: Arno Press and The New York Times, 1971), details life in "Usturdi" (Ust'-Orda) and the surrounding area during the two months that Curtin spent there between mid-July and mid-September of 1900. He also recounts a number of Buryat legends and myths. Many of Curtin's descriptions of Buryat life at the beginning of the twentieth century are remarkably similar to what I observed during my short visits to Ust'-Orda in the spring and summer of 1994.

James Forsyth's *A History of the Peoples of Siberia* presents a wealth of information about the indigenous peoples of Siberia, including the Buryats, in a well-balanced history of the native peoples and the Europeans who ultimately conquered, colonized, and settled in Asian Russia. Forsyth also challenges Soviet-Russian claims about the indigenous peoples of Siberia and Soviet historical interpretations of the colonization and settlement of that land.

For additional information on Buryats in the modern era, see Caroline Humphrey's *Karl Marx Collective: Economy, Society and Religion in a Siberian Collective Farm* (Cambridge: Cambridge University Press, 1983), which contains a mass of economic and social data from Soviet sources as well as from Humphrey's own fieldwork among the Barguzin Buryats, east of Lake Baikal, during the 1960s and 1970s. See also the chapter titled "Buryats," by Caroline Humphrey, in *The Nationalities Question in the Soviet Union*, edited by Graham Smith (London and New York: Longman, 1990), pp. 290–303.

The Russians and some of the Buryats I met in the area around Lake Baikal referred to "Burkhan" as if that were the name of one particular spirit or god (usually associated with Lake Baikal itself). But in Jeremiah Curtin's book there are many Buryat myths and folk tales that include references to "the thousand Burkhans" and also to specific "Burkhans" with individual names—which strongly implies that "burkhan" is the Buryats' general name for gods or deities, or at least a certain category of deities. Later I learned from personal sources that the term is often used in reference to visual representations (statuettes) of various deities, usually Buddhist ones, although "burkhan" is also used by the man in the street as a general term for Buryat gods.

Little has been published about Buryat cuisine, which is not well known in Russia outside the Buryat areas. For more information on traditional Buryat ingredients and prepared dishes, see *Buryatskaya kukhnya* [Buryat Cuisine], a cookbook by G. Tsyndynzhapov and E. Baduyeva (Ulan-Ude: Buryatskoe Knizhnoe Izdatel'stvo, 1991); "Molochnaya pishcha barguzinskikh buryat [The Milk Foods of the Barguzin Buryat]," *Etnograficheskiy Sbornik* [Ethnographic Collection], vol. 2, (Ulan-Ude, 1961), pp. 137–40; and "Raw Liver and More: Feasting with the Buriats of Southern Siberia," by Sharon Hudgins, in *Food on the Move: Proceedings of the Oxford Symposium on Food and Cookery 1996*, edited by Harlan Walker (Totnes, U.K.: Prospect Books, 1997), pp. 136–56.

The quotation on page 143 is from Curtin's *A Journey in Southern Siberia*, p. 91.

CHAPTER 7. THE HIGH-RISE VILLAGE

For information on the history and development of Soviet cities, see *The Contemporary Soviet City*, edited by Henry W. Morton and Robert C. Stuart (Armonk, N.Y.: M. E. Sharpe, 1984); *Modern Soviet Society*, by Basile H. Kerblay (New York: Pantheon Books, 1983); and *Quality of Life in the Soviet Union*, by Horst Herlemann (Boulder, Colo.: Westview Press, 1987). A very informative work on domestic architecture in Russia from the late nineteenth century through the late twentieth century is *Russian Housing in the Modern Age: Design and Social History*, edited by William Craft Brumfield and Blair A. Ruble (Washington, D.C.: Woodrow Wilson Center Press/Cambridge: Cambridge University Press, 1993).

The dollar figures for ruble prices quoted in this chapter are based on the average exchange rate for each relevant five-month period (that is, each university semester that I spent in Vladivostok and Irkutsk), since the rate changed so rapidly every week during that time because of high inflation in Russia.

The quotation on page 163 is from Eugenia Ginzburg's *Within the Whirlwind*, p. 174.

The problem of undependable municipal utilities in Vladivostok and Primorskiy Kray not only persisted, but even worsened, during the second half of the 1990s. See "Fear and Freezing in Vladivostok," by Nonna Chernyakova, *Russian Life*, January/February 2001, pp. 62, 64; originally published on the Internet in Transitions Online, *www.tol.cz*, but not currently located in the archive there.

CHAPTER 8. FEASTS AND FESTIVALS

For twenty-five years prior to going to Russia, I had been collecting cookbooks published in the Soviet Union, most of them printed in the Russian language. Assuming that Russian-language cookbooks would be readily available to me in the Russian Federation, I carried with me to Vladivostok and Irkutsk only my favorite Russian cookbooks published in English: *The Food and Cooking of Russia*, by Lesley Chamberlain (Hammondsworth, U.K.: Penguin Books, 1982); *A La Russe: A Cookbook of Russian Hospitality*, by Darra Goldstein (New York: Random House, 1983); *The Art of Russian Cuisine*, by Anne Volokh (New York: Macmillan, 1983); *Please to the Table: The Russian Cookbook*, by Anya von Bremzen and John Welchman (New York: Workman, 1990); and *Classic Russian Cooking: Elena Molokhovets' A Gift to Young Housewives*, translated, introduced, and annotated by Joyce Toomre (Bloomington & Indianapolis: Indiana University Press, 1992). Russians who saw those cookbooks in my apartments were amazed to discover that any books about Russian cuisine had been published in the United States and England. They fingered the pages carefully, commenting on the high quality of the paper and printing, which was far superior to that of cookbooks published in Russia. And when they read the texts, they were even more surprised at the accuracy of the recipes. It was a revelation to them that people living in other countries could write so authoritatively about Russian cuisine.

For additional information on Russian foodways from Kievan times to the present, see *Food in Russian History and Culture*, edited by Musya Glants and Joyce Toomre (Bloomington & Indianapolis: Indiana University Press, 1997), and *Bread and Salt: A Social and Economic History of Food and Drink in Russia*, by R. E. F. Smith and David Christian (Cambridge: Cambridge University Press, 1984).

Notes about calendars and holidays. The dates on which certain holidays occur in Russia can be confusing to people in the West, because of historically different ways of calculating the calendar. In 45 B.C. Julius Caesar introduced to the Western world a calendar that closely approximated the time it took for the earth to make one complete revolution around the sun. But the Julian calendar's minor deviation from true planetary motion added up over the centuries, causing it to become increasingly less accurate as time went by. A new, reformed calendar, introduced by Pope Gregory XIII in 1582, calculated the time more accurately, dropped ten days from the old Julian calendar, and changed the points at which leap years occur. By the twentieth century, the difference between the older Julian and the newer Gregorian calendars had become a total of thirteen days. Much of the Christian world adopted the Gregorian calendar several centuries ago, but Russia continued to use the Julian calendar until shortly after the Bolshevik Revolution. On February 1, 1918, Russia's new government officially changed from the older Julian calendar to the Gregorian one commonly used in the West. That's why the Soviet Union's annual celebration of the Bolsheviks' 1917 October Revolution was always held thirteen days later, on November 7. But the Russian Orthodox Church continued to adhere to the older, Julian calendar. Hence Christmas Day (December 25 on the Julian calendar) occurs on January 7 on the current Gregorian calendar, and New Year's Day (January 1 on the old Julian calendar) now occurs on January 14.

Calendrical differences between Eastern Orthodox and Western Christian churches are sometimes also a source of confusion in regard to the dates of other religious holidays. When I was in Siberia in 1994, Easter was observed on April 3 by Roman Catholic and Protestant churches, but not until May 1 by the Russian Orthodox Church (and other Eastern Orthodox churches). In some years, Easter occurs on the same Sunday for the Roman Catholic, Protestant, and Eastern Orthodox churches alike. In other years the date of Easter for the Eastern Orthodox churches (Russian, Serbian, Greek, and so on) can be anywhere from one to four weeks after Easter has been observed by Roman Catholics and Protestants.

In all these Christian churches, Easter is initially determined as occurring on the first Sunday after the first full moon following the vernal equinox (around March 20 or 21). But unlike the Western Catholic and Protestant churches, the Eastern Orthodox churches have an additional criterion for determining the date of Easter: it cannot fall on or before the eight-day Jewish spring festival of Passover, which always begins on the fourteenth day of Nisan on the Jewish lunar-based calendar—a date that occurs in March or April on the calendars used by most of the Christian world. Since the Hebrew calendar, the Gregorian calendar, and the Julian calendar all differ in the ways in which they are calculated, in some years Passover might occur at the same time as Easter, whereas in other years the difference between the dates of these two major religious holidays can be as much as two weeks apart. Whenever the lunar-determined Easter Sunday falls during the time of Passover, the Eastern Orthodox church pushes back the date of Easter, observing it on the first Sunday after Passover. Hence the sometimes differing dates on which Easter is celebrated by different branches of the Christian religion.

CHAPTER 9. THE MARKET ECONOMY

Most of the information in this chapter comes from my own experiences of the emerging market economy for consumer goods in Vladivostok and Irkutsk and from reports published in *Vladivostok News* and local newspapers in Irkutsk between August, 1993, and December, 1994. For further information on the subject of food markets, see "Onions with No Bottoms and Chickens with No Tops: Shopping for Food in the Emerging Market Economy of Siberia and the Russian Far East," by Thomas C. Hudgins, in *Food on the Move: Proceedings of the Oxford Symposium on Food and Cookery 1996*, edited by Harlan Walker (Totnes, U.K.: Prospect Books, 1997), pp. 157–76. Another useful article about the early post-Soviet economy is "Winners and Losers in Russia's Economic Transition," by Elizabeth Brainerd, *American Economic Review* 88, no. 5, (December 1998): 1094–1116.

On January 1, 1999, the Russian government issued new currency to replace the inflated ruble, dropping three zeroes from the old ruble. Thus 1,000 rubles under the old system became 1 ruble in the new system. All bank notes issued from 1993 to 1995—with denominations such as 1,000 rubles, 5,000 rubles, or 10,000 rubles—ceased to be legal tender, although Russians were allowed to trade in those "old rubles" for new ones without losing the value of their money. At the same time, all prices were changed to reflect the new system, too. However, prices in this book are given in the "old ruble" value at the time that I lived in Russia; hence most of the prices cited are in the thousands of rubles. An item that was priced at 1,000 rubles when I lived in Russia would today be priced at 1 ruble (not considering subsequent inflation, of course).

CHAPTER 10. SCHOOL DAYS

Established in 1947, the institution known today as University of Maryland University College (UMUC) is one of the eleven degree-granting institutions of the statewide University System of Maryland. Since 1949 UMUC has offered university courses in more than fifty countries—primarily, but not exclusively, for U.S. military service members, U.S. government employees, and their families stationed around the world. University of Maryland University College was the first U.S. university to offer baccalaureate degree programs taught on site at U.S. military bases abroad (1949); the first to confer bachelor's degrees at U.S. military installations overseas (1951); and the first to send its faculty to teach in a war zone (Republic of Vietnam, 1963). In 1994, the last year that I taught for UMUC, it was offering programs (both military and nonmilitary) at more than two hundred sites in twenty-two countries. As the UMUC administration was fond of saying, "The sun never sets on the University of Maryland." See *Never an Ivory Tower: University of Maryland University College—The First 50 Years*, by Sharon Hudgins (Adelphi, Md.: University of Maryland University College, 2000).

University of Maryland University College was not the only U.S. university to establish ties with Far Eastern State University (FESU) and Irkutsk State University (ISU) in Russia. Prior to 1991, when the UMUC program began, various groups of faculty and students from other colleges and universities in the United States had visited institutions of higher education in both Vladivostok and Irkutsk, primarily as a result of Gorbachev's policy of glasnost. In 1987–88 Washington State University was the first U.S. university to establish a formal academic relationship with FESU in Vladivostok, and by 1994 FESU had more than twenty cooperative agreements with universities in the United States, China, the Republic of Korea, and Japan. Although a number of U.S. colleges and universities established programs with various institutions of higher education throughout the Russian Federation after the breakup of the Soviet Union, to my knowledge University of Maryland University College was the first, and only, American university to offer an American-accredited bachelor's degree program taught entirely in Russia. Some of the other joint Russian-American education programs did not offer American-accredited bachelor's degrees; those that did required their Russian students to spend at least one or two semesters studying at the American institutions' campuses in the United States.

In the Russian Federation, education was compulsory through the eighth grade, at which point each student had to decide whether to continue his or her secondary education in an academically oriented school (in preparation for higher education at a university or professional institute), in a professional-technical school, or in a vocational-training school—or to leave school after the eighth grade and enter the workforce. Reforms of the Russian education system from the mid-1980s to the early 1990s included increasing the total number of years of primary and secondary education from ten to eleven, with students starting the first grade at age six and graduating from high school at age seventeen. However, when I was teaching in Russia during 1993 and 1994, many of the proposed reforms had not yet been instituted, at least not uniformly throughout the school system. Meanwhile many Russian primary and secondary schools were operating with substandard facilities, from a Western point of view, and were drastically overcrowded, with different groups of students attending school in shifts each day: morning, afternoon, or evening. According to *Russia: A Country Study* (p. 260), "In 1993, Russia was forced to close about 20,000 of its schools because of physical inadequacy. . . . In 1994 one of every two students attended a school operating on two or three shifts."

For a good description of the education system during the late Soviet period—the system that educated the Russian students I taught in the mid-1990s—see Richard B. Dobson, "Soviet Education: Problems and Policies in the Urban Context," in *The Contemporary Soviet City*, edited by Henry W. Morton and Robert C. Stuart, pp. 156–79. For additional information on the Soviet education system, see *Soviet Education under Perestroika*, edited by John Dunstan (London: Routledge, 1992); *The Soviet Secondary School*, by Dora Shturman (London: Routledge, 1988); *A Guide to the Soviet Curriculum: What the Russian Child Is Taught in School*, by James Y. Muckle (New York: Croom Helm/Methuen, 1988); and *Education in the USSR*, by Joseph J. Zajda (New York: Pergamon Press, 1980).

A NOTE ABOUT WEBSITES

Websites dealing with Russia have mushroomed since I first went to that country in 1993. Some of the most useful for up-to-date information on the Russian Federation (in English) are *www.rferl.org*, Radio Free Europe / Radio Liberty's Website, which publishes "Newsline," a daily report that includes current news about Russia; *www.russianobserver.com* and *www.moscowtimes.ru*, both with daily news reports from Russia; "Transitions Online" at *www.tol.cz*; *www.vladnews.ru*, the online, English-language edition of *Vladivostok News*; *www.russianfareast.com*, which has good links to other sites dealing specifically with the Russian Far East; *www.iews.org*, the EastWest Institute's site with links to other sites about Russia; and REESWeb at *www.ucis.pitt.edu/reesweb*, the University of Pittsburgh's index of electronic sources on the former Soviet Union and Eastern Europe. An interesting online source of historical material is the United States Library of Congress's "Meeting of Frontiers," found at *www.international.loc.gov*, which is described as "a bilingual, multimedia English-Russian digital library that tells the story of the American exploration and settlement of the West, the parallel exploration and settlement of Siberia and the Russian Far East, and the meeting of the Russian-American frontier in Alaska and the Pacific Northwest."

INDEX

Page numbers appearing in *italics* refer to illustrations.

ISBN 1-58544-237-2